Back in Two Weeks

JG Debs

Copyright © 2014 JG Debs
All rights reserved.

ISBN 13: 9780578150994

Library of Congress Control Number: 2014902436
CreateSpace Independent Publishing Platform
North Charleston, South Carolina

For Bishop

This is the story of the most challenging five years of my life I spent striving to be the best person I could and almost failed. A lot had to be omitted, most of the names and places have been changed, but the journey is all there.

PROLOGUE

It wasn't much after midnight when I tiptoed into our dilapidated pine green house and hoped Dad was asleep or, at the very least, had the TV up loud enough so he wouldn't hear me come in.

"Get in here, and do the freakin' dishes," he called out as soon as I'd closed the door.

My skin prickled. I wondered if he'd been waiting for me, waiting to pick a fight, until I realized he was watching TV, inhaling from his pot pipe and just happened still to be up. He coughed hard as if he was about to choke, and I walked into my room hoping he would.

"Get your ass in here," he called louder. "I'm not going to tell you again!"

I knew he'd only get louder if I ignored him, but all I wanted to do was finish my research paper, keep my grades up, so that I could one day get out of this shithole, like my brother Ryan had. He'd always gotten the worst of it though.

The last big fight between him and Dad had been a few years ago when I'd heard a commotion from the living room. I saw Dad on top of Ryan, smacking his face while Ryan not the fighting type, barely blocked him.

"Stop it, goddamn it!" I'd tried to pull Dad off of him. When that didn't work, I punched him as hard as I could, but that only made him laugh and say, "I'm going to make him into a man if it kills me, just like my father did with me."

"You fucking asshole!" I'd cursed because that was the sure thing that ticked him off.

He'd wasted no time coming after me, pulled me by the hair until I fell, dragged me to the bathroom and stood me upright then forced a bar of soap into my mouth.

"Stay the hell out of this," he'd pinned me to the wall. "And stop defending that little shit. You think you're a princess who has to protect her poor little brother?"

My nose had started bleeding, not from the force of his hand around my neck but from the stress of me thinking about killing him, and he let go once the blood flowed onto his hand.

I didn't know how long Ryan had been planning it, but the day after High School graduation he joined the Air Force, just like that. It didn't matter how much I missed him, I couldn't blame him.

Feeling emboldened now, I thought, I'm older and stronger and I don't have to take this anymore. If I didn't take a stand now, this would go on forever and I was really getting tired of his shit.

I marched into the living room to give him a piece of my mind but lost my courage when I saw his vegetative state, the potato chips and cookie crumbs all around him and the TV reflecting off his shiny bald forehead. Jerry Springer was on in the background, the most pathetic show on Earth that Dad had once claimed made him feel better about his life, when all he had to do was stop smoking and being so goddamned lazy, and I thought if he wasn't such an asshole, I'd have felt sorry for him.

Studying him, I thanked my lucky stars I only inherited his greasy skin and that everything else about me was like Mom: blonde, blue eyes, 5'4", 120 pounds, and although Ryan had his olive skin and brown hair, he was nothing like him either.

"I'm sick of threats from you," I shouted, to get the ball rolling. The sooner this started, the sooner it would be over. "I'm sick of you!"

"You're sick of me?" he sat up much quicker than I anticipated and I clenched my fists trying to look tough and said, "Yeah."

"How about I'm sick of you," he shouted back. "How about doing something around here?"

"I fucking do enough."

"What did you just say?" He looked aghast I'd cursed and back talked all in the same sentence, which made me realize I'd have to get even bolder, couldn't back down or we'd end up at square one again, so I repeated, "I've fucking had enough!" which made him leap off the couch.

I hadn't expected that, not in his high and usually lethargic state, but he came after me, yelling "I'll show you enough!" and chased me into the kitchen. My lungs were already wheezing from all the smoke in the house and I thought if I just stop now, turn around and kick him in the leg before he pummeled me to the ground, I'd at least get one good hit.

Then my eyes fell on the knife drawer and I quickly reached in looking for the biggest handle I could find, raised it up and threatened, "I fucking dare you to come after me!" He realized I was serious and backed up.

His eyes looked sad and shiny as if he was about to cry which made me ashamed for having given in to poor judgment and violence when all I had to do was shut up and do the dishes, although they were never ever the point anyway.

"Get the fuck out of here!" he raised his hand in the air. "I don't eva wanna see you again! I'm callin' the cops and when I get back in thirty minutes you betta be gone or you're going to jail!"

And with that, he disappeared, the front door slammed shut, and I sank to the ground letting the knife fall to the floor and thinking what the fuck had I done?

Outside the snowflakes were already falling, the first Nor'easter that had been predicted had actually arrived on time and I didn't know where to go or what to do. Even if I did have the money, I didn't know where to find a hotel, and really, how long could I stay there while I was trying to finish school and make something of myself?

Jake would know what to do. He had a quick response to everything, whether it was for a joke or not, but he'd have to pick up first at this hour otherwise Mrs. C would chew us out for calling at this hour and hang up before I could say another word. Then I'd be shit out of luck.

The sound of the ring tone made me cry and wish I could turn back time. If only I'd ignored Dad a little longer. I knew his short fuse, his fits of anger, and still thought I had a chance of staying here until I was done with school. But it was inevitable. He never understood we didn't want to follow in his footsteps, in a regular nine to five job that had him exhausted all the time. Then again, maybe I didn't know what I wanted except to get the hell out of here and now that I had my freedom, I didn't know what the hell to do with it.

ONE

Ryan, a Senior Airman in the United States Air Force, and my recruiter Sergeant Pearson, a Staff Sergeant in the Air Force who had more experience than Ryan and undoubtedly should have told me himself but hadn't, had failed to mention one very important detail about basic training: it started the very second you landed at the San Antonio airport, as soon as you got off the plane, and not after a taxi ride to a meeting or some kind of building as I'd originally thought.

All I wanted to do was rescue my heavy bag from going in circles at the baggage carousel when a body builder, a bull dozer of a man dressed in green camouflage pajamas and a big blue hat approached me and shredded my ear with his voice.

"Get your stinkin' luggage airman, sit down over there at attention, and don't move!"

What I had done to piss him off I didn't know and didn't want to find out, and decided this was the end of the line for me. This was not what I'd signed up for. I searched for the nearest exit, which I couldn't find, and instead stared down a lady and mouthed 'help me.' She must have thought a scene of big men screaming at adolescents in the middle of an airport was normal because she kept on walking.

Reluctantly, I dragged my luggage to an area with neatly aligned metal chairs and sat down next to a young guy with messy hair who looked like he hadn't blinked in days. He stared straight ahead at what I saw was two guys in green pajamas sitting behind a desk, and I searched for our uniforms and our weapons and thought, why were we just sitting here?

"What's your problem, Nancy?" an ogre barked behind me. "What's so special over there?" Then another guy yelled "Grillo." That was me, and involuntarily I leaped out of the chair, in the direction of crazy guys who appeared geared up to tear me a new one.

Trembling up the aisle, I did my best "Full Metal Jacket" marching impression and instantly remembered why I hadn't watched the whole movie in the first place. I hated yelling, which brought me to another point: why had I joined? Why had I believed Ryan when he'd said, "Everything is going to be just fine?"

"Why on God's green earth are you walkin' like that, ya dumb air-min?" one of the guys joked, turning my palms sweaty.

I wiped them on my favorite sweater, the dark blue and white striped zip up that Ryan had given me last year, and wondered what he'd gone through on his first day, which made me relax only slightly.

"And what are you supposed to be?" the other one chimed in but I didn't understand the question, and just as I opened my mouth he answered his own question with, "A light house?" which caused both of them to laugh so hard they nearly fell over.

"It was a gift," I said defensively, feeling the same anger well in me when Dad picked on me and I wished they'd just shut up.

"You're Airman Grillo?" the guy on the left stopped laughing long enough to shout.

"Yes I am," I replied sincerely and he shouted, "Shut your pie hole and get back to your seat!"

I had to stop myself from running.

At my chair, my hands rested on my thighs again, and this time they were shaking. Biting the inside of my cheek kept tears from falling, but I didn't know how much longer I could hold on. How had Ryan survived here when he was more sensitive than me? All this time he'd said, "You'll be fine if you just don't think about it," and I thought it'd be a walk in the park. But how could you not "think about it" if everyone was in your face shouting at you?

After roll call, we piled into a school bus. I was shoved into a window seat as the stampede of scared airmen pushed past me and the big military men stayed behind, making me think the worst was over. Then the bus driver stood up, a friendly Native American looking guy wearing a Veterans baseball cap and glasses.

He smiled timidly and said, "I'm Bob." Then somehow his demeanor changed to angry and he threatened, "Don't think for a second that this is going to be easy!"

Never had I thought this was going to be easy, I wanted to tell him as I hugged my backpack for comfort and getting anything but. Why the hell did he have to act this way?

"All of you are going to grow up now," he growled meaner than both the first two military guys put together. "This isn't a game and you're not gonna escape and go running home to your mommies!"

Who said anything about games or mommies? Just get me the hell off this bus! The guy next to me looked too scared to even breathe. I glanced out the window but saw nothing but black sky and a few orange street lights and was forced to look at the kid again whose lip was now trembling. What the hell was this place?

Bob stood for another second, as if to pierce us all with one final glare before he sat down, closed the door and let the bus lurch forward. I wanted to know where we were going and what time it was, but I didn't dare to move or open my mouth.

When the bus stopped Bob screamed, "Up!" in a tone that let me knew I was supposed to be scared. I was pushed towards the door and off the bus with more screaming angry men in pajamas waving flashlights with yellow cones on them to get us into some type of order.

"Grab your luggage and line up, line up, line up! File into the dorms! Males to the left, females to the right. Females on the second floor, males downstairs. When you're in the dorm, pick an empty bed and lay down!"

Without really looking at anyone, I followed someone in front of me, watched as the yellow glow stick flashlights danced on the pavement until I found myself in a white concrete stairwell, something I pictured a mental hospital to look like, and walked upstairs.

"Move it," someone's voice boomed behind me, but I couldn't. My suitcase felt like a car and the handle its bumper, and the voice boomed again, accompanied by stomping boots, "Hold on to the handrail, airman! Move it!" I couldn't hurry *and* hold onto the handrail. Make up your mind angry man!

Suddenly I was already on the second floor and he rushed in front of me and unlocked a thick heavy door with a tiny window that reminded me of a prison door and said, "Get in there and find a bed!" I hurried inside, heard the door slam shut, and kicked a foot up in front of me as everything turned black.

By the time I stubbed a toe, I could make out rows of bunk beds, and I dropped my suitcase to pat the bottom bed. When I found it was empty, I slipped under the covers fully dressed and listened to the eerie silence.

This was it, I had arrived.

Turning to the side, I saw more rows of bunk beds, shapes of feet and heads, and the windows close to the ceiling that reminded me of the home I'd left behind. Then again what was home? Dad's, the basement I'd been living in, or God forbid, this place now? I thought of my friends Jake and Pam who helped me through all the tough times before and who I'd repaid by running away, just like Ryan had done. I hoped they missed me as much as I missed them! It'd only been hours ago since I'd left, but it already felt like weeks. What had I done? Why had I thought running away was the answer?

Then I thought back to the fight and how Jake had come over that night with a puffy coat over his pajamas, glasses instead of his contacts because they were usually a hassle, so that he didn't have to waste a single minute.

He'd burst through the kitchen door that was always unlocked and screamed, "What the hell is that?" when he spotted the knife on the floor. When I didn't move or answer, he took charge like I knew he would, picked me up off the floor, hugged me tightly, quickly, and had said, "We'll talk later. Come on, we don't have much time to get you the hell out of here." He tossed the knife in the sink and said, "Grab some trash bags for your clothes and meet me in your room."

I'd known him since eighth grade, met him after I moved here from Germany, exactly one year after Mom had sent Ryan to live with Dad. She had said he was a handful, especially because he and I fought with each other every day, but once Ryan was gone I realized I couldn't live without him and decided on summer break that I was moving too.

Dad didn't own much, just a tiny sparsely furnished condo in Massachusetts and a motorcycle. Ryan didn't seem to mind so I didn't either, until school started and all the Puerto Rican kids ignored me. I'd never felt so alone. When Dad suggested a private school, one like Ryan's, except that he was a year younger and therefore in a different school, I walked into the class and saw Jake, and instantly felt at home.

The desk next to his was empty and I'd decided from across the room that he was shy and nice enough when I sat next to him and studied his pale face and oversized glasses that wanted nothing more than to slide off his nose, but then he surprised me. He leaned in and smiled and said, "The moment I saw you I knew we were going to be friends," and I, thinking I'd found my reason to stay, had shrugged, "Okay," and we'd been friends ever since.

Once I'd made it back to my room from the kitchen, I couldn't believe the progress Jake had made. He'd torn the sheets from my bed and tossed clothes and shoes he'd helped me pick out after all these years of shopping and bundled it together like a makeshift suitcase.

"Wow," I'd said, thinking I'd have never come up with that so quickly, and he feeling proud too had asked, "Is there anything that asshole owns that you wanna break?" I'd pumped my fist in the air and screamed, "Hell, yes, everything!" but couldn't find a single thing worth breaking.

Back in the room, we decided to drag the bed frame along the wood floor and minutes later it looked like a skating rink and left Jake feeling really good about himself but me feeling even worse because how did a beat up floor compare to me being kicked out of my home with nowhere to go but the streets?

Outside it had been freezing cold, the snow coming down in sheets. I remembered the Beta fish I'd bought after Ryan had left that I'd hoped would fill the void (which of course it hadn't) and screamed, "Wait!" while Jake waited by his car.

I hurried through the kitchen and felt sick to my stomach. This was where it had all began and this was where it ended. I felt emptier than the fish bowl I'd drained most of the water out of and met Jake outside trying not to cry. The tears would freeze to my face I told myself. I could cry when I got to his house.

"That's it," I said to Jake, getting into my car and wedged the bowl between my legs.

I followed his green Saturn onto the street. I'd know his car anywhere, in a snowstorm or in a full parking lot, because a jagged piece of fender was missing above his left front tire from when he'd forgotten to put the emergency brake on before running into his house to get something and the car rolled down the long driveway and into a pine tree. He then dubbed the broken fender, 'the shark bite,' which it did indeed resemble and always made me laugh, except for tonight.

Then I realized we weren't driving to his house at all but to Pam's instead, and I thought oh no, anywhere but there, because Pam had enough on her plate: a two-year-old son, an ex-boyfriend in and out of her life and in and out of jail, and her mom dying of cancer. The last thing she needed was me.

"Stop crying or you're going to crash," I said aloud to calm my nerves. "Everything's going to be okay." Who was I trying to convince, me or the fish? Nothing was okay! Nothing was ever going to be okay again! I barely had enough money for school, not to mention gas and books, and now my asshole father had thrown me out into the cold!

Pam opened the screen door as soon as we drove up and I thought Jake must have called her before he'd left his house. I parked the car and trudged through the heavy snow that felt as heavy as my heart and stared up at her feeling nothing but self-pity. She kissed my cheek and whispered, "Jake said you were on your way. I'm so sorry about what happened with your Dad."

"Thanks for letting me stay." I bit the inside of my cheek, ready to throw up because it sounded so much worse than in my head. Technically, I was homeless, desperate, and more dependent than ever, when all I'd wanted in life was to be on my own and make something of myself!

"Come in, it's cold," she smiled when I hadn't responded.

Then Jake squeezed past us with the trash bags and she said, "Jake, be quiet, everyone's asleep. You can throw her stuff in the basement." I thought that even a basement felt more like home than my Dad's but I sure as hell didn't want to sleep there. I'd only seen it a few times before; a brown paneled room with brown paisley carpet, a fireplace, and a hutch filled with liquor and all sorts of drinking glasses. Once upon a time, Pam's parents, Mr. and Mrs. B., sat down there drinking nightcaps after a long day of teaching, but that was way before her cancer hit. Then Pam's son Danny's video room, although he was too young for video games, and now it was my room, which sounded depressing to me.

I was a good kid and didn't deserve this. Kids on drugs got kicked out and slept on couches or in basements, but not me. How could Dad do this to me?

Jake whizzed upstairs to Pam's room before I was finally able to put one foot in front of the other, just getting into the front door. That's when I saw Mr. B passed out in the living room, his head cocked to the side, with a glass of melted ice and rum remnants. Pam had mentioned he liked to drink, and I wondered how many glasses it took for him to forget his wife had cancer.

Once in Pam's room, I plopped down on her four poster bed where we'd solved many problems before. Somehow, this one took the cake and I knew I'd be stuck here for a while. How was I going to make enough money to get out of here?

Then I told them the story, and Pam pulled her long brown hair into a ponytail (she reminded me of Liv Tyler with her natural beauty, pale face, and pouty pink lips) and said, "It's always something with him."

I'd met her a year after I met Jake. She and I became driving buddies in Driver's Ed after everyone had found a buddy except us, and one week I'd suggested the three of us hang out Jake, her and I and we'd been inseparable since.

"You're safe now. You can stay as long as you want," Pam added and I replied, "I didn't know where else to go. I'm really sorry about this."

I had no desire to be there whatsoever and felt what I could only call jealousy of her and Jake for having parents who not only loved and supported them but also paid for their very expensive colleges, while mine had flaked out at the last minute forcing me to go to Community College so that I wouldn't lose any time or sight of my goal: to be something! But where the hell was living in a basement going to get me?

"No, problem, honey," she stretched and yawned, which I took as my cue to venture down to my new room. Jake took the hint too, stood up and hugged me, and said, "It'll be alright. I'll call you in the morning."

Standing in front of the basement door, the sound of the tumbling dryer and the smell of dryer sheets reminded me of how low I'd sunk. With my hand on the knob, I managed to open the paper-thin door and fight back tears as the cold musty air hit my face.

Home sweet home. I rubbed my hands together thinking that sleeping in my car might have been a better choice, and I turned on the thermostat. Pam usually kept it on in case Danny ventured down here, but Mr. B. shut it off because he was an accountant by trade (even if only a high school teacher accountant) and therefore counted pennies. As I watched the dust blow up from the vents, I prayed my asthma wouldn't trigger because I'd forgotten my inhaler and there was no going back to my Dad's. There was no turning back, period.

I sorted through my sheets and plugged in my alarm clock so I'd get up in time for work tomorrow as if nothing out of the ordinary had happened. Then I found my pajamas, turned off the light, and sneezed, while trying to get comfortable on the sagging couch, thinking at least I was safe from her pets' dander that would trigger my asthma in a second, but were never allowed down here.

I shivered to get warm and watched the moonlight from the small windows, knowing I should feel comforted but didn't. My eyes fell on the black tree roots outside which reminded me again how low I'd sunk. To make matters worse, something was scratching from behind the walls, as if trying to dig its way in. Why had my Dad done this? I started crying, wishing I could call my mother in Germany and tell her how I felt, but all she'd want to do is push her agenda on me and call my dad every name in the book.

"You're father's an asshole," she'd start the conversation like she always did. "It's all his fault! Move back here! Be a flight attendant and see the world."

She never understood why I wanted to go school and that I'd already seen half the world thanks to her flying benefits, and that it had satiated all my traveling thirsts.

"How about an au pair? I have friends that need English-speaking nannies," Mom would counter, regardless of the fact I'd told her I didn't want kids and that I sure as hell didn't want to raise someone else's!

So I promised myself I wouldn't call her, not until I was really desperate, and right now I was still borderline. All I had to do was figure out how to leave Staples, get a better job, maybe be a waitress and make tips or get some corporate gig in Boston, which I, of course, needed a degree for, and couldn't worry about yet because I was already overwhelmed with the news about being homeless and had to worry about tomorrow. Yes, tomorrow things would look brighter. Tomorrow I'd have a newspaper to search for jobs and a clear head after I got some sleep. Only I didn't sleep at all.

Penny, or "Stupid Dog" as I called her, started barking at four in the morning and no one came downstairs to shut her up. I didn't know what the hell she wanted so I ignored her barking while cursing every insult in my head at her, and by the time she shut up and I had forgiven her because I could then go back to sleep, Gus Gus started meowing. I couldn't tell if he was inside or out and wasn't going to go searching for him, and therefore started all the cursing again, wishing the pillow-over-your-head trick in movies actually worked.

Then there was the choking incident, gagging sounds coming from the kitchen that instinctively made me leap off the couch and up the eight steps two at a time while running through the CPR checklist from high school in my head.

Sure enough, Mr. B. had been sprawled out on the floor in his tightie whities, only he wasn't choking or having a heart attack. His elbows were raised and his body twitched an inch off the floor and back down again while he grunted, "Won, hew, hee, fo," during a drunken attempt at a push up.

Slowly I backed up, wondering why of all things something like this wasn't mentioned to me? How was I going to last another night here?

The minute I'd crawled back under the covers the first rays of sun came up and I listened as Pam attempted to hold Danny still and get him dressed, but he kept slipping away and running up and down the hall, which made her count to three ten times until he was ready to go.

When they left, Mr. B.'s got up to shower. Once he was gone and everything was silent, I forced myself up because it couldn't hurt to be on time for school just once, and carried my clothes and toothbrush upstairs to the only bathroom in the house.

Upstairs, Mrs. B's door closed and I felt relief I wouldn't have to talk to her and pretend like we didn't know how sick she was. Then I wanted to kick myself for thinking that way, for being so unbelievably selfish, a nineteen-year-old brat worried about a silly goal and where she'd end up in life because she was in a basement and not a four-year college, versus a woman on her literal death bed.

Then it hit me that this was probably what I deserved for being so selfish in the first place: staying in that basement until my hair fell out. I thought what the fuck could I even do about it if this was where I was meant to be?

TWO

There was nothing in the newspaper that I qualified for, absolutely nothing that could advance my career and launch me out of the hole I called home, so I settled on the words "no experience necessary" under a hair salon receptionist position, and called for an interview although I knew it wasn't for me.

I didn't own make-up, a blow dryer or even hairspray, but it paid more than Staples, and although I thought they'd just tell me no, to my surprise, Julie, the woman on the line, was enthusiastic I'd called and wanted me to come in as soon as possible.

With the small parking lot adjacent to a little stream, the salon looked like one of the laundromats Dad used to take us to on the weekends, and the fact that it was in the back alley of a Cadillac repair shop didn't give me any more confidence to step in either, except that I really needed the money.

A small sign above the door read, 'Hair and Skin Care,' and once I got the courage to open the door and saw the beautiful floor to ceiling mirrors, glass shelves, and shampoo bottles I couldn't afford, I was hypnotized.

"I'm here for the interview," I told the blonde behind the counter who I assumed was Julie, and her dimples appeared instantly, revealing big teeth and an even bigger belly once she approached me.

"I'm Julie," she extended her hand.

I said obviously, "You're pregnant!"

"Ready to pop any minute," she beamed, and I stared at her perfect blonde highlights, feeling intimidated because I'd never had highlights before. I reminded her, "You know, I don't have any experience."

She waved her hand like it was no big deal and opened her mouth to speak, but the phone rang and she excused herself so my eyes fell on my reflection again. I studied my flat hay hair that Jake said made me look like Tom Petty and I knew I'd made a mistake by coming, that I'd never fit in, and this was the perfect time to leave.

Almost at the door, I bumped into a short brunette with a blunt bob, purple eye shadow and bright red lipstick who eagerly shook my limp hand and said, "I'm Jean. This is my place. Welcome. I really need a receptionist. You're the only one who showed up for the interview and I'm desperate. Can you start right away?"

"Well, I don't have any experience," I said, almost telling her I almost hadn't shown up either, and she said, "It doesn't matter. Julie will teach you everything you need to know." Then she winked at Julie, which made Julie smile back as if she had supersonic hearing even though she was on the phone. Jean leaned in closer as if she wasn't going to take no for an answer, and I offered, "I guess I can give it a shot?"

"Great, see you tomorrow," she smiled, and I pushed my way outside wondering why I couldn't ever say no?

Filled with anxiety the next morning, I waffled back and forth, do I go, do I not go, then decided to go, which made me ten minutes late. But no one noticed and no one chewed me out like they would have at Staples.

The salon was packed, women chatting, sipping coffee, and laughing with the radio on in the background as if they were in someone's living room. The smell of nail polish and hairspray filled the air and I thought that it might make me feel light headed but didn't. It made me curious. I wanted to know more, wanted to belong, wanted anything but to have to go back to Staples and pick up pens kids liked to knock from the shelves and kick around the aisle, I just didn't know how.

"Grab some coffee and attach yourself to Julie's hip. I'll check on you later," Jean suddenly shook my shoulders from behind then disappeared again.

Julie was pinching a phone between her cheek and shoulder, flipping through a huge calendar on the desk while simultaneously running a credit card through the machine for a client and making it all look easy. I was in awe of her.

"Here, give this a try," she handed me a pen once the customer left and played back an answering machine message that sounded like static and gibberish.

"Me?" I asked with surprise and she giggled.

"Yes you. These are messages from last night while we were closed. Write down the messages and call the clients back to schedule their appointments."

"But I don't know what they're mumbling after 'hello,'" I said, perplexed.

"It gets easier the more you do it." She started the message over. "And let me show you an example day in the appointment book for when you schedule an appointment."

The book was worse than the answering machine. The lines were too small, the stylists names too many, and the list of services, infinite. I'd never even had a pedicure before.

"First, turn to the date then find the stylist the client wanted to see and block out how long the service would take and add the client's information."

"I don't even know what a mani-pedi is," I wanted to laugh, cry, and walk out.

"There's nothing to it. You can do this."

"Yeah, right," I sighed at her optimism. Where the hell had Jean found this girl? More importantly, how was I going to emulate her?

By some miracle, I finished the messages and the appointments and followed Julie through the salon for the grand tour.

"Sometimes you want to look alert and just stroll around to see if anyone needs something," she whispered over her shoulder as I followed her like a lost puppy dog. "You know, like coffee or water, or sometimes I even sweep if the stylists are busy."

As if she didn't have enough to do already!

"Everyone, this is Jen." She suddenly stopped in the middle of the salon so that everyone looked up, which made me cower behind her, too embarrassed to speak.

"Oh, Julie," one of the women eyed me up and down critically, "No one can replace you. I'm going to miss you so much."

Thanks a lot, lady, I wanted to say, although I couldn't deny it; I'd never be as sweet as Julie if I were rolled in sugar. But then another woman who was much older said, "Welcome," and everyone seemed to hush as if she were the Godmother of the salon and wanted to hear what she had to say. She said, "I hope you're ready to take care of me as well as Julie has. Did you see how big Julie is? She's ready to explode!"

Jean glanced up from her manicure, winked at me and smiled before going back to buffing a woman's nails again, and to the right of me a stylist was trying her best to hide a smile that told me she was digging the drama a little too much, and I thought no way in hell was I coming back to this!

"See, they're not that bad," Julie spoke over the laughter. "Come on, I'll show you the rest," then waved a cordless phone in front of me and said, "So I don't have to make a mad dash to the front when the phone rings." She took me down a long hallway to the back rooms.

"After a while, they'll be like family," she said, as if she could tell I felt a little beat up, and I thought, I never knew a job could be like family, like what Ryan, Jake, and Pam were to me.

The laundry room was on the left, filled with long white shelves that bowed in the middle from all the cluttered shampoo bottles and towels. In the hall was a large make-up table and bar stools for bridal parties. Beyond that was a bathroom, massage and facial room.

Julie fluffed her hair in the mirror and raised her eyebrows playfully. "When it's slow, you'll be able to get a facial or your hair done. The biggest advantage of being a receptionist here is that they love to play with your hair."

"Your hair looks great," I said, feeling envious that it was perfect and dubious that I'd ever look like her.

"Thanks," she smiled, and suddenly we were at the top of the hall again by the laundry room where she told me how to run the washers, fill the bottles, and stock the manicurist tables with cotton. She was truly impressive, impossible to mimic, and I wondered how the hell she thought I was going to keep up?

Returning to the front desk, a stylist suddenly patted me on the back and smiled, "I'm Kathy, can you ring up my client and book the next appointment?"

"Of course." I blushed and searched for help from Julie, who of course hadn't missed a beat, was right behind me, and walked me through my feeble attempts to get the register open and book the next appointment.

"See, you've got the hang of it already," Kathy smiled encouragingly, but all I wanted to do was fall to the ground and hide under the desk.

"Now we look at what's next," Julie distracted me from beating myself up. "Okay, a facial, which means we have to get the room ready by putting on fresh sheets and heating up some towels. After that, a pedicure is coming in."

Watching her duck and move around the pedicure chair, I was amazed she hadn't gone into labor two months ago. Into the boiling water she poured a carton of Epsom salt, which I'd never heard of before, and smiled, "It's good for the muscles."

When I didn't reply she asked, "How do you like it here so far?"

"You make this look easy," I sighed.

"All of this is easy once you learn all the services." She paused to load the towels into the little oven so that they'd be warm for the facial. As if reading my mind, she said, "I know you can do it and trust me, you will love this place. Everyone here is wonderful and will help you. Just tell me you're coming back tomorrow because I know I'm going to deliver any minute now and I can't leave knowing you won't come back."

The last thing I wanted was to stress out a pregnant woman but this wasn't for me, even if everyone was sweet as pie, but before I could reply the damned phone rang again and she handed it to me like I knew what to say and I said, "No, I can't."

"Say your name and how may I help you." Julie wiggled the phone as if that was going to tempt me, and I lied, "Fine, don't worry, I'll be here tomorrow," and pushed the receiver at her.

She pushed it back and reluctantly, I answered with my heart thumping wildly and said, "Hi this is Jen. How may I help you?"

Julie silently clapped her hands together and flashed those gigantic white teeth at me as if she was so proud of me, and all I could think was that now I didn't have a choice but to come back and that I never really thought about anything before I leaped off the damn cliff; I had a tendency to just go for it and in mid-fall, think what the fuck have I just done?

THREE

Gazing through my windshield at the recruiter's office, I wanted nothing more than to jump out of the car and rip the "Aim High" stickers from the door. Joining the Air Force wasn't aiming high. It was scraping the bottom of the barrel.

They took people who were desperate, lost, and void of hope, people who didn't think they had any other choice but to go, people like my brother, people like me, and I knew I shouldn't have parked in the first place, should have made a big loop in the lot and left and laughed about it with Jake and Pam later, but I didn't. I got out of the car and went in.

A tiny bell rang as the door opened and fell shut behind me. A man dressed in a blue uniform was typing away at his computer and didn't look up although I expected him to, so I sat down in the metal chair in front of his desk and waited.

"Recruiter Pearson." his desk plate read, sitting next to stacks of bumper stickers, pencils, and other *Aim High* crap I wouldn't be caught dead with. Hell, I wouldn't have been caught dead in here either, but I didn't have a choice on this one. I'd promised Ryan I'd check it out and give it a real try so I could get out of the basement. A year was long enough.

"If you're here to join the Air Force," Pearson said finally glancing up, "come back in a week. I won't be here. I appreciate you stopping by to defend your country, but I'm retiring."

"Oh, okay." I stood up, the relief sliding from my shoulders.

I had asthma so badly as a kid I couldn't even participate in gym class, and although I had recently tried to jog around Pam's block, realized instantly my body couldn't handle it at all and that I'd never survive basic. All of that had been for nothing because I couldn't go! They weren't taking people, hooray, and the best part was I didn't even have to lie to Ryan about it. I'd tried, boom, end of story.

Then my hands rested on the door and I stared at my sometimes cooperative red Escort and thought, what was I going to do with the rest of my life, how many more years was I going to waste in the basement? How much more money was I going to throw at a Psychology degree that wasn't going to get me far?

Hadn't Mom always said I was a fighter? I was born prematurely, six weeks early, and therefore didn't have the fully-developed lungs I was supposed to and lived in an incubator for nearly two months before my parents could take me home, and the doctors and nurses all marveled at my will to live. I. Was. Not. Going. To. Give. Up!

So what was I doing now?

"You're back," he sighed when I sat down again.

I folded my hands on his desk to show him I meant business and said, "Yes," which didn't motivate him the way it motivated me.

He said, "Let me give you some advice. You're a cute kid. Don't join the Air Force, go to college."

"I thought you're a recruiter, not a comedian?" I said. "And I wish it were that simple but you see, my brother is in the Air Force. He told me to join and that's why I'm back."

Pearson sighed, reached for a binder and placed it on his desk facing me, showing me a list of some sort and said, "Pick a job."

"Ryan thought I'd like linguist, learning a foreign language." I smiled as if I knew what I was talking about. "But I don't see it on here. All I see is numbers and letters."

Pearson typed something on his computer and leaned back with a smile as if he had me beat and said, "There's a nine month waiting list. Come back in a year."

"Sign me up." I smacked the desk, thinking it would give me enough time to think this through. "Nine months is fine with me."

Sliding a few forms at me, he said, "Take them home and sign them, then make an appointment at the Boston MEPS to get your physical. And take the written ASVAB, the Armed Services Vocational Aptitude Battery test."

He stood as if he couldn't get me out of his office soon enough, shook my hand and said, "Good night, Missy. If you pass, which I doubt, I won't be the one to see you in nine months, but the new recruiter will get the good news, and you'll be an Airman."

"Okay," I replied, unsure of what to do with that information, his eagerness to get rid of me, and the nine month waiting list that maybe meant I really shouldn't join.

Instead, I went to Jean the next day and said, "I'm leaving. I'm joining the Air Force," thinking that maybe if I just did it and left, failed and came back, well, at least I'd tried and of course she'd be supportive, she was always someone I could count on for guidance, and wouldn't hesitate to take me back.

But she was frantic unlike her usual poised self and pleaded, "You can't do that to me. Julie told me a few months ago she is definitely not coming back. She's staying home with the baby. I need you." I thought to myself that was strike two, I should definitely not go.

I wanted to tell her I wasn't going and to never mind what I'd just said, but a fire rumbled within me as I thought of the musty cold nights in the basement, and I thought no way in hell did I want that for the rest of my life so instead I said, "I'm sorry, Jean."

"Well, what do we do now?" she glared at me.

"Can I take tomorrow off so I can take the physical?" I asked which made her laugh out loud, her sour mood gone, and she said, "I don't think you're the Air Force type, but sure go if you're going to be stubborn, I guess you're going to have to find out for yourself that even if you do go, you'll be back in two weeks, tops!"

I wanted to be in on the joke and cackle alongside her, but then the fire in my stomach died and I realized that she was absolutely right. I didn't have a snowball's chance in hell, as they say.

FOUR

Alone on a street on the outskirts of Boston stood MEPS, a gray, creepy eyesore like the Addams Family house that made me check the hand-scribbled note twice to see if I had the right address.

Inside wasn't any better. I stepped into the ancient elevator with the flickering yellow fluorescent lights and decided that if one thing went wrong, anything at all, I was out of there.

On the top floor that appeared deserted, I found an office with a handsome man with black slicked hair like Clark Kent, dressed in blue like Pearson, who courteously stood up when he saw me, shook my hand, and asked, "Are you Grillo?"

I nodded, thinking I could get used to this, and he continued, "I'm Sergeant Anderson. Follow me to take the ASVAB before we talk about anything else."

Down the hall he opened a double door for me where inside were rows of desks and computers but only two skinny young guys in there clicking away on the mouse with their backs to me.

"Everything is explained once you tap the mouse," Anderson offered, his hand already closing the door behind me as if to say *you're on your own kid*. Then he quickly glanced at his watch and said, "You have two hours. I'll see you when you're done."

Swallowing hard, I approached the front row, knowing I wasn't going to do well on this test because I was a poor test taker. Even when I'd taken the

SAT's after countless practice tests, I still only scored less than average, and what the hell could I possibly know about the military?

"Welcome to MEPS, Military Entrance Processing Command. Click to start the ASVAB, Armed Services Vocational Aptitude Battery," the screen read.

What a mouth-full I thought, wondering if the rest of the test was going to be this confusing and difficult to understand. Then I read the first question, which seemed easy enough, like it had been written for third graders, and I thought hell yeah, I was way on my way! But by the time I made it to the mechanical section, I was back to reality and knew my military career was over before it even began.

Anderson surprised me outside, standing there as if he'd been waiting for me all this time, and handed me a piece of paper and said, "You have the best test results of the day, pick any career you want."

I couldn't decipher the letters and numbers and when I noticed the two young guys who looked like they could have been my sons, I asked, "Is that saying much?"

"Keep up that sense of humor, airman," Anderson chuckled, walking me down the hall to an exam room and said, "Go ahead and step behind the curtain for your physical." He pulled back a white curtain to reveal a gurney and then pointed at a gown and said, "That's for you. Change and get on the table and I'll see you later."

It seemed a little too easy I thought, kicking my legs in the air as I sat on the high table in my white and blue speckled gown. A test and a physical and I was in, just like that?

"I'm Doctor Morrow." An elderly man in a white lab coat suddenly appeared in front of me.

He had to be at least one hundred and two with those deep wrinkles, thin gray comb-over, and dentures so loose his name sounded like 'marble' until I read his name tag.

"Lay on your side for the rectal exam." A cheery nurse with a brown ponytail joined the party.

I asked, "What kind of exam?" already turning on my side thinking I'd misunderstood until, sure enough, I heard the snap of a glove and felt a crooked finger in my rear and gasped.

"You can sit up now," Marbles mumbled.

"Is this all of it?" I asked even though I felt extremely violated.

"Good luck," was all he said, and left as though he hadn't heard me.

"Follow me," a cheery nurse smiled. I followed her to a room that resembled a small basketball court where three young bored looking girls were already standing, chewing gum and adjusting their ponytails in the mirror.

I looked nothing like them, couldn't even imagine how they fit all that eye shadow and mascara on their faces, and thought if the military was looking for call-girl looking girls, I was in the wrong place. I stood off to the side.

"Out with your gum, the trashcan's in the corner," the nurse with the short black curly hair standing behind them snapped. I was so intimidated by her I nearly marched to the trashcan myself so that she wouldn't even look at me.

Then one of the girls spit loudly and marched back with an attitude as if she was going to punch someone, and I thought I couldn't wait to fail and get the hell out of here.

"Everyone face the wall and lean into it, raise one foot. I'm checking for flat feet," the nurse announced. Not exactly what I'd had in mind when Cheery Nurse had said "test."

"Okay, good. Now, down on your knees and walk to the other side on your knees, like a duck."

It was hard to believe this was for real.

"Grillo!" The door suddenly flew open and a nurse with short red wavy hair waved when I looked at her. She barked, "Follow me!" and in my hospital gown I followed her back to Anderson's desk. He sat with his arms crossed and was scowling.

"Why didn't you tell Pearson about your shoplifting record?" He slapped a folder in front of me.

Funny story, so funny I avoided telling anyone about it. To Ryan, I'd explained it was an unpaid parking ticket. Jake eventually weaseled the story out of me once he found out I'd had to go to court and my measly savings account had been wiped out from the fine. But, two years ago, weeks before Christmas, I went Christmas shopping (Jake called it Christmas shop-lifting) walked into an empty store, and walked out with a pair of shoes I didn't need.

Shaking my head, I wasn't about to tell him that Ryan had told me to lie about any ticket I ever had. His rationale was that all recruiters lied and it didn't matter if I gave it right back to them because they deserved it.

"You will write an apology letter," Anderson slid a pen and paper towards me and motioned for me to sit down.

Picking up the pen, I didn't know what to write or to whom and said, "I already wrote one to the store manager a long time ago and he said he forgave me. He'd also said not to steal when the store was empty, or right in front of the camera, and that if I'd asked him for the shoes he would have given them to me."

"You're writing this one to the Air Force," Anderson replied angrily. "You are going to write how sorry you are and that it will never happen again. It's going into your permanent file and if anything else happens, we'll kick you out on the spot. Is that clear?"

Not really I thought, scribbling the silly words on the paper before I slid it back to him. He then slid a thick binder towards me and said "Pick another career field."

"What?" My mouth went dry. How many more strikes were there going to be against me?

"You have a criminal record." He enunciated every syllable as if he were about to lose his temper. "You will never be able to get the highly classified clearance needed to be a linguist or any other job requiring that clearance. Pick another career field."

"I need a minute." Tears filled my eyes. I'd been trying to forget the incident and now I realized it was going to haunt me for the rest of my life!

This was the sign, the final sign to leave and never look back. But this wasn't how I'd wanted it to happen! I'd wanted it to be my asthma or the ASVAB I'd thought would be impossible to pass, but now this?

"Okay. Go finish your physical." He tapped his fingers on his desk. "Then we'll talk." I stood up and went back out to the hallway. Standing in front of the emergency exit, I became distracted again. Maybe this was the right time to say goodbye, just slip out without anyone noticing, and it would be over.

"It's this way." Someone tugged at my elbow.

I glanced up and saw Cheery Nurse smiling encouragingly, as if she'd seen frustration like mine before, and I wanted to tell her all about it, tell her that maybe I was making a mistake and this wasn't for me, but before I could say anything we were already in the next exam room and she said, "Sit there, put your forehead against the black bar on the microscope. I'm testing your depth perception."

Obediently, I looked through the scope, scanned the black rows of circles, ten in all, and called out the ones that popped out at me. The last one, however, would not pop and suddenly tears filled my eyes as I blinked at the now foggy circles because I didn't have a plan B. I wanted to be a linguist. Beyond that, I didn't know. All arrows pointed at the basement and how I was doomed to be there forever.

"Keep looking," Cheery Nurse sang, making me want to impress her and tell her where that flipping circle was, but I just couldn't see it.

"It's alright if we call it a day," I accepted my fate. It was over. Time to go home.

"Take your time," she coaxed and I guessed indifferently, "One."

"Try again," she said and I replied, "Four," hoping she'd get the message. She didn't and said, "Try again."

"I'm sorry," I looked up at her and said, "This just wasn't meant to be."

"Look harder," she pointed at the scope like she wasn't having any of my pity party.

Glancing down again, I suddenly saw the circle popping out at me as if to tell me *This is it! This is where you're supposed to be!* I shrieked proudly, "Three!"

"Outstanding!" she clapped her hands together, "Now, get into that booth, put the headset on, and when you hear a beep, raise your arm on the side you hear the beep and say, 'I hear it.'"

At first I sauntered over there with all the enthusiasm in the world, but then I sat in the hot box, put on the headphones, and started sweating, started questioning how many other people she'd helped, and thought what was the point of being here if I couldn't do the job I wanted?

"What's going on?" Cheery Nurse pulled the door open so that cold air swished all around me, she lifted up one side of my headphones and asked, concerned, "Don't you hear the beeps?"

"I'm sorry. I forgot to listen," I admitted.

"Oh, okay, let's try again. Listen for the sound, then raise your arm on the side you hear it, okay?"

I nodded, unconvincingly I guessed, because she then said, "I know you're upset, but you can learn another language any time you want. The Air Force has so many other jobs. Don't let this one little thing get in your way."

And instead of admitting to her that I didn't have a plan and that she was probably right, I said, "Okay," which satisfied her enough to close the door and conduct the test, which I passed.

After the hearing test, I was supposed to be back in Anderson's office, but when I saw the payphone in the hall I couldn't resist and had to call Ryan, who, I knew would know what to do.

"They won't let me do linguist." Nervous tears rolled down my cheeks. I wiped them from my face when a blonde girl my age walked by and I whispered, "What am I going to do now?"

"Oh, that's great!" Ryan shrieked as if he hadn't heard anything I'd just said, so I asked, "What?" He replied, "You didn't want to be a linguist anyway. The Tech school is three years. Air Traffic is what you want. It was my dream job but I failed the eye test and they wouldn't let me retake it."

"I don't? What do you mean?" I felt better just hearing his voice, but didn't know what the hell he was talking about. "What's 'Air Traffic'?"

"Only the greatest job in the world! It's my dream job. Now walk back into the recruiter's office and tell him Air Traffic Control. Just like that. But promise me you'll visit a tower before you leave for basic, so you know what to expect. Promise me!"

"Alright, alright, I promise," I agreed, thinking this was the second blind promise I'd made, but forgot all about it when Anderson leaned back in his chair a minute later and said, "Well, you do qualify, but it has an 80% wash out rate."

"That's what I want." I folded my arms across my chest with certainty, although I had never felt so uncertain about anything before in my life. "Air Traffic!"

"Okay," he leaned forward to type on his computer. "In three weeks there is one seat available for class. You're lucky, someone just washed out."

I gasped, "Three weeks?" My mind was racing. How was I going to explain this to Jean? Jake and Pam? Pack everything and go, just like that?

"See you in three," Anderson reiterated, as if he was personally challenging me and I croaked, "Yeah, see you," and headed for the elevator, thinking what the hell had I done?

Jake and Pam were going to kill me! And if they didn't, my mother would. And if by some miracle all of them didn't, I knew sure as hell the military would!

FIVE

August 11 was my report date. The weeks leading up to it, had me excited in anticipation that I was finally going to get out of here and start a new life, but now that the day had arrived, I couldn't pick myself up off the couch in fear of the unknown. Had I done the right thing?

Suddenly the couch felt comfortable and the basement not so bad; in fact, I liked having a view to the bottom of the tree, grass, bugs. Why would I leave a room, a home I could finally call mine? Why would I leave, pretend to be a soldier when I had asthma, didn't stand a chance, and had become the running joke to everyone around me: Bye Jen, see you in two weeks!

"It's alright, Jenny." Pam sat by my feet frowning as if trying to understand my fear, but I barely understood it myself. If Ryan had left and now raved about it, why couldn't I?

"You don't have to go," she tried to comfort me, and she was right, I didn't. Ryan had explained it too. It was the last signature, the third and final one that they needed when I arrived before it was official, but then why did I feel so torn? Why was I so afraid to leave if that was what I'd wanted?

There was heavy knocking at the front door as if whoever it was wanted to bang it down and I knew that it had to be for me and begged Pam, "Please get the door! I can't face him!"

"Okay Jenny." Pam got up slowly and took her sweet time opening the door as if his time meant nothing to her.

"Is Grillo home?" Pearson barked, although he should have been retired by now, and I wondered if he'd made it his last mission to get me, storm through the house, drag me by my collar, throw me in the car and haul me off to the airport, but he stayed right where he was.

Pam answered firmly, "No," like this was a chess game. Now it was his move.

"She was supposed to be at the airport this morning," he replied angrily. "But she wasn't on the flight. Do you know what happened?"

"Yes," she said so calmly, I wasn't sure what she was going to say next. Then to my horror, she said, "We were at the hospital all night with my mother. She has cancer. We couldn't get to the airport in time."

"Oh," Pearson lowered his voice. "I'm sorry about your mother. Here's my card. Could you tell Jennifer to call me as soon as she can? There's another flight tomorrow."

"Sure thing." She slammed the door in his face which made me laugh and as soon as Pam came back downstairs she laughed too. "He's gone Jenny. Let's call Jake and go to Dunkins."

"You were good," I stood up.

"I wasn't going to let him take you, Jenny."

"Yeah," I glanced at the boxes in the corner of the basement. My things that Pam had made me pack to make room for Danny, which reminded me that I had to go. I'd made a promise, to the military and to myself. All she did was buy me a small window of time and the countdown was on. Again.

"I'm here," Jake called from upstairs a few minutes later, and Pam went to her room to change out of her pajamas and put on a pair of jeans.

"You okay?" Jake asked.

"I think so," I lied, but how could I be? Leave for the unknown or stay here treading water.

"I'll drive," Jake said when Pam joined us again. We didn't say another word until Jake asked, "Drive thru, or go in?"

"We've got time, let's go in," I said, hoping it would calm my nerves, but as soon as we were seated and I took my first swig of coffee, I thought I was going to throw up.

"It's going to be okay, honey," Jake squeezed my hand.

Pam squeezed the other and said, "Don't go. You don't have to go."

"I do at some point," I replied. "I can't stay in your basement forever."

"Yes, you can," she smiled then Jake reached under the table and grabbed my knee, a move he'd seen Dad do before, which made me scream because it tickled.

"Jake!" I screamed so that everyone looked at me, which was why he loved to do it, and he took a sip from his coffee as if nothing was out of the ordinary and giggled, "What? It wasn't me."

"Jake, don't. It's not funny!" I said when he reached under the table again.

"Yes it is!" he chuckled.

"Let's get out of here," I stood up. "I don't want to sit still today. Pam, do you have Pearson's card?"

"No, I thought you had it. I slammed the door in his face before he could give it to me."

"Pam!" I said, trying to be serious, but she raised her eyebrows as if to say, "what?" and I said, "It's okay. I'm sure I have it somewhere." I looked at Jake and asked, "Can I use your phone?"

To my surprise, Pearson wasn't mad after I promised I'd be there, and I felt relief, almost a victory for scoring an extra day with my friends. I told them, "The flight doesn't leave until five p.m. tomorrow," after I hung up.

"Whatever, you're not going," Pam shrugged, and I smiled because I didn't have the heart to tell her that I could not live in that basement for the rest of my life. I just couldn't.

Before I knew it, it was the following day and I was in Pam's driveway trying hard not to cry and think of the unknown road that lay ahead. On the phone, Ryan had said I'd be fine, there was nothing to it and that I'd see him on the other side, but that didn't tell me what to expect, so I tried not to think about it.

Mr. B hugged me and said, "You're doing the right thing," while Mrs. B hugged me and said, "I'm sure you'll love it, Jen." I replied, "I hope so," as Jake loaded my heavy suitcase into his trunk.

"Remember to take care of the fish, Danny." I squatted down to his eyelevel and he immediately put his head on my shoulder and asked, "Where you going Jenny?"

"I'll be back soon, okay muffin?"

"Yeah, but where you going?"

"The Air Force."

"Can I go with you?"

"No, muffin, but I'll be home soon, okay? I love you, okay?"

"Okay. Love you too, Jenny."

Danny was still waving after I got into the front passenger seat and Jake put the car in drive. It was all happening too fast I thought, but no one else seemed to notice. Jake and Pam were giggling as usual, and Jake asked, "Dunkins?" as if my life wasn't ending, then remembered, "Oh wait, you still want to go to the tower right?"

"Oh, yeah," I said, having completely forgotten I'd promised Ryan to see one. I almost told Jake to skip it until he said, "There's a small airport on the way," and ten minutes later we were there, parking in the lot and standing at the bottom of the short tower trying to figure out how to get in.

"Yes," a man's scruffy voice said when I picked up the receiver and pushed the button I assumed was a doorbell.

"Hi, I'm Jen," I stood on my toes to reach the speaker. "I'm here with Jake and Pam, my two friends. I'm joining…"

Something buzzed, the man hung up, and Jake pushed the door open and cast me a glance that said *this was your brilliant idea so you can climb the stairs first.*

"I would kill you if I could breathe, Jenny," Pam gasped after the first flight and Jake said, "Yeah." It was me who should have been coughing because of my asthma but was doing surprisingly well, so I said, "Both of you need to quit smoking."

I reached the top first and wanted to run right back down when I saw a room surrounded by windows with the perfect view to everything around us. This was an office in the sky, surrounded by puffy clouds, a horizon that stretched to eternity, and the buildings and cars looked like toys in the distance.

I wanted to kill Ryan for getting me into this. A few planes in the sky flew around us like bugs, and the chunky man sitting halfway on the consul dangling one leg as if he didn't have a care in the world, as if planes weren't circling the tower, was mind-boggling. I'd never seen anything like it. I'd never heard of anything like it!

"Hi. Welcome to my tower cab. I'm Steve," the man stood up and shook our hands.

"Hi, I'm Jennifer," I replied. "I, uh, promised my brother to visit a tower, to see what it's all about because I'm joining the Air Force today. In a few hours actually."

"You are going to have so much fun." He chuckled and looked at the floor as if he'd remembered something funny. "I was in the Air Force too, a long time ago, and you'll love air traffic. It's the greatest job in the world."

"That seems to be the consensus," I said, thinking about what Ryan had said. "But I've never even heard of it."

"Come over here," Steve waved me over. "Let me show you some of the equipment you'll be working with."

He turned a few knobs, pointed at a small computer screen, and said, "See, this is what we use for our weather. It's called the ATIS."

"I see it," I said. "It looks like a computer screen and yet it doesn't make any sense to me."

"It takes a while to understand all of it, but once you get the hang of it, it's easy, you'll see."

"I'm not sure if I want to see," I admitted, something nagging me in the back of my mind to call Pearson and tell him to get me out of this Air Traffic thing pronto!

Steve pointed out the window and said something inaudible. To me he said, "I'm talking to planes."

"Talking to planes? I didn't know that was even possible!" I gasped.

"Look over here." He was suddenly excited, as if he wanted to share all of his air traffic experience with me. "This is a 'crash phone,' we use it for emergencies. And this," he pulled a small black barrel from the ceiling, "It's a light gun and used to signal to planes that have lost their radio communications."

He pointed the barrel at the floor, pulled the trigger that shined red, white, and green, and asked, "Isn't that awesome?" I wiped my sweaty palms on my jeans, thinking it wasn't awesome at all, it was overwhelming and scary as hell and he might as well have been talking Chinese because I didn't know what he was talking about, and I sure as hell didn't want to see an airplane with an emergency when I was supposed to get on one in a few hours.

"Sorry," Jake shrugged when I glanced back at him.

"Don't look at me," Pam said.

"Thanks, but we really have to get going." I waved at Steve, heading for the stairs.

"Yeah, thanks." Jake and Pam followed.

"Already?" Steve called after us, disappointed. "Okay bye, enjoy the Air Force. You'll have a blast!"

Have a blast my ass, I fumed, running to the car. I asked, "How could Ryan do this to me?"

"I don't know Jen," Jake shook his head as he unlocked the door.

"No, really, I want to know. Give me your phone please." I extended my hand and took it from Jake.

"Ryan!" I got in the car while Pam and Jake smoked a cigarette. "I just saw a tower. There is no way I can do that. Why did you tell me to do that?"

"It's going to be okay," Ryan laughed. "Trust me, you'll love it."

"I don't think so. That's your dream job, not mine."

"Well, if you don't make it, you'll wash out and go home. It'll be like nothing ever happened. Hey, don't you have to catch your flight? Have fun when you get there. Remember, the drill Sergeants will try to cut you down, but don't change who you are, ever."

"Those are your last words to me? You're scaring me now," I said.

"Never mind then. Just be you. And oh, I told Mom you joined, she's happy that you'll be able to take care of yourself. Bye."

"Huh?" I said, but he was already gone and my stomach turned in anger because I'd thought she would have been upset at me for leaving. Instead, it was worse than what I'd thought she'd say after she found out I was living in the basement. I *had* been taking care of myself. That was the whole freaking problem! And I was getting nowhere! God, why was it so hard for her to understand anything?

"Let's get out of here." I said. Jake got into the car and reached for my knee. I slapped his hand and said, "Quit it!" and they both laughed out loud.

"It never gets old, right Pam?" Jake smiled in the rearview mirror, but she was laughing so hard she couldn't answer.

"Okay, you asked for it," he said, turning on the radio and surfing the channels.

"Oh no," I groaned, knowing exactly what he was doing: looking for a Phil Collins song because I'd made the mistake of telling him years ago that

Phil Collins was all that played on German radio, as if everyone was still living in the eighties, and he'd thought that was the funniest thing he'd ever heard. Since then, everywhere we went seemed to be playing a Phil Collins song, the mall, a restaurant, and it never got old to him.

"Su-su sudio!" he turned up the volume and all of us started singing and laughing until he pulled into the airport parking lot. That's when I stopped laughing and talking altogether and almost couldn't move. I stood in front of the security check point, Jake and Pam holding onto me in a group hug.

"It's going to be alright," I sniffed, unsure of whether I meant for them or for me.

We stood for so long, I heard the announcement to my flight, that they were about to board, and I said, "I have to go."

"Don't go Jenny," Pam whispered back. "Let's run."

"You know you don't have to go, we'll figure it out like we always do," Jake said. In my head I said "Okay. Let's go home," but the words got stuck in my throat and somehow I lifted my head and stepped away. This was my one chance out of the basement and I had to take it.

"I love you both so much," I managed to say. "Don't worry. I'll be back in two weeks, ha, ha?" They nodded unconvinced, wiped their tears, and watched me as I placed my backpack on the scanner.

On the other side I waved one more time and watched them disappear around the corner. This was it, isn't that what they said? Now or never, time to get this show on the road, time to grow up, do or die? Well, then here it was, and here went nothing.

SIX

Bright lights exploded overhead then a crazy trumpet, what I guessed you could call music, blasted from a loudspeaker.

I jumped out of bed, my heart thumping in my throat, and wiped the hair from my face that was stuck in a puddle of drool on my chin. I watched a bald Hispanic man stomp up the aisle between the row of beds, his fists clenched at his sides, his face contorted in anger and the light shining off his bald head, thinking this must be some type of fire drill, the building was on fire and he, looking like a New Age Teenage Mutant Ninja turtle minus the Katana sword hanging from his back, had to get us out of here.

Girls leaped off their bunks beds, blankets in trail, spinning in circles and throwing their hands up as if they didn't know what was going on either, and I looked around for smoke and came up short and thought, it's still dark outside, what the hell is going on here?

"Do you need any help, princess?" the turtle leaned into my face, nearly smacking me with his flaring nostrils.

I stared back at him not knowing what to say, although I really did need help, and instead stuttered, "Uh," because Dad called me princess when he was in a foul mood, and this turtle didn't know me at all so why would he be: a. pissed at me and b. calling me princess?

"Uh, uh, what air-man?" he screamed, and that did it. The tears that had been in my eyes started flowing, and I thought of Mom who called me her tough cookie and then remembered that I wasn't four anymore and certainly no longer a tough cookie either.

"This is reveille, ladies," the turtle leaped into the aisle when the music stopped. "It means Get u, Get up, GET UUUPPPP air-men!"

He said airmen like air-man, as if to emphasize something, then said, "My name is Perez," which he said like P-rez. "An' I'm your trainin' instructor. You will address me as Sergeant P-rez, and if you have somethin' to say, you address me as, 'Sergeant P-rez, air-man whoever you are, request to speak. Every mornin' when you hear reveille, you will get up, make your bed, and get ready for physical trainin'. You un'astan'? Let's go!"

I didn't understand shit, but followed suit when all the girls ran to the door and stood along the wall. I was sure we resembled some sort of line, although I think hugging the wall was a way to ensure that we were as far away from him as possible. Then he opened the jail door and we fled past him, down the steps and away from him as fast as if the room really had been on fire.

"Hold on to the han'rails, air-man!" he called after us, but as not to cause even the slightest delay, no one did.

Outside it was so dark I wondered if it was still night and not morning. The air smelled like fresh cut grass, my favorite smell in the world, but the air was so thick and humid I thought I could fall backwards and it would catch me and I'd be able to fall right back asleep again.

This had to be a dream, I told myself, standing in the group that had now stopped like a gang of grazing cattle. Nothing looked real, nothing felt real either. Suddenly another forty or so guys came running down the stairs from behind us with another T.I. (Training Instructor) who met up with Perez and together, we marched to a large concrete slab the size of a football field, illuminated like one so brightly that I realized this sure as hell was no dream. This was for real.

Hundreds of other airmen dressed in gray gym shorts and shirts that said "Air Force" stood in rectangles, perfectly still. All of us were still in our street clothes and stuck out like sore thumbs.

"Line up like everyone else, unda'stan? Like everyone else!" Perez yelled, then sauntered off to the side like a coach and a tall, very white bald, T.I. stepped in the middle of the slab, put a megaphone to his lips and shouted, "Time for the Air Force song!"

"Off we go into the wild blue yonder…" a chorus exploded around me, people spitting, smiling, excited to sing a song I'd never even heard of, so I mouthed the words in case Perez saw I wasn't singing.

"Daily reminder," the bald T.I. announced when the song was over. "Always wear sunscreen. You are military property now and if you get burned you are damaging Air Force property." Then he handed the megaphone to a shorter and more tanned T.I. who commanded, "Drop those arms to your ankles and stretch!"

I bent over but I don't think I stretched; my tendons ripped and my legs tingled. About to lose consciousness, a whistle blew and the T.I. said, "Run," and we scattered to the outside of the concrete and started running.

Kicking one foot in front of the other, I thought I'd better go slowly just like Ryan had said, or I was going to get airlifted out of here. My lungs wheezed like a damned steam engine and people passed me, dodged me, glanced back as if to ask, what is that sound, but I wasn't going to stop until I fell over. I was not going back to the basement or Germany, not now, not yet!

Then I coughed so hard I thought my lung was going to flop out, but instead, it was just a big hunk of phlegm I spit to the side. Side effects of asthma. At least I hadn't fainted yet. I was hurting and couldn't tell what was worse: my legs that had never been used like this or my lungs. But still, I was doing it!

By some miracle, the whistle blew again and it was over, and I fell to my knees in exhaustion. Someone stood over me, extended his/her hand to pull me up, and said, "That's not good for you, you should stand up." I said, "Okay." Because I was happy I'd survived that. Now to shower and get all that sweat and grease off me!

But Perez had other plans. Instead of going upstairs, we stared at the staircase to the dorm for what felt like an hour until I started hallucinating, thinking I smelled food.

"First row go in the chow hall," Perez barked, and I smiled because it was food and was pissed when the first row didn't include me. Neither did the second and third. I was in the last row and could barely keep from running by the time I made it in and smelled toast, eggs, and sweet syrup.

It looks like any other high school cafeteria, I thought, reaching for a tray and glancing up at the lunch ladies in hair nets then back down at the most beautiful food I'd ever seen behind the glass.

"Eyes front, air-man," Perez snapped in my ear when I happened to glance at what the guy next to me was getting. He'd said, "Biscuits and gravy," which I'd never heard of and couldn't believe existed once I saw the slop on his plate.

"Keep your hands on your tray an' step sideways. Don' worry about what Sally next to you is orderin'!"

"What'll you have," the lunch lady looked bored and I said "Everything," and pointed at the hashbrowns, eggs, toast, pancakes and sausages.

Excited to eat, I skipped the drinks from the soda dispenser marked milk, water, and orange juice, and walked straight past the tables where two T.I.'s were eating their breakfast and laughing snottily as if they were insulting someone, just like what I remembered from the airport the night before.

"Airman!" one of the T.I.'s roared and I stopped, my tray shaking, wondering how in the hell I was going to get out of this one.

"You need three glasses of water, airman, now get back there and do it right!" The T.I. on the left had gotten up out of his chair to yell, but I saw it wasn't at me when I turned around. It was the poor guy behind me, so I booked it to the nearest open seat, at a table where three girls were already shoveling food into their mouths, expressionless and in a hurry like they were fugitives.

"Don't get caught in the snake pit," the blonde one suddenly gazed at me before stabbing at her eggs. Her ponytail was messy like mine and she had pale, beautiful, even skin and a long, regal nose.

"What?" I whispered surprised she looked so calm about all this. Her eyes darted left and right as if to make sure the coast was clear and said, "The T.I.'s sitting at the table over there is called the *snake pit*."

"Thanks," I whispered, and bit into my hashbrowns that were surprisingly fantastic. "These are like McDonald's," I marveled, thinking about Jake and Pam and wondering what they were up to without me.

The blonde smiled as if stifling a laugh, and introduced herself as "Stefanie Oslo, but call me Oslo since we have to use last names now."

"I'll call you Ozzie." I said. "I'm Grillo."

"You know you sleep under me," she replied, and I nearly dropped my fork because how in the hell had she noticed anything in the chaos this morning?

Then Perez's voice boomed as he pounded his fists on the table and shouted, "Move out, let's go! Leave your tray an' get up!"

Stuffing another forkful in my mouth, I hurried outside where the orange sun started creeping up in the sky, making the air feel like it was on fire.

Wanting to wipe my brow, another kid did the same with his forehead and Perez instantly ripped that poor kid a new one, so I said nothing.

"The plan for the day air-man," Perez announced, "Is to march around until half of you drop like flies!" I thought, I hadn't even thought about marching!

"It's just one foot in front of the other, air-man!" Perez barked at me, and I said, "I'm trying!" because it really was hard to do it right with the sun in your face, sweat stinging your eyes, and a lunatic buzzing in your ear, but that only pissed him off more.

"Stop trying and do it!" he yelled, and I accidently kicked the guy in front of me which instinctively made me say, "Sorry," and had Perez really livid, screaming, "Stop socializing air-man!"

"Keep your eyes up, ain' no gold on the groun'!" he yelled when I happened to glance at my feet. How in the hell did the marching band do it? How in the hell hadn't I passed out from the heat yet? I needed water! I needed a pool filled with ice! I needed to be back in New Hampshire!

"Don't move and don't lock your knees or you'll drop!" Perez shouted once we finally stopped.

Glancing up, I saw we were in front of a putrid brown military building that looked the same to me as all the others, and I wondered if we'd been marching in circles for the last few hours and just randomly stopped here.

Perez hopped up the few stairs two at a time and disappeared inside and was back less than a minute later, smiling like a jerk when he saw a kid hunched over and throwing up. Then he said, "Alright, inside air-man!"

Inside it was nice and cool, and we lined up against the wall where I thought about sitting down and curling up on the floor to take a nap and bask in the air-conditioning for the rest of my life.

"We're at the den'ist. Smile for your x-rays!" Perez burst through my thoughts, and a few minutes later the Technician called out, "Grillo!" and I made my way up the hall to meet him.

Perez snickered as I past him and he said, "These x-rays are for when you're blown to bits and they have nothing to identify you with…" I gasped, wanting to run the other way, down the hall and outside and back to the dorm, until he stepped in my way. So I followed the Technician obediently, wishing my last name started with 'Z' and not 'G'.

"Stand here," the Technician said without as much as a glance. I was just another name, another number to him. "Lean your forehead here and hold on right here."

But I couldn't hold anything. My hands were limp as I imagined my Swiss cheese bullet holed bloody body in a field somewhere with a team of experts holding up x-rays next to my blown off jaw trying to identify me.

Then it was over, I was done, all of us were done, and we were melting outside again.

"Vaccines boys and girls," Perez announced when we stopped at the next brown building, and I thought if we were only running errands, why the hell couldn't we take a bus?

"Roll up your sleeves and prepare to be a pin cushion." Perez grinned once we were inside then said, "Don' worry it won' hurt, because they're practicing on you, he, he."

Staring at the assembly line of nurses, I pulled my sleeve up, closed my eyes and winced when I saw the first nurse getting ready to stab me three times, but I hardly felt a pinch and she had to remind me to, "Keep moving!" I decided to stop taking Perez so seriously.

Outside marching in the heat again, I knew exactly how horses fell asleep standing. I was exhausted, as if I hadn't slept in days, and felt lightheaded. For a second I lost my balance and my head bounced off the shoulder blades of the guy in front of me, but he barely even noticed. Then I heard the cadence of another flight and looked up, and was in awe when I saw people our age, like us, except with green pajamas looking like soldiers, square serious jaws and shoulders, and puffed out chests like they meant business. I wanted to look like them, wanted to be them, until suddenly they changed their cadence from "Hup two three four" to "Rainbows, rainbows."

I didn't give it a second thought, but Perez stumbled sideways with laughter, wiped a fake tear from his face and said, "You rainbows because all of you are still in your street clothes. Ha!"

So they were making fun of us like they weren't one of us just a few weeks ago. Well, screw them.

"You don't have your uniforms yet, undastan'?" Perez reiterated, and I fumed, thinking yes, we fucking got it, big deal! I'd rather sleep in my white and blue cotton GAP shirt forever if it meant I didn't have to be a cocky asshole like them! Nothing pissed me off more than poor sportsmanship or being an ass for no reason. They could shove their pajamas up their asses for all I cared.

In the next brown building we were seated for the first time, writing our names on a note card, and I, enjoyed the air conditioning. As if Perez could tell I'd temporarily let down my guard and felt relaxed, he opened his big fat mouth and said, "These cards are for your dog tags an' when you get them, never take 'em off because you only get two, one for your toe an' one to be jammed into your teeth once your face is shot off."

The recruiter had definitely failed to mention this, I thought, and I started thinking about Jake and Pam, holding on to me at the airport, telling me not to leave, telling me to go home with them, and how I'd decided to leave anyway. Oh, I was kicking myself now. They had been right all along, I admit it! I wanted to go home!

Less than an hour later we were outside marching again, and this time it included the steady *clank-clank* sound as the metal dog tags rubbed together just above our sternums. It was only a matter of time before I was dead, this cadence bringing me closer to my deathbed with each step, and there was nothing I could do about it. I had decided to join and there was no turning back.

Inside the next brown building there wasn't much to look at, just an open space, dark blue carpet and three large cardboard boxes that could have once held refrigerators before they'd been sawed in half.

"This," Perez picked out a black pouch from the first bin, held it up, and unzipped it to reveal a blue instruction book the size of a notebook, "is the BMTM II, the Basic Military Trainin' Manual, part two, otherwise known as the finest military read the Air Force has to offer. You will eat, sleep, and breathe this book, undastan? That means when we are outside an' waiting for an appointment, you are not dreaming about your boyfriends and girlfriends, you are learnin' the Air Force, because the Air Force is hurry up and wait, undastan?"

Not even a little bit.

I reached into a bin and skimmed through the "finest military read" and was stunned when one of the paragraphs described in ridiculous detail how to zip up a zipper on one of the military coats. I'd rather study calculus. I'd rather leap from a cliff.

Bin number two contained drab olive green Batman web belts, which were pretty cool once fastened around the waist, and from bin number three came a green canteen that attached to the belt.

I danced all the way to the water fountain when Perez said, "Fill it up an' drink 'til it's empty. Hold it upside down to prove it!" because I couldn't remember the last time I'd felt this parched. But as soon as the canteen hit my lips and the smell of raw sewage enveloped my senses, I couldn't drink. My audacity and ungratefulness towards Air Force fountain water, however, sent Perez into a fit of hysteria and he jumped around like a marionette, flared his nostrils in my face and screamed, "They've been sanitized just fine, princess. Now hydrate! Lock an' load! Next up pee pee test. Drink up!"

This day was never, ever going to end, I thought marching up to the urinalysis building where other rainbows were waiting to go in. I was ready to lie down until I noticed some of the other rainbows awkwardly turning their heads because, as I noticed, they'd peed their pants. As if the first day in basic wasn't hell enough, the T.I.'s couldn't let those guys go to the bathroom?

"Get used to it. Hurry up and wait. It's the military way," Perez winked before he hopped up the stairs and disappeared inside and I aped what everyone else was doing; reading the BMTM II and knowing I'd never retain a thing.

"Air-man Grillo, get in here!" Perez hollered a second later. Curse my last name!

Inside, I signed on a clipboard, was handed a cup, and followed a woman in green pajamas to a bathroom where the stall doors had been removed. If anyone had ever smuggled old urine into this place after a day of running, barely eating, all this marching, the vaccines, dental records, and the overall shock to their system of being here, I say they deserved to use it!

When I dropped my pants the woman said, "I have to watch to make sure," and I nodded, wondering what the hell she'd done to get this job.

"Next brown buildin', last stop," Perez announced when we started marching again, and I thought there was an end in sight, thank God, and felt a new energy, a second wind, and excited for the first time that day.

Then we got there, sat on the floor in the hallway of this building while Perez lectured us for fifteen minutes on the green pajamas as if it was the most important speech he'd ever given in his life.

"Lemme tell you a little som'in' about the BDU, the battle dress uniform." He stopped to make sure all of us were looking at him. "They are uniforms designed especially for soldiers in the field, but are also worn every day. You will wear them with pride an' make sure they are clean an' serviceable at all times. This means if you see a string hangin', clip it. If there's a hole, don' wear it. Unda'stan'? Follow me."

Eagerly, we jumped up, turned the corner, and found an entire store of green camouflage pajamas waiting for us.

"All the uniforms are designed for men, an' come in four inch increments. That means if you are 59" inches, you will have to wear 60", undastan'? Males can change behind the left partition, females on the right. Go!"

I made it to the shelves last and surprise, surprise, my size wasn't available. When I turned to see if anyone had any to spare, I saw that everyone was modeling in front of a tall mirror, looking like a soldier, looking how I wanted to look like.

"I can't find my size," I told Perez and he snapped, "This isn't Macy's airman!" When I didn't move, he explained so that no one else could hear, "We at the end of the fiscal yea' undastan'? No more money 'til October. Suck it up an' get the next size up."

The next size up made me look like a human green tent, and as I sulked at my clown like reflection, I realized the smallest boot size was two sizes too big. I couldn't believe my luck.

"The trick is to double up on socks, air-man!" Perez said when I'd wobbled over there, and by the time we tried on hats I was in luck because I had the smallest childlike head of anyone there and at least looked good in that.

"If the hat ain' on your head, it goes into yo' right cargo pocket so you don' lose it," Perez demonstrated, folding his green BDU hat into a burrito and then shoving it into his cargo pocket. "Like this." We did the same and followed him into the next room.

In more bins were the gym clothes. The only size for me were shirts that were skin tight and made my tiny B-cup boobs look huge, and shorts that were too long and wide so that I looked pregnant, making me think I could use the shorts as sails when a gust of wind kicked up while I was running.

Then we picked out our 'blues' uniforms, the same as the recruiters had worn, and I was ready to walk out altogether because they looked and felt hideous, scratchy, and unflattering.

"Wrap it up," Perez called out.

Everyone gathered his or her things, but I thought I'd use the bathroom one more time if he was going to march us in circles all night.

Raising my hand in the air I said, "Sergeant Perez, I need to use the bathroom," and he took one glance at me and turned away.

Oh no he didn't, I thought, calling after him, "Sergeant Perez! Airman Grillo requests..." because I was about to pee my pants!

Then he charged at me, like a bull, like Dad, and stopped on a dime and almost touched his nose against mine and growled, "This ain't no summer camp, Grillo! It's called a latrine, air-man! Get it right!"

"Sergeant Perez," I nearly growled back, why the fuck were we getting technical about a toilet and instead asked, "Can I use the *latrine* please?" because I was too tired to argue semantics. He stood up and waved his hand at me like I wasn't worth setting straight, and I sprinted to the bathroom where I stood for a second to catch my breath, feeling ever so victorious that I'd stood my ground.

But the victory was short-lived when I saw my reflection in the mirror: deep rings under my eyes and shiny skin that revealed new zits getting ready to break through, not to mention my disheveled hair. What the hell was I doing here? I didn't belong here!

"Fall in!" Perez shouted from the hall, and I held my breath trying to calculate how far and fast I could run out of here once they left. I could make it home, at least find a payphone and call someone to get me the hell out of here, right? More like, yeah, right.

Then I exhaled deeply. I had to get my act together. This was only the first day and everyone else was feeling the same way. I dabbed my face with a wet paper towel, fixed my ponytail, and stared deep into my eyes and said, "You can do this! The basement can wait two weeks, right? Lock and load, air-man!"

SEVEN

You would have thought I'd seen it coming, the God-awful lights and trumpets at 5:30 in the morning, but it was even worse the second time. My skin prickled as though I'd heard a gunshot, and I groaned as I rolled off the mattress remembering that oh no, I was still here!

Ozzie and I stood on either side of our bed and took turns tightening our wool sneeze-attack-causing-blankets. We were already dressed in gym clothes; it was one of Perez's tips he'd given us before 'shut eye,' before he turned off the light and slammed the prison door shut, but it didn't make me feel like I was one step ahead of the game at all. Human beings weren't meant to be awake before the sun, so how could I concentrate on a task when I was still half asleep and half dreaming I was at the mall with my friends, trying on clothes?

"What are you waitin' for air-man?" Perez stormed up the aisle, roaring at no one in particular, just roaring for the sake of roaring. "Make your bed! Let's go, let's go, let's go, move it, we don't have all day, undastan'?"

Thank God he passed me as I tied my shoes.

"You call this making a bed you pitiful air-man?" Perez scowled in the distance. Then Ozzie nudged me to get up and we pulled at our blankets again. This time she yanked so hard I was pulled up on the bed.

"Get that rats' nest off of you' neck an' get you' shit together air-man!" Perez caught me pulling my greasy hair into a ponytail as I hustled to the front. "No hair past the neckline, undastan'?"

Sneezing from the dust in the air, I cursed myself for not stuffing my pockets with tissues and having to use my arm as if I was some kind of heathen.

"Lock and load! Move with a sense of urgency air-man!" he screamed after us. The only way to run quicker down the stairs, I hope he realized, was if we all swan dived.

This time the boys from downstairs were already outside and together. In the dark and thick humidity we marched to the concrete slab where the tall bald T.I. wanted us to sing the Air Force song again. Another T.I. then took the megaphone and screamed, "Drop into a plank position!" which only told me one thing; we weren't running.

I dropped to the ground and Perez's boots walked past me. As if reading my mind, he said, "Today is *calisthenics*, the best damn workout program in the world, designed by scientists to get you in shape so you can be America's finest."

Somehow I knew I preferred death.

"Get up! Jumping jacks!" the megaphone exploded, right along with my heart as I tried to keep up.

"DROP!" I dropped, more like collapsed. "Put your noses to the concrete and get your elbows up!"

With my nose smooshed into the concrete, I would have cried if I'd had the energy. Then I tilted my head to the side and stared past the rows of sneakers and into the black sky, once again calculating how far I could run before they caught me.

"Up! Down! Up! Down! Push-ups airmen, let's go! Stick your butt in the air when you want to rest. Do not lie down on the ground! Up! Down!"

Half a push up and my body shook like a seizure, and I rested with my butt in the air until I realized it was harder to rest than to do the actual push up. I was so weak it was appalling, and the guy next to me was eating it up, clapping his hands together once he'd hoisted himself up like he was a trick seal at SeaWorld. Boy, was I in the wrong place.

"Sit on the ground." The whistle blew and I rolled over, coughing, sweat dripping into my eyes, thinking I wasn't going to last another second. "Look to your right and find a sit-up buddy. One of you do sit-ups, the other hold ankles!"

The Hulk next to me nodded. We were partners, and I thought, this is not going to be good.

"I can't remember the last time I did a push up," I admitted, almost blinded by his bright white skin, red hair, and freckles.

"Are you kidding?" he wrinkled his forehead as if I were crazy. "This workout is nothing. This will be the easiest six weeks of your life."

"Easiest?" I whispered thinking, easy for him to say. He looked like he'd been working out all his life. Then the Hulk pushed one finger against my toe as if holding me in place was one big joke and he asked, "How do you like Disneyland so far?"

"What do you mean, Disneyland?" I asked, but wanted to say cut the shit already. Then he pointed in the distance at a huge golf ball-looking thing and said, "Our squadron nickname is 'Wolfpack,' but it's also known as Disneyland."

"Who came up with that crap?" I wanted to know but the whistle blew and it was time to shine. I brought my shoulders up to my knees and exhaled deeply and the Hulk counted, "One." The fact that I'd already completed one sit up already impressed the hell out of me.

Then I cranked out another, but my baggy shorts rode up to my crotch and I was suddenly self-conscious about the view I was giving. The Hulk was cool about it though, he looked away, counted under his breath, and said, "Don't give up, keep going," when my body slowed down and twitched.

The whistle blew, thank God, and the Hulk said, "Watch out," and we changed places, which was easier said than done because I couldn't wrap my tiny fingers around his gigantic ankles to pin him down.

"Turn around," he said, "Sit on my feet and wrap your hands under my knees," I thought it was never going to work but it did, giving me the sensation I was going to be launched into space with each powerful upward thrust.

"Reverse push-ups!" the T.I. screamed, "Sit on your butts and put your hands behind you and lift."

It sounded like that was the one thing I could do, but then the whistle blew and when I attempted to lift my body that one inch off the ground I thought my arms were going to snap off.

Shortly after, the T.I. announced, "Last exercise," and I kissed the ground until I realized we had to jump up and run over to the pull up bars off to the side.

"Pull-up bars. When you're not pulling yourself up, you're jogging in place!"

Another arm exercise, I whined silently, and everyone made it look so easy! Then it was my turn and I dangled like a beaten rug and hung my head in shame, wishing lighting would strike me dead already.

"Pull it up, princess," Perez scolded, but I couldn't, and finally, the whistle saved me from further embarrassment and Perez commanded, "Line up air-man!"

This time we didn't go to breakfast right away. This time Perez brought us back upstairs and announced, "Combat showers!"

Two days I had waited for this moment, a hot shower to make my aches go away and to make me feel clean and all better, except that combat showers didn't really mean "shower," as Perez explained, it meant, "Shower sixty females in three minutes like you're in a combat zone. Grab your crap, get wet, shampoo, soap up, brush your teeth, rinse off and get out! Unda'stan?"

The prison door slammed shut and all hell broke loose.

Gym clothes flew to the ground and sixty women sprinted to the shower, attempting to carry every toiletry item they owned. By the time I got there, the benches were piled so high I didn't think anyone knew whose stuff was whose, but it didn't matter, there wasn't any time for it to matter.

I squeezed my way into the shower between two, then ten bodies, trying to get a few drops of water on me, but was quickly pushed to the back and past all the other shower heads. I soaped up anyway, was elbowed in the shoulder while someone brushed her teeth, and suddenly felt someone crawling on the floor wailing about her razor. Why did she think she had time to shave?

Then I brushed my teeth and tried to lift my head to rinse, but got soap in my eye instead as someone rinsed her lathered up hair. The soap on my body was starting to itch too, but the more I tried to force my way under the water, the farther away I seemed to get.

Screw it, I decided and got out, snatched the first towel I could find, and took off running to my locker until I hydroplaned in my flip flops on the linoleum floor and fell right on my ass, wondering how many people had fallen before me and broken a leg or their neck? That kind of a fall could get someone sent home, and I did not want to get sent home for something like this. Why the hell did we have to shower and hurry to our lockers in a dangerous stampede?

At my locker my legs tingled from the fall, but there was nothing I could do about it. It wasn't like I could file a lawsuit or complain to Perez that I was hurt. He was already pounding on the heavy door like he didn't give a damn if we were naked and screamed, "Thirty seconds. Tick tock!"

I tore the BDU's from the hangers and dressed, combed my fingers through my wet hair and tied it into a bun, and by the time I buttoned the last button on my BDU blouse, Perez burst into the dorm room, staring at his watch, "You're too slow! Too slow air-man!"

For a second I was discouraged. That man was out of his mind. I almost broke my neck and still he was pissed! Then I reminded myself I'd already made it through an entire day and that I was already stronger than the day I left, and wasn't that part of the reason I'd left? To make something of myself?

Bring it Perez, I silently dared him. Is that all you got?

EIGHT

Next to the *latrines* in our dorm was the conference room. About two weeks into basic Perez said, "Park yourselves in there and wait," although there weren't any chairs to park ourselves on. We had to sit on the floor and stare at the blank walls. The only window in there faced the back of a hideous brown and boring building and thank goodness, was in the back of the room so that we didn't have to look at it.

When the prison door opened and shut again, we heard a swishing noise and seconds later, Perez appeared in the doorway with a stack of envelopes pinned under his armpit kicking a plastic mail bin with a package sticking out of it.

I pitied whoever that package belonged to because when Ryan was in basic and we'd accidently sent him a care package, he called us crying a week later saying the T.I. had made his life a living hell and had made us promise not to send another.

Sitting up straight, I tried to guess who'd written me. All week I'd written letters to Ryan, Mom, Jake, and Pam telling them about crazy Perez and that the only time we could unwind was right before lights out where some people wrote letters. Others like Ozzie polished their boots. Why, I had no idea. One girl danced the hula up and down the aisle.

Perez picked a letter from the top of the pile in his pit and studied the name, but instead of reading it aloud he said, "Mail day, air-man! Now, before I pass out your mail, I just want to warn some of you that you may have received a Dear Jane or Dear John letter, undastan'? That means your boyfriend or girlfriend or whatever, is writing to tell you that they don't love you anymore, boo hoo, because you are here. If you don't get the letter this week, you will get it next week. Don' be pitiful. Do your cryin' somewhere else. And before I forget, you are not allowed to receive any packages. This isn't summer camp air-man. Tell your parents not to send packages!"

He glanced at the letter again and called, "Smith," who then smiled and jumped up to get it from him, except that he chucked it blindly so that it sailed past her head and into the wall. The next one hit Minnow in the forehead, but when he called my name, I was expecting it and leaped up and caught it in mid-air like when Dad, Ryan, and I played Frisbee.

Hi Sunflower, I read the letter from Mom. She had called me that since Kindergarten when my teacher had told her I lit up the room when I walked in. It had been a nice way of saying I was too talkative and never shut up, but Mom loved the name and so it stuck. *I miss and love you so much. I am proud of you and can't imagine what you are going through. Is your asthma okay? It's all your father's fault you and Ryan had to join. If I was there, none of this would have happened...*

Hearing everyone around me sniffle, I suddenly couldn't hold the tears back either, even though I couldn't believe she was still ragging on Dad. In fact, I almost believed it was Dad's fault I was here until Perez broke my thoughts as he mocked, "Boo hoo," then screamed, "Air-man!" and I wished he'd just shut up once in a while! Couldn't he see we were reading?

"Air-man! Get up!" I glanced up and saw his shiny boots in front of me.

My letter fell to the floor as I stood up in horror. He was talking to me!

He pushed the package at me hard and I said, "Oof," and pushed it back. "That's not for me." Then I saw Pam's address from the corner of my eye and thought oh shit, how the hell didn't she remember not to send me anything?

"Oh, well, in that case air-man, it must be for me then!" Perez ripped the tape from the box so hard chunks of cardboard came off with it. "Ladies this is what happens when you get a package..."

He unfolded the note in such haste that it tore, then he coughed for emphasis and read the note to everyone in the room. "Ahem, Dear Jenny, we love and miss you. Blah, blah, blah. Hope you are doing okay, here are some cookies…blah blah blah," then let the note fall to the floor and asked, "Do you have water in your canteen, air-man?"

When I nodded, I caught Ozzie's wide eyes staring at me. Never did she have fear in them! Why did she have to look like that now?

"Then grab your canteen an' start eatin'!" Perez shoved the box of cookies into my chest and clumsily, I opened the cap and tried not to gag when he screamed, "Hurry! We don't have all day!"

Reaching for a cookie, I thought this was going to be the worst moment of my life until I took a bite and tasted the sweet crumbs and morsels on my tongue. I couldn't remember the last time I'd eaten a cookie and wow, it tasted amazing!

Cookies two and three were just as awesome and I took my time as I chewed the cookie into a nice mush, mashed it against the roof of my mouth before I swallowed and thought yum! This was not a punishment, this was pure delight! I reached for another and another and savored every bite as if I'd never eat another.

Cookies five through ten, I was in a sugar coma, my eyes half shut, imagining myself in Pam's kitchen with Jake, laughing as we made fun of Dad, a ritual we'd fallen into after he kicked me out, until I suddenly felt a hot breath on my face and saw it was Perez in front of me, not Pam and Jake.

"You think this is funny and that you're at summer camp?" Perez scowled. "Do you think I am here to entertain you, because I had nothing better to do this summer? You will eat every cookie in that box and if you throw it up, you can eat it off the floor, undastan'?"

Unfortunately, I understood too well. At cookie number nineteen, my stomach was so full I could barely breathe, my mouth was raw and my jaw so sore I couldn't part my lips to sip from the canteen. I couldn't even taste the water anymore.

Then Perez snatched the box from me, crumpled it in his hands and screamed, "As you can see, air-man Grillo really loves those cookies! Tell your parents and little friends not to send cookies!" I sank to the floor feeling bloated, sick and anxious, but relieved because I had survived another day!

NINE

"It's all about attitude," Sergeant Cass explained, his arms exaggeratedly wide amid the middle of a story I wasn't listening to.

The scrawny man with the bushy mustache paused for emphasis, to make sure we were listening to his every word, but all I saw was a man who'd been picked on in high school and joined the military to gain respect. I couldn't pay attention to someone like him. My eyes wandered around the room, along the bland white walls as I soaked up the soothing air-conditioning, a nice relief from the boiling outdoors, and zoned out from the boring BMTM II lectures and now, Cass's personal boring anecdotes.

"Attitude is what you make of any situation," Cass continued, strutting around with his chin in the air was if he was God's gift to the Air Force. "You can get through anything in life if you have the right attitude. If you have the right attitude, you can be outstanding!"

He couldn't get enough of that word either, said it a thousand times like it was the word "the," like it was supposed to be used every five seconds, and how did he expect me, for one, to keep up a positive attitude with Perez constantly yelling in my ear?

"My job is top secret, the most secret and highest level of security clearance out there," he bragged, and I suddenly couldn't remember if I'd dosed off, didn't understand what he did, or he just hadn't mentioned it before. Then again, I didn't care. I wanted to zone out and feel like I was taking an ice cold shower. "And it's not just any old top security clearance either, only a select few have the clearance I have. Isn't that outstanding?"

I waited for a punch line, something outstanding, but all he finally said was, "I save your lives every day. You, you, you, and you," he pointed, "and all of your families too, every day. Outstanding, isn't it? I sit in a top secret building with my top secret clearance and monitor everything in the sky. And nothing gets by me, no sir. Birds and airplanes? I see 'em. UFO's? You bet. I've seen 'em all. Missiles? All day, even now, some are flying in from different countries, to see what they can get away with. Not on my watch. And speaking of my watch, all of you should be thanking me for being so outstanding and keeping you safe."

I thought he was trying to be funny, but he really did want applause or something. In unison we thanked him and immaturely he smiled, as if that really did satisfy him, and he said, "Outstanding!" making me decide right then and there never to date a military man, ever.

"Today, you may also be aware that you're halfway through basic," he said, and I sat up as if I'd been punched in the gut, thinking, it couldn't be true, only halfway? "Just today, you are making your beds right, marching and exercising to the Air Force standards, you know, trying to be outstanding, and pretty soon you'll be a part of the "real" Air Force."

I perked up in excitement. Light at the end of this tunnel?

"I don't mean Tech School either- that's one step closer, but not the real Air Force yet. In the real Air Force you live in dorms or base housing and have a regular job. You call everyone by their first name. You don't have to march around all day. You can buy a car and drive around base, even off base. You don't answer to a drill sergeant or shine your boots all the time, as long as they look good like mine, see? Outstanding, right? Trust me, it's where you want to be, but you can only get there if you are good. If you graduate basic."

He meant 'good' as in "don't get washed back for doing something stupid," like some of the other *sisters,* as Perez called us, who'd in the last few weeks been washed back.

The first one happened all of a sudden one day when we'd returned from lunch and Perez caught Ryland and Miraz kissing in the hallway, tongues and all, arms exaggeratedly wrapped around each other and moving up and down their bodies like they were in a play or something.

"What the hell? Come downstairs with me ladies!" Perez had screamed almost confused because he knew they weren't lesbians, that all they wanted to do was get the hell out of the military, but he'd said he had to take them downstairs anyways and we waited for over an hour, biting our knuckles and wondering if we'd ever see them again.

"I didn't have no choice," Perez had come back with his head down and without our *sisters*. 'It's the rules. And they ain't even goin' home. The place they goin' is horrible. They have to sit in a buildin' for months waiting for a ticket home. You'll graduate and be gone a long time before they get outta here. For any of you thinkin' about any more stunts, it's easier to graduate."

I, for one, believed him and wanted to assure him that no matter how many times a day I thought about running away, I didn't have the intention of trying.

Dixon, another one of our sisters, was caught stealing food from the chow hall last week. None of us knew she'd been doing that regularly, and that night she'd flooded the toilet by trying to flush the evidence: chicken bones.

"Stop stealin' food air-man!" Perez reamed her after the plumber left, so she didn't, and the following evening, she fell over in the shower and cracked her head open from what the paramedics had explained was a disease where she needed to eat all the time or else she'd faint. Perez had said, "No kiddin," to the EMT then "Anyone else have a crazy disease I need to know about?" to us, but all we could do was stare at the blood and Dixon lying helplessly on the gurney as it was carried away, wondering when she'd be back, although she never did come back.

McQuin disappeared two nights after that, literally in the middle of the night. In the morning her top bunkmate Hudson found her bed perfectly made with her suitcases set neatly to the side, as if they too were waiting for her to return, and she'd told us that two guys with flashlights had woken her in the night and said to McQuin, "Your career field needs you now. Pack your shit, let's go."

I' could recall wishing I'd known what her job was. I definitely couldn't recall that she was a genius, only very quiet, unless you started talking about her red frizzy hair that she said she dyed that way because she was Wiccan, which she'd explained to me many times on her stroll around the dorm before lights out, and yet it still hadn't made sense to me. Now I wished I'd talked to her more, found out what her career field was so I too could get the hell out of here.

Mohr was the hardest story to bear and had also left in the middle of the night. She too had been quiet and anxious looking, constantly fidgeting and with deep rings under her eyes, and the only reason I remembered her tics was because Perez reminded her ten times a day that as soon as she could she was to dye her 'two-tone' hair one dang color because it was not within "regs, air-man!" and she'd reply in her deep Georgian drawl, "I prah-miss to chain-ge it when I ca-n, suh," and I'd always thought her accent funny although her story sure as hell wasn't.

She never did sleep. That's why she had the rings under her eyes, because she had recurring nightmares from when her stepfather used to come into her room at night. Perez didn't elaborate, only muttered "she'd have been a lot safer here" and "Where was she supposed to end up now?"

Cass suddenly jolted me back to his lecture and I was reminded that I was here for a reason, that I had a chance to change my life if I didn't get kicked out, and listened enthusiastically when he recited the Air Force core values, "Integrity first, service before self, and excellence in all we do. Isn't that outstanding? These are the Air Force core values. Learn them, breathe them, live by them, got it? Outstanding!"

It *was* outstanding, I thought for the first time since joining. I'd never heard of "integrity" before, but I knew I had it once Cass spewed the definition: doing the right thing even when no was looking. "Service before self" was a tough one since I hadn't been in for very long, but I thought I was doing okay so far, and "excellence" was definitely all I strived for.

This was where I belonged, this was where I was going to prove myself because now it all made sense, and I wondered if I'd made it past two weeks, how much farther could I go? What else lay ahead for me? Could I make it all the way to the "real" Air Force?

TEN

Perez called us into the conference room right before lights out, handed us an enormous list of things to pack in our duffle bags, and announced proudly, "Tomorrow is FTX. Field Training Exercise, airman! If you don't make it through FTX, you do not make it to graduation, undastan?"

All too well, I thought. We were close to the end but it didn't matter because basic was just one never-ending list of tasks, and graduation the never-ending dangling carrot in front of us, close but never in reach.

"I can't wait to go," Ozzie beamed as we packed our bags.

Astonished I replied, "What do you mean? I can't wait to get out of here!"

"You don't really mean that," she pushed my shoulder playfully and I begged to differ.

I said, "You're absolutely right! I don't mean it. I swear it!"

And the following morning it seemed just as blazing as ever as we carried our duffel bags downstairs, leaned them against the chow hall wall, ate breakfast, then returned to get them.

"Get them duffle bags up, air-man!" Perez screamed as we struggled to lift the duffle bags and stand upright. "Then grab three MRE's. Without 'em you'll starve, air-man, undastan'?"

To the side was a large box filled with brown plastic packages, the words 'Meals Ready to Eat' written on them, and after I shoved three of them into Ozzie's bag and she did the same with mine, Perez explained, "They're designed to keep you alive in the field, air-man," as if that was any explanation at all. Where the hell were we going and why the hell didn't he have his own duffel bag?

"You sure you packed everythin', princess?" He smacked my back and I struggled to regain my balance. Then he moved to the front of the flight and screamed, "Lock and load Wolfpack! Forward, harch!"

"Hua," we shouted back and marched forward, out from under the awning and into the blazing sun.

Within a few minutes my knees didn't ache anymore and besides the streams of sweat down my face, neck, back, and armpits, I thought I was doing just fine, that maybe this last task wasn't going to be so hard after all. But after twenty minutes, once we reached the edge of the base, left the concrete behind, and found ourselves surrounded by dirt and tall dry grass, I wondered if we were hiking to the end of the Earth.

Perez stopped and stared into the sky as if we'd arrived at our destination already, and then I really got excited thinking it wasn't bad until I realized he was just watching a bird in the sky, and I wanted to remind him that we were melting over here, carrying the equivalent of a small motor vehicle on our backs while he was sightseeing!

"Hydrate!" he suddenly barked, and we took little sips of sewer water that I'd thought with enough hope had miraculously turned cold or for once, would taste like water, but each sip was stinkier, hotter, and thicker.

I looked at the sky and guessed that if the sun had moved at all it had only moved closer and wished Perez would just leave me behind, leave me in the dirt under a tree until my BDU's dried and wouldn't chaff my skin anymore and I could catch up on six weeks' worth of lack of sleep.

"Flight, halt! Hydrate! Hydrate! Hydrate!" Perez commanded a few minutes later. "You see that truck back there?" Perez pointed, wanting us to look at a stupid truck behind us, which all of us eventually did, unimpressed. "Last year, an air-man got himself dehydrated out here and fell over dead. His folks are suing the Air Force now, so guess what? Hydrate! Damn it! Turn your canteens upside down and I'd better not see a drop! Go to the truck and fill your canteen with water and drink it and fill it again! You undastan'? Then lock and load, let's go! Let's go!"

He wanted us to die out here, I was sure of it, and just when I thought I couldn't take one more step, I saw the abandoned warehouse in the distance and thought, hooray, finally, we're here! One step closer to graduation!

"This is not FTX, airman!" Perez read my mind and broke my heart in the same second. "We're takin' a break for M-16 trainin', undastan'? Leave your duffle bags and get inside!"

The duffel bag slid from my wet shoulders without any effort and I left it in the dirt feeling like I was floating. Inside the air was so cold I thought my sweat would turn to ice, and I was going to let it.

Besides a shiny linoleum floor and a large American flag mural on the wall there was nothing inside, and I couldn't figure out why we marched all day to get here until I saw the two gun racks in the middle and realized Perez had saved the worst for last.

My stomach did a flip and I wanted to take off running because I hated guns more than anything in life. Dad used to take Ryan and I out in the woods where we practiced shooting a BB gun and it was fun, but this shit was for real, with real bullets and the real power to kill. Accuse me of having an overactive imagination all you want, but I didn't want that kind of power and I sure as hell didn't want to see someone's head explode, or for that matter have mine explode.

Carefully I laid the rifle on the table in front of me and noticed I'd been so consumed with fear that I'd lost Ozzie, my one anchor in all of this, the only who'd make me see the bright side, and then some hillbilly next to me bragged, "I can't wait to shoot this darn thing. I used to shoot them there squirrels in my backyard and watch 'em explode! It was awesome!"

"Sergeant Perez!" I stood up with my arm in the air, but Perez was gone and in his place stood a six foot, dark haired Sergeant with a thick black mustache.

He closed the door and said, "Welcome, airmen. I'm Sergeant Sanchez, your M-16 instructor. Today, we'll learn about rifle safety, taking the rifle apart and putting it back together again."

Sinking back into my seat, I felt lightheaded and trapped and tried to push away all thoughts of exploding squirrels until Sanchez pointed a red laser pointer above my head and said, "See that red circle on the ceiling?" I slowly looked at the hole in the ceiling circled in red and thought, please don't let that be what I think it is. "See that dot in the middle? Yes, that's a bullet hole. Some knuckle head fired his weapon in class thinking his M-16 wasn't loaded. Luckily, he was pointing it upwards and no one got killed."

I wanted to ask Sanchez to let me go, please let me get the hell out of here before the trigger-happy knucklehead next to me inadvertently fired his M-16 and killed me, but I couldn't get the words to leave my throat and Sanchez smiled, "Let's begin!" and I thought maybe if I didn't look at the rifle, I could manage to get this over with.

"Let's disassemble your M-16, you'll first start…" he said, but I didn't know what he was saying and somehow, minutes later, wasn't even sure if I'd even taken it apart when he said, "Wasn't that easy?"

All I could think was, thank God that is over, let's go to FTX now, bye!

"Now it's time to go outside and shoot!" He pointed at the door. This was never going to end! "Use the door over there, it leads to the range. An' don't forget to take your ear and eye protection, gun clip and two boxes of rounds."

Everyone jumped up excitedly, hurried to the table, pocketed his or her ammunition, donned the ear and eye protection, and disappeared outside, but I couldn't move, and a second later Sanchez stood in front of me, his palms on the table, and asked, concerned, "What's your problem, airman?"

"I'm not ready. I can't do it. I don't know how," I stuttered.

He said, "Stand up and watch me," not accepting my defeat. "Just load the bullet in this chamber and cock it. Your finger goes on the trigger. Aim and breathe slowly. Shoot when you exhale. Now you try."

"No, really, I don't want to," I pushed the rifle towards him, but he just pushed it back so that I had no choice but to pull it close to me, check the chamber as he instructed and place my finger on the trigger like I was ready to shoot, like it was second nature.

"There you go. You've got it, kid. You're a natural," he nudged my shoulder like a proud Dad.

I reiterated, "No, I'm not. I'm not ready to go out there. I can't. Please."

"Sure you can," he insisted. "All you need is some confidence. Go out there and give it your best shot, ha ha. Don't forget your stuff. I'll be out there in a minute."

His face was so friendly I couldn't think of another stall tactic and had no choice but to don the ear and eye protection, pocket the bullets, and remind myself to breathe as they rattled in my pocket.

Outside, it was so hot I thought I'd have to crawl to the shooting bay. The only one open of course was next to the hillbilly, and as sweat poured down my brow I thought this is how I am going to fail out of the military forget all the push-ups, sit-ups, pull-ups and laps that nearly killed me.

My heart pounded in my chest as I laid down, compounded like a big Chinese drum booming through my body because of the ear plugs cutting off all other sounds. The nasty rifle was next to me and clumsily I loaded the clips, noting the crow in the sky circling overheard, awaiting my death, so it could pick the skin from my carcass.

"Ready?" Sanchez's voice echoed through a megaphone and I nearly wept. No, I wasn't ready at all and yet I didn't want to go home, not like this. "On my count, hold your rifles tightly. I'm counting back from three to one. Three…"

Holy shit! Why was I the only one who didn't want to do this? Oh my mouth was so dry, why hadn't I thought to drink water?

"Two…"

I had to calm down, I knew it. I just didn't know how. I also couldn't fail, I reminded myself, not like this, and I exhaled so deeply dust flew off the concrete and swirled in front of me. A sneeze attack was the last thing I needed. I tried to blow the dust away, and then "One!" and a thousand fire-crackers exploded *boom, boom, boom,* and I screamed as hot shell casings from the hillbilly hit me in the forehead, cheek and ear.

"Ouch! Stop!" I screamed, but my voice was drowned out, and although I wanted to stand up and make a run for it back to class, I stopped myself, gripped my rifle tightly, and realized it was insane of me to run into gunfire and that I had to suck it up, face my fears as Ryan always said, and just do it.

Pulling the rifle close, I aimed, exhaled, and ignored the images of bloody bodies as I pulled the trigger. I thought my shoulder had been hit with a sledgehammer, but pushed through the pain. What a kickback! But I couldn't stall any longer if I wanted this done, and I aimed, exhaled, and pulled the trigger again until all the bullets were gone, and stood up when Sanchez announced, "Next position is standing."

My palms were soaking wet, my sternum felt like it had been inverted and was squeezing my heart and lungs, but I kept telling myself I was almost done with this shit and that a silly little rifle wasn't going to keep me down, and before I knew it, it was all over and Sanchez instructed us to get our targets and bring them to him.

"This is accurate as hell, kid," he whistled when he saw mine, but I was only halfway listening and said, "What?"

"Did you know there's a ribbon for marksmanship?"

"No," I replied indifferently. Then I looked over his forearm to see for myself and said, "Really?"

"Wait a minute, there's an extra bullet hole," he exhaled then recounted. I almost told him to forget it if it meant I had to reshoot, but then he said, "Looks like one of your neighbors hit your target. It disqualifies you from the ribbon. Sorry, airman."

"That's okay. Am I done?"

"Here's your score card. Put your rifle back then you're done. Good job."

I said, "Alright," and almost ran back to the rack.

Afterwards, I joined everyone else on the picnic benches outside but couldn't eat, could barely even stand the smell of the cooking food with my sick stomach. In the distance the dead grass and leaves swayed in the hot breeze making the landscape look like a scorched Monet painting, and I hoped I'd chosen right, that this was where I belonged, the path I was supposed to be on, and that somehow it would all come together in the end like a puzzle and I wouldn't feel like an outsider any more. Then I thought about how much I wanted to be a normal kid, back home, or just able to shave my legs and shower in peace!

"Lock and load!" Perez brought me back to my nightmare, and as I strapped my duffel bag to my shoulders and nearly buckled under the weight, wondered how in the hell I'd made it past two weeks.

Again, we marched in the sun for what seemed like hours until the guy in front of me stopped so that I nearly slammed into him. Perez shouted, "That's right air-man! Suck it up, you're walking through it," and I glanced to the side and saw that we were expected to wade through a stream up to our chest and come out on the other side. Disgusting.

Instantly my boots, pockets, and underwear filled with water and I closed my eyes to stay focused. Perez definitely had a knack for making a bad situation so much worse. I felt refreshed for a second and like Swamp Thing the next. Oh, I just wanted a shower, Perez!

And then he said, "Almost there air-man!" as if he read my mind and as I stared past him and saw the camp ground with camouflaged tents, an amphitheater and trees all around it, and knew it was true. We made it. We had arrived at FTX, the final test!

The first cabin we stopped in front of was marked *Office* and Perez barked, "Wait here. Drop your bags," before he hopped up the four steps and disappeared inside.

Suddenly a tall, thin, sandy-haired and green-eyed happy Sergeant came out and smiled, unlike all the other T.I's and Perez who wore a constant frown. Who was this guy?

"My name is Sergeant Stanton and I'll be in charge the next few days. You are the very first flight to go through FTX and I hope you're excited, even though it will be grueling. I promise you all," he annunciated "you all" although I could tell he wanted to say y'all, "will learn a lot here. Remember, attitude is everything."

Oh great, another attitude fanatic.

"So let's jump right in. There are some rules you all need to follow, of course." He pointed at a large bin on the side of the office. "One. Wear a Kevlar helmet when you're outside. This is a simulated war zone."

Everyone grabbed a helmet, they were so cool looking, and put it on, but all I wanted to do was rip it from my head when it scrunched my vertebrae together and gave me a headache.

"Two. Have a buddy with you at all times."

That was a no-brainer. Ozzie and I glanced at each other.

"Three. Carry an M-16 with you for protection. They are hollowed out, but don't be fooled, they are still important. Four, camouflage paint."

Next to the Kevlar bin stood the rifle racks, which didn't bother me at all because a bullet couldn't fit into the chamber. Next Stanton passed out paint cans resembling shoe polish and although I didn't want that crap on my face and clogging my pores, Ozzie pried the lid open, dabbed the back of her hand to admire the color, and said, "Oooh."

"Whoever has the best paint job gets a prize," Stanton said.

Ozzie bounced with excitement and said, "I love it!" as she smeared the thick paint on my face. I groaned, "No prize is worth it, Ozzie. I'm going to break out all over."

"No you won't," she countered. "You look great, like we're in a jungle. Do mine now." Minutes later, Stanton walked around with his hands behind his back as if really studying us and said, "You all did a great job! I can't decide who to give the prize to, so I'm not going to hand one out," and I thought, this isn't Kindergarten, pick someone!

"How about your assignment for the day?" He smacked his hands together as if giving himself a high five. "It's not as exciting as what we're doing tomorrow, but like I said, you guys are the first ones here and this area used to be a landfill, and I need you to grab a garbage bag and pick up any debris you find in the near half mile radius."

"Come on!" Ozzie pulled me up as if that was the most exciting thing she'd ever heard.

I said, "We're picking up garbage!"

"We're out in the open! Can you smell the fresh air?"

"It smells like dirt and heat," I answered, but Ozzie pushed my shoulder as if I had made a joke, then skipped ahead of me gleefully picking up trash.

"Hey, look at me!" I leaned against a camouflage building labeled, *the latrines*, and laughed. "Psst, Ozzie, can you see me now? How about now?"

"That is hilarious!" she giggled. "Let me try! Can you see me?"

"I can't! Ozzie, where are you? I can't see you!"

Stanton's voice suddenly exploded over the P.A. system. "All airmen rendezvous at the amphitheater. All airmen to the amphitheater," and we took our almost empty garbage bags to the amphitheater and watched as Stanton did a headcount and sat down.

"In a few minutes I am going to dismiss you all for your dinner MRE. But first, I want to let you know that the sleeping tents are set up. The first three by the latrines are the females, the last three males. After you eat, bring your duffle bags to your tents. There are sixteen airmen to each tent and you'll sleep by alternating head-to-foot. You have permission to shower and lights out will be in two hours. Everyone is expected to pull a half hour guard shift through the night and I will check that you do. Good night! I'll see you in the morning hours."

This time I devoured my spaghetti MRE, although it didn't taste anything like spaghetti. Ozzie of course said hers was the best meal yet, whatever it was, and afterwards we claimed our cots and decided we had enough time to shower. I couldn't wait to scrub the paint from my face.

The showers, however, were nothing more than a concrete slab with a chain hanging next to the shower head as if it was something straight out of a concentration camp, and when I pulled the chain, ice water stabbed my face and I screamed, "Ozzie, you do not want to shower! It's pure ice!"

Even though I couldn't keep my teeth from chattering, she said, "It can't be that bad," and stepped in anyway. She of course, screamed too.

"Let's polish our boots," she said once we made it back to our cots, and I agreed although I could hardly keep my eyes open. Then I fell asleep and awoke to Ozzie shining her flashlight in my face telling me to get up for guard duty, another one of Stanton's rules.

"It's 2 a.m." Ozzie turned off the light and I turned on mine, wondering when this would all be over, when I could finally sleep?

Standing by the front of the tent, I stared out onto the FTX camp and the stars and felt more alone than I had in a while.

Who was I kidding, pretending to be a soldier, a guard, in my oversized BDU's? I didn't even know what I was doing here. What was I doing here? Where was I going to end up? Why did I feel so lost and why wasn't any of this clear to me?

Then the timer went off. I put those questions on hold again, ducked inside the black tent, and eagerly woke the next girl, who groaned like I had.

I laid down in my sleeping bag and decided it didn't matter whether or not I knew where I was going or if I'd made the right choice. I was young enough, and more importantly, still here. I had held on this long, all I had to do was keep holding on, and in just a few more days I'd be out of here. Just a few more days!

ELEVEN

I didn't know how "Reveille" found us at FTX but it did, and when Ozzie and I leaped out of our cots instead of our bunk bed we stood confused for a moment, searching for Perez and wondering why the lights weren't on but the sun was up.

"Let's go, you all!" Stanton called through his megaphone from outside, sounding overly eager. "We've got PT in your BDU's! Let's go!"

Of all the crap Perez made us pack, of all the things he made us stuff into that ridiculous duffle bag to make it weigh sixty pounds, he couldn't let us take our PT shirt and shorts?

"Here we go," Ozzie smiled. "This will be fun!"

"Fun?" It was not the first word that had come to mind, although admittedly, the definition of fun had changed in the last few weeks. I'd settle for taking a hot bath, having the time to floss and shave and put on deodorant without getting my ear blasted off. Any of those would be fun.

Ozzie's definition, however, had stayed the same. All she wanted to do was travel, which was why she'd joined; her job description required her to travel every few months, and it was all she ever talked about. Basic was her first travel destination, but to me it was just in the way. I needed to get past basic, start my career and my life, and I hoped it was all waiting for me on the other side, if I graduated.

Outside, Stanton jogged in place in his BDU pants, tan t-shirt with a whistle that bounced around his neck, and a huge smile. The megaphone went to his lips and he said, "Half a mile run followed by calisthenics," making me wish I'd had the eight cups of coffee he'd drank that morning so I could feel that awake.

"Come on airmen, you all cheer up!" Stanton blasted us. "Enjoy the morning! The sun is up and beautiful."

"Hua," We groaned, and he said, "I can't hear you airmen!"

"HUA!"

HUA nothing, my boots felt like concrete blocks and the insides of my thighs couldn't take any more chaffing from the constant sweat and hard materials rubbing against me, and I was suddenly worried that Perez had left us out here for good and that we were in fact never going to graduate.

"The same rules apply," Stanton said after the run that hadn't been as hard as I'd thought. Then he told us to huddle together and said, "You all need to repaint your face. Wear your helmets and rifles and I'll see you after you eat your MRE's in the amphitheater."

After we showered, Ozzie studied my face and envisioned a new paint scheme that I hoped would cover up all the new zits that had popped up overnight. Then we donned the rest of the war crap and ate a tasteless MRE. When we met Stanton in the amphitheater again he was even more amped up than before. He pumped his fist in the air like a superhero and said, "You all follow me!" and led us to a large dried-out grassy field with three piles of something I couldn't identify until Stanton said, "We're going to build tents!"

"Yeah!" Ozzie shook my shoulders excitedly.

Sarcastically, I replied, "Who said this day wasn't going to get better by the minute?"

I'd been camping once, with Dad and Ryan, at the beach when we were ten or twelve, and an hour after we'd roasted a can of Spaghettios over the fire it started to rain, and we hung out with an elderly couple who had an RV with an overhang. We sat there until the rain stopped and then went home because none of us wanted to sleep in a small tent on top of wet sand.

"You all will be separated into three teams," Stanton announced. "Each team will set up a tent and rely on each other for team work. Follow the directions that are attached to the front and don't worry, it's written for the Army, so the directions are dummy proof." He laughed at his own joke, checked his watch, and said, "Go!"

Ozzie dove for the side of the tent and read aloud, "First…" while I was pushed off to the side, sweat pouring down my face and wondering why in the hell we were doing something so impractical in this heat? When would we ever build a tent?

"Good job, you all. Team Two finished first. Gather 'round. Let's review," Stanton called after what felt like hours, and then afterwards announced, "Chemical Warfare training is next! And we'll be in air-conditioned tents behind the office."

I smiled at Ozzie and had to keep myself from skipping. Air conditioning!

Inside the big white freezing cold tent were rows of metal chairs and an aisle like we were attending a tiny wedding. On each chair was a spiral bound notebook and a pen for us to take notes with, but by the time Stanton played the part of the video where puppies and kittens curled up and died from the effects of chemical agents, I was too stunned to write anything down.

"In the field," Stanton hit pause on the video, "you'll wear detection tape over your chemical warfare gear, here, here and, here." He pointed at his bicep, wrist, and shin. "That way it's easy for you to recognize when you have been exposed. And the cure," he held up a large syringe missing a needle, "is an injection called Atropine, also known as a 'cocktail' because of all the different vaccines that mix to combat the chemical attack. You shoot it in your leg, here, not in your rear as before. Soldiers were shooting it into their tail bone and messing up their backs. So remember thigh. Not rear."

I curled my lip at Ozzie who was too engrossed in the video to look at me. I'd rather die than stick that thing anywhere into my body.

"UXO's are next." Stanton cued the next video and said, "Take good notes," and minutes later, I once again couldn't take my eyes away from the screen as buildings, cars, and people were blown to smithereens from homemade bombs planted by terrorists. It was unfathomable to see such devastation and destruction willingly caused by a few people whose hatred ran so deep they'd kill anyone in their paths.

"Not only are the detonated bombs dangerous, as you can see, but so are the UXO's, Unexploded Ordinances. Here's a checklist. Take look and then place your notebooks on your chair because we're going outside to do this for real."

"Come on," I groaned. It was noon, the sun blaring and high in the sky. We had no business being outside without as much as a twig for shade. I preferred to watch more puppies die than stand in that heat!

Not that Stanton cared. He pressed on and once outside, he dragged two huge duffle bags over from somewhere and led us to a sandy area. He spilled the contents out of the bags and said, "This is your chem gear. They look like BDU's but they are much thicker and lined with charcoal. You can see the charcoal has leaked out from all the demos so they aren't good for the real world, but you get the idea. Put them over your BDU's. The gas masks are in the pouches. Strap those to your leg and buckle them around your waist. In the real world, the cocktail would be in the pouch. Don your masks!"

Slowly, I covered myself in another layer of clothes as thick as a snowsuit and wondered why Stanton didn't just light us on fire. Then I donned the mask, something out of a zombie apocalypse movie, with a beat up plastic visor someone had tried to carve their initials into, a black can attached to the outside by the mouth, and a cape that covered the back of the head to my shoulders. It might as well have been a plastic bag that someone wanted to suffocate me with. I struggled to breathe, my vision blurred, and beads of sweat formed on every pore.

"Check your masks for the seal," Stanton placed a hand over his mask canister until suddenly his visor caved inward as he sucked in the last air in his mask.

I placed my hand on the can and started choking. This was how I was going to die.

"Put on your gloves!" Stanton ordered as if he just didn't know how to quit.

I was so wet from sweat I thought I'd peed myself and I was way beyond the point of overheating, I was a soufflé and I wondered how firefighters ran into burning buildings if they felt like this? How did astronauts walk on the moon, so close to the sun?

I waved my hand at Ozzie to signal that I was about to pass out, but she waved back as if to say hello, and before I could wave again Stanton screamed, "Drop down! Air raid!" and everyone dropped in the sand, surrounded me with dust, and crawled in different directions like spiders trying to get away.

I dropped too, but only because my knees had buckled and my chest felt as though a bus had parked on top of me. Mom's voice echoed in my head: "I knew this would happen, this is your father's fault. I told you not to join the military. I told you, you were going to drop dead!"

She was absolutely right, I thought and struggled to rip the mask from my face and failed. Then I pulled at my gloves, finally got them off and then tore the mask from my head and felt the hot heat that now felt cool swarm all around me. I managed to pull at the chem gear top then kicked off the pants.

When all the clothes were off I thought Stanton would spot me and yell at me for breaking the rules of his war game that I hadn't understood in the first place, but all I heard in the distance was, "Great job you all. Hydrate and get back to class," and everyone came rushing past me, took off their chem gear, and headed back to class, where I wanted to stay all day.

Stanton cued another video, but when he caught someone yawning, decided we needed a break and said, "You all put your notebooks under your chairs. Take five outside and stretch."

No one stretched as we shuffled out and I joined Ozzie standing next to a skinny tree and stated the obvious: "It's so damn hot!"

She whimpered, "It's getting to me too," and wiped her forehead.

"Who put their notebook on top of the chair when I specifically asked you to put it underneath?"

It took me a second to realize that it was indeed Stanton who was yelling because I'd never seen him in a bad mood before. "Following orders correctly is exactly what the military is all about! You all have been the best group I have taught in the last two weeks, but this will not be tolerated. You all spread out. Stand in a circle!"

Not knowing what to expect from this usually nice guy, we dispersed and made a huge circle as if we were going to sing Kumbaya around a campfire, and glanced at each other in wide eyes all thinking the same thing: what was he going to do to us?

"Drop Down!" Stanton screamed, and after six weeks of being yelled at and learning to do as you're told, we dropped.

Sand hit my face and danced in front of me and tickled my nose.

"Noses in the dirt, I'd better not see any eyeballs! Now UP!"

Instinctively, we went up.

"Down!" We went down and I didn't know what came over me, but I giggled.

Weeks ago I couldn't do half a push up and now I was pumping them out at will! Ryan would be so proud! If Jake and Pam could only see me now!

"Enough you all!" Stanton frowned, his hands on his hips. "Twenty is enough. Get back to class so we can finish up and get to bed early. No guard duty tonight either!" We clapped and cheered, and I wished all T.I.'s were as awesome as he.

Then we went to bed when the sun went down, and sometime in the middle of the night Stanton and a few other T.I.'s stormed through our tent like a S.W.A.T. team raiding a building, waving flashlights in our faces and shouting, "Exercise, exercise, exercise! Rendezvous at the flag pole," and disappearing seconds later.

"There's no way we're doing calisthenics," Ozzie said.

I replied nervously, "I wonder what's going on."

Outside, we stood in the dark, staring up at the flag pole and at the only light bulb on in the camp. It started to rain and I shivered, wondering how this night could get any worse.

A crackling sound came over the speaker like an old record player and suddenly a voice came alive and said, "This is the President of the United States of America and I am proud of each and every one of you. I have a special mission for you today…"

I didn't know if it was from sleep deprivation, chemicals from the MRE's, or if I'd been brainwashed, but all I felt was pride and patriotism. I was Captain America, ready to follow the call, ready to jump into action for the President, HUA, and follow Stanton to wherever he led us! No longer was I the scared and helpless girl. I was a soldier now, an airman in the United States Air Force and ready for anything!

The recording stopped, the cabin office door opened and slammed shut, and Stanton and a few T.I.s in camouflage ponchos appeared.

"War games and sleep deprivation is what the military is all about," Stanton said, as if we didn't know that already. "Tonight you all are on a special mission to take over this Fort and take hostages if necessary. Try to strategize, make sure you have code words agreed upon by your team to defeat the enemy. Lock and load."

Everyone dispersed behind the trees like they'd done earlier after he'd called air raid, and I wondered how they'd gotten wind of a plan when I had no idea what was going on. All I had was questions: what codes, what strategy, where was Ozzie, and wasn't it enough to have a rifle, helmet and face paint? Why all these games?

Running to nowhere in particular, I wanted to get away from everybody and ended up next to a wooden fort. I leaned against it to get shelter from the rain but couldn't. When I wanted to climb to the top, I noticed a T.I. was pacing back and forth, standing watch over something, and I couldn't remember if it was one of the forts I was supposed to protect or take over. I decided I didn't care and ran in another direction, wishing there was some place to hide, rip off this helmet, and sleep!

It could have been minutes or hours that passed. Either way, I was completely drenched when I heard the whistle. It was over, and I went running for the amphitheater. But I knew there was trouble when I arrived and found a shocked crowd staring at Stanton, who wouldn't take his eyes off a guy next to him, his head hanging low in shame.

"You all better get here within ten seconds, or else!" Stanton screamed angrily then flicked his index finger out for a quick head count. He roared, "Why are you all here?"

No one said a word.

"Well, I'm going to tell you all why you are all here," he spit. "Airman Andrew here decided to sleep. Why would he do a selfish thing like that? Why would he let down his team, airmen who are counting on him?"

He walked around Andrews as if to intimidate him, as if Andrews wasn't intimidated enough, and I knew he wanted all of us to be as mad at Andrews as he was, but the truth was I wasn't mad at all. I was envious. I wanted to know what corner he'd found to sleep in and how long he'd slept for, and then I wanted to imagine what even a little cat nap might feel like.

"Now you all will be punished for his actions. Raise your rifles out in front of you. Two minutes," Stanton screamed, making me wonder if he'd lost his mind. What kind of punishment was that?

It didn't take long to find out. Ten seconds passed and my shoulders felt as if someone was hacking at them with ice picks. Someone groaned, someone else sneezed and Stanton screamed, "Four minutes," and nearly all of us gasped and he said, "Five minutes," and it was silent except for the rattling of our rifles as our muscles tensed and wanted to give out and the clenching of our jaws.

"Did all of you learn your lesson?" Stanton paced around us like a hungry shark.

"Yes sir!" we screamed.

"Six minutes!" he screamed, but a second later said, "Alright, you're dismissed for breakfast," and all of us dropped our rifles to the ground.

In the amphitheater, Ozzie and I ate silently and watched as the sun came up over the horizon. I couldn't remember the last time I'd seen a sunrise but knew I didn't want it to be like this.

"I can't wait to get out of these muddy BDU's and take a shower," Ozzie said.

"You're not kidding," I said, and added, "Did you get the newspaper? I wanted to check out the comics!"

"Grillo!" Stanton's voice suddenly boomed.

Ozzie said, "Get up, you've got to go."

"Do you think he heard me? This can't be good."

Sprinting towards the office, I attempted to get in, but was blocked by a linebacker T.I. who stood there for a minute before he said, "You have a phone call."

"What?" I flew past him, hoping it wasn't the only person I thought it could be, because if it was it wasn't good news. I was sure getting a phone call out here was nearly impossible unless it was really bad.

"Are you Jennifer?" a woman's voice asked after I picked the receiver up off the table and said hello.

"I am, but who are you?"

"I'm with the Red Cross, can you hold for a transfer," she said, and I fell into the chair and sniffed, "Yes," as tears formed in my eyes.

"Jenny?" Pam asked.

I tried to sound as strong as she did and replied, "It's so good to hear your voice Pam. It's felt like a year since I've seen you!"

"How are you doing over there, Jenny?" She avoided the obvious, and I played along.

"I don't know, okay I guess. I miss real showers and shaving."

She laughed, "It never bothered you before not to shave for a while, you're so European!" Then she added quietly, "I can't believe they found you. We're at the hospital and the Red Cross said they could find any military member so I decided to try."

"I don't know how they did it either," I agreed sadly, feeling like I was living on the moon and not just a few states away, and wished they hadn't found me, because what could I possibly say to my best friend whose mom had died, whose mom I'd felt pity to talk to? "I actually have no idea where I am right now."

"My mom passed away," Pam sniffed.

I replied, "I'm so sorry Pam," knowing that it sounded flat and that it didn't even matter if it hadn't been flat because I wasn't even there and that was all that really mattered. Instead I'd run away, and worst of all, couldn't come back, couldn't hug her and tell her how sorry I really was. "I'll come home right now, okay? I can't believe I'm not there. I know I'm the worst friend in the world. I should have never left."

"No! You can't." She quieted. "I know I said you'd be back by now, but you're doing it. And you're almost done. You can't come back. You have to finish. I was just sitting here and the nurse told me about being able to find you and I wanted to try it out."

"You have no idea how good it is to hear from you." I pressed the receiver into my ear with two hands, as if that was going to teleport me home, and listened to her breathe, which made me ache and wish I'd never left, wished I'd found peace in that damned basement so that I could be there for her.

"I am so sorry Pam." Tears streamed down my face. "I am so sorry I left and that I'm not there."

"It's okay," she replied, as though she didn't hate me like I hated myself. "I love you. I didn't want to bother you. I'll let you go."

"You're not bothering me. I love you. I miss you. Your voice, it's so good to hear your voice, please don't go."

"Finish up there Jenny. I love you."

"Please don't hang up. I love you too, no! Please come back!" I screamed but she was gone and the T.I. was behind me as if he'd been listening, and held me by my forearm so that I wouldn't fall, handed me a tissue and asked, "Are you okay to go out there?"

No, I am the scum of the Earth I thought, but said "Yes," and he replied, "Take your time," although all I wanted was to find Ozzie and hug her.

"You all have done a great job the past few days," Stanton said after I'd made it back outside and found Ozzie. "Even though we had a few sticky situations, you have set the bar high for everyone after you. There was supposed to be a ceremony, but the Air Force coins haven't been printed yet, so you can wash the paint off your face, return the helmets and the rifles, and go pack your bags. You have thirty minutes, then line up over here for the march back."

"Let's go," Ozzie smiled at me, but then Stanton pulled me aside.

"Sorry for your loss," he said. "You don't have to march back. There is a bus waiting to take you back. Your duffle bag is already on it." Ozzie waved goodbye, although I wished I could tell her to stay with me.

Getting on the bus as the only passenger would have been exciting two days ago. Now it was just another reminder that I didn't belong here, that I needed to stop running around in the mud pretending to be something I'm not and find my way home to the people who loved me.

The driver said, "We're here," as if he had said it at least a few times already, and it took me a moment to remember where I was and where I was going until I recognized my dorm. I ascended the stairs and plopped onto my bed, wondering what I was supposed to do now, when a girl in BDU's approached me and said, "Grillo? I'm Airman Willow. Perez assigned me to you."

"For what?" I croaked.

She replied uncomfortably, "Well, suicide watch. I will be with you for the next twenty four hours. Come with me."

I followed her downstairs and said, "I don't feel like eating."

Willow didn't take me to the chow hall. She took me past the laundry room and into the courtyard where the payphones were. Perez was there too, with his arms folded on his chest, and looking mean as ever.

"You have five minutes, Airman," he said, and I stumbled into a booth and called Ryan, thinking of how he had called me from here a year ago, hadn't said one word besides "hi," and started crying. All I'd wanted to do was reach through the phone and yank him back home, and now I wished he could do the same for me.

Ryan hadn't heard about Pam's mom yet and promised he'd call then surprised me with, "By the way, Dad is getting married tomorrow."

"I don't care," I said. "He can go to hell" which he could. I wanted Ryan to be there at my graduation and if he was going to Dad's wedding, it wasn't going to happen.

"I understand," I corrected myself, although I'd never in a million years understand, and he said, "I'll see what I can do."

Next I called Jake, who was about to meet Pam at her house, and I thought at least someone was there to take care of her, not like me who'd run away from her problems. I didn't dare to ask about whether he was going to my graduation since all this happened, and so I tried to hang up, but he had another bombshell to drop. He said, "I'm gay. I told my mom and she kicked me out of the house and I just couldn't live with it anymore."

Trying to recall if I'd known all along that he was gay, I decided I didn't care, and I asked, "Are you okay? What are you going to do now? And what the hell is going on there since I left?"

"Everything's fine," he said trying to sound convincing. "I'm going to my dad's. Just take care of what you're doing over there."

I said, "Easier said than done," and hung up.

Then Perez, Willow, and I stared at each other like a stupid triangle, and I bit the inside of my cheek before I said something I couldn't take back, like "Get Willow the hell away from me and get me out of this hell hole, you ogre!"

"Take her to the chow hall," he said to Willow, and I said, "But" to argue, until he narrowed his eyes at me.

"You should at least drink something." Willow filled a glass and carried a tray of food for me to a table, trying to be nice. But I didn't want nice. I wanted out, and said, "Thanks, but I don't feel like doing anything right now, Willow. Can we go back to the dorm?"

She hesitated but eventually agreed, walked me back to dorm, and watched me lie in my bed with my eyes closed while on the inside I screamed my head off, what have you done? What the hell have you done with your life?

TWELVE

"I don't need to tell you ladies nothin'," Perez beamed as he strolled up the aisle.

He was right about that. Ozzie and I were done making our beds in seconds and as we lined up by the wall seconds later, it was almost as if we'd been waiting for him for an eternity. Then we burst through the door without him, hurried downstairs, and lined up again.

"It don't matter that this is your last day today," he said once he caught up. "If you can't meet Air Force standards, you're not graduating tonight. You're not graduating unless I say so!"

But he didn't scare me, not anymore, and he sure as hell wasn't going to hold me back unless I broke my neck.

The timed run was first and although I thought I was going to die of an asthma attack, I passed, which was all that mattered. Then I cranked out the minimum forty sit-ups, rolled over and did the push-ups with effortless glee, and thought I was doing just swimmingly until Perez yelled, "Pull-up bar!" My arch nemesis. But I passed that too, even as Perez circled around me like an alligator in a moat, even as my arms felt like spaghetti after all those push-ups. I held on and I pulled up because I was not failing, not today.

"An' that's all air-man!" Perez blew the whistle and smiled broadly as if he wanted all of us to know that he was proud of us, but I didn't want his pride. I wanted to get as far away from him as I could.

Then he screamed, "Chow hall!" and we lined up like pros, went in row-by-row and without missing a beat I slid my tray with ease, stepped sideways along the glass display, and picked every food except biscuits and gravy because success equaled hunger, and I was famished.

With my tray piled high with hash browns, scrambled eggs, pancakes, and three very filled glasses of water, I executed a perfect right flank past the snake pit without so much as an expression on my face. I hoped they'd call me back so I could say hello, but they didn't even notice me.

I swallowed my food whole, leapt up for seconds, a bowl of cheerios that never got the chance to get soggy, and by the time Perez parted his lips to say "Let's go," Ozzie and I stood up and hurried outside.

Upstairs he said, "You will have 'nuff time to shower because today is picture day…" And all hell broke loose, more than what I'd seen on the first day at "Reveille," and he screamed, "Calm down ladies, this isn't Miss America!" to get some order, but it was too late. How could he expect us to be calm after six weeks of being away from civilization and then hurling us in front of a camera? I had at least three new zits on my chin, and when I looked down at my legs, saw that I'd transformed into Wolverine!

The bathroom was a mosh pit, the most coveted item being mirror space, where girls tried to pluck, hairspray, and apply make-up.

"I need hairspray!" someone shouted, and someone shouted back, "I have hairspray," and sent it down an assembly line of hands. Someone else said, "Can I borrow foundation?" and the call was answered with, "Over here!" and so I decided to try and said, "I need foundation," and Ozzie raised her hand, pinned between four shoulders, and said, "I've got mascara and eye shadow if you need it!"

When I was dressed, Ozzie checked my gig line, smeared foundation on my face, dabbed light eye shadow on my lids, and showed me the fantastic results in a compact mirror.

"You're a lifesaver," I smiled. "I actually look like I've slept."

Then Perez rapped on the prison door, opened it, and said, "Move it out, lock and load!" I thought, this couldn't be happening, the end is so near!

One of the classrooms downstairs had been transformed into a little studio, and when it was my turn to sit in front of the marbled back drop and flag, I felt an overwhelming sense of accomplishment because I was doing what Ryan and Dad had done before me, like my uncles and grandfather had done before them. I was a part of something big.

"Make me look good when you do the touch-ups," I told the photographer after he snapped the flash, but all he said was, "Book or t-shirt?" as if he really didn't care about my zit dilemma, and I replied, "Book," because the last thing I needed was another oversized item of clothing.

"I got the book too," Ozzie shook my arm happily. "I can't wait to sign yours."

"This isn't summer camp airman, undastan'?" I cracked up, doing my best Perez interpretation, then realized Perez was right behind me.

He narrowed his eyes at me like he was about to explode but all he said was, "You have a three hour pass to go aroun' the base before graduation. Don't be late or you ain't graduatin' and you'll be washed back, undastan?"

I had completely forgotten about the day pass and could have cared less. Ozzie, however, tugged my arm, jumped up, and said, "Wohoo, the mall, I can't wait!"

"Isn't there anywhere else we could go?" I pleaded because I didn't feel like doing anything other than sitting in the dorm, watching the clock until graduation, and hoping like hell everyone had come to see me.

"What's better than the mall, airman? We gonna do some shoppin', you undastan?" Ozzie mimicked Perez better than me and I laughed and said, "Okay fine," and thought it really would be until Ozzie reached for the door at the mall and opened it.

That's when I saw the sea of blue airmen, shoulder to shoulder and all the same, and I said, "I'm not going in," not because there was no place to actually get in, but because I didn't want to lose myself in that crowd. I wanted to stand out not blend in. I wanted to be me.

"There's a table over there!" Ozzie ignored me, pushed me through the crowd to a dirty table covered in trays and crumbs and said, "Wait here, I'll get us some pizza." As I watched her dance through the crowd I wondered what was wrong with me. Why couldn't I be happy like everyone else here? Why did I want to be so different?

"Here you go." She slid a slice of pizza my way.

"Thanks, Ozzie," I said, feeling guilty when I took that heavenly bite because I should have been at the mall eating pizza with Pam and Jake.

"Look," Ozzie waved her hands in the air to the music. I noticed everyone else was doing it too, like a concert had broken out in the food court. "Didn't you miss the real world?"

Of course I missed the real world, I wanted to say, but Ozzie closed her eyes as if she was dreaming of a far off place and swayed to the music, and again I wondered if I was the only one who was scared, who didn't know what the future held, where I was going to end up.

Then the music got even louder. It was the Dave Matthews Band, "Ants Marching," and everyone sang along, "*And all the little ants are marching, red and black antennae waving. They all do it the same.*" even Ozzie, who then wanted me to sing along. I did, all the while thinking about Pam and Jake because we used to sing like this when we were out too.

I worried. What if they couldn't make it?

"What time is it?" I asked when the song was over.

Ozzie jumped up from the stool and said, "Time to go to the mall!"

"Ugh," I said, but she didn't hear me, and when she said, "My mom and sister are flying in," I said, "That's awesome," because it was. I lied, "Mom and brother are coming to visit me too."

"I can't wait to see San Antonio after the graduation," she said, but I'd forgotten about that too.

I said weakly, "Oh yeah, San Antonio," because I didn't want to get her down.

"It's time!" Ozzie suddenly exploded. "Time to graduate! Come on." That was all she had to say to light the fire under my ass. I took off running and when she caught up she said, "Wait! We're not going to be late!" Even as my lungs protested, I couldn't stop.

In the distance, Perez stood under the overhang by our dorm with his arms crossed over his chest, and as we trickled into formation he said, "This is it, don' embarrass me." He explained, "We're gonna march to the graduation field, go aroun' once, join the other flights, and stan' at attention, undastan? Then you wait for your family to get you. Don't take one step without your family comin' to you first! Tonight, you have five hours in San Antonio and don't even think about running away either. You won't make it far. Trust me, everyone knows who you are and will report you, undastan?"

Yes, yes, we undastood just fine, shut up already!

"Now," he boomed. "For the last time, forward, harch!" Eagerly we marched, and for the first time, I relished the sound of our boots on the pavement. This was it. Almost over. Just a few more steps, two, three, four!

And there it was, past the PT concrete slab: the football stadium with the bleachers filled to the brim with our families! Just a few more yards, I thought, until out of nowhere, three other flights joined us and we were no longer first, no longer clearly visible, but now a vast ocean of blue airmen, unidentifiable to anyone trying to spot me!

"Flight, halt!" Perez commanded and faced us.

He stood for so long I thought he was going to reprimand us for something, but then he bowed slightly and left and the crowd descended on us like a tidal wave and I couldn't wait to get knocked over.

Enviously, I watched as girls were hugged, kissed, and engulfed in tears and I love you's. Where were my hugs and I love you's, I tried not to cry. My head swiveled, where were they? Balloons and clusters of people blocked my view. Anyone?

Then Mom appeared, bright blonde hair and red lipstick smile, Pam's long legs, Jake's grin, and Ryan pointing at me. They'd seen me! I could die at this very moment and all would be okay, I thought. They'd witnessed the end of the hardest thing I'd ever done in my life and came to see me!

I stepped forward even as someone hissed, "Grillo, not until they're here," and took off running. To hell with Perez! They'd come for me, all of them!

"My big girl!" Mom planted an indelible red kiss on my cheek. Ryan, Jake, and Pam completed the sandwich around me and I thought this was it, if I died at this very moment, I would die happy, and said, "I love you Mom, I love you Ryan, I love you Pam, I love you Jake!"

"I can't believe you did this," Mom cupped my hands in her face and wiped my tears. Ryan smacked me on the back, "You did it!" and Jake said, "Oh my God Jen, I can't believe it."

Pam was quiet; she missed her mom. But when I asked, "How are you?" she ignored me and said, "How was it, Jenny?"

"Hell!" And everyone laughed.

"Can we get out of here, away from all the blues?" I pulled Mom's hand toward the opening between the bleachers.

Pam reached for my hand and I whispered, "You doin' okay?" and she nodded as if she'd tell me all about it later. I said, "I'm sorry I left," and she squeezed my hand as if to say she understood, and I realized that no matter how difficult the journey, I was stuck. I couldn't turn anything back no matter how sorry I was and no matter how much I regretted it.

"I want to see your dorm," Mom said as if she'd remembered Ryan's from the year before and wanted to compare.

"We'll grab a smoke," Jake said, waving a pack of cigarettes in the air, and I said, "Okay, we'll be back in a few," and took Mom upstairs.

"Aren't these girls amazing?" Ozzie's mom asked mine, standing by our lockers.

Mom studied my bed and locker like a homicide detective and said, "Yes, and living like animals," to no one in particular. She muttered, "Your father, your father." I said, "Who cares about Dad after everything I've been through? Look at me, I survived this! Marching and push-ups, and M-16 training!"

"We're going to catch the bus," Ozzie interrupted, and her family moved toward the door and waved.

I said, "Okay see you," and Mom snapped, "Fine, let's get out of here."

At the bus stop I fantasized about renting a car and driving home from here, and on the Riverwalk I barely paid attention because all of us had been there the year before for Ryan, and now were simply going through the motions. Them being here was almost like a cruel joke, a small taste of what my life was once like. And nothing could ever be the same, it was gone forever.

Hours later we ended up at a burger joint and I knew what I wanted the second I walked in - I'd been dreaming about it since the day I landed: the biggest, fattest, and juiciest burger on the menu.

Everyone else took forever to order, and even longer to squeeze ketchup and add salt on the fries, arrange the napkins just so, and take a sip of soda. But I didn't waste any time at all. I picked up that big fat burger with two hands and savored the fireworks of hot juicy beef, lettuce, tomato, pickles, guacamole, and onions on my taste buds and wished the sensation wouldn't end.

I wiped the last remnants of burger from my lips when Mom said, "Huh," and eyed my empty plate. She hadn't even eaten her first fry and I could tell she wanted to get up, all those years of table manners down the drain.

"It's because she's been in basic, Mom. Remember I was the same way?" Ryan patted her shoulder and she dipped her French fry angrily, which made Jake and Pam laugh, maybe to ease the tension, but then Mom looked at Ryan and said, "So tell me about Dad's wedding."

"He can go to hell," I said.

"It was a small ceremony," Ryan admitted, and I thought Mom was going to burst into flames at the mention of his name.

"Look at what your father did to you. Both of my children in the military! When you should have been in school…"

"Mom, please," I begged, not wanting to hear about my train-wreck-of-a-life all over again.

Ryan said, "Well, I'm okay now, Mom. I'm getting stationed in Las Vegas. It's not where I wanted to go, but at least it's not in the middle of nowhere…"

"I'm just saying it's all his fault, that's all." She threw her hands in the air, and although I wanted to change the subject, Mom beat me to it and asked Jake, "How are things with you?"

But then my eyes fell on the clock and I jumped up and said, "Oh my God it's time! We have to go now to catch the bus or we'll be late!"

We hurried down the street, along with a few other straggling families with their airmen, and I suddenly knew why Perez had warned us not to take off because that was all I wanted to do: run away, change my name, and rebuild my life.

On the bus I rested my head on Mom's shoulder, wishing I didn't have to go back, and once we stepped off the bus I started crying. "Please don't leave me. I miss you all so much!"

"Don't go Jenny, don't go back," Pam hugged me.

"What will happen if you don't go?" Jake hugged us both.

"Come back to Germany with me," Mom joined the pack.

Ryan pulled me out and said, "You'll be going to Leavenworth if you don't go back. You'll be AWOL and you didn't make it this far to go backwards." He hugged me too.

"I love you all." I stepped backwards, wishing I could stay there forever and knowing I couldn't. I'd made the decision to join and I had enough curiosity to see where I'd end up, even if it was the hardest thing I ever had to do.

I sprinted toward the dorm and thought I was late, but Perez was in the hallway closet digging through our suitcases and didn't even know I'd snuck up.

Behind him, everyone screamed and pointed excitedly, "That's mine over there, that one," and when he hovered over mine, I did the same and said, "Yes, that's the one."

"You alright?" Ozzie pushed my shoulder like old times and I said, "Yeah, it's just weird to see my old clothes. This was my favorite shirt, although Jake always hated it..."

Then Perez sauntered through the middle aisle, interrupted us like he always did, and said, "Two knuckleheads from your brother flight got into trouble." He shook his head as if he'd told this story a million times before and said, "These two knuckleheads got drunk, went to a tattoo parlor and came limpin' back to the dorm, and when the T.I. saw they were limpin', he thought they had broken their legs, but they kept sayin' no, no, no, we ain't hurt, and then finally, they opened their shirts and showed him their tattoos. Both knuckleheads tattooed the entire Wolf Pack t-shirt on their bodies, includin' everyone's names. What knuckleheads!" He held his stomach and laughed.

"So what happened to them?" someone asked, and he said, "Kicked out. Pfft. Gone. On the last day. You don't mess with the Air Force, undastan?"

Collectively we gasped, and then he said, "Yeah, wow is right ladies, and on that note, I wish you goodnight and good luck, air-man!"

THIRTEEN

It is hard to believe that yesterday I was still in basic, and today, I am in beautiful Biloxi, Mississippi, in a comfy bed surrounded by cheerful cream colored walls and the sun smiling on my face.

Never have I felt this well-rested, so well rested I convinced myself that the last six weeks of sleep deprivation and hell were worth it to feel this good. Almost. How else would I have slept over twenty-something, maybe even thirty-something hours, right?

I stood up and stretched, admired the little tree outside my window that faced an empty parking lot, and couldn't believe my luck at having the double room all to myself. The other bed, dresser, and desk were bare, and I took the liberty to undress, toss my BDU's on the floor, dig through my suitcases naked, and shower for as long as I wanted to in my very own shower, and damn if I didn't look like a million bucks afterwards! Not a single zit on my face or sagging bag under an eye.

Messing with the radio dial, I stopped once I heard dance music and couldn't believe how good it sounded. Then the DJ said, "That was 'Waiting for Tonight' by Jennifer Lopez…" and I calculated how long I'd been cut off from the real world that Jennifer Lopez, who I knew as an actress, was now a singer?

Sounds from the hallway echoed through the room: slamming doors and girls yelling, "Wait up!" and "Hey! What's up," reminding me to get a move on, get to a payphone and call everyone I knew, and scope out my new surroundings, because all I remembered from last night was that we were in the newest looking dorm on base. After that, I'd passed out. Not only was the bus ride too long and soothing with the sound of the engine, but the bed was so comfortable I'd fallen asleep as soon as my face hit the pillow.

Stepping into the hall I practically skipped into the hotel-like foyer, my eyes deadlocked on the phone room, and I thought, wow, what a difference from the basement, how far I'd come. I'd really made it!

Then someone said, "Grillo? In here please," and I wondered who the hell knew my name and what she wanted with me.

"Oh, hi." I spun on my heel and recognized Nelson, now casually dressed in a t-shirt and jeans instead of the BDU's from yesterday's in-processing briefing. She was the Commander's sidekick, assistant, helper kiss-ass, and had assigned us extra duties called AFI's, Awaiting Further Instruction. They were kind of like chores, unless you couldn't start school right away then they were kind of like your job, and thank God I started school bright and early Monday morning because I wouldn't know what the hell I'd do if I had to be here one day longer than I had to be!

Inside the laundry room, ten bored girls in pajamas I didn't recognize leaned against the machines as if they hadn't slept all night. They didn't look a day over fourteen either, making my nineteen feel like thirty.

"Okay. Make sure all of the washers and dryers are free of dust and lint." Nelson removed a lint trap and held it in the air as if we'd never seen one before. Then she pretended to wipe down the top of a washer so that she wouldn't take the duty away from one of us, and said, "I will check each one on a daily basis and if they are not clean, I will have to pull a 341."

That was almost the most ridiculous thing I'd ever heard. A 341 was a little post it sized paper with our name, rank, and squadrons written on them and was intended to be handed to someone who was tattle-taling on you. I'd heard the threat all the time, but I never saw anyone pull one and I couldn't believe she threatened it now.

She lifted her watch to her face and said, "Okay, now clean up!" I turned to face the dryer, pulled out the lint trap (which was as empty as I'd expected it to be because that was Doing Laundry 101) and was then handed a rag from someone who'd already wiped down her gleaming dryer next to mine.

When I tried to pass it on to the next girl she refused because her dryer was already clean too. I glanced at Nelson making the rounds with her clipboard like a scientist in a lab, I wondered how long she wanted to keep this charade up.

"Are we done?" Someone sighed at Nelson inspecting her "work."

"Well, uh, no, we're supposed to clean for at least fifteen to thirty minutes," Nelson stuttered.

"Are you serious?" someone else groaned, and I folded my arms across my chest, suddenly feeling claustrophobic. I had phone calls to make! I needed fresh air after sleeping for an entire day!

"I guess you're right," Nelson frowned at her watch. "Fifteen minutes is a long time. You're dismissed. Please make sure…"

But the door was already open and I was the third one out, sprinting into the phone room without looking back. I dialed Jake's number and thought I'd misdialed when he didn't answer, but neither did Ryan and Pam and I wondered why no one was by the phone waiting for me! Didn't they know how much I missed them?

"Hello?" Ryan finally answered when I called again and he said, "You made it! How is it? Did you get your key to the mailbox yet, because I sent you a pager?"

"What do you mean you sent me a pager? I don't know how to use a pager!"

"It can't be that hard to use," Ryan said dubiously. "There'll be instructions and if you still don't know how to use it, I'll help you figure it out. It should be easy enough though and once you have it, anyone can reach you like a phone. I'll pay the monthly fee. It's cheap. You'll love it."

I glanced at the empty payphones around me and felt that sinking feeling in my stomach again, like I'd made the wrong choice by leaving, and wished my life had been so much easier so I didn't have to join in the first place and leave everything behind.

"It's lonely here," I said. "How do you stay so upbeat?"

"It gets better. I felt the same when I first got there. Just wait until school starts and time will fly."

"Okay," I sighed, feeling very uneasy about school and fearing failing out. I had thought basic was the hardest part but now that it was behind me

I knew I had another uphill battle ahead of me. And besides, I knew nothing about planes. This was Ryan's dream job, not mine.

I hung up and walked outside. Next door was the cafeteria, and I ordered a roast beef sandwich because I wasn't in the mood for breakfast. The server was an Asian woman who had even less enthusiasm than I did, as I noticed when she let the sandwich fall onto the plate before she handed it to me.

For a second I contemplated sitting with one of the other loners in one of the booths, then decided nah, I had friends back home, why did I need friends here?

Back outside twenty minutes later, I passed a tiny strip mall, a short dull brown building I had no interest in checking out. The NCO (Non-Commissioned Officer Club, which was an enlisted person with a rank four stripes and higher) was a block further. I already knew I'd never be caught dead in there because I didn't want to date a military guy, much less hang out with one.

Across the street was Ryan's old dorm with a bulldog mascot painted on the side wall. Our squadron mascot was the gators, which I remembered from the dorm rule book Nelson had given us. I'd paged through it just to see what was in there, but the rules were so self-explanatory I couldn't believe they wasted the paper to print it out.

The post office was next. Although we'd had our addresses since the last day of basic, we didn't get our box numbers and keys until we met Nelson at the briefing.

Walking back, I noticed all the parked cars had Mardi Gras beads hanging from the rearview mirrors. Ryan had seen New Orleans at least six times and loved it, but because I'd only be in Tech School for four months if everything went well, I'd never hit the curfew and would never get the chance to go, which only made me want to go even more.

Out of boredom I ducked inside the strip mall and saw almost everything in it was closed: the pool hall, dry cleaners, alterations place, and video rental place, although I couldn't imagine who had a VCR in his or her room. The BX, however, was open, so I bought a few magazines, thinking back to how Jake, Pam, and I sat at Barnes & Noble some Friday nights after a Dunkins run flipping through magazines, gawking at things we'd never be able to afford. God, what I wouldn't do for a French vanilla iced coffee right now!

I sulked all the way back to my room. I had nothing to do, no one to call, and it wasn't even noon yet. Then I unlocked my door and gasped unexpectedly when I saw a girl with long black hair and raccoon make up smoking a cigarette on my window ledge in front of my little tree.

"Oh, sorry," I said as if I'd done something wrong, and hoped it would prompt her to apologize to me and get the hell out of my room. Then I saw her two suitcases sprawled on the floor and clothes everywhere and waited for her to explain herself, but all she said was, "You're not going to tell anyone are you?"

"Who would I tell?" I asked. I had no friends and I certainly wasn't going to have a career if I stayed in this room one minute longer. Didn't she know smoke permeated? And that she was sitting in front of a window with a clear shot to the parking lot?

I could see it now, me explaining myself as her accomplice in front of the Commander: "Yes sir, it's G-R-I-L-L-O," as he printed out the paperwork kicking me out of the military.

I glanced up at the smoke detector. She stubbed her cigarette into a Sprite bottle cap, and crouched low to exhale through the crack in the window, then said, "Don't worry, you won't get caught," as if she was amused at me being so scared.

"Oh." I thought of handing her the dorm rule book. Hadn't she heard of RMT? Remedial Military Training where all the bad airmen went, as if it was prison, and for any little thing!

Why me, why now after I'd made it past basic, did I have to be confronted with this troublemaker? I just wanted to skate out of here in peace, see how far I'd get in my career, and didn't want it to be over before it even started.

"My room is torn up," she said as I stepped over her clothes. "My shower isn't working. I live in the hallway to the right. A pipe burst under my shower and this was the only room with a bed available. The showers suck as it is. Sometimes you'll wake up and the water is ice cold."

I bit the inside of my cheek and let the magazines fall on my desk to let her know I was not cool with her being here, and she said, "Hey, I was going through my closet to sort out some clothes. I gained forty pounds since I've been here. Do you like these?"

She held a pair of pants up at me that could fit a toddler, and I asked, "What? How did you gain forty pounds? You don't look it."

"Thanks," she smiled. "You need to watch out too. Now that you're not in basic and you can eat whatever you want when you want, it's real easy to gain weight. There's popcorn and Ramen by the microwave that I brought over. Help yourself."

"Okay," I said, knowing I wouldn't and she glanced away as if deep in thought and said, "Yeah, in basic everything was different. I didn't eat much. I had an affair with the T.I. and when it was time to eat, we went off to fool around."

"What?" I asked. "What about fraternization and all that?" I asked, wanting to throw up at the thought of even kissing Perez, and she said, "Fuck those stupid rules. He was hot and getting divorced. He really loved me. Here are some of his letters."

She rummaged through a pile on top of her desk.

I said, "I believe you. I just don't believe *it*. Yeah, he's cute," I lied, because he was no Brad freaking Pitt. But even if he was, he was a T.I! The enemy!

"I'm Jen, by the way. Where are you from?"

"Alanis. New Mexico. You?"

"New Hampshire," I said. "Close to Boston," I explained when she didn't respond. I didn't want to elaborate about the basement, Dad, or Germany, and was grateful when she said, "Cool, and don't worry about school. You look like a worrier, but I'll help you study. The girl that lived with me just graduated and gave me all her notes. I'm halfway done too, just started the radar portion. Never did I think I'd make it this far, but I did and now I know that if you stick with it, you'll get it too."

"Isn't that cheating?" I thought about getting kicked out.

Defensively, she replied, "No. It's how it's done. Believe me, you'll need them. Oh, and another word of advice. Invest in NyQuil."

"NyQuil the cough medicine?"

"Yes, it'll put you to sleep on nights where you've studied all day but can't fall asleep at night when you need it, when you have a grueling test the next day. And believe me, they're grueling!"

"Okay, got it," I said getting even more worried.

"Oh, I didn't realize it was almost one!" She dove into a pile of clothes, picked out a sweatshirt, and said, "I'm going to a sports bar and maybe New Orleans today with some friends. Word of advice, find someone here that has a car and be their friend. If someone asks where I am, just tell them the mall. Technically, I'm not allowed out to New Orleans because of the curfew. Okay? Thanks."

Then she let the door slam and was gone, making me wish she'd invited me to go with her. Trouble or not, she was all I had. Then again, there was no way in hell she was twenty one and I thought, better stay as far away from her as I can. That girl was trouble and trouble was the last thing I needed.

FOURTEEN

My alarm went off at 5:30 on Monday morning. Alanis groaned and faced the wall as if she was hung over. She had afternoon classes and therefore could sleep longer, but I was tempted to ask her what time she'd strolled in because I had tossed and turned all night and knew she wasn't in her bed at three a.m.

The shower didn't get hot until I stepped out, just like Alanis had promised, and I tried to tell myself I didn't have to rush anymore, that I wasn't in basic anymore and that I could relax, but Dad used to say that to me all the time, relax, you're too uptight! No kidding! I didn't want to be like him and not to be like him meant not to end up a vegetable on a couch, I had to keep moving.

I buttoned the last button on my BDU top, fixed my collar and pushed my hair into a bun, reached for my new blue Air Force messenger bag Nelson had given us at the in-processing briefing, and took a deep breath. It was official: I was an adult now, doing something important. If only I knew where to go from here.

Gently, I closed the door, scanned the hall, and found no one. The laundry room and foyer were empty too. Outside it was humid and cool, unlike the hot and sticky Texas air, and I almost turned back to get a coat until I noticed two smokers huddled on the side not wearing coats either, and I thought surely more people would be out any second but no one came.

When they finished their cigarettes they went next door into the cafeteria, and I nearly smacked my forehead for not coming up with that myself.

They dropped their bags on the floor in the hallway, on top of fifty others. I didn't want to do it, but when in Rome I thought, and plunked it down. Inside, every seat was taken and everyone looked alive and happy and as if they knew what they were doing. I looked like a kid, holding a tray and a bowl of oatmeal, too afraid to ask anyone if I could sit.

Then as if I'd missed the trigger, everyone stood up, formed a line, and trickled out. I found my bag lying on its side and hurried out where all the same groups at each table formed the same groups now, reminding me of grade school and not the United States Air Force.

Suddenly, a whistle blew and everyone scrambled into perfect rows in front of a wooden platform I hadn't noticed before. A minute later, two guys and a girl stepped onto the platform, looking like a singing group, each wearing a different color cord on their shoulders.

The first guy was short, looked Hispanic under the light from where I was standing, and had the red cord. I wondered if the rope would look just as good pinned to one of my sweaters as he raised his arms to the sky like he was Caesar and became distracted by the screaming crowd, cheering and whistling like we were at a football game. Who was this guy and what the hell was this circus?

"Off we go into the wild blue yonder..." everyone sang. The guy next to me roared with excitement, but I still didn't know the words.

Then the second guy stepped to the edge of the platform. He was fair-skinned, tall and skinny, with glasses and a green cord around his shoulder. He leaned forward, even though there wasn't a microphone to lean in to, and announced, "Highs of eighty five today, slight chance of rain with 76% humidity."

There were more cheers, but not as loud, and I wondered why I'd gotten out of bed for a choir rehearsal and a weather report.

"Hi, and welcome new recruits!" The girl with the yellow cord stepped forward, her voice so whiny and pitchy it made me wince.

No one else shuddered, so I thought she was done, but then she sucked in more air and screeched, "Welcome to the morning briefing! For those of you who don't know me, I'm Airman Shanks, the green rope is Scotts, and the red rope is Diego. And today is his last day as a red rope. He graduates next week."

More cheers erupted like a frat house party, and I pitied the rooms on this side of the building who were trying to sleep through this nonsense. The only thing so far I liked was her using the word "graduate" because it had to be the most beautiful word in the English language, and hopefully one day, someday, it was going to be me.

"Fall in!" Diego screamed, and I thought this couldn't be happening. This was Tech School, basic was behind us, why were we marching?

"Good morning!" Shanks screeched next to my ear. Just perfect, she was going to march my flight to school and had her place right next to me. I closed my eyes, wishing she'd disappear, wishing her voice would mute, but then she said, "Please turn on your flashlights," and I realized I'd forgotten mine and then I wanted to disappear.

Yellow dots appeared on the pavement, and she screamed, "Ready, harch!" and I gritted my teeth, not only because of her godawful voice, but with the realization that I was in the military and yet was unable to walk myself to school.

I thought that would set the tone for the rest of the day, we were going to be treated like babies forever, but then we turned the corner and the morning sun broke over the horizon and illuminated big puffy clouds and almost took my breath away and I forgot all about it.

Diego screamed, "Flight halt! Fall out!" and everyone stopped and dispersed, but I couldn't move. We were standing on the tarmac of an airfield and our school was a hangar. How cool was that?

"Is this your first day?" Diego looked at me sincerely. His voice was smooth, his teeth brilliantly white, and his smile so perfect I knew why everyone had been screaming this morning. All I could do was nod.

"You can go through either door," he pointed, amused. "The first class is always in room 102. Don't be nervous, you'll do great. Study hard."

"Okay," I said, thinking he was a comedian. How do you study airplanes?

It took me two laps around the building to find room 102, and I sat down just as the teacher walked in, a short woman with an orange afro who chewed gum and smiled at the same time, like I imagined a truck driver would.

"Hey y'all," she clapped as if she were a coach and then let her hands rest on her hips as if we were about to start a scrimmage. "I'm Kathy."

I smiled and remembered Cass and his promise about the "Real Air Force." This was so much better already.

"I'm your instructor for the next few weeks and will teach you the tower portion of ATC. We'll do book work, hands on learning, and simulator training. We just got that bad boy a few months ago. It beats the static lab. We used to hold airplanes and stand around the room. Anyway, here's a quick ATC run down. Out of any career field in the Air Force, it has the highest divorce rates, suicides, alcoholism, and drug abuse. That's right, because spouses do not understand the constant stress you are under, unless you marry an air traffic controller too, but that's another story. ATC is also the only career field where you can resign if you feel you are too scared to work, being in charge of all those lives, you know. If you ever say, "fear of controlling" you will no longer work planes and no one will question it. This here schoolhouse is not the real ATC world, it is meant to overload you with information to see if it sticks and for us to see if you can hack it. The washout rate is just above 60%. Look around you, half of your fellow students will not make it, but I'm gonna try my damndest to get y'all through!"

Everyone glanced at each other as if the realization hit us all at once; the recruiter had coated that part in sugar and we didn't understand its true meaning until now. Immediately I thought of Alanis and her notes. I never did well on tests. I was going to need a miracle.

Kathy then dropped a phone book-sized binder in front of each of us. She said, "Here's the FAA 7110.65, Point Sixty-Five for short, our air traffic bibles. Someone told me they were gonna sue me for saying that, but that's just phooey. This book is where every rule of Air Traffic is written and that's all there is to it. But first things first; as controllers, you'll need controller names. We use initials in ATC so you don't have to say your full name and waste time and it will become your name. I go by HR, the first and last letters of my last name, but you can use any combination. Eventually, you won't know anyone's real names anymore, just their initials, and every time you move to another base, you'll have to make sure those initials aren't taken, or you have to change them. Don't worry, it will make sense soon."

Kathy pointed at the albino-looking guy in the first seat. He squinted through his glasses and said, "I'll go with DN, I guess."

I already knew I wanted JG, it sounded good, strong.

"Great! Delta November," Kathy grinned. "You'll have to learn the phonetic alphabet as well. It's in the back of the point sixty-five. Quiz ya tomorrow on it."

Great. A test already. I frowned as Kathy pointed at the brunette from Jersey, and I then put two and two together: her name was Jennifer too and her last name started with a G too. Silently, I begged her not to pick my initials, but she did.

"Please," my hand shot up. "Can I be JG?"

"I wanted that too," a guy interjected two seats down, but when my head snapped to look at him he said, "but I can pick something else."

Jennifer wasn't as lenient though. She stared me down until I was ready to tell her it was only fair she keep JG since she was first.

"Shu'a," she suddenly said. "I'll just be G ah-R."

"Okay, Golf Romeo for you, and Juliett Golf for you." Kathy moved on as if it was no big deal, but I exhaled hard because I'd been holding my breath. A new name, a new beginning. No longer was I boring Jennifer, now I was JG, Juliett Golf, the new me!

"Alright, down to business," Kathy smacked her hands together again. "Let's talk about pilots, how they get from the ground to the sky and to their destinations...Jeppesen maps...beacons..."

It was hard to pay attention because she might as well have been speaking Chinese. How had the Controller I visited before basic made it look so easy? Dangled a leg and laughed like there was nothing to it?

He had said I was going to love Air Traffic but how could I love it if I couldn't even repeat anything Kathy was saying! I wanted her to slow down, repeat what the "highway in the sky" was, and explain it ten more times so I wouldn't have any doubt. Who could keep up writing as fast as she was talking? My hand cramped, my brain was tired, and she kept going as if she were reading from an encyclopedia.

"If you say "roger" it means "I heard you." "Affirmative" means yes, and "wilco" means, "will comply," as in, he will do whatever the heck it is you tell him to do..."

Scanning my page of notes, I cringed at my awful handwriting and incomplete sentences. I wasn't keeping up, not even close. I was drowning in a sea of pencil scribbles, unable to decipher a thing. Jersey Jennifer and I looked at each other with open mouths and I could tell we were thinking the same thing: 60% washout rate? Try 100!

As if Kathy had read our minds, she said, "I guess y'all deserve a break from this fun stuff!" She glanced at the clock. "The break room is down the hall or you can stand outside for five minutes."

I had to stop myself from running. I needed air! I needed to be resuscitated! I needed to wake up from this crazy dream where I was in the military thinking I was going to be an Air Traffic Controller!

Outside, I sat on a picnic table with my head between my knees and was ready to throw up. A minute later, Jersey Jennifer sat down next to me and glanced up at the sky as if she wanted to fly far away from here.

"Hey, thanks for letting me have those initials," I said.

"Not a problem," she smiled and poked me with her elbow. "I didn't want to mess with you."

"Me?"

"Yeah, you." She looked at me as if I should know. "There's something about you, JG. You have a good smile, like you're really nice, but there's something dangerous behind that smile, telling me to watch out. You're tough."

My smile grew even bigger. She thought I looked tough?

"Like that," she said. "There's something there telling me not to mess with you."

"That's the nicest thing anyone ever said to me," I said, but she didn't hear me. Her eyes were back in the sky and I thought of the last six weeks, how far I'd come, and maybe that she was right. I was tough, and although I didn't have a clue about planes, I'd figure it out.

At least that's what I kept telling myself when I returned to class and tried to keep up with Kathy in round two. But there was no more trying, only doing. Jennifer Grillo only tried, but Juliett Golf was doing it!

FIFTEEN

Fearing I was late for school, I hurried through the foyer only to be stopped by a group lollygagging in the doorway. I was still groggy from last night's NyQuil and still trying to remember if it was real or a dream when Ryan had paged me nine times only to sing "Happy Birthday" to me with his drunk friends, knowing my birthday wasn't for another three months. I was supposed to graduate in three months, but every day at school made me feel more and more behind, and Ryan partying on the weekends and paging me all night didn't help.

Then I heard Nelson talking loudly with her arms flailing all around dramatically from the middle of the huddle, "I don't know her name, Alanis maybe. She was right there. I don't know who she is, but they dropped her drunk ass off and ran away."

Then I put it together: Nelson had been on midnight duty and I was sure I hadn't seen Alanis in her bed this morning. Why the hell hadn't she paged me and what kind of friends left you drunk in the middle of a foyer like road kill?

"Heck yeah, I called the Commander! And he called the ambulance after he saw her. She was passed out cold. I checked her I.D., she was underage! She's in remedial training right now where she belongs…"

There it was, all my fears realized: Alanis was the only person I knew who didn't fear Air Traffic control or anything really and was one of the reasons I thought I could do this because I had her beside me. Now she was locked away in airman prison with a minimum thirty day sentence that with her attitude and defiance, would no doubt give her a year. What the hell was I going to do now?

All week I thought about visiting her, but I couldn't get past the idea that I would look disappointed (which I was) and then make her feel worse than I'm sure she was already feeling. Then, at the cafeteria, I saw her in a group of what I thought must have been the RMT gang that had been "arrested."

She was sitting at a table in an orange jumpsuit, and eating something that resembled oatmeal, and no one spoke with one another, didn't even look at one another. Their bowls stood six to eight inches away from them as they ate in a weird pattern, tracing an invisible triangle with their spoons: plunging them into the bowls, lifting them up and then into their mouths.

I lost my appetite and wanted to leave, but not without trying to make her notice me as I walked past her table and coughed. But when she didn't look up, I looked down and saw the mud on her pants and wondered if the rumors were true, that they dug holes in a yard all day then filled them back up again.

Too distraught to return to my room, our room, I opted for the mall, a quick bus ride away. I'd been there twice already, once to get my first haircut after basic and then again to shop for clothes, which had only made me homesick; I only shopped with Pam and Jake, so I tried to stay away.

The bus wasn't scheduled for another hour, though, and when I saw the guy in front of me take off walking, I decided to follow. I'd heard it wasn't far, thirty minutes maybe, and though it would be a nice walk to take my mind off everything.

It took me almost fifteen minutes to get to the front gate and I knew then that it was going to be a hell of a lot longer than thirty minutes, but with nothing better to do, I decided not to turn back. Then I noticed the sidewalk which consisted of a jungle of roots breaking through the concrete, and wanted to cross to the ocean side until I saw the gray water, water that was not supposed to look like that, and the gray sand littered in seaweed, and thought that everything had to be miserable here, every little thing!

An hour later I was in the food court, one of those loners on a Saturday night, and swallowed my Panda Express whole. I went to the GAP for some retail therapy. I needed clothes, since the boxes of my clothes that Pam and

Jake had sent never arrived, and opted on a sweatshirt and jeans I wasn't even sure looked good on me.

I left to catch the bus after two hours, cutting through the back parking lot and towards the old strip mall where the movie theater used to be a strip club, and next to that was one of Alanis' old stomping grounds, the bar called The Sports Bar. Hotel parties were the only other places she drank at, and I had the privilege of going to one of them last weekend. I didn't stay long.

I'd arrived alone and only under the impression that everyone in my class was going to be there. I took a drink from the makeshift bar, which was a plastic tub filled with ice and random drinks, and enjoyed the buzz for a few minutes until someone pounded on the door. It was the pizza delivery guy, but it sparked an urban legend about one of the pizza guys also being one of the instructors at school who then busted all the underage students in the room.

I'd heard enough and left. Even though I found it hard to believe that a four or five striper in the military had to have a second job in the first place, I wasn't about to push that theory. I wasn't getting kicked out for something as insignificant as this.

The bus stop was right in front of The Sports Bar, and for the first time it was surprisingly quiet inside. The last two times I'd stood here I heard the "hooah's" loud and clear, so I decided to go in and check it out. I regretted it instantly.

Inside it was dark and smoky, the fake turf carpet trodden down and spotted black, and the sports paraphernalia on the wall so crooked so that it seemed not even the owner seemed to give a damn about this place. I sat down anyway (what else was I going to do?) and studied the fat guy in the camouflage baseball cap three stools down. Obviously he was not military, but the three kids with their tapered buzz cuts in the corner shooting pool definitely were.

"What will you have, young lady?" The bartender approached me. He looked young, his hair slicked back, and I wondered if it was the same one Alanis had bragged about not checking I.D.'s. Look where that had gotten her.

"Coke," I replied flatly, and noticed one of the kids from the pool table staring at me. Then he leaned his stick against the wall and walked towards me, even as it fell to the ground with a loud crash. He sat down next to me, boldly extended his hand, and said, "Hi, I'm Kenny."

"I'm just waiting for the bus." I sipped my coke and whispered, "Aren't you a little too young to be in here?"

"You don't need a bus. I have a convertible," he ignored me. "I'll take you back to the base later. You're military right?"

I nodded, deciding not to question whether he was old enough to drive.

"Want to join us in a game of pool?"

"No, thanks," I tried to sound friendly. I could have been his mother!

"Come on," he coaxed. "Just one game. No strings attached."

"I'm really not looking to date or anything like that," I said. "I'm sorry, but I just want to sit here."

"No date," he said. "Just a game of pool, okay? Saw you sitting here all by yourself and thought I could offer you a ride. What else you gonna do?" He smiled as if he was about to get lucky, but then I smiled even bigger, because I realized it was me who was about to get lucky.

If there was one thing Alanis told me to do, it was to get a friend who had a car. I said, "I'll play winner."

SIXTEEN

"Y'all are halfway there," Kathy announced after lunch one day. "You'll test out of tower in two weeks before you start radar and oh, in case y'all weren't told, the school house closes for two weeks for Christmas so make sure y'all buy tickets home or y'all be sitting here by yourself in the dark!"

I couldn't believe we were almost halfway done and worse, I hadn't even thought about Christmas and that it was right around the corner, as if I'd been living in a cave! I couldn't get to the dorm fast enough that afternoon, away from Shanks' godawful voice, and right to the travel office to book my ticket home. And before I knew it the week was over, I tested out of tower with flying colors, got on the plane home, and ran through the terminal and outside into Pam's and Jake's arms, feeling as though I'd never left.

And that was when the fantasy ended and real life kicked in.

I climbed into the backseat of Pam's neon green VW bug and studied the scenery as it went by. Surprisingly, everything looked the same, and although I couldn't pinpoint what I'd expected, all I could come up with was "different." But nothing was different. The songs on the radio, the conversations about college, parties, Dunkin Donuts and pizza were all the same, as if indeed I hadn't left, except that everything in my insides was telling me that I had.

Not one comment was made about how I was doing, or that they were proud of me, or how that "Air Force thing" was going, so I stared at the trees and said nothing and doubted that I should have come back at all, until I convinced myself it would be fine once we got home and when I saw my room. But that was worse than I expected too.

It wasn't home or a room. It was a basement and I didn't belong there. How had I ever belonged there when it was so dark and cold, dirty and smelling like soot? How desperate had I been to live like that?

Then my eyes fell on the fish bowl and the thick dirty water where nothing could live and I was furious with Pam for not telling me that Mississippi had died. Then suddenly his little nose nuzzled the glass, as if he was welcoming me back, and I thought, what a fighter he was, a fighter like me, and decided I was taking him back with me.

The following morning I woke up to an empty house, feeling colder and more alone that I had the previous day. I showered and dressed in my blues and went outside to scratch the snow off my Ford Escort so I could get to "work" on time to the recruiter's office, where it would be my job to recruit for the next two weeks in exchange for two weeks of free vacation days. It seemed like a good idea a few months ago when I'd signed up, but who could I recruit when I barely knew my place in the military or where I was going to end up? My fate was still undecided. I could wash out at any minute.

I made it to the office ten minutes early and considered the irony of how I once used to pride myself on being late and was now early for everything. At least the Air Force had succeeded in that.

When I walked into the recruiter's office I expected to see Pearson, even though I knew he'd retired a long time ago, and was greeted by a tall guy with light brown hair parted to the side. He stood up without smiling, picked up his hat from his desk as if he was leaving, and said, "Grillo, right? I'm Sergeant Oliver. I'm heading out of the office so you can sit at the desk, but keep your coat on, the heat isn't working. Man the phones and here is a stack of flyers you can pass out at restaurants, libraries, or at the mall after lunch."

"What do I say when someone calls?" I asked, in disbelief that he was leaving. This was the "recruiter's assistance" program, not "airman recruiting by the seat of her pants" program, right?

"Tell them they've reached the recruiter's office, what else?" he replied, and added, "I'll be back in a couple of hours," although I could tell he had a whole list of better things to do running through his mind.

A minute later I sat in his chair, watched as he peeled out of the parking lot, and wondered why in the hell the Air Force couldn't afford heat around here. Then I glanced from the phone to all the mismatched furniture, wondering why I'd ever felt intimidated here.

Tempted to snoop through the file cabinet, my eyes fell on something better, a stack of letters on the corner of his desk. The first one said, "Hello Sgt. Pearson, you lied to me," and I was hooked. I scanned the next page, a new letter, same message that said, "You said this was going to be easy," and the next, "Sergeant Oliver, you are a fucking liar!" After that one, "How could you?" And "It was nothing like you said it was going to be…I cry every day."

I felt like crying with them. If it wasn't for Ryan I would have been another letter in that stack. What was the big deal about telling the truth anyway? Then I answered my own question: because no one would join, and for a second I thought about writing all of them back to let them know that there was an end in sight, but the letters were dated months ago. They were all somewhere else now and there was nothing I could do.

Suddenly the door swung open and I expected to see Oliver, but it was a grungy familiar-looking guy my age, black hair and sunken-in nose like a boxer.

"I remember you," he smiled as if he was elated to see me and not Oliver. He said, "You look different- I mean, you look good. Like basic was good."

"Mark, right?" I stared him down, wishing I was him, still here, living my life like nothing had changed. The odd thing was he stared back at me longingly, as if he wished he had gone, and like me, was now done with basic.

Then I remembered why he hadn't left with me- silly unpaid parking tickets- and I became angry that he'd weaseled out so easily while I, as much as I wanted to, hadn't.

"What are you doing here?" I pictured Pearson banging on his door a hundred times.

Mark said nothing, sat down in the chair across from me, eyed the bumper stickers and pens I knew he'd probably seen a million times before, and popped his neck for good measure, as if to impress me. I wanted to say, don't bother, we both know I'm tougher than you.

"Basic was hard. Don't do it. It's not for you," I said, thinking if Oliver had sent him here so I could convince him, it wasn't going to happen.

"Yeah," he stood up slowly and sighed. "That's what I thought. I started a construction job anyway."

"Good luck with that," I waved. "Bye." And to my surprise he left, just like that, and I felt like crap for having said all the wrong things.

Either way, I knew that recruiting wasn't for me and I was tempted to post a note on the door that read, "Don't do it." Instead, I took the flyers off Oliver's desk and left thinking that if Oliver called and questioned my leaving, I'd blame the cold weather and tell him I'd left to hand out flyers.

I had every intention of parking at McDonald's to tape flyers on the bathroom stalls, but after I parked, I couldn't get the stack of letters off my mind. I got out of the car and threw all the flyers into the trash, and then drove around aimlessly until I ended up at my old high school, where I parked the car and walked around the halls.

I was surprised at how small my locker seemed, how small all of it seemed, and remembered how badly I'd wanted nothing more than to get out of high school and prove myself to the world. But what had I proven? I was living someone else's Air Force dream, Mark's Air Force dream, and still feeling clueless about what lay ahead. Then I passed the empty cafeteria, thought back to the few students I remembered who'd joined, who'd set up a table and tried to recruit while students laughed at them, while I laughed at them, and now I was one of those people. Funny how fate worked sometimes.

I stopped in the doorway of Mr. B.'s class and said, "Hello," thinking he'd wave back and continue teaching, but he waved me in and said, "What a surprise, Jennifer! Look class, this is Jennifer, one of my former students. Look how sharp she looks in that Air Force uniform!"

No one had ever said I looked good in that ridiculous uniform, and as I walked in I blushed and tried to walk a little taller, but half the kids were asleep and the other half tried to catch a glimpse of my butt.

"Do you have time to tell us about the Air Force," he beamed, and said, "and how exciting Air Traffic is?" Then he moved to the back of the room so I could shine in front of the class, which was exactly what I didn't want to do.

Staring at the blank faces, I thought of how much I hated basic, how much I cried and cursed every day, and knew I couldn't tell them that. Tech School was better- sure, kind of, if you liked the constant fear of failing out every minute of every day and the "real" Air Force was the goal. But I didn't know if I was going to make it there, and then there was the chance of being shipped off to war; we were always fighting someone somewhere. And of course you couldn't drink, and had to follow orders...

Mr. B. waited patiently. He sort of knew what I'd gone through because a hundred years ago he was drafted into the Army, except that after basic he was shipped off to Vietnam. When he got there, he proclaimed he could type so that he wouldn't have to go on the front lines and get shot, although he couldn't type worth a damn. Six years later he was home, started teaching, met his wife, and had Pam, which sounded like a great story to me, like I'd end up with a good story too someday, although the moral of the story was that it was all based on lies.

The recruiters lied to get you in. I lied so I could get in. Mr. B. lied to survive. I had to lie to Oliver about the pamphlets and lie to the kids in front of me because I couldn't stand there dressed in my sharp blues spewing anti-military shit because it would be a little hypocritical, and would be extremely confusing to them and me.

I couldn't remember what I'd said by the time I was done or by the time I fell back onto my couch, but I knew I couldn't keep up the charade for the next two weeks, and the following day seemed to go worse than the first.

Oliver had taped a note on the door for me with instructions to drive twenty miles to the next office because the temperatures had dipped too low to sit in his office. What I couldn't figure out was why he hadn't picked up the receiver to call me instead of making me drive here. Or, more importantly, why he didn't call someone to fix the damn heater.

The new office was nice though, tucked in the corner of a strip mall next to a sub shop and a China Express restaurant. Inside the office it was bright and warm, furnished with three matching wood desks haphazardly placed around the room, with three large bookshelves to accompany them. A chunky blonde girl whose desk plate said Sergeant Amanda Crayfield smiled like a cheerleader into her compact mirror giving off the illusion she was a nice, honest person who didn't have to lie to get someone to sign up for the military. I couldn't wait to see her in action.

"Call me Mandy." She showed me to my desk, and although she was at least four inches shorter than I, she had pep in her step, and I studied her perfectly pinned bun, unlike mine which hung loose and was still damp from the shower.

"You don't have to answer the phones," she explained. "And I don't expect much traffic in here today, either. It's a small location and we're lucky if we get five a month."

"Okay," I smiled, thinking five people giving up their lives was still pretty high, but was relieved; the less entertaining I had to do, the better.

Tidying the pamphlets on my desk for the tenth time, I was prepared for a long boring day of listening to Mandy chat away to her boyfriend on the phone, until the other line rang and she quickly switched over, then relayed the message to me that another recruiter closed up shop due to a forecasted storm coming. I wished I could be snowed in here forever so I didn't have to go back to Tech School, so that I could figure out my life here again.

Then I noticed the chunky guy in the doorway trying to catch his breath, and I said, "Hi."

"Hi." He walked over to my desk and smiled as if he was auditioning and said, "I wish to enlist. My name is David."

I studied him and concluded Perez would eat him for breakfast; he was too overweight and his face too sweet and innocent. He'd cry as soon as the clippers mowed over his beautiful chestnut brown curls.

"David," I replied. "The Star Trek convention and comic book store is next door."

"No, no, you don't understand," he begged. "I'm qualified. I have a Master's degree in Political Science."

"You want to be an officer? That's great, let me think about what I know about the officer's program," I tapped my nails on the desk.

"No," his shoulders dropped impatiently. "I want to be enlisted. I want to start from the bottom again."

"You're in the wrong place David," I snapped. "You cannot throw away your hard earned degree. Being enlisted in the military is worse than starting at the bottom. You will be a nothing, a nobody, and you're already on top. Why would you want to do that to yourself?"

"I just do," he shrugged.

"Not good enough," I shook my head just in time for Mandy to overhear what was going on, slam the phone on the receiver, and hurry to his side before I could tell him to get lost.

"I can help you over here," she cooed. "David, you said your name was?"

I knew better than to start pulling out my hair and make her look bad in front of a stranger, but what was she thinking? Then I watched fascinated, like I was seeing a car wreck in slow motion, as she pulled a form from her desk, told him where to sign and pick a career field. Then she showed him where to mark the contract for "open general," as in, he could be a bus driver, a chef, a cop, something random, except he'd be a bus driver, chef, or cop, with a Master's degree, and I couldn't tell who was worse: her for doing that to him or him, for throwing away his hard-earned degree that I would have killed for.

"I'm going to lunch," I slammed the desk drawer angrily.

"Oh, I'll get something," she called after me, but I couldn't look at her, and as I thought about getting his last name so that I could track him for the next few months, I thought twice, because what could I say to a grown man who wanted to play Rambo?

Then I glanced back at her smile and wondered how she slept at night, and sat in my car because I couldn't sit and watch the rest of the car crash blow up in flames, and had lost my appetite anyway.

SEVENTEEN

Sandwiched between Jake and Pam on her queen sized bed, we watched Seinfeld just like we used to, before I joined the military. Jake held the remote and impatiently flipped through channels during commercial breaks while Pam twirled my hair pensively, until she suddenly blurted out, "Jenny, are you doing okay in the Army?"

"I used to call it Army too when Ryan joined," I laughed uneasily and somehow felt vulnerable, wondering where she was going with this, and clarified, "I'm in the Air Force, you know that right?"

"So how are you doing?" Jake let the remote fall in his lap.

I squeaked, "Fine, really," knowing they saw right through me. Pam buried her head in my shoulder and Jake stared me down.

"I miss you guys so much," I started crying. "I thought I was doing fine, but I'm not. You know I don't belong there and I should have been home by now! I don't even recognize myself. I don't know who the fuck I am anymore!"

"It's okay, Jenny," Pam whispered into my neck. "You'll be back in no time."

"Four years? It's forever away!"

"Don't worry, we'll be here when you get back," Jake hugged me.

I wiped my tears and replied, "I know. I just never thought I'd be gone this long."

"Do you want to go to a party tonight? To take your mind off of everything for a while?" Jake asked.

"Being here with you guys is all I need," I said, and Jake teased, "You're always such a homebody. Come on, we don't want to go without you. It will be like the old days."

"The old days is me saying no and you guys trying to convince me all night to say yes."

"Yeah, so stop being such a homebody, come on," Pam nudged me.

I said, "If that's what you guys want to do on my last night here, then I guess that's what we'll do," and as if I'd spoken the magical words, they leaped off the bed. Pam checked her make-up and Jake patted down his zip up sweater in the mirror and said, "Alright let's go."

Before I knew it, we stood in front of a white vinyl sided house in the dark, listening to reggae music blaring loudly from the other side.

"We're not going to stay long, right? I can't get into trouble or anything. I could get kicked out," I said uneasily.

"You won't get kicked out," Jake laughed as if I was being paranoid. "Nothing's going to happen."

"His name is Andrew," Pam knocked on the door as if she couldn't wait another second to get in. "We met him when you, you know, after you left, and his parents bought this place for him so he could be close to school."

"Uh-huh," I glanced around uneasily, as if the cops were about to show up and arrest us for being there. As if on cue, Andrew opened the door. He was a tall kid with a beer gut, holding a beer can with a cigarette dangling from his mouth.

The collar on his bright green polo was flipped up and his baseball cap was backwards, like he was some preppy kid, and for a second we stared at each other like a game of chicken, waiting to see who'd say hello first. Instead he walked away, as if saying hello wasn't cool anymore, or as if to say he didn't care whether we came in or not. Pam followed eagerly. Jake pushed me in.

Inside, Pam veered left into the kitchen, opened the fridge, and studied whatever was in there like she owned the place. Jake disappeared behind a door as if he thought he was being inconspicuous, as if I didn't know he was about to score pot or pills or something I wouldn't approve of, and therefore had to sneak it.

I settled on the couch next to two drunk guys who were half asleep, cigarettes hanging out of their mouths and beer cans held sideways, and studied the house, how I'd decorate it and how cool it would be to live here, right across from college and without having to worry about bills. Yet this Andrew guy left this house in complete disarray, trash all over the floor, half the furniture sideways and knocked over, and from what I could tell from the dimly lit space, had a few holes punched in the walls. What a shame. What a waste!

Then I noticed Pam disappear behind the same door Jake had, and Jake reappeared looking sleepy. Suddenly I wished I was back in nasty Mississippi rather than on the nasty-ass couch feeling as though I was invisible.

"You're a bitch-skank!" Andrew's voice suddenly boomed over the loud reggae music.

Everyone looked up at him scolding a girl who had make-up running down her face, and not one person moved a muscle as he raised his hand as if to hit her. Instantly it conjured up images of old fights with Dad, and more recently Perez in my face and how I'd lacked the courage to fight back. Until now.

"Hey," I stood up and screamed. "Don't you ever talk to her like that again!"

"Who the fuck are you?" Andrew screamed back. "This is my fucking house and my fucking party!"

The louder he screamed the more emboldened I felt, and I raised my fists in the air knowing he'd knock me over if he so much as sneezed and said, "Never mind who the fuck I am. Talk to her like that again and I'll deck you!"

"Are you kidding?" he laughed.

"Do I fucking look like I'm kidding, bitch? Do you want to take this outside and find out?"

Suddenly, Jake appeared next to Andrew, whispered something in his ear and hooked his arm in mine and tried to push me towards the door. He said, "She didn't mean it," and I pulled my hand away.

"The hell I didn't!" I yelled back. Then Pam had her arm around my waist and managed to get me to the door.

"She just got out of basic training," Jake said as if I was the one who'd done something wrong, and dumbfounded, I stopped struggling. Never mind that poor girl who almost lost her face, or our seven years of friendship.

Then all three of us sat in the car in silence. Jake looked at Pam as if to say "What the hell is wrong with her?" and I, in the backseat, crossed my arms wondering what the hell was wrong with them.

"Why did you pick a fight?" Jake finally turned the key and drummed his fingers on the steering wheel as though he was deep in thought and choosing every word carefully.

"I didn't mean to." I glared out of the dark window. "I just couldn't stand to see him yelling at her."

"You don't even know them!" Jake argued. "You shouldn't have done that!"

"I would do it again," I said unapologetically, "But you're right, I don't know them and I can't take it back, now can I?"

No one said a word, which said everything. I was different now, a monster compared to who I was before. But I only had one shot, at what exactly I didn't know so I couldn't explain it to them, and I was going to take that one shot as far as I could.

EIGHTEEN

The dorm, once I'd returned, reminded me of the abandoned hotel from the movie "The Shining" as I wandered the halls for signs of life and heard nothing. Outside everything was dead too and in the cafeteria only instant bags of oatmeal and cereals had been left out as if to say, "You're on your own. Good luck, whoever you are."

Off to the mall I hiked. The busses weren't running, and after I'd made an entire loop and passed every store, I realized that it too was boring and decided that I was better off being lonely in my dorm.

Out of habit, I crossed the parking lot where The Sports Bar and bus stop were and saw that the movie "Three Kings" was playing, a movie I didn't know much about except that Mark Wahlberg and George Clooney were in it and it had something to do with the military. That should have been my first hint not to go in, but I did and bought a ticket.

Inside the theater were lounge chairs and tables, remnants of the former strip club, rather than rows of movie seats. I sat down with my pack of Twizzlers, half expecting a stripper to come out and give me a lap dance.

There was no one else in the theater and I felt even lonelier than before. I'd never gone by myself before, and I wondered what I was doing there, not only in the theater but in life. I'd just left my friends and everything I knew behind, but I wasn't doing much better here. All I wanted was a shot at a future, a career if I held on long enough, but how much longer could I keep hanging on and waiting for something to happen?

Then the screen went black and the following words appeared: "March 1991. The war just ended."

I sat up, thinking it was a happy movie, until the next scene showed Wahlberg in the desert somewhere, dressed in DCU's, the desert uniform, and a Kevlar helmet, unable to determine whether to shoot a guy waving a white T-shirt in surrender.

Wahlberg chose to shoot his head off and I nearly choked on the Twizzlers, thinking this was not the movie for me. But seconds later the scene changed again this time to Wahlberg and his buddies celebrating in a tent. He was a new father.

I calmed down and convinced myself I was hypersensitive from having just returned from my home and friends, and needed to stay away from my dorm where I'd throw my very own pity party and cry for days.

The plot thickened. Someone discovered a map to Hussein's bunkers and the amount of gold locked inside. Wahlberg and Clooney hatched a plan to find it, get filthy rich and get out of the military, which was exactly what I would have done and would do today if I'd found suitcases full of gold.

Of course they found it, which unleashed a fury of everything going terribly wrong: civilians got shot up, others tried to steal the gold back from them, Wahlberg got kidnapped, and the kicker of them all, Clooney and Ice Cube get engulfed in chemical weapons, my personal nightmare. The next scene was of Ice Cube decked out in full chem gear, holding up the atropine shot, the cocktail, to be plunged into his leg.

Completely spooked, I bolted out of the theater and nearly threw up outside. Why had I joined if I was so sensitive to war and yet that was all the military ever was? What the hell was I doing here?

"I don't want to be here anymore! Get me out of here!" I called Ryan, sobbing. He blamed my hysteria on being homesick and said he'd gone through the same thing when he was in Tech School and had accidently flown back a day or two early like I had.

"You don't understand," I said. "It's not the loneliness. It is and it isn't, but I just don't belong here, I know that now. I need to get out. I don't want this anymore. I'm not okay and I wish I'd never signed. I want to get out for good!"

"Are you sure it's what you want, because this will pass."

"I am. Ryan. Please. Get. Me. Out." He paused for a full minute before he whispered, "There is a way, but it will be a dishonorable discharge, or medical, and all the hours you have put in will be a total waste, down the drain. You know that right?"

"I don't care!" I wailed, and he said, "Go to the "Mental Health" building, tell them you're depressed, and keep pressing the issue. They'll send you home eventually."

"Okay," I exhaled, ready for my next mission: to go home and get out of this mess.

Once I made it back to the base, it started raining. I found the Mental Health building and when I walked in was surprised someone was there.

"Here you go." The receptionist handed me a clipboard with a packet and I sat down, blew my nose, and wondered why in the hell I had to fill out a book of information when the military knew every little thing about me.

"It's quite a lot, huh?" A man in a long white doctor's coat stood in front of me and I said, "Yes. I'm sorry, but I can't fill this out. I don't need people thinking I'm nuts."

"It's a little misleading," he replied. "But trust me, all of that information is confidential and believe me when I tell you this, everyone during his or her career comes to see us sooner or later. It's not going to be used against you."

"It's not that. It's just that…" I felt damned if I did and damned if I didn't. What if they locked me up or what if they didn't take me seriously?

"Follow me," he said. "We can take care of it later." I followed him down the hall, where he pointed me in the direction of a small room and said, "Have a seat," making me feel a whole hell of a lot more comfortable. He understood me. He'd listen to me and send me home.

But when I looked up, an Asian woman with a blunt black bob sat down across from me, flipped through a folder I'd never seen before, and snapped, "What seems to be the problem?"

"Who are you?" I asked.

"I'm the one who'll help fix what's wrong. So tell me, what's wrong?"

"I don't fit in," I burst into tears. "The military isn't for me. I don't belong here. I really tried, but I can't stay."

She studied me and handed me a box of tissues as if she knew exactly what I was going through, but then her eyes narrowed as if she was angry with me, and she said, "I've seen your kind before."

I asked, "What kind?"

"You're homesick and think you can't make it."

"It's more than that!" I sobbed louder, feeling as though I had to lay it on thick for her to believe me. "Please help me!"

"Listen to me," she reached for my arm with one hand and glanced at my file with the other. "You're going to have a wonderful career in, what is it? Air Traffic? Now go call a friend. I'm not letting you go home and give up your career just because you miss your family. Take care." Then she stood up and left me there as if she hadn't heard a single word I'd said.

Walking back to the dorm in the rain, I felt worse than ever, more confused than ever. Where did I belong? I didn't want to quit, but what did the future hold if I stayed here?

With nothing better to do, I thought I'd sleep. I took a few swigs of NyQuil and woke hours later to someone standing in front of me asking if I was okay. I wiped the drool from my face and studied the girl with her perfect pony tail, freckles, puffy vest, and jeans, as if she was a GAP commercial, and asked, "What?"

"I'm your new roommate, Alison," she smiled, as if me waking up was the greatest thing that had ever happened to her. "I just got here. I thought you were waking up but maybe you were talking in your sleep. You look sick. Are you okay?"

"Oh," I replied, and thought, oh crap, a new roommate, a young little whipper snapper who looks as though she is about to go skiing or run through a meadow to pick fresh flowers, not be an air traffic controller.

"Hi Alison." I stood up and tried to be civil, although I wanted nothing to do with her. The second I made friends with Alanis she was gone, and who knew how long Alison would last here looking like that. She'd fail out in a day. "I'm Jen and I'm fine."

"I'm so excited about Air Traffic Control," she hugged me unexpectedly. "I can't wait to be an air traffic controller. But I am a little scared."

"About Air Traffic..." I wanted to warn her about the stress, the wash-out rate, the nightmares, but I stopped. She was me two months ago: fresh, alert, and eager to learn. The cycle had started all over again and as much as I wanted to push her out the door and save her from the anguish, I was still standing, and who was I to judge what she could and couldn't handle.

"This came for you while you were sleeping." She handed me an envelope and I sat on my bed and opened the letter from Alanis, telling me she'd graduated out of RMT and out of school during the break. She'd learned her lesson, had gotten orders to Arizona, and wished me luck.

"So about Air Traffic," I looked at her big brown rabbit-like eyes, unable to tell her the truth and crush her dreams. "Don't worry about a thing. It's fun when you get the hang of it. And I have some notes for you if you get stuck along the way or when I'm not here. Let me show you around the base and then we can grab a bite at the cafeteria."

"Okay, great!" she beamed, suddenly finding enough space to do a cartwheel. "Because I have a million questions."

"I did too," I laughed, thinking that maybe Alison was going to help me a lot more than I was going to help her, and told myself I'd tell her anything she wanted to know. I said, "And I've got a million answers."

NINETEEN

Sitting next to Kenny at the hockey rink, I shivered and said, "I didn't realize how cold it was so close to the ice."

He smiled as if he'd known all along, then put his arm around me and said, "Come closer."

"I'm not really that cold." I leaned forward so that his arm fell and said, "You know we're just friends, right?"

He nodded as if he understood, but said "You do know we're good together, right?" He pointed at the puck and said, "I love hockey, don't you?" and put his arm around me again.

"Kenny, you're too young," I whispered so that his friends couldn't hear me, which was partly true; the rest of it was that I didn't want to get involved with anyone in the military because that might keep me in longer and throw me off course, wherever my course was supposed to lead me. It was confusing enough. I didn't need to add another obstacle.

"Let's go to New Orleans tomorrow," Kenny said as if he'd been waiting to play that card for a while, one last stab to win me over since he knew how badly I wanted to go.

I said, "Really? Yes! What time?" Which made me feel a little like a hypocrite because I should have said no.

"I'll pick you up early," he said coolly. "Eight? How does that sound, guys?" he glanced at Luis and Tyson, although we both already knew they were going because they didn't go anywhere without Kenny.

"Sure thing," Luis replied, bobbing his head sadly as if I'd stolen his puppy, and I almost told him I didn't want to steal his friend from him, all I wanted to do was see New Orleans.

In the morning, however, I dragged my feet getting ready and going to the cafeteria because technically I wasn't allowed to go to New Orleans and if anyone caught me, I'd get kicked out. Then I decided to go anyway, because my fate was already written and if that was the way I left here, so be it.

Minutes later I slid into Kenny's booth and whispered, "I'm ready to go. I don't want to eat."

Kenny smacked the table excitedly and said, "Let's go guys," although Luis and Tyson were only halfway through their toasts.

When they glanced at each other as if to state the obvious, that they weren't finished yet, Kenny stood up, pulled my hand, and said, "You heard her, she doesn't want to eat," and they got up too and together we walked to the parking lot. I skipped ahead like a little kid, and Kenny held the door for me.

On the highway, I had my window down even though the wind was cold, and as much as I wanted to pay attention to the scenery, Kenny kept talking to me about Mardi Gras and how he wanted to take me. Before I could argue for the tenth time that I might not be there if all went well, he pulled into a parking garage.

"This is it?" I studied the lot around us and Kenny said, "This is where we park. We always park at the mall. It's free and close to downtown."

"You can't beat free," I smiled. "Where do we go from here?"

He took my hand and smiled, "How about Mardi Gras," and I pulled my hand away, suddenly self-conscious about Luis and Tyson watching us- I was leading Kenny on just by being here because going to New Orleans was all I ever wanted, and all Kenny wanted was me.

"Look at these," I ran through the door and up to a push cart at the mall where most of the stores were just opening up. "Are these the beads I see all over the cars here?"

"Yes." Kenny caught up with me, picked up a voodoo doll, and said, "Aren't they awesome?"

"They're freaky." I backed away and said, "I don't believe in black magic, but I don't want to take my chances."

He laughed. "Alright, now what about Mardi Gras, you're going right?"

"Kenny, you know I'm not going to be here- don't look at me like that. I have two weeks left and a final test, and if I pass or fail, I'm out of here either way."

"You don't know that," he said and I shrugged as if to agree, although I knew in my heart that a few weeks from now I was moving on to bigger and better things.

"Is she going to stand there all day?" Luis snapped.

Tyson piped up, "Yeah, I thought she wanted to see this place and not some stupid cart."

"Geez! I'm sorry, let's go!" I surrendered and ran ahead bursting through the doors that led onto the street, and stopped cold when I saw the City. What a city it was!

The air smelled like rice, and as I inhaled deeply Kenny caught up to me and said, "It's jambalaya," which sounded like jumble to me, and before I could ask him what he'd said, I became distracted by a kid playing a trumpet as if Louis Armstrong had been reincarnated into a five-year-old. I asked, "How can a little boy play like that?"

"Oh boy," Luis smacked his forehead like I was naïve and Tyson laughed, but in all my travels when I was younger, I'd never seen anything like this before, a city so alive!

"Then you'll love Bourbon Street," Kenny tugged my hand.

I asked, "Can we eat, that, aya stuff I smell?"

"Jambalaya," Kenny laughed, and as we turned the corner to Bourbon Street and I saw even more kids playing instruments and tap dancing, smelled new spices in the air, and saw the different colorful houses and thought I was going to faint.

"This is awesome, Kenny." I wriggled my hand free of his and before he could reply, a shopkeeper placed a string of beads around my neck and said, "Here ya go, miss."

"For me?" I gasped at Kenny and smiled. "See? Where else but N'awlins would this happen?"

"Look here, Jen," Kenny pulled me to another stand. "I'm going to eat alligator meat."

"I'm going to throw up if you do!" I looked away and glanced at Luis and Tyson trying their best not to look annoyed with me.

"Come here and try it, or do you prefer snake meat?"

"Neither, yuck!" I pretended to gag and so Kenny decided not to eat anything crazy and walked me down to Canal Street instead, the hustling and bustling city part of New Orleans.

"Can I buy you something?" Kenny asked as I stood frozen in front of Gucci.

"I just want to take a look," I replied solemnly, reminded of Pam and Jake and our Barnes & Nobles days. I walked in and glanced around.

"Jen, let me get you something," Kenny said, following me around.

I replied a little snarky, "You can't afford the tissue box," wishing once again that I wasn't here but back in New Hampshire where I belonged.

"Come on." I finally took his arm and held it, wondering if I was meant to be here then why did it hurt so much?

Outside the air was cool, and I thought I'd better get my act together before Kenny bombarded me with questions and really got me thinking about home again, when a cab driver leaning against his car smoking a cigarette asked, "You kids military?"

"How did you know?" I became hypnotized by the way he slowly drew the nicotine from his cigarette.

Kenny put his arm around me protectively and the guy smiled and said, "Ahh," and dropped his cigarette. "I see you folks all the time. D'y'all need a ride?"

"No," Kenny gently pushed me to walk the other way, but I pushed back.

"How you likin' it here so far, little lady?" the cabbie asked.

I shrieked, "I love it! I can't get enough of it!"

"I love this town too," he said mysteriously, then pointed at the other side of the street where clouds cast a shadow on the buildings. He said, "But you see the other side of the street over there where it's dark? Y'all better stay away from there, 'cause the crime is high. People get shot over there. Stay close to your men."

"What?" I said but he was already in his car and rolling away, and I thought, how could people get shot here when this place was magical?

Then, as if it was something like black magic, it started to rain and Kenny said, "Maybe we've seen enough for the day. Let's head back." We took off running down Canal Street, back to Bourbon and to the mall again, where we collapsed in his car and caught our breaths.

"Thank you for driving here today." I hung the beads around Kenny's rearview mirror.

He looked at me and smiled. "The usual this Friday? Hockey and pizza, same time?"

And I held his hand and said, "I'm sorry Kenny," which made Luis and Tyson smile.

"Come on." Kenny looked at me as if he was about to cry, and I shook my head no, although I kept thinking, oh yes. Soon I would be out of here, one step closer to my future, one step closer to destiny.

TWENTY

Nothing was going to be easy for me in the military I thought, opening my manila envelope and seeing Tyndal AFB, Florida. Radar.

"What the hell!" Dave huffed next to me as if he'd read my mind. Then Jersey Jennifer shouted, "Hey, I didn't have any of this on my Dream Sheet!"

My thoughts exactly. What the hell was I going to do in Florida when one of the reasons I'd joined was to be close to Ryan? Why had the military wasted the paper asking us to fill out our Dream Sheets if they didn't give a crap?

"Dave," I glanced at his orders. "How did you get Vegas when you wanted Florida, and I got Florida when I wanted Vegas?"

It reminded me of a story I'd heard of two guys joining under a "buddy program," where the recruiter had told them if they joined together they'd be stationed together, but once they got out of basic they were split apart. Lies, lies, lies! I had counted on, at the very least, getting somewhere close to Ryan, and now I was far from everyone.

To make matters worse, Shanks spotted me kicking a pebble ten minutes later before we got into formation and snapped, "Is there a problem, airman?"

I shook my head no, because if I heard her voice for one more second on top of the trough of bull crap I'd just gotten, I swore to God I was going to lose it. How could this happen to me? I'd tied up my loose ends, said goodbye to Kenny, passed all the scopes (barely, but I did it) and passed the

CTO this morning, only to get my orders to nowhere. Why was there always one more hurdle?

"Ready flight?" Shanks shrieked, and I wanted to scream no, I'm not, I do not want to go to Florida!

"Forward, harch!" she shrieked anyway, and my heart pounded right up to my ear drums and my temples, making me think I couldn't take one more step, but she gasped for air and I decided I'd had enough, plugged my left ear and smiled when I barely heard, "Column left, harch!"

But then she screamed, "Flight, halt," and I almost bumped into the guy in front of me when she was suddenly in my face. "What do you think you're doing?"

Before I could shove my finger in her nose, she stepped back and screamed, "Give me a 341!"

"I don't have a 341!" I almost laughed. She couldn't be serious. We carried it around in basic training in case we got into trouble, but here?

"Oh, you don't?" She took a notepad from her pocket and scribbled. "The Commander's gonna love that!"

"Please! Not the Commander!" I begged, realizing the trouble I was in. He could kick me out or worse, send me to RMT.

"You think you can put your finger in your ear when I'm marching you? I'm telling on you! That'll teach you a lesson, airman!"

"I was just protecting my ears!"

"You can explain that to the Commander! He'll know what to do with you."

She stuck her nose up in the air like I imagined a prissy bitch would and called the flight into action again. Five minutes later when we were in front of the dorms, she dismissed the flight, curled her finger at me, and said, "Follow me." I did, and obediently waited in the hall in front of the Commander's office as I listened to her rendition, which made it sound like I'd been so disobedient that I kicked her in the face.

"Send her in!" he ordered, and she passed me with an I-told-you-so smirk and I wished I had the nerve to trip her as I went in, and thought, here goes nothing.

For a moment I stood in front of the Commander's desk and realized it wasn't the old raisin like Commander at all, but a short fat guy named

Sergeant Keats who'd substituted a PT class before. The only reason I remembered him was because he looked like he hadn't done PT himself in at least twenty years and had the most unforgettable, flattest flat top haircut I'd ever seen, and Jack Nicholson's voice. Even now, it was hard not to laugh when he spoke.

"At ease, soldier!" he whined, shuffling papers on his desk as if I had interrupted him. When I glanced down to see what they were, he suddenly slapped a folder shut and said, "It's come to my attention that you have a problem marching to school."

I bit the inside of my cheek, dying to ask him, "You know you sound like Jack Nicholson from "A Few Good Men?"

"Do. You. Have a problem, airman?" He stared at me.

"Sir," I schmoozed him. Perez had taught me that. How much military men loved to be called "Sir." "Her voice-"

"Spare me the details, airman," he sighed. "I'm not interested. It's airman Shanks' job to march you to school, and it's your job to march, not stick your finger in your ear. Is that clear, airman?"

"Sir. Yes, sir."

"I trust this will never happen again?" He relaxed back into his chair as if my ass kissing had worked and he was going to let me go, then lazily slid a piece of paper towards me and nodded, "Consider yourself counseled."

"Sir?" I was unsure of what just happened. My punishment was to sign a piece of paper, not be sent back home or to remedial?

"Is there anything else you'd like to discuss?" He folded his hands in front of him expectantly.

"Yes, sir, there is, actually. My orders are for Tyndall, but I'd like to go to Nellis Air Force Base in Las Vegas."

He perked up as if he'd discovered a secret about me, and asked, "Is there a gambling problem I don't know about, airman?"

"My brother is stationed there and I'd like to be there too."

"You twins?"

I shook my head, wondering if this was going to take all day.

"Fine," he huffed as if he couldn't think of any other stalling questions. "You find someone who is willing to switch and put both copies of orders in my box on the door. And don't get your tickets or your hopes up until it's a done deal. Now get the hell out of my office. I'm busy!"

Making an about face, I thought about finding Shanks and thanking her! Her ridiculous voice could stop a clock, but had put me right on track to where I wanted to go!

"Don't go buying your tickets yet, because you never know, the orders might not go through…" he called after me again, but military advice was the last thing I was going to heed. I had one mission and one mission only: convince someone he or she wanted to be in a beautiful ocean oasis town in Florida instead of the drab desert, and get tickets out of here, ASAP.

Forty-eight hours later, just like that, as if all I'd had to fix was a typo, as if everything I didn't let the military take care of turned out fine, I was on a plane, clutching the fish bowl between my legs, staring out at the night and trying hard not to feel overwhelmed. Another step closer.

I thought of Alison and smiled. She'd caught me at the last minute, as I was trying to leave and get the hell out of the dorms and to the taxi, except that my suitcase wouldn't shut. She frowned, and as she tossed her school bag on the side, plopped herself down on my suitcase so that I could zip it shut and sighed, "I'm going to miss you."

"I'm going to miss you too," I'd said, tearing up and hoping she'd get a good roommate after me. "I left my notes for you in the closet. Do you think I'm a bad airman for throwing away some of my blues and gym clothes to close this suitcase?"

"I'm starting radar soon," she shook her head sadly and pouted. "I won't know what to do without you."

"You'll be fine," I tried to convince both her and me because even though I was done with school I had no idea what else awaited me. "I'll miss you too."

"We'll stay in touch, right?" she hugged me and I nodded, knowing I wouldn't. If I found out she failed, I couldn't take it, the fact that maybe she'd lose that spirit or that the Air Force would have one up on her. Anyone but her!

Then she'd rummaged through her desk drawer and handed me a picture. It was of us from the first day we met, after she'd woken me from my NyQuil haze and I'd agreed to show her around the base. In the picture we were standing there laughing because she'd tried to jump on my back but had slipped because of her puffy vest.

It seemed like so far away and yet like yesterday.

"You know you're going to be just fine, right?"

She'd nodded and smiled that smile, and said, "That's right, because things can only get better from here!"

TWENTY-ONE

I couldn't think of anything better than flying into Las Vegas the day I turned twenty one, Tech School behind me and Ryan welcoming me with open arms and hugging me until I thought I was going to pass out.

"I knew you could do it, sis! Happy Birthday!"

"Thanks, Ryan." I let him take my suitcase, throw it in the back of his white beat up Honda, and he said, "I've got a night planned for you! I can't believe it's been four months already! We are going to celebrate, big time!"

I couldn't say much, I couldn't say anything, as Ryan drove down the strip and let me gawk at the bright lights of the city, the casinos, Disneyland for adults. How did I get this lucky? How had it all worked out so smoothly? How had I made it this far?

He finally parked at the MGM, the big green casino with a gold lion in the front and led me through the parking lot to an open bar called "Fat Tuesday," which aptly means Mardi Gras. As we stood there and waited, guys popped up out of nowhere and slapped his hand as if they'd been waiting for him to get this party started, as if he was the Bat Signal, and I thought that this was a side of Ryan I'd never seen before. Usually I was the popular one and he'd tag along with me and my friends, and now we'd flipped roles.

"Grillo-o-o-o," a tall skinny guy in a cowboy hat slapped Ryan's back. I studied him for a moment, handsome for a cowboy, if I was into them. He was at least a foot taller than Ryan with thin lips and a pale face, and chocolate brown hair that would have started to curl had it not been for the short faded haircut. He was holding a beer can as if he'd started his own party hours ago, and he said, "Oh, I forgot there's two of you now."

"Martin-in-in-in," Ryan sang back, and Martin chuckled as if he was drunk already and said, "Grillo one and Grillo two. You ready to part-ay?"

He nudged me when I didn't respond, tossed his beer can in the trash and said, "Follow me. I'm going to show you the cheapest way to have fun in Vegas."

At the counter at Fat Tuesday, I gazed at Martin, who ordered six slushy drinks, wondering why he wanted me to follow him, until he nudged me and grinned. "Show 'em your I.D., Grillo-o-o-o," he said and then paid.

I flashed my just-turned-twenty-one I.D. and was handed three slushy drinks, and before I could turn to walk back to Ryan and the rest of the guys (whose names I couldn't remember), Martin said, "Take a sip and follow me up the escalator. We don' wanna get caught handing those drinks to minors."

"Good, huh?" He watched me take a sip.

I said, "It's dynamite. Sweet and then you get a strong kick of alcohol."

The last time I drank was at the cheap Hotel Tech School party and I couldn't remember the last time I drank before then, so I felt pretty tipsy already. Combine that with being on the corner of Las Vegas Boulevard in the middle of the night, and I was feeling pretty good.

"I'm so glad you're here, sis," Ryan said coming up from behind and hugging me sideways. "Jen, I want you to meet Winston."

"Hey, hey," Winston said almost shyly.

He was even taller than Martin, lanky, and pale except for the bridge of his nose that looked sunburned, and before I could say hi, Ryan said, "I can't ever tell if he's serious or kidding either. Don't ever take him seriously. In Pennsylvania they have a very different sort of dry humor."

Next to Winston was Joe, a guy my height and weight with hair so wispy it moved with every step he took. He didn't say anything, only smirked quietly while the others joked, reminding me of a cartoon character.

"You have the wrong number!" Jeff huffed into his cell phone, "I swear."

Jeff was also my height and blonde, but muscular and balding. He wore a permanent frown like he was an old cranky man stuck in a young buff body, and after the phone call he angrily shoved his cell phone in his pocket and said to no one in particular, "I was the first Jeff Gordon. It's not my fault my number is in the phone book and they lost touch with the other one!"

"Let's go, Gordon," Martin winked at me as if I were in on some inside joke and hooked his arm into mine. I could get used to this: feeling like a rock star among five brothers.

"Give me your number, sexy!" Martin let go of my arm to chase a girl, but he came back with this arms out wide calling after her, "Aw, why not? Come on, girl."

"Way to get her number," Winston said.

Martin said, "Whatever, man," as if we (or Winston) hadn't seen the last of his skills.

We stopped at another Fat Tuesday, this time a small stand outside of Caesars's Palace, and Martin didn't even have to tell me to get my I.D out. I already knew the gig.

"Where's Ryan?" I came back with the drinks, only to see Joe, Winston, and Jeff joking around.

"I don't know," Winston scratched his head. "A few more guys showed up while you and Martin were ordering. He must have left with them. He won't answer his phone and I've got to take a piss."

"Me too," Martin sauntered over with his arms full of drinks. "We'll find him later, we always do. Let's go in hea'."

"Hea" was the Monte Carlo, and we stumbled in only to find out we had to walk three miles to the nearest bathroom. Too drunk to stand on my own, I held on to Winston's arm and followed them into the men's room. I was escorted out by security ten seconds later because they thought I was a prostitute about to conduct some personal business.

"Come on, just let me take a leak, man!" Martin pleaded, but they didn't let up until we were outside again.

"Fine, I'll just drain it hea', then," Martin unzipped his fly when they disappeared. Joe and Winston joined him, peed their names onto the casino column while I laughed, trying not to look.

"It's got to be, like, two in the morning," I said when they were done. "Are we going home soon?"

"Ryan should be at his car by now." Winston glanced at his watch, but by the way he dropped his arm I could tell he couldn't read it. "Don't worry. We always find him sooner or later."

We took off towards the MGM again until a girl stopped me, causing everyone else to stop, and said, "You are so hot."

"Thanks." I didn't know what else to say to the skinny brunette in the pink tank top and mini skirt, but what I said wasn't enough for her to let me by.

She asked, "Can I kiss you?" which caused Martin and Winston's jaws to drop and grip my hands so tightly I couldn't move at all.

"Sorry guys. I'm not into girls," I said, and as the girl waited for me to change my mind, Martin pouted, "Aw come on." That gave her the courage she was looking for. She honed in, took my face in her hands, and plunged her tongue into my mouth as if I was an ice cream flavor she'd never had before. When she started moaning, I realized it wasn't doing for me what it was for her, and I pulled back and said, "Sorry."

"Can I get your number?" She followed me as I broke my hands free from Winston and Martin, who were too dazed to move.

"Yeah, Jen," Martin whistled and told the girl, "I'll take it for her. Write it on my hand. She'll be calling you tomorrow."

"No, I won't," I promised when he caught up to me, and he said, "I will remind you of it every minute until you do!"

"Why are guys so nuts about stuff like that?" I suddenly felt sober, and said, "And we need to find Ryan!"

"There he is," Winston pointed through the car garage as we walked in and saw Ryan sitting Indian style on the hood of his car.

"I've been calling you guys all night." Ryan slid off the hood and said, "It gets later every night!"

"You too, man!" Martin laughed. "You wouldn't believe what happened to us."

"Sorry," Winston said to me after Ryan unlocked the door and Martin, Jeff, and Joe wedged themselves into the backseat. "But you have to sit on my lap in the front."

"Make it quick, Ry." I squeezed onto Winston's lap, my head sideways against the roof as I managed to clutch the oh-shit bar above the passenger door, close to the mini fire extinguisher Ryan had added to make his car look sporty. Sporty or not, the extinguisher was already empty. Ryan had told me how they'd installed it and immediately drove to the outskirts of town and unloaded it in the desert.

"Mwah." Ryan sped through the red light then kissed his hand and pounded the dashboard as if that was going to keep us from being killed.

"What are you doing, Ry?" I shrieked.

"Best not to look," Martin called out from the back, and the rest of the guys laughed as if this near death experience was normal.

"I'm not going out with you guys anymore." I held my breath. "I didn't make it this far just so I could die my first night here!"

"The hell you're not!" Ryan blasted the Wu Tang Clan on the radio. "We've only just begun!"

"Only just begun," Martin, Winston, and the rest of the guys started singing, reminding me of their midnight choir sessions when they pranked me at Tech School, and suddenly I couldn't help but smile, feeling for the first time that I was right where I belonged, right where I was supposed to be.

TWENTY-TWO

My clammy hands stuck to the wheel as I tried to signal and make the turn on the long windy road to my new tower. I was grateful, at least that Ryan had let me use his car (he took the bus to work), but when he'd handed me the keys and wished me luck on my first day, he'd also commented that I looked like I was playing dress-up in my oversized uniform, which shattered the only shred of confidence I had.

I tried to focus on the big red-orange mountains all around me, unlike anything I'd ever seen in New Hampshire or anywhere, and tried to formulate how I'd describe them to Jake and Pam. All I came up with was "beautiful" which wasn't enough then again how could I explain anything that had happened to me in the last five months? From basement to Las Vegas and on my way to becoming an Air Traffic Controller, all of it was breathtaking.

I parked the car and exhaled deeply, glancing at the runways, the pebbles in between, and hangars across the way. It was soon to be my playground, and I thought, wow, this is awesome. Then I made my way to the door, and stood dumbfound as I studied the number lock on the handle. Should I even take a stab at the numbers to get in?

Suddenly the door swung open and a very handsome young man with olive skin, green eyes, and black perfect hair held it open and smiled so that I could see every perfectly spaced tooth, as if I was a cute little stray puppy. He said, "You don't need the hat."

I didn't know what he meant, but knew I was in trouble if all Air Traffic Controllers were as gorgeous as he. Then he pointed at his head, revealing a wedding band that shattered my dreams, and he said, "Your hat is FOD," as if that cleared everything up.

"Of course," I muttered, making a note to ask Ryan what FOD was, and went in as he went out.

Standing by myself in the beige-tiled hall, I looked straight ahead at the elevator. To the right was a classroom-type room with a table and white board, and in the office to the left stood two desks side by side, the left desk occupied by a black man with an angry scowl on his face as he stared at me.

"Hi!" I walked in with my hand extended and was shut down immediately when he growled, "I know who you are airman. Have a seat."

His desk plate read "Chief Controller," which told me nothing, especially about how he knew my name and what I'd done to him. Had Perez given him a call?

"You are the most abrasive airman I have ever seen." He stood up and with my eyes I followed his slow strut around the room, waiting to be enlightened and making yet another note to look up the word "abrasive."

"Do you know what it takes to be an Air Traffic Controller?" he asked as though he'd rehearsed this speech a million times, and before I could answer he asked, "Do you know where you are, airman?"

I thought I was in the "real Air Force," I wanted to say as I followed his gaze out the window. Had I walked into the wrong tower? If I'd ducked into the elevator instead of loitering in the hall so damn long would I still have made myself a target?

"When my military career started," he continued. Somehow I must have missed what he said afterwards because he then asked, "Are you serious about becoming an Air Traffic Controller. Are you ready to learn, airman?"

"Well, yes," I replied, confused. Wasn't that why I was here?

Then Chief Satan sat down, folded his hands in front of him, and stared at me while I stared at his perfectly shaven face, manicured nails, and wedding band, thinking who the hell would marry that asshole? Then he picked up the phone as if he couldn't think of any more speeches to give and snarled, "She's on her way up." And as he smashed the phone into the cradle as if he was trying to smash my dreams, he said, "I'll make you one promise, airman. I'll teach you the true military ways, airman, and if you don't learn them, I will wash you out, got it?"

"Yes," I replied, thinking his threats didn't bother me as much as his horrifying smirk did.

"Go on now, airman, shoo. Show some initiative." He waved his hand at me as if he hadn't been the one to suck me into this black hole he called an office and hijack my time in the first place.

I leaped out of my seat (he didn't have to tell me twice to get out of there), and I dropped the idea of setting him straight because unbeknownst to him, I was the very epitome of initiative.

I must have hit the elevator button at least eleven times, and once I was inside I watched the display as if my life depended on it. Then the doors opened to another beige-tiled hall. This one was bigger, with a soda machine, a door to the bathroom, and another door to the stairwell that I had to take. Quickly, I rushed up the last flight of stairs only to be blocked by another coded door. Thinking I was never going to get inside, the door buzzed and I was suddenly numb as I climbed the stairs. This was what I'd fought for, to be here, and I couldn't believe I'd made it!

At the top, I nearly fainted when I saw the runways, desert landscape, and the Vegas strip in the distance. This was my new world, my future, my tower cab, and I was ready!

"Hi!" I beamed, and immediately the fat supervisor spun in his chair, flashed a smile, and put a stubby finger to his mouth as if to shut me up. He whispered, "I'm LZ, the Watch Sup." Then he pointed at the controllers and rattled off their initials, although no one turned around to greet me, and said, "Don't worry, you'll get used to their initials. Pretty soon you won't know anyone's real name. And in the corner over there is the SOF, a pilot, the Supervisor of Flying, in case a pilot needs help with something, like being talked down through an emergency, like we have coming in now."

"Emergency?" I searched the sky for smoke and flames and stared at Local Control wondering what I'd do, what would I say? This wasn't a computer scenario; this was real!

But the controller remained calm as if he barely noticed anything was amiss, and minutes later when the F-16 came into view, zooming past the tower so loudly my ribcage rumbled, I wondered if the Chief had me pegged correctly. Did I have what it took?

The F-16 landed smoothly, taxied to the end of the runway, and turned into the revetments, where the emergency crew checked him out.

"See, that was it," LZ read my mind. "No sweat. Don't look so scared. If I can do this, so can you," he joked, but my head was swimming.

This was nothing like Tech School. I was in way over my head, trying to swim with the big fish, and God help me prove that devil of a man downstairs wrong. God help me not get sent home tomorrow!

TWENTY-THREE

The room across from Chief Satan's office was called the "Batcave," and I was told every tower had one, that that was where all trainees started their Air Traffic career, and that I was stuck there for two weeks no matter what, to learn all the important airfield information like radio frequencies, runway lengths, and which aircraft were stationed here.

It didn't bother me so much, except that I was an extrovert and only had contact with Sergeant Behr, a Watch Sup from upstairs who was also in charge of the training program and therefore gave me assignments and tests throughout the day. Otherwise, I was on my own and subject to Satan's phone calls, as if he forgot both our doors were open, as if he thought I wouldn't listen.

"'Xactly, 'xactly," was his favorite thing to say, followed by a random Bible quote, making me want to bang my head against the table hoping he'd stop.

To be fair, not all conversations went on for hours. When his kids called, he'd only give them a chore to do, a chore that sounded simple until he explained it in excruciating detail, like how to dust a shelf correctly by removing every item, then spraying said shelf and moving the dust rag clockwise then counta'clockwise, which I was sure made them wish they'd hadn't called to say hello. His wife's calls were even shorter, always a long sigh as if he was swamped with work, and the standard, "Uh-huh, I'll call you back soon," which he never did.

"This should be the last of 'em," Behr walked into the room smiling.

I said, "Hey," because I was happy he'd stopped the monotony, and more importantly, brought another test, something for me to do.

"Any more crazy stories?" he teased, making me wish I hadn't told him about all my adventures on the strip, which I hadn't if I wasn't stuck in this dungeon-type room, desperate for social interaction and I shook my head no, embarrassed.

"You're just holding back," he joked, waving my test in the air. "This is the last test! Two weeks are done! As soon as you finish this, I'll bring it to the Chief and then, well, we'll see."

I could barely contain myself as I hurried through the test and handed it to him minutes later. Then he said, "Be right back," and practically skipped into Satan's office. But as soon as Satan ordered, "Close the door," Behr's enthusiasm was gone. His shoulders slacked, his eyes turned towards the floor, and his smile was replaced by a frown as I watched him close the door.

"Are you sure?" Satan's voice was muffled through the door. "I mean, are you sure?" I thought, what an asshole! Yes Behr was sure! What was the big deal? Why was there a problem every time I took a test?

Silence followed for a full minute, and I thought my heart was going to stop from the suspense. Then the door whipped open and Behr stepped back into the room with a frown still on his face, and he sighed, "I have no choice in the matter," and handed me the test.

"Oh," I replied, scanning the page thinking. This wasn't how I'd imagined I'd fail, at week two.

"I'm just messin'!" he grinned. "You passed your last test! You're done in the Batcave. You can go upstairs!"

"What? Really? I passed? That's it? I can go up?"

"Congratulations," he nodded proudly. "Just get a headset from the Chief and I'll see you up there."

Satan glared at Behr as he hurried past the door and into the elevator, and when his gaze fell on me I could tell he wasn't pleased.

I entered the office and noticed Satan's firm grip on his desk, his knuckles strained as if they were about to break off and his nostrils flared as if he was a bull about to charge, because I was his worst nightmare.

"What are your initials, airman?" He finally let go of the desk.

"JG," I replied proudly.

He said, "We have a JG already." I hadn't even thought of an alternative. "But he's leaving for another base, so you can have them."

He wrote them on a piece of paper along with all the other initials, as if to make it official, and I thought, yes, he could not keep me down!

"He was a good controller. You'll have big shoes to fill," he continued, and I almost told him to keep the pep talk to himself. I was going to be an Air Traffic Controller no matter how much he tried to push me down. Then he dug through his desk, unraveled a cord, and handed me my very own headset, which almost made me burst with excitement, until he snapped, "Mind that headset! If you break it, you're not getting another one. They're expensive."

I wrapped the cord around the headset again and let my hands drop to my side. He asked, "You got the code for upstairs?" which he knew I damn well didn't have, and said, "Four, two, two, one. I ain't gonna tell you again. Dismissed," which had to be the most beautiful word in the English language.

Skipping to the elevator, I pushed the button fourteen times and stepped in, feeling like a whole new person. Upstairs I punched in the numbers four, two, two, one, waited for the click, and turned the knob. The kingdom was mine!

"Hi," I entered the cab like a newly-adopted puppy, thinking, where do I go, what do I do? But Behr was the only one who smiled. He pointed at the Flight Data position and said, "CB is waiting for you."

"Hi CB!" I extended my hand excitedly.

He said, "You done socializing?" and stood up as if to intimidate me, although he was shorter and skinnier than I, reminding me of a little Chihuahua with glasses. His bark was probably worse than his bite.

Then he slapped a binder on the counter, flipped it open, and read from a checklist like an auctioneer. "Runway two one in use, Bravo on the ATIS, men and equipment at the approach end of 21 right, got it?" I didn't. He pushed his glasses into his forehead and wrote our initials on a piece of paper, which meant we were taking responsibility for the flight data position. He snapped, "I'm signing you on in case something goes wrong, then you'll get blamed, not me. Got it?"

I couldn't figure out if his little smirk was serious or not and therefore said nothing.

"Now, when the phone rings," he softened, although I felt my confidence had already been shot, "I'll cover my boom and tell you what to say. You be a parrot. Don't question it if you don't understand. We can go over it later. Before you hang up, give your initials. Don't say bye or some shit like that, just JG. That means the conversation is over and your name is on the record. At the end of the shift I'll write up an evaluation, or eval, of your progress or lack thereof. Then it goes downstairs to be signed, and then into your folder. If you're not in position, you're reading the point sixty five. If you're not reading, you're mopping the stairwell. Copy?"

"Copy."

Then the phone rang as if on cue, and CB's eyes narrowed. Although I knew I was supposed to answer, all I could do was stare at the consul and compare it to how similar it looked like to the one in Tech School, knowing this wasn't school at all. This was real and scary as hell.

"Now!" CB gritted his teeth as if stopping himself from calling me a dumbass. "Answer that *cat* as soon as you hear it, not five rings later." I successfully picked up the line but couldn't speak, so CB covered his boom and whispered, "Tower."

"Tower," I stuttered.

"Hey tower, this is Base Ops," a friendly female voice said. "Sweeper is going out there in a couple of minutes. He's a little late because of some radio problems earlier, okay? TL."

It was a simple statement, but I couldn't think of anything to say to her, especially with CB breathing in my ear so loudly I couldn't hear myself think. Then he nudged my shoulder and whispered, "It ain't rocket science JG. Just say 'Copy, JG' and hang it up!"

I hung up without saying a word and CB was forced to call back and fix my mistake.

"Hey, this is Air Traffic, missy. You can't freeze up like that. Talk, say something stupid, I don't care, but say something. What the hell are you gonna do when you got planes lookin' at each other and you gotta fix it? And don't keep secrets. Ground is sittin' right next to you, tell 'em verbatim what you got!"

"Ground, sweeper will be out in a few minutes. He was having radio problems," I relayed softly, but Ground didn't even look in my direction.

Neither did anyone else, making me feel invisible and praying the phone would never ring again.

"Did you hear that?" CB hopped off his seat, reached for a grease marker next to me, and started scribbling all over the clear plexiglass counter. "While you're busy daydreaming, Local is working an IFE, an In-Flight Emergency. Pay attention. That cat is ten miles out, left engine out. Ring the crash phone."

My mouth gaped as if he was speaking Chinese, as if I hadn't done this a hundred times at Tech School, and CB screamed, "Godamn it JG! Ring the Goddamned crash phone! The red phone over there!" and I picked up the receiver, shaking, and wondering what the hell I was supposed to say as all the other agencies picked up and waited for my information.

CB stood shoulder to shoulder with me, cocked the receiver close to his ear so that both of us could listen, and whispered, "Wait 'til they're all on, then say everything that's on the glass."

"IFE," I read from the counter. "F-16. Left engine out. Thirty miles out. No other information," and I nearly hung up, my throat so dry I wanted a gallon of water to drink.

CB whispered, "Not yet. Wait and see if they have questions."

"Any questions?" I coughed and thanked God when no one said anything.

"Okay, hang that cat up," CB said, and once the receiver was down, he put his hands on his hips and said, "Alright, you almost fucked that up. Now pay attention to what Local and Ground do and assist them if they need it. And for God's sake, answer the damned phone when it rings. What the hell is the matter with you? You have one job and one job only! Answer that cat! How in thee hayll didn't you wash outta Tech School?"

TWENTY-FOUR

"Call me Sid," the Weekend Sup said with his bottom lip tucked under his two front crowns.

He'd lost his real teeth in a car accident and so he played it up, sucking on his bottom lip when he spoke to females. I turned and replied, "Oh, yeah, Sid," although I couldn't remember why he went by Sid when he looked nothing like the British singer at all. In fact he was the opposite, built like a matador, chest like a bull, and toothpick legs.

"Because I like Sid Vicious from the Sex Pistols, get it," his eyebrows bounced as if waiting for me to react, which I didn't, and so he continued. "So I go by SD, or Sid."

He waited until I looked at him again and this time narrowed his eyes, batted his eyelashes, stared at my boots, and said, "Tell me about your toes." He rubbed his tongue along his front teeth as if I wouldn't notice, and asked, "What color are they? When was your last pedicure? Are your toes straight or curved? Do you have a toe ring?"

I answered, "Uhm," because I knew he wanted me to tell him something sexy, when in fact I'd never had a pedicure and my toes were boring as hell.

"It's just what he does. He has a foot fetish," the Ground Controller whispered next to me. "Don't you remember all his books on his coffee table when he had the BBQ? They were all about shoes and feet."

I hadn't noticed. Who would notice such a thing? But now that he mentioned it, I did recall his girlfriend's purple sausage toes in her strappy sandals, asking everyone if he or she liked her new kicks. I'd agreed, but only so she'd leave me alone, and I suddenly realized how much I missed hanging with Ryan and the guys and wished my schedule wasn't always changing so that I could see them more.

"What color were they, you said?" Sid cleared his throat.

I answered, "Red," which I hoped would settle the issue but only made him hungrier, and he said, "Tell me more." I couldn't, and luckily the Ground Controller shook my sleeve and pointed at the Scrabble board and said, "Your turn, JG," because that was what we did on the weekends when there weren't any planes in the sky or Chiefs in the downstairs office.

I had wanted to study since my Flight Data certification was coming up, and I was nervous I'd fail because CB had pounded that idea in my head since day one, but Sid didn't like to do much on weekends except kick his feet up on the consul and relax and made sure everyone else was relaxed too.

"I'm going to do the trash and check the stairwell." I excused myself from the awkward conversation and boring game, and before I reached the stairs, Sid caught my wrist and gripped it hard and asked, "Is that where you're really going?" as if he didn't believe me, making me wonder how rough he was with his girlfriend.

"I need to get out of the cab and think of something other than my cert coming up," I explained quickly.

"It's only flight data," he smirked.

I insisted, "I know, but I'm nervous," and he finally let me go.

I was in the hallway twenty minutes later when he snuck up on me mopping the floor.

"You think you have it covered tomorrow?"

He startled me, and I shrugged, "I guess so," wondering why his eyebrows weren't playfully jumping.

I reached for the elevator button and said, "I'm taking out the trash." Before I could pick up the bag from the floor he had me pinned against the wall, his hand on my throat, and hissed, "You guess so?" reminding me of when I was a little girl, helpless against my father, and even more helpless now against a bipolar lunatic I didn't know.

I thought of kicking him in the balls, but his breathing was heavy, as if he was extremely focused, and I knew that with one hiccup I could be spitting blood. I stood perfectly still.

"You count as one of my crew because I work with you, even if it's just on the weekends, so you "guess" doesn't fucking cut it. You better not make me look bad tomorrow. Got it?" The only thing I got was that I was alone. Satan would laugh, CB didn't care, and Ryan simply wouldn't get it.

Pleading with my eyes for him to let me go, I suddenly saw something familiar as I stared deep into his; fear. The same fear of failure I had because Satan had the same grip around his neck that he had around me.

It wasn't a secret that Satan thought of Sid as a fuck up. He'd been in the military eighteen years without a single promotion and had the balls to flaunt ignorantly that he didn't want the responsibility because he already had everything in life he needed: a car, an apartment, and a girlfriend with whom to split the rent. All he wanted to do was relax, and all Satan wanted to do was light a fire under his ass, and if I failed, in Satan's eyes he failed too, and the hell would start all over again.

"I'm sorry." He blinked as if he'd snapped out of whatever trance he was in and let go of me. Then he patted my neck as if to erase his handprints and asked sincerely, "Are you okay? I didn't mean that. I was just worried for you. I hope you do well tomorrow."

"I will, Sid," I whispered, feeling even more pressure than before and wondering what would happen if I didn't do well.

Besides, what was he worried about, he was already rated. It was me who was struggling to get my foot in the door and prove myself before I was sent home and lost everything. And I wasn't about to let Satan get the best of me. No matter how hard he tightened his grip, I was not going home.

TWENTY-FIVE

Sitting in Ground Control, I almost wished I'd failed Flight Data. CB chucked the checklist binder against the window and barked, "Damnit JG, are you gon' answer that dang pilot?"

"I can't hear anything but static," I whined.

He sighed loudly and keyed up for me, as if it was the easiest thing in the world to taxi the F-15's to the runway. He said, "Rip the dang strips. Sort 'em out and line 'em up. That way, you'll know what to listen for."

Ripping the flight strips out of the printer, I glanced at all the flight information I needed: call signs, destination, and altitude, then slid the strips into plastic trays and sorted them into alphabetical order, wishing they'd call me in that order and make my life easy. I wondered why Tech School had been so much easier, the frequencies clearer, and everyone doing what you told him or her to. Here, I couldn't understand a damn thing.

"JG, say something. I don't give a flying fuck if you say 'say again' a hundred times. Talk to the dang planes!"

"Last calling ground, say again" I pushed the button to key up the headset to transmit, not because I wanted to, but because I was getting more scared of CB's rage.

"JG, you're not a phone sex operator. Say it like you mean it!"

I looked at him as if the airplanes were on his face, and I noticed the angrier he was with me, the more Southern he became.

"Keep yo' dang eyes out the winda! Don't test may JG, not to-day!" As if that was different than any other day.

"Hear that faint whistlin'?" CB finally softened. "You can tell that cat is a lawn dart, and his call sign had a 'one one' in it. All they want is an engine run or to taxi out. That's why we have phraseology, so you know what to listen for. Go with what you know. Ask him which F-16 he is and tell him he can taxi out. Get 'em movin'. They don't have time for your shit. If they hear that stutter in your voice, they'll ignore you and taxi themselves out and we don't want a pilot thinkin' for hisself."

"Say again," I repeated, listened, and could almost make out the pilot's reply, but before I could say anything else, CB sighed, "Get your head outta your ass girl," and I knew he was right. If I didn't get my head out of my ass starting now, I wasn't going to last another day.

"I'm going to tell him to taxi, okay?" I glanced at CB for approval.

"Well, yeah, JG," he replied sarcastically.

"F-16 calling ground, uhm, runway 21, uhm, taxi via..." I said and I couldn't tell whose sigh of relief was louder, mine or his, maybe even the pilot's. I had said something!

Sliding the flight strip to Flight Data, CB snatched it up and explained, "You're not done yet. Mark it up, so everyone knows what that cat's doin.' Like this. Now it's ready."

"Say again?" I keyed up then. "Cobra41 taxi to runway 21," I said shakily, but felt as if I was almost getting the hang of it.

The pilot read it back. "Taxiing to runway 21, good day," and I just about died! He heard me! Understood me and was now taxiing because I had told him to!

"Good day, Cobra41," I smiled, feeling in charge and wanting more.

"I will strangle you with that dang headset if you don't cut out that god dang cowboy phraseology!" CB burst my bubble. "You can say 'good day' when you're rated. Right now I need you to pay the hell attention!"

Then the phone rang and LZ shouted across the cab, "JG, the Chief was listening downstairs. No more 'good days' to the pilots!"

I said, "Wilco!" but really wished I could tell Satan where to shove it. Then again, if that was his only complaint, maybe I was doing okay. Maybe I didn't sound like a moron on the radio. I was doing it! I. Was. Doing. It! And just like that, the crash phone rang. Inbound emergency.

"Aw hayll, JG, an IFE." CB whistled like he was fishing and had caught a big one, making me want to crawl under the consul and disappear. In Tech School, I'd worked one emergency. Here there seemed to be one every hour!

"You betta' get your head out yo' ass. Groun' contro' is the most important position for an IFE, In-Flight Emergency. Anyone can clear 'em to land, but you gon' make sure you know where all the vehicles are and get 'em through to that emergency. An' you betta' not cross them without permission. You watch Local Control like a hawk and make sure you know what the hell is goin' on! Now watch me, so you don't fuck shit up agin'!"

Everyone talked above me. LZ and the SOF, Flight Data, CB, and Local spoke calmly, methodically, and like I didn't exist. And I wished nothing more than to be like them.

Minutes later the IFE touched down safely, without flames or a single hint that anything was amiss. CB coordinated with Local Control and vehicles met the F-16 within seconds, making it all look easy, as though I could do it too.

"Unplug and stick your head in the point sixty-five," CB ordered.

I asked, "That's it? But I'm just getting the hang of it. I don't want to read it in a book, I want to do it for real!"

"There'll be more, later." He pulled my headset out of the jack for me.

"But..." I attempted to plug in again because I didn't understand why I couldn't get more practice if practice was all I needed.

CB warned, "JG, don't argue."

"But..."

"But nothin', I said, go!" He yanked the headset from my head, hurting my ear as if he'd pulled that instead, and chucked it downstairs. He said, "Now go chase your headset and get the hell out of the tower cab!"

Angrily, I left and stood next to the soda machine one floor down, staring at the window and trying not to cry. I knew I'd bitten off more than I could chew, but I also knew that no matter what, I couldn't go back home. I wasn't the same anymore, I wasn't someone who could work a nine-to-five job anymore and pretend that what I'd been through the last few months was normal.

The door opened a few minutes later and LZ leaned on to the pane next to me and said, "I've seen grown men cry in training, JG. Training is rough, but believe me one day it will all click. The light will come on. Some get it on the first day, some on the last, and of course some not at all. The timing is different for everyone."

"I don't even know what I did wrong!" I squeaked. "And I'm tired of being pushed around."

"I'm your supervisor," LZ smiled, making me feel like I could confide in him. "I might not be your friend, but you can tell me anything. In the meantime, you gotta keep pluggin' away, that's all there is to it."

"Okay," I said, wondering if maybe I did have to get used to the idea that eventually I would have to go back home and work a nine-to-five, no matter how much I couldn't picture it. Sometimes the facts of life were just that.

Then he turned to leave and said, "Oh, and the Chief wants you in his office." I thought, great, as if I hadn't had enough for the day, now him, and pushed the elevator button.

"Shred those papers over there," Satan said as I walked into his office. "Remove the staples before you load them into the shredder."

"Huh?" I gasped when I saw the small table by the door piled with a stack of papers the size of three phone books. Next to it sat a staple remover, and on the floor a shredder that seemed to be smiling at me as if he was in on the joke with Satan. Now that I was in Ground Control training the chores should have stopped, but they seemed to have increased, as if I had the name Cinderella sewn on my name tag.

"Excuse me?" He glared at me.

I whispered, "You really are the devil," thinking he hadn't heard me, but suddenly he smiled and said sarcastically, "Why JG, whatever do you mean?"

I wanted to tell him what I really meant, that he was a flaming asshole, like Dad, like Perez, who didn't know a damn thing about what I needed. What I needed was a mentor, a teacher. I wanted to learn, that's all I ever wanted, and I was tired of being pinned down! Why couldn't he help me soar?

"And make sure you pull the weeds around my car. I had a plaque ordered for my spot that reads 'Chief Controller' and it's getting installed today. In fact, make that your daily detail. Inspect the rocks around the lot and make sure you nab 'em before they get big. And speaking of cars, wax the emergency vehicle when you're done with that and then polish the elevator. I know it'll take you a while, so you can spread that out for the next few days and when those tasks are complete, I'll have some more for you. Is that clear?"

He resumed typing but noticed I hadn't answered, and repeated, "I said, is that clear?"

I muttered, "Yes, sir," hating the very sound of it.

Then I promised myself to get rated as an Air Traffic Controller no matter what, even if it was just to piss him off, and I thought, rot in hell Satan. Rot in hell!

TWENTY-SIX

Three intense months later I made it to Local Control, which was more pressure than Flight Data and Ground Control put together. I had learned to take one minute at a time, because it was impossible to predict even the next ten seconds. And as if to prove my point, as I stared out the window waiting for a plane to call me, the tower cab burst to life when the door opened and a bubbly female voice giggled, "Hi!"

Pretending to unravel my headset cord so CB wouldn't breathe fire down my neck as I turned to peek, I saw three new trainees. The blonde, the one who'd said hello, couldn't stop smiling. She waved to no one in particular and said, "I'm Mandy. And that's Kimmie and Evan."

Mandy had chubby cheeks which made her look fourteen. Evan was tall and skinny, with a big nose and teeth that he tried to hide by nervously chewing gum. Kimmie had dark eye raccoon make-up like Alanis had worn, brown hair she had slicked back into a tight bun, freckles, and square tomboyish shoulders.

"Aw shit, not another JG," CB said. Hospitality died in this tower, as if it was frowned upon to say hello. But I'd waited six months for this. I was no longer alone!

"Yes, sir, fresh out of Tech School," Evan crooned at LZ, in a deep smooth voice I hadn't expected from such a lanky guy. It made me risk another glance and this time I appreciated his odd features and shyness. There was something about him, something more than a sly smile and bright blue eyes I wanted to dive into, and I thought, we could really be friends. I couldn't wait to talk to them all.

"JG, unplug," LZ hung up the phone and I hadn't even noticed it had rung. I feared I'd have to sweep the parking lot, but instead he said, "Go show the new trainees around." I unplugged, not having to be told twice.

At the elevator, I had to stop myself from squeezing the air out of them and said, "I'm JG and it is so great to finally have trainees here!"

"It's so great to be here!" Mandy mirrored my enthusiasm so much I didn't dare give her the rude awakening about Satan.

"Is there a place to smoke?" Evan glanced around, antsy.

I replied, "Uhm, I guess outside, downstairs, although I think you're the only one who smokes here besides CB, my trainer. But he says he only smokes because of me. Never mind that, follow me." I took them downstairs and outside and asked, "Where are you guys from?"

"Well," I'm from Montana," Mandy replied, her mouth like a faucet, "and Evan's from Maryland and..."

"B'More," Evan interrupted calmly and flashed a sideways peace sign with his index and middle finger, as if I was supposed to know what that meant, which made Mandy giggle, push his shoulder, and snap jokingly, "I wasn't done yet. Kimmie is from Florida."

Kimmie looked away as though studying the scenery, and I understood that she, and Evan were a little more guarded than Mandy. So I said, "Okay," wondering how Mandy had made it through basic when she acted so much younger than her years.

"Right over here is the executive closet," I led them back inside and into Satan's office without looking at him. "This is where we keep all the cleaning supplies. We have to clean the facility, the bathrooms, and empty the trash after each shift."

"Show them the right way to do things around here, JG," Satan chimed in as if trying to sound important, but, I ignored him and took them back upstairs.

I said, "We can start with the trash first."

"I wanted to be a nurse," Mandy said as she helped me toss the trash bags in the dumpster outside a few minutes later. "But back in Montana, we didn't, like, have enough money, so I joined to go to school and I just can't believe I'm here. This tower is so big. I'm from a farm. And jeez, I can't even believe I passed basic…"

"I can't believe it either." Evan lit another cigarette and exhaled slowly, which somehow hypnotized and roped me in, as though his smoke were a lasso, and I realized I was in awe of how calm he was, completely opposite of me, and how nothing seemed to bother him.

Mandy pushed his shoulder again, which made him exhale in short little bursts and smile, but just for a second he stared off into the distance again as if remembering the time he spent on a beach somewhere swinging in a hammock. I wanted him back in the conversation and asked, "So how did you get through basic if you couldn't smoke?"

He slowly finished his cigarette, rubbed the butt between his thumb and finger until the burning ash flew away in the wind, flicked the butt into the big dumpster as if he had coolness down pat and didn't mind making me wait for an answer, and finally said, "I told myself, 'soon you'll be able to smoke.'"

"That's it?" I wrinkled my forehead and he shrugged, "Yup," as if whatever he said was gold and there was no point in questioning him.

Mandy started talking again, but I studied Kim and how she fit into the equation. Before I could say another word it was time to go, and we were in the parking lot going our separate ways.

"Hey, JG," Mandy's head popped up from behind Evan's black beat up Honda. "Do you want to join us at Applebee's tonight? We go every Friday since we've been here, which, like, has only been twice, but you know what I mean. So what do you say?"

I wasn't sure why my eyes fell on Evan, who was so focused on lighting another cigarette, but something inside me wished he would have asked me. Although I wanted to say no because I didn't want to force my way into their clique, I thought I saw Evan smile, just slightly as though he was amused at all of this, and I called out, "Yes! I'd love to."

Mandy squealed, "Great, like around six thirty-ish? Right Evan?" But he got in the car without a glance, making me regret my commitment.

"Evan can pick you up if you want," Mandy offered, trying to shrug off his smugness. "He drives us everywhere too because he has a car."

"He drives alright," Kimmie added sarcastically as she rolled down the window from the front passenger seat. "He just learned how to drive stick after he bought the thing and rolled it off the lot."

"I can meet you there," I said, thinking Evan was going to need some time to warm up to me, especially if I reminded him of Mandy.

Then he pulled out of the parking spot, flashed me his sideways peace sign, and pealed out of the lot.

At 5:50 p.m. I sat in my car in the Applebee's lot, fidgeting with the radio until I saw Evan's Honda roll up. Not wanting them to think I'd been waiting for a long time, I waited and watched as Evan got out and lit a cigarette. He looked a little out of place with his oversized sports jersey, saggy jeans, and a backwards baseball cap, and I thought he had to be single because no girl would let her man leave the house looking like that.

Mandy hopped out of the back seat in jeans and a t-shirt and danced on the curb like a ballerina with her arms out wide to the side, and Kimmie got out of the car slowly and adjusted her black t-shirt, the very same black uniform t-shirt worn under our BDU's, which along with her jeans and combat boots made her look like an off duty mall cop.

When Evan flicked his cigarette on the sidewalk everyone walked inside. He held the door as if he thought his mother was watching and I got out of my car and waved, "Hey guys, I just got here too!"

We slid into a booth as Evan lit another cigarette and ordered a beer with the hostess, who nodded her head excitedly. But when he said, "And a sampler as an appetizer for all of us," I was a little thrown off, because how did he know what we wanted to eat?

Then I noticed his bitten fingernails on the table and nearly lost my appetite, until I watched him blow smoke circles up to the light, and thought, what was it with this guy that has me so fascinated? I hate smoke. Mom and Dad nearly killed me with all their smoking when I was a kid with my asthma, and now I thought this guy was cool?

"I can't drink for another three years," Mandy pouted. "But I love Vegas! All of us came here together. We were in basic together, Tech School together, and now, we're here, together."

"Yeah, lucky us!" Evan smirked. I looked at Kimmie and asked, "So how do you like it here?"

"I miss home," she turned her palms up indifferently. "I want to do my six years and go back. But I guess it's fine for now. It sure makes me regret blowing the scholarship I had. It was my fault though, I partied it away."

"Me too, kind of," Evan chuckled at his beer before he took a sip.

I asked him, "What did you study?"

He said, "Naw, I was kidding. I was a little rowdy before I joined. My brother's the brainiac in the family. I'm the complete opposite. I broke into cars and got caught for the third time. Even though my Dad's a retired cop, he couldn't bail me out anymore. The judge had enough of me and said, jail or Air Force. Here I am."

"I stole a pair of shoes when I was eighteen," I tried to make him feel better.

He snapped, "That's cute," as if he was the clear winner.

I replied, "I didn't think so, at the time. I guess it's funny now, but my parents still don't know."

"Shit, I wish my parents didn't know half the shit I did," he exhaled smoke too close to my face and I tried to wave it away. "My poor mom, it almost killed her when I was addicted to coke. I plowed through so many eight balls with my friends that in my first week of basic when I coughed, I tasted coke in the back of my throat that had been lodged there for I don't know how long."

"That's our Evan," Mandy pulled on his sleeve.

Kimmie admitted, "We kind of have the same story. It was meth for me. I was forty pounds lighter and fucked up all the time!"

For a second I was fascinated by how they all got along so casually, especially when talking about addictions, when I thought it was the worst thing on Earth, almost unspeakable to talk about much less joke about, and not knowing what else to say, I said, "I'm sorry," because I was. How could she blow away a scholarship like that?

"Be right back." Evan excused himself to go to the bar because the waitress had taken too long to refill his beer.

I didn't know what possessed me to ask, but I glanced back and forth from Mandy to Kimmie and said, "Does he have a girlfriend?"

"Yeah, she's coming here next week," Mandy curled her lip in disgust. "We met her in Tech School, but I think he's planning on breaking up with her."

"No, that's not how I meant it. I was just curious, that's all," I backpedaled, but it was too late. Kimmie couldn't help but smile and said, "Ahuh," as if she had suddenly figured everything out.

"I'm serious. I don't want a boyfriend. I'm like you. I want to do my time and get out and go back home…"

"Serious about what?" Evan slid back in the booth holding a tall beer.

I said, "Nothing," which only made Kimmie look away and chuckle, "Ahuh, sure," as if to taunt me.

Suddenly I doubted my policy on dating military men, whether I was really attracted to Evan or if his smoke rings had me so dazed that all I wanted to do was fit in.

TWENTY-SEVEN

Fast forward a few Friday nights, and Evan and I could've been mistaken for lovers in the booth at Applebee's, laughing uncontrollably at everything like children. He had said Mandy and Kimmie couldn't make it that night because they had something to take care of, although he couldn't remember what, and I rambled off the list of chores Satan had me do that morning, one of which was scrub bird shit off the tower welcome mat I'd never even noticed before.

"And when I was done, he gave me a lecture on a drug bust in one of the dorms, and I was like, why is he telling me this? Do I look like I'm on drugs?" I cracked up.

Evan said, "He's a funny guy. I don't know what his deal is with you and CB, woah, like Local isn't hard enough. He makes kicking your ass a sport!"

"You see it too?" I slouched back into the seat, elated, feeling as though I'd finally found someone who understood me.

"And you know Satan told Mandy not to hang out with you because you were a bad influence, right?"

"Me?" I stopped laughing. "What did I do besides all those unsat evals, which aren't even my fault!"

"You really don't get any position time do you?" Evan gulped down his beer then patted his nose to make sure the Band-Aid was still in place. He'd broken his nose at touch football when someone else, who was drunk, accidently tackled him. I'd volunteered to drive, stay for the surgery, pick him up and take care of him, which I felt had only made us closer.

"All my years of coke," Evan chuckled, "and I'm so freaked out my nose won't heal. The doctor said he couldn't figure out why my nasal passages were so weak. It's not like I could tell him."

"It's not funny," I replied seriously. "You could have died back then. Think about what you put your family through. And you're lucky the doctor didn't know or he might not have straightened that pretty nose of yours."

"Ha, ha," Evan muttered. "I'm not the same person anymore." He reached for my hand apologetically and said, "I'm different now."

"Okay," I patted his hand to change the subject, but he must have taken it for sarcasm or insincerity and snapped, "Your hands look old," which caught me off guard, causing me to drop my hands on my lap and stare at them.

"You don't have to be so hot or cold around me. I don't get you. One day you're nice to me and the next, it's like we've never met."

"I was kidding," he chugged his beer as if he wasn't then blew smoke in my face, which I could tell he hadn't meant to do, but instead of dispersing the smoke, he looked away.

"Tell me about your brother," I fidgeted with my empty Long Island Iced Tea glass, feeling really buzzed and like I really wanted to change the subject. "What did you call him, Ken Doll? That's funny."

"Maybe you've had enough." He signaled for the waitress and said, "Why don't I take you home?"

"Not yet!" I realized I was slurring, but I wanted to stay all night gazing into his eyes. What was I going to do in my room alone? I was always alone. "Did I upset you? I was just trying to make small talk."

He didn't reply. Instead, he quickly paid, took my hand, and helped me out of the booth. With his arm around my waist, he pulled me close and walked me to his car, and I inhaled him, the smell of faded cigarettes, beer, and cologne.

After he'd fastened my seatbelt in the passenger seat, he lit a cigarette, rolled down his window, and backed out of the lot, making me wonder why the hell I was so into him. There was nothing special about him, except that he was funny and made me feel like I was funny, and I could talk to him about anything, especially training, things that Ryan, Jake, and Pam didn't understand squat about because I was too embarrassed to tell them I was one foot out the door.

Then everything went black. I woke up freezing, in total freezing darkness, clutching my chest and trying to breathe. Evan's cold naked body lay next to mine, and as I climbed over his snoring corpse, I nearly gagged on the overwhelming smell of beer and smoke, and wondered if I'd undressed willingly or if he'd pulled off all my clothes by himself.

Kneeling on the floor I found my clothes and got dressed, saw that it was 3:08 a.m. on his alarm clock, and wondered how in the hell he hadn't suffocated in his sleep from all the thick stale smoky air.

I hurried to my room one building over and felt lonely as I climbed into bed. Then I wondered how I could ever see him again if he smoked in his room so damned much. It wasn't like I could exactly tell him I had asthma. I couldn't tell anyone. What if Satan found out and used it against me to wash me out for lying?

My phone rang several hours later. The sun blinded me as I opened my eyes and I croaked hoarsely, "Hello?"

"Where did you run off to in the middle of the night?" Evan giggled.

I cleared my throat and said, "How are you awake right now? I can barely open my eyes. Damn that Long Island!"

"I see how it's going to be," he snapped. "You're with someone else. I'll talk to you later."

"Hey! What are you talking about?" I caught him before he hung up. "There's no one else. I left your room because I couldn't breathe. It's worse than a bingo hall."

"Okay, whatever." He exhaled deeply as if smoking a cigarette, and I was suddenly worried he didn't believe me and that our entire relationship that wasn't even a relationship depended on me having one pretty darn good answer that he believed.

"I mean it," I protested. "Listen, I didn't want to tell you or anyone, but I have asthma. I lied to the recruiter to get in and I could die from an attack."

"Whatever you say," he replied, snottier than before, and I became defensive.

"I haven't told anyone my secret, so if you don't believe me just keep your mouth shut. I don't need Satan to have another bullet point against me."

"I guess you'll tell me why you really left when you're ready," he suddenly giggled flirtatiously, as if my anger had squashed whatever insecurity he felt. He asked, "How about you join me for breakfast? I'll pick you up in fifteen?"

"I don't think that's a good idea," I replied, confused. Did he like me or not?

"Come on, I really want to see you," he cooed, and I glanced around my room at the lonely government issue furniture and black and white TV, a fifteen dollar Salvation Army Special that got more use than I was proud to admit and was my only friend since my schedule fluctuated so much and kept me isolated from Ryan and the rest of the guys, and was going to continue being my only friend if I kept saying no to Evan. So what if he had a few mood issues.

"Yes, I'll go."

Fifteen minutes later, Evan's Honda zipped through the parking lot like it was on fire and with rap music cranked so loud I thought it was an amp on wheels.

"Come on, get in!" he shouted, and I got into the passenger seat wondering why he'd agreed to meet me in fifteen minutes if he hadn't bothered to shower, brush his teeth or pick out clean clothes from his closet.

"I can't hear you," I turned down the radio.

He laughed, "Everyone gets used to my music eventually."

I said, "Well, I'm not everyone."

"How about this," he moved my hand, changed the music to an "oldies" station, blasted it, and sang along. "Sha la la la la la means I love you." He took my hand and kissed it as if he was about to propose, which made me stare into his blue eyes and notice the tiny freckles on his nose because he'd finally removed that silly Band-Aid.

I thought he was about to kiss me, and wanted him to do it. Then he let my hand fall so he could turn up the dial some more. He sped out of the lot, three blocks down the street into the cafeteria lot, making me feel duped because I kept thinking he liked me with every little gesture.

Angrily I got out, slammed the door, and went inside, indifferent as to whether he was right behind me or not. I took a tray and loaded my plate full of French toast, hoping it would settle my stomach, and sat down at a table and started eating without him.

"The reason I thought you were with another guy was because of my ex-girlfriend." He sat down quietly and moved his fork around the plate, poking at his toast and over easy eggs as if he couldn't decide whether to eat them. "She cheated on me. A lot. She'd come over unannounced, even though we broke up, would do anything to seduce me. I always wanted to say no, but I couldn't, and this went on for years."

"If you want to be with your ex why did you break up with her?" I asked, annoyed. Didn't he know that mentioning an ex was taboo in a new relationship, or whatever it was we were?

"Not her," he replied agitated. "My last ex before that, before I joined the military. About five years ago."

"You're upset about a girl you dated five years ago?" I stared at him. "She must have been some girl."

"She was like Pamela Anderson," he sighed as if fighting back tears. "But with brown hair."

I couldn't take another bite. How was I supposed to compete with that? I didn't look anything like Pamela Anderson, nor was I a brunette, and the last thing I wanted to hear was how much in love with her he still was. But he didn't care.

"Sometimes I'd drive five hours north to her college just to put a note or rose on her car and picture her smiling in the morning when she saw them." I looked at him pouting over his food and wished he'd love me like that.

"But it didn't make her smile. In fact, it annoyed her that I did it. She said it was because I was checking up on her. And when she broke up with me, she said, 'I love you, but I'm not in love with you.' Can you believe that? Can you believe how cruel someone can be?"

"Besides the cruelty of someone telling you how much they're thinking of someone else?" I took another bite of French toast and realized he wasn't listening, so I thought if he wasn't interested in me like that, maybe I could be his friend, and suggested, "How about getting some closure?"

"No!" He crumpled his toast so that it fell into pieces all over his plate and the tray and growled, "I don't ever want to talk to her again! She broke my heart for good. I'll never love anyone as much as I loved her. I'll never love anyone again."

"You're twenty six," I said, hoping he realized he was too old for that shit. He was in the Air Force training to be an Air Traffic Controller for God's sake, but when he said nothing, I knew it was time to get out of there. I said, "Take me home. I definitely don't need this shit."

He didn't argue and dropped me off at the same spot where he'd picked me up. Without a word, he pealed out of the parking lot blasting his damn music, making me feel guilty. Had I overstepped a boundary?

All calls to him went unanswered and when I bumped into him at work he never said anything more than, "Hey," neither angrily or cheerily. I was even more confused when he called me the following weekend and asked me to come over for pizza and a movie.

"Am I hallucinating? Is this Evan? Are you sure you don't have the wrong number?" I teased.

He said sheepishly, "Yeah, it's Evan. So what do you say?"

"I say I don't know," I replied while knowing I didn't want to spend another second alone. I offered, "Why don't you come over here so I'm not in all that smoke."

"I don't like to leave my room," he countered.

I, feeling like a child playing tit for tat, said, "Well, I don't want to leave mine either."

"Please," he whined, making me wonder why he was sweating me so much. All of a sudden he was over his ex and wanted to move on with me?

"Fine, I'll be right over." I hung up the phone and stared at my wall for ten minutes so I wouldn't appear desperate since it would only take me sixty seconds to get there.

His door was propped open, and when I peeked inside I saw him crouched on his futon holding a video game controller.

"Oh, hi." He put the controller down, met me at the door, and kissed me on the cheek as if he was nervous, and smiled, "I opened the door so you could breathe."

I was too distracted by the nylon sock on his head to feel any excitement from the kiss, and said, "Is that a do-rag? You look like a homeless person. Do you have any gang affiliations?"

He giggled and let me pull it off his head and toss it onto his bookshelf as I walked in and nearly tripped over an empty beer can.

"Are you going for a world record?" I was stunned when I saw all the empty cans on the floor and his overflowing ashtray.

"Ha, no, I was about to clean up." He picked up a few cans apologetically and said, "I got a little lazy on my days off. I'm used to my ex cleaning up after me. Oops, I'm sorry, I won't mention her again."

I stared at him, wondering how long it must have taken him to drink all that beer. It just wasn't possible for one person to drink all that. Then he sat down next to a pizza box on the futon and patted the spot next to him and said, "I didn't know what kind you liked, so I just got cheese. Is that okay? And I already watched Gladiator five times this week, only because I needed something to fall asleep to, but it's great. I wanted you to see it with me."

"Black olives and mushroom is my favorite," I smiled.

He said, "Next time," although I wondered if there would be a next time because we were so damn different. He needed the TV to fall asleep to and I needed absolute dark and quiet. He smoked constantly and was a slob and thought he had gang affiliations because he came from Baltimore. Was this a sign to run away or a sign that opposites attract?

"There will definitely be a next time," he said, smiling and I thought, maybe it can work. His ex is toast.

Excitedly, he stood up and pushed play on the VCR, and as the credits rolled, I was happy I'd decided to come over and give him another chance. Before sitting down again, he rummaged through his book shelf, handed me a stack of pictures, and said, "I wanted to show you these. Of my family."

"You look like your mom." I smiled at the resemblance, and although she was about half his height, she had the same hair color and eyes. His Dad, although he was taller in the picture, had an angry scowl on his face as if he'd been mad at Evan when they took the picture, but I didn't ask him why and instead shuffled through the next few pictures of white cats in different sleeping poses.

"I love my little fluffies." He scratched the picture as if he thought he was petting them, and I thought it was definitely time to leave because we didn't have a thing in common besides Air Traffic and if this was to go any further and one of his "fluffies" came near me, I'd be dead.

"I need to go," I stood up but fell right back down when I saw the next picture of Evan looking like a half-dead skeleton, and I gasped, "Evan, I've never seen anyone so skinny!"

"I know," he giggled, as if his drug past was hilarious. "Whew, I lost a lot of weight from the drugs back then. What do you think about my pierced eyebrow? I had to take it out when my loofah got caught on it in the shower. My poor mother heard me screaming for help and I felt so badly for her because she had to see me naked!"

"You look like a pirate!" I laughed when I noticed the matching gold hoop earrings. "Maybe a drag queen even, those earrings look huge on your skinny body!"

"Chicks loved my earrings." He snatched the pictures from my hands, stood up angrily, lit a cigarette, and said, "I got a lot of action because of those earrings."

"Okay stud," I replied, forgetting how sensitive he could be. "Come on, it was funny, you wear a sock on your head for crying out loud! Don't you think you're taking yourself a little too seriously?"

He stormed outside and leaned against the railing, so that I took my cue to leave. I said, "Thanks for the pizza. I'll see you tomorrow." That made him change his tune yet again.

"I don't know why I snapped. Come back inside." He flipped the cigarette off the balcony and took my hand.

"We'll watch the movie and cuddle to make it alright?" I put my arm around his waist, but that set him off again.

"I don't do cuddling. She ruined my life! I don't ever want to cuddle again!"

"I'm obviously saying all the wrong things. So I'm gonna go, okay?"

"No, don't go," he pleaded and he took my hand and brought me over to his futon, making me want to scream. He was a genuine nut case and yet I couldn't say no to him, and before I knew it, like déjà vu, I woke up in the dark cold, climbed over him, and got dressed.

This time I did remember the awkward sex attempt. He drunkenly fumbled at my jeans and by the time we were naked, he was unable to perform and blamed it on the beer. I said nothing and fell asleep, grateful not to be sleeping by myself, although the truth was I was too afraid to leave and hear his crazy accusations, but by four in the morning I woke up choking again and decided my lungs couldn't take it anymore.

He didn't call me in the morning, however, and played strangers on a bus at the tower with me until I cornered him in the stairwell and asked him what the hell was up.

"I don't want anyone to know we're dating," he whispered, as if anyone was around. "You know, give Satan more fuel for the fire."

"That's very kind of you," I snapped, tired of his games.

That only made him angry, and he stormed off for another cigarette. Then I stormed back in the direction of Satan's office broom closet, until I noticed the newspaper on Satan's desk he must have left open in a hurry to get to his meeting, and I flipped through it looking for the horoscopes that I hoped would give me an answer.

I read my horoscope, Aquarius, then his, Scorpio, and our compatibility level that said, "Don't be in the same room together..." before I crumpled the section into the garbage. What the hell did a newspaper know anyway?

TWENTY-EIGHT

"Vrooom, vroom, rrreeehhhh," Winston screamed across Ryan's room, trying his best to imitate the sound of a motorcycle for the tenth time in two minutes.

"No, you've got it all wrong," Ryan argued. "It's like this: vreeeeeh, vrrooom! Yeah, bad ass!"

"You guys are driving me nuts," I sighed, wishing I was with Evan, who was in the middle of his few-days-of-ignoring-me game again.

"How about vurrooom, vureeeh." Joe held up both wrists and squatted as if he were riding a motorcycle, and I wondered if Evan did have a point about my immature brothers he'd dubbed "The Goonies," after the 80's movie about a group of guys causing all sorts of mischief together.

"Can we get out of here, maybe to the chow hall or something and forget about engines? I'm going crazy in here with you guys."

And although they agreed, they took their magazines with them, and as we sat and ate in the cafeteria they spread the pages out all over the table, causing me to look over my shoulder to make sure no one I knew would see what they were doing. Mainly Evan.

"When are we going to finally meet him?" Ryan broke through my thoughts.

I replied, "I don't know. He likes his alone time," although I knew it sounded ridiculous.

"Why don't you just tell him he can hang out with us?" Ryan shrugged.

I said, "He's just not like that. He's an old fart who likes to be by himself in his room."

That wasn't true either, because on weekends when his friends called from Arizona, he was gone in the bat of an eye if they asked him to visit. Not to mention when he went to his usual bar at night or to gamble.

"We're taking a motorcycle safety course," Winston waved a hand in front of my face to get my attention. "Why don't you sign up and take it with us?"

"Me? Not only no, but hell no! One, I'm terrified of motorcycles and two, I know my luck, I'll die on that damn thing."

"Yeah, Jen," Ryan interrupted, "it's a good idea. Come on. Face your fears."

"Ryan, the last time you told me that I ended up in basic!" Not to mention the glorious tower I was in now, where I was failing miserably, which made me feel like each day here was my last.

"It'll teach you confidence," Joe smiled. "Even if you don't like bikes, it's just a safety course. Your insurance will go down."

"Absolutely not," I shook my head. "The last thing I need is to learn another skill." I really could use the confidence, though, and so I changed my mind and said, "Okay, sign me up."

By Saturday morning, though, I regretted it but knew it was too late to get out of it, and grudgingly, I got into the backseat of Winston's lowered bright red Acura.

"Dude, you took off the windshield wipers?" Ryan adjusted the front seat so I'd have more room, but it barely gave me another inch. "What else have you done to it since I last saw it?"

"I lowered it a little more…"

"Why in the world would you take off the wipers?" I struggled to lean forward so that I could see for myself.

"It's the desert," Winston retorted proudly. "Who needs wipers to weigh you down?"

"But you don't race. How heavy could a windshield wiper be?"

"It's a Pennsylvania thing," Ryan added, and we laughed and joked for twenty minutes until we made it to class and sat down, and instantly I was reminded of how much I loved the learning environment and wondered how I'd veered so far off track and from my dream of going to school.

By the second day, I couldn't wait for class to end so that I could register for classes at the local college. Then Bill the instructor announced, "Class time is over, let's go outside and ride!" which made my mind go blank as I recalled M-16 training and the fear I felt then about doing something for real.

"You guys didn't tell me about this! I can't ride! I can't! I won't know what to do!" I told Ryan and Winston, who didn't understand my complaint at all.

"You'll learn." Winston handed me a helmet and said, "Confidence, remember."

"I didn't mean it," I muttered, wondering if I would have agreed to this if Evan was even slightly more receptive to me.

"Throttle on the right, brakes on the left." Bill sat on his bike at the top of the semi-circle and held up his hands while twenty of us sat on our bikes in a circle watching him.

"What if I drop it, Bill?" I raised my jittery hand, thinking about how I should've been at home watching reruns on my black and white TV instead of risking my life to prove the point that I didn't need Evan to entertain me. "The bike is too big and wobbly and so is the helmet, and that's unsafe, right?"

Winston snickered at Ryan as if he'd noted that comment to make fun of me for the rest of my life, and Bill looked at me encouragingly and said, "You'll be fine. Just give it a try. No one's ever dropped a bike in my class and I've been teaching for ten years. Now, everyone turn your keys."

Patiently, Bill and everyone else waited for me so that I was forced to turn my key. If I died, it would be Evan's fault for ignoring me. Then I pulled the throttle, held my breath, and something amazing happened. I moved forward easily, as if I'd been doing this all my life, riding a motorcycle at five miles an hour, and let the warm breeze all around me calm my nerves with the illusion that I was flying.

"I'm doing it!" I shouted into my helmet.

Winston must have sensed my satisfaction and waved at me, and although I wanted to wave back, I didn't dare let go of the handlebar. But oh, was he right. What a feeling!

The next task involved cones and a whole lot of slaloming, which put my paranoia right at square one again and made me drop the bike when I was almost stopped.

"You know you're the first one to ever drop a bike in my class," Bill rushed over to me, although I kept telling him I was okay.

"It fell while I was trying to put my foot down," I explained to anyone who could hear me so they would stop looking so impatient.

Bill said, "You have to look up, not down," and although I was supposed to have motorcycles on the brain, it reminded me of my own life. If only I could look up and feel a sense of security instead of being stuck in a mouse trap with Satan and CB dancing around me with a piece of cheese.

When I had the bike rolling again, the breeze through my helmet seemed to lift all the bad thoughts away from me and I suddenly understood why Winston and Ryan loved riding so much. This was as close to flying as you could get, and although the engines were loud, it was peaceful. Then I slowed down to get another cone and somehow dropped the bike again.

"You know, you're the only one who's ever dropped the bike in my class twice," Bill helped me up. "Although class is over, make sure you practice when you leave here. Only practice will make you better."

"I will," I said, although I had absolutely no intention to. I had other things on my plate: Air Traffic Control, getting a degree, and sorting out this Evan thing.

On the ride home, however, Ryan and Winston were amped up talking about motorcycles and making plans to go riding that night. I butted into the conversation. "How are you going to ride if you don't have motorcycles?"

"Jen, where have you been?" Ryan craned his neck towards me. "Didn't you hear me talking about the Ninja I ordered?"

"No," I replied, confused, and just as I wanted to ask him more about it, we were back in the dorm lot and Ryan shouted, "That's it" at a truck that was rolling a neon green bike down a ramp. "It's early, woo!"

"Yeah, where have you been, Jen?" Winston grinned facetiously. "I bought mine a few days ago."

"Take the first spin, come on!" Ryan hopped out of the car, took hold of my arm to help me out of the car, and pulled me over to the new bike that half the dorm stood around gawking at.

"I think I've had enough practice for one day," I said, but Ryan wouldn't take no for answer.

"Come on, just once around the lot."

I agreed, made the lap on the little bike and actually enjoyed it, but afterwards I dismounted and said, "Okay, that's it for tonight. I have to get up early and still have to iron my uniform. See you guys tomorrow." And then, thinking of Evan, I added, "Maybe."

"Can you hold on to the keys? And my helmet and gloves?" Ryan handed me his motorcycle gear and said, "Winston and I are heading back to his place and I'm too lazy to bring them to my room." I agreed, went to my room, set my alarm, ironed my uniform, and went to bed.

In the morning I hit the snooze button so many times I was in more of a rush than usual. As if to make matters worse, as if everything always had to happen at the same time, my car wouldn't start.

For a moment, I worried about Satan and that if I was late he'd have one more reason to get rid of me. Then my eyes fell on the motorcycle silhouette. I couldn't wake Ryan and ask for his car because it hadn't started either, which was the main reason he'd rushed into buying the bike in the first place. But I couldn't take the bike without telling him, could I? Well, I could because he took the bus to work, and I'd call him in time so he wouldn't think it was stolen. As if that was the most foolproof plan I'd ever come up with, I ran back to my room, grabbed the keys and helmet, and hurried back to the bike, thinking I had Satan beat. I wasn't going to be late and he wasn't going to be able to kick me out.

The bike started up easily, as if to settle my nerves about taking it, and I eased out of the lot through two stop signs and onto the long winding road to the tower, enjoying the breeze all around me and smiling as I gazed dreamily at the sun coming up over the horizon. Today was going to be a good day.

Then I checked my mirrors again and suddenly saw Evan's familiar black Honda behind me, a trail of cigarette smoke from the driver's side window and Mandy jumping in the passenger seat, pointing at me because she'd recognized my backpack. Evan's face looked squinted and angry, and I thought, yeah punk, while you forgot about me and went partying without me, I was busy getting a motorcycle license.

I waved back but the bike wobbled and I realized I didn't have time to think about what Evan was going to say, I needed to pay attention to the road up ahead of me. But when the final turn came up so quickly that I didn't have time to lean, I became nervous and instead of hitting the breaks, I twisted the throttle and sailed right into the curb, over the bike, and helplessly crashed to the ground and skidded for what seemed like forever as dirt and gravel pounded me from all sides.

"Jen, Jen, Jen!" Mandy screamed as I struggled to stand up in the cloud of dirt, wondering how I wasn't dead.

"I'm okay," I said when Evan patted me down, his cigarette flopping between his lips.

He snapped, "No you're not. What are you doing on a motorcycle? Look at that lump on your wrist."

"It's nothing, I'm fine." I gasped when I saw the newly formed egg on my wrist and said, "It doesn't even hurt that much," but he was already walking back to the road and flagging down a nearby truck that had stopped, and together, he and the stranger lifted the dented bike onto the truck bed while Mandy walked me to Evan's car.

"Ryan is going to kill me," I glanced at all the scattered neon green pieces and she opened the door for me and said, "Shh, don't worry about that. Evan will drop me off at the tower and then take you to the hospital. Everything's gonna be fine."

"Nothing's going to be fine." Tears welled in my eyes. "How could I have been so stupid? Ryan's going to kill me and then Satan's going to have his turn!"

Minutes later, Mandy hopped out of the car and said, "I'll tell the Chief what happened. Take care of yourself." As Evan pulled out of the lot, he put his hand on my leg and said, "You're in shock. See what happens when you hang out with your Goonies?"

"Yeah," I replied, sadly realizing my plan had completely backfired on me.

"I'm going to take care of you like you took care of me when I was in the hospital."

He suddenly tightened his grip around my thigh, and I said, "I didn't think you cared. You were so mean to me afterwards, remember that?"

"Of course I cared," he said hurt. "I was in pain, that's all. You know I can get a little grumpy, and there's nothing pleasant about having gauze up your nose with weak nasal passages. Damn all that coke!"

Then he helped me out of the car and into the empty emergency room, where a nurse said, "Come with me," right away, walked me to a triage room in the back, and after a few questions, proceeded to scrub pebbles from the palms of my cut-up hands.

"Aren't you supposed to wear gloves?" Evan gagged at the flopping skin and I said, "They were too big," as if that was a good excuse.

He put his hand to his mouth and said, "I need a cigarette."

"I need one too," I joked, but when he disappeared, so did the calmness I felt, and I started rambling, "Do I need to be on meds because if I'm on meds I can't work and if I can't work I can't get rated!"

"You don't have to take the meds," she replied, but I wasn't listening because I'd dug my own grave and Satan was probably chomping at the bit, waiting for me to get to the tower so he could send me home.

"You have your cast and you're free to go," the nurse said cheerily, and I wanted to ask her, go where? Run away?

Then I met Evan in the waiting room. He studied my cast and said, "Ryan was worried about you," making me feel worse than before.

I asked as though I hadn't understood, "You called him already?"

"Yeah, call him back when you get a chance." Then he paused and said, "And Satan, well, he wants you to report back immediately. I think for a lecture on safety or something."

"I hate him." I hugged Evan, burying my head in his chest and wishing I could stop time and stay in his arms forever.

"Don't let him do this to you," Evan wrapped his arms around me tightly and said, "You didn't do anything wrong. Everything's going to be fine."

"Everything's fine until we get back to the tower," I soaked his shirt with my tears.

He kissed the top of my head and said, "Don't give up now that you're close to the end, this is nothing! You're going to show them! You're going to show them all, right?"

He lifted my chin until our eyes met and wouldn't let go until I repeated, "Yes, I'm going to show them all," although I felt like no matter what I did, nothing could save me now.

TWENTY-NINE

Evan pulled my shirt over my head, took off my bra, unbuttoned my pants, and let me fall back on his futon as if I wasn't hampered with a cast on my arm.

"Hang on." He rushed to his bookshelf, waved a pair of white plastic handcuffs at me, and smiled. "These glow in the dark," he said, as if that was going to get me excited.

"Since when are you this kinky?" I asked, accustomed to our lack of foreplay and small talk, but he didn't answer as he slapped one cuff on my good wrist and the other on the metal futon and giggled. "Well, since I'm banging a crippled girl, I want to go all the way."

"Hey, come on, don't leave me hanging like this," I said, as he rummaged through the shelf again and then blinded me with the flash from a disposable camera.

"Evan!" I screamed instinctively, trying to cover myself up with one hand, suddenly self-conscious because I'd gained a few pounds since the addition of the cast. "This is not funny. Stop taking pictures of me!" But he laughed harder, stumbled backwards as he held his stomach and replied, "Nah, this is too much fun."

He stopped when the phone rang, and although I had an inkling our romantic evening was ruined, he confirmed it with, "Hey man, what's up. Oh yeah man, I just gotta ask." He'd be off to Arizona to visit his boys, without me.

"Can you help me with this?" I couldn't believe his audacity when he hung up and ducked into his closet without as much as a glance, then pulled out a small black duffel bag and piled some clothes on top of it.

"I'm still here, you know!" I felt like I'd been set up as usual, and this time I couldn't even free myself from a flimsy plastic cuff, get dressed, and storm out without him helping me.

"Oh, yeah, sorry," he smiled apologetically. "That was Dave, you know from Tech School, and all our buddies are getting together."

"Yeah, I know. And let me guess, you'll take me along next time, right?"

"I'm sorry." He kissed my cheek, but I turned away and said, "I'm tired of your sorry's and I know you're not even sorry. You ditch me every chance you get."

"You can stay in my room if you'd like," he offered me like a consolation prize.

I gasped, "In this smoke stack? Why would I stay here?"

"I'll call you when I get there, I promise." He helped me into my jeans, then gently put on my t-shirt while I wished I could spew venom into his eyes.

"I'll hold my breath," I managed to open the door, but as I tried to slam it shut behind me, it bounced open again, making me feel like the entire universe was against me.

"I promise I'll call," he called after me.

I said, "Whatever, I'm done with you!" wishing it was that easy to rid myself of him, not just his smell on me, but his smile, and his promise to me that I'd never find anyone else who loved me the way he did, which I didn't always believe until he did something sweet for me, like call me at midnight when he got to Arizona like he'd said he would.

"I'm sorry to wake you," he whispered in my ear. "Just wanted to hear your voice. I miss you."

"I'm asleep, not stupid," I whispered back. "I can tell you've been drinking."

"I told you I'd call, right?" he giggled. "I was thinking, why don't we go to the Christmas party together when I get back?"

"You want to go to the Christmas party with me?" I nearly sat up in bed to make sure I wasn't dreaming. "You know that will mean that everyone knows about us, right?"

"Yeah, that's the point."

"What's the catch?"

"No, catch, come on," he whined, and although I was on the verge of saying yes because I wanted to believe it was true, I said, "Evan, I'm tired of the games. And what are Mandy and Kimmie gonna say? Or everyone else when they see us?"

"Who cares about them?" he asked as if that hadn't been our problem all along.

I replied, "You do. Now get serious."

"I'm only serious about you."

"I'll go," I caved. "But only 'cause there'll be free food. You know I can't resist free food." Or you, I wanted to say, and felt it when he picked me up for the party one week later.

I waited in my parking lot because I still couldn't put on a coat with my cast. He pulled up, got out of the car and opened the door for me, kissed my cheek, and said, "You look nice," even though I was in black corduroy pants and a red shirt with a motorcycle on it that I thought was both festive and humorously self-deprecating.

"This old thing?" I got in, inhaled his scent of cigarettes, beer, and cologne, and said, "You don't look so bad yourself," thinking that even though he was wearing the same oversized jersey and jeans, seeing his smile was always worth the wait.

We parked at the local VFW, a small bar across from the base that made a low-cost Christmas party feasible this year, and Evan got out of the car to open the door for me.

I spotted Kimmie five spots down getting out of her car too, and by the time I waved and said, "Hey, Kimmie wait up," she'd already connected the dots between me and Evan and ran into the building.

"I think she saw us." I glanced at Evan, wondering how he'd take the news. "She knows."

"It doesn't matter," he finally said, but by the way he sucked on his cigarette until half of it disappeared, I knew it did.

"We don't have to say anything to anyone. I'm fine with it," I offered, but he squeezed my hand and flicked his cigarette to the side, determined to carry out what he'd promised.

He said, "It's okay," then opened the door and eased me forward with the back of his hand on my lower back as if to say, "I'm behind you all the way baby, no matter what."

"Oh, boy, look what we started," I joked, temporarily immobilized from the heat of all those bodies packed in such a small venue and the smell of spicy hot wings in my nose. "You ready for this?"

I turned and realized that the reason for his silence was that he was no longer behind me; rather than the blaring Christmas music tuning out his voice, I discovered him in the opposite corner with a beer in his hand, at least twenty people between us. He was talking with George, who was the new tower trainee and who everyone said was my twin brother because of his blonde hair, blue eyes, and knack for pissing off Satan, yapping and laughing it up like they were long-lost buddies.

Kimmie and Mandy waved me over to their table, but I raised my cast in the air to buy myself another minute to formulate a plan and get over the disappointment and humiliation.

My eyes fell on the hot wings I'd waited all damn day for but now couldn't eat because Evan had stolen my confidence, along with my dignity. Instead I opted for a plastic cup of boxed wine and drank it one gulp. Then I refilled and gulped and refilled before I felt a slight buzz and was strong enough to proceed to the table for my round of questioning.

"Oh my God, girl, you'd better start talking," Kimmie said before I sat down. "How long has this been going on? Are you two serious? Are you having sex?"

"Nothing about my shirt? You don't you think it's funny?" I pointed at my chest, but they weren't having it, and Mandy gripped my arm and shook it so that wine almost dripped all over me.

"Spill the beans Jen. What's up with you two?"

"I'll be right back." I stood up again, although they begged me not to, and instead of smacking Evan's beer out of his hand like I wanted to and demanding to know how he expected me to answer all these questions without him, I made another visit to the boxed wine, dumped another two cups into my system so that I really had to think about walking in a straight line to the table, and somehow stole someone's cigarette in the process.

"Alright, I'll tell you everything you want to know."

I sat down again and Kimmie asked "You smoke?" surprised at this new side of me she'd never seen before.

I coughed, "No," and pushed the butt into the ashtray, which made Mandy giggle, "Jen, that's a pretzel bowl, not an ashtray!"

"You wanna hear it or not?" I blinked, so tipsy I couldn't tell Mandy and Kimmie apart already. I said, "It's true. Evan and I are together. We've been dating for the last four months. Yes, sex all the time, every weekend, well, almost every weekend."

They looked at each other as if they wanted to burst and I was reminded again how Evan had ditched me. I stood up, embarrassed, wishing it wasn't freezing cold outside so I could run home.

"Wait! Tell us more." Mandy held onto my arm, but I needed more liquid courage, as they say, and also food, because a headache was starting to set in.

Opting for another cup of wine again, I walked back to the table and somehow passed right by it. Red, green, and white lights blinded me as I stepped onto the dance floor, which was just a small cleared-out area where a table once stood.

"How you doin'?" I felt an arm around my waist, lips against my ear, and I said sternly, "I thought you don't like to dance, Evan?" although my heart was pounding in my chest with excitement he'd finally decided to join me.

"I like anything you like to do." He kissed my ear and gently twirled me around so that my head rested against his chest.

Stay like this forever, I thought, and said, "I love you." Instead of being angry like I thought he might be, he tilted my chin up to his and kissed me like he'd never kissed me before.

"Your nose is so much smaller than I remembered." I looked up, but was suddenly yanked backwards and pulled to the door, trying hard not to stumble.

"Come on, Jen, you're drunk." Evan kicked the door.

Cold air rushed all around me and I said, "But we just got here, Evan! What the hell is going on?" and "Ouch," when he angrily opened the passenger door, pushed me in, and slammed it shut.

"What the hell?" I said again, but by the time he lit a cigarette and turned the engine I passed out. I woke up in his bed to him screaming, "Jen, wake up, wake up, oh God please don't let this be happening to me! Please, no, please, wake up," wishing he'd just shut up.

"What?" I squinted and the light from his windows felt like high beams on my face and said, "Why are you kneeling on the floor like you're praying?"

"Oh thank God you're alive, Jen." He hugged me as I stood up, like a little kid around his mommy's waist, and I said, "Can I please go to the bathroom? What's going on? What is that smell?"

"I thought you were dead." He paced when I emerged from the bathroom, and I asked, "What are you talking about?" I coughed, "It's so damn smoky in here," then rubbed my forehead. "I feel like I've been hit with a sledgehammer!"

"That would have been much better than what really happened." He put his hands on his hips. "I thought I had to take you to the hospital," he ran his fingers through his hair anxiously. "I thought you were going to die."

"Nonsense," I said, then saw the devastation in his room, my clothes and paper towels everywhere, and I said, "Did I throw up? What happened last night? When did you dress me in your clothes? I love these but you never let me wear your comfy pants and it looks like a bomb went off!"

"You don't remember?" Evan stared at me in disbelief.

"Did I throw up last night?" I repeated. "I couldn't have. I've never thrown up after drinking before."

"You don't remember," he replied dubiously.

"Oh yes. I think I told you I loved you. It's too soon, I know. I'm sorry."

"It doesn't matter." He put on a pair of jeans and said, "Let's grab some breakfast."

"Listen, I'm sorry," I pleaded. "I know you're sensitive about the L-word and I shouldn't have said it."

"That's not it." He helped me into my clothes and then his car, kissed my cheek, and said, "I'm glad you're okay, okay? Let's enjoy breakfast."

And everything was okay until Monday morning when Mandy and Kimmie snickered at me, as if they knew something I didn't, and finally told me what happened after I begged them to. I'd practically had sex with one of the radar controllers on the dance floor before Evan dragged me out of there.

I searched every floor of that tower until I found that smug punk in the break room and hissed, "How could you feed me to the wolves then disappear? How could you let me find out this way when you knew I was drunk?"

"Hey." He put his hands up as if it wasn't his call and said, "You can do whatever you want or whomever you want!"

I raised my middle finger and cursed, "Fuck you. That is not fair! Did you do it on purpose? Set me up so that you could throw it in my face and treat me like your ex-girlfriend? So you can pretend not to trust me, ever. You know I love you. How fucking could you...?"

"JG," CB poked his head through the door, an amused smile on his face and said, "Chief wants to see you."

"Of course he wants to see me," because when it rained it poured and somehow it always seemed like Satan had another bucket above my head in reserve.

"This is your fault and I don't ever want to hear about this again, ever!" I sneered when he said nothing. "And let me guess, you took that disposable pictures to Arizona and showed your friends all the naked pictures of me, right?"

Evan's face when blank as he silently retraced his steps, and he admitted, "I don't have the camera. Tom took it from me and took pictures of the girls in the bikini contest and I know I asked to get it back, but I never got it."

"Perfect!" I ducked into the elevator and into Satan's office. He handed me a piece of paper and smiled. "JG, this is for you," which should have been a warning to me before my eyes fell on the sheet.

"I can't do this, please don't make me. I beg you." My hands trembled, and he smiled as though he enjoyed reviving my old nightmares and said, "You have no choice. Your training is due every year and I see that you're overdue."

"No one else has to go." My bottom lip quivered as I counted the zero times anyone had ever been assigned M-16 requalification training. "No one else gets pulled out of position for the things I do. Helicopter rides, squadron tours. I need to practice to get rated, you know that."

"Don't worry about anyone else," he stood up angrily. "You don't talk back to the Chief when he's given you an order!"

I stuttered, "Does CB know that you're signing me up for all these extra duties on purpose?"

"I don't give a hoot who knows what. You will do your M-16 training whether you like it or not, and you'll pack a lunch and do as you're told or starve to death. I don't give a shit, airman!"

THIRTY

The only other time I'd seen the First Lieutenant at the tower was when he was first stationed here a year ago. He came up for a visit, plugged, in and a few minutes later was told he was able to work traffic. We called this a "paper rating" which meant, we'd never let him work traffic, but for the sake of his job, because he represented us somehow, somewhere at some meeting, it proved to everyone else he knew what he was talking about. But now that he was back and called me down into Satan's office to talk to me, I knew it couldn't be good.

"You have the highest record of unsatisfactory evaluations in the entire history of this tower, airman." He folded his hands on top of my folder and tried not to smile, although I could tell he enjoyed my anguish.

The Lieutenant was one year younger than me, chunky like a baby waiting to lose his fat and with thinning brown hair. Sitting there smirking at me, I wished I could smack those cheeks and tell him he wasn't better than me because of the little Lieutenant stripe on his lapel, and no shit I had the worst record in history. All I ever did around here was chores!

"Here's your washout packet." He slapped my folder on the table for emphasis and I almost stood up and walked out on this stage production.

Hand me the pen, I wanted to say, so I could get this over with already. This is what had been promised me the day I'd walked in. Now it was here, and after a year and a half I was tired of fighting. It was time to go home, and as much as I wanted to blame everyone else for this, the truth was it was my fault for letting them steamroll me. Welcome to the real Air Force.

"It's just how it's done," he said as if wanting to hear himself talk. "They write you up like you're going to fail, even when you're not. I know this must be tough." He paused as if he was going to say something meaningful, then stood up instead and said, "Well, good luck," and left.

"You have one week to decide." Satan sat down across from me, pointed at his wall calendar, and said, "Today's Monday? How about you take the week off and think about whether or not you're serious about Air Traffic and getting your ratings, since there's obviously a lack of integrity on your part. Next Monday morning, you let me know what you've decided."

"I don't need a week," I protested, nearly telling him to send me now, until he raised his finger to silence me. I cleared my throat and said, "Yes, sir," wanting nothing more than to take the dagger from my back and hand it to him and tell him he could never defeat me, ever.

But I had nothing left and it wasn't the decision itself that had me sulking all the way to my car and to the dorm. At least I knew where I stood now. It was over and I was no longer in limbo. My problem was still with myself; I had nowhere to turn to because I'd pushed almost everyone away, everyone but Evan who, for the last month or so, was out on the town showing his childhood friend around Las Vegas and unreachable. And for the first time, Ryan was gone too. He was in Italy, on a routine deployment, and if I could get a hold of him and told him all the problems I'd been having he'd say, "How? Planes are easy!"

So I sat in my room with my black and white TV and cried, waiting for my phone to ring and hoping Evan would check up on me, which he didn't, because he was so preoccupied with Amber who couldn't find her way around town, ever. I contemplated how long it had taken me to figure out the roads of Las Vegas, which were without a doubt tricky, but thought two months of going out almost every night, seemed a bit much. Then I realized it wasn't her hogging my boyfriend's time that bothered me, but the inscription she'd put on her Playboy spread of her on a bed pulling off her panties with the words, "love your little sister, Amber," making me feel like I'd missed something about their relationship.

When the phone rang days later, I thought I was hallucinating, and let it ring until I realized I wasn't.

"I've missed you, Jen," Evan whispered in my ear as I shielded my face from the sun shining through the blinds.

Instead of saying hello, I asked, "What day is it?"

"Thursday, silly," he giggled, annoying me. He knew what deep shit I was in and none of it was funny.

"Just wanted to tell you I love you and I miss you and I'll see you after work today."

"Great," I replied, getting up. Then I froze when CR's voice boomed in the background, "Is that JG on the line?"

CR was the certifier, the guy who certified me in Flight Data and Ground Control, and only came to the tower for that specific reason, to certify. Right now I was the only one up for a certification, whether the process was on hold or not.

"Yes, sir," Evan stuttered as if he'd been caught by surprise, both from realizing CR was standing behind him and realizing CR knew Evan and I were a couple.

"You tell her to get her happy ass over here," he barked, then took a deep breath and called out louder than before, "But only if you want your rating! JG, do you hear me? Do you want to go up for your rating today?"

"What does the Chief say?" I asked Evan, who asked CR, who snapped, "Stop asking questions, damnit! Tell her to get over here! If she's not here in the next ten minutes I'm leaving. Flying is about to start and I don't have time for this shit!"

My arms shook in the shower as I tried to comprehend the chance I was being given, the chance of a lifetime, behind Satan's back. Minutes later, I ran to my car, tied my wet hair into a bun, and drove with white knuckles to the tower, thinking, what if I wasn't ready?

At the tower I parked the car crookedly, hopped out, and saw Evan holding the door for me.

"Evan." I said, and he kissed my cheek like I was a boxer about to enter the ring.

He said, "Good luck. I love you." I wanted to say I need a miracle not luck, and I was surprised Satan wasn't in his office. I wondered if he was upstairs waiting for me, until Mandy held the elevator door open for me and said, "Go get 'em, Jen."

Upstairs, I hurried into the cab sweaty. CR smiled, "What took you so long, JG?" and without waiting for a response said, "Glad you could make it. You ready? Plug in. Runway 21 in use, you know the rest."

When I had a second to breathe, I glanced around and noticed LZ was the Sup, thank God. Most controllers might not admit they are superstitious but they are, and to go up for my certification on a Thursday rather than a Friday (when pilots had parties on the brain) and to have LZ in my corner set me a little bit at ease already.

Last week when CB had gone on vacation LZ had plugged in with me and chuckled, "You know you're going about this all wrong. First of all, you have to leave your shit at the door and relax. A controller can't work with stress bogging him or her down. Secondly, take a quick second to think before you key up. Focus on three planes at a time: one on the ground about to take off, one about to land, and the one that's a few miles out. Then shift it as they land and depart. Remember, three at a time and always scan the runways before you do anything. A quick right to left or left to right, whichever is easiest to you, but do it the same way every time, make it a habit, so you know your ass is covered, because a pilot will take you down hard if you don't watch 'em."

I had learned more in five minutes with him than the last year and a half with CB, and wondered why all training couldn't be that calm and collected. But that was last week and this was now. The moment to prove myself was here, and I was terrified of fucking it all up.

"You got this," LZ mouthed and I nodded, wiped my wet palms on my pants, my armpits already soaked, and wished I felt the confidence that LZ had for me.

Then Ground passed a few strips to Flight Data, who then loaded them into my bay and raised his brows as if to say, "Got it?" I nodded, back thinking I had good people around me and that if there ever was a time to get my head out of my ass it was now.

"Can I take off my BDU shirt?" I glanced back at CR like I would if CB was behind me.

Annoyed, he replied, "Do whatever the hell you want JG," and shook his head side to side as he made notes on his clipboard and said, "You own the skies. You do whatever you want, just don't look at me. Move 'em out!"

Outside, the big boys like the B52's, B1's, and B2's inched closer, reminding me of whales. As a rule they always left first because they had more fuel than the fighters and were easy to work, except for the delay they caused in between departures from all the wake turbulence.

Then I saw my first Israeli flight of F-16 fighters. There were only two in that flight, but I saw another one with eight behind them. That's what this rating was all about: working all the different aircraft from all over the world so that they could dogfight in the desert sky, and when it was all over, get them all back before they ran out of fuel.

It took a little over an hour before they were all gone, but gone they were. I let my shoulders hang a little but I knew I couldn't relax. The departure phase was easy and although it was dead outside now, it was just the calm before the storm. In an hour when the first dot appeared in the sky, all hell was going to break loose.

I glanced back at LZ to get a feel for how I was doing, but he turned and pretended to type on his computer, and I thought if he was nervous, poor Evan had probably bitten his nails all the way down to his knuckles.

"JG," CR tugged at my arm as if he'd been trying to get my attention for a while. "If you need to step out to use the facilities, I suggest you do it now."

"I'm fine," I replied, trying to read the notes on his clipboard, but he placed it face down on the counter and said, "Up to you."

I quickly changed my mind and said, "Okay, I'll go," unplugged, and hurried downstairs into the bathroom where I splashed water on my face and gave myself a pep talk. "Halfway done! Keep it up!"

Back upstairs, time seemed to stand still as if no one out there had the desire to get home. But as they say, "Be careful what you wish for" the first dot appeared on the horizon and I thought, oh shit, they're going to be here any minute!

"Nellis Tower, Snake 11, seven miles out," the first pilot buzzed my ear.

I answered, "Snake 11, Nellis tower, report initial," like a reflex and thought, don't get overwhelmed now. We've only just begun and there's no turning back. It's on.

Seven miles out and creeping closer, Snake reported base. I cleared him to land but wasn't done with him yet. I scanned the runways and let him cross. Now I was done and thought, whew, only a hundred or so left to go!

"Cowboy 41, report initial," I told the next flight of F-15's, and a few seconds later a flight of six, followed by a flight of five.

One quick peek at the horizon and I counted at least twenty more dots and held my breath until I thought of LZ ("Three at a time JG, three at a time, scan and stay calm."). Within minutes the F-15's landed, but only half the flight had enough time to cross before the next flight landed. Another six F-16's entered the pattern, hauling ass as if to test me, to keep me busy so that my nerves wouldn't eat me alive.

Now there were twelve fighters in between the runways looking like little ducklings waiting to cross the busy street, and I knew I'd better get them over because they were running out of room. And just as I was about to key up, make a hole, and send them across, the phone rang, and LZ explained, "Oh. Yes. She's in position. Yeah, CR is here. Right away sir," and I knew I should have stayed home instead of messed with fire.

"JG, work your planes," CR snapped. "Don't worry about this."

"Viper 54, cleared to land," I stuttered then cleared my throat and thought, voice, confidence, don't leave me now! Get it together, breathe, think, scan, three planes, breathe, you got this, forty more to go, almost done, hang in there!

"Nellis tower this is Hog 11 flight of eight requesting to split to land, four straight in four for the overhead."

"Hog 11 approved for the split, report initial. Hog 44 report five mile final," I gripped the reigns again and almost thought I was having fun. In the past something different like a request like this would have freaked me out. Now the picture was clearer than ever and I thought, bring it!

"…Requesting to taxi across," the faint voice of a pilot was in my ear and I suddenly remembered I'd hadn't made a hole yet, hadn't crossed the gaggle that now resembled a pile up, and there sure as hell wasn't any room now with the A-10's coming in.

That, however, meant nothing to the rogue pilot who then broke loose and crossed without my permission, causing me to nearly jump out of my skin as I keyed up and screamed, "F-15 in between the runways, do not cross, do not cross!" until CR keyed up over me, "F-15, crossing, say your call sign! You just crossed in front of landing traffic."

Then I went quiet, Ground and Flight Data looked at me with gaping jaws because we all knew what it meant when CR keyed up for any reason: automatic failure. I was suddenly livid, ready to go downstairs and punch that pilot in the face for ruining my life.

"Sorry tower, I wasn't paying attention," he finally muttered and I thought, not paying attention? It was his job to pay attention! There were a hundred planes around and he thought this might not be a good time to pay attention? Why of all days did he have a death wish? Let me at him CR! Let me at him!

But there was no point in arguing. A failure was a failure, no matter how close to the end I was. And I was close. The big boys were on the horizon coming in. I'd been in position for almost five hours and felt exhausted, like I'd run a marathon. Damn that pilot!

"What the hell are you doing?" CR barked, "That dumbass pilot has nothing to do with you. It wasn't your fault, keep working," and suddenly my batteries recharged. I couldn't believe it!

I cleared the first cargo aircraft to land, but then CR said, "I've seen enough. There isn't much left out there, not enough to sequence anyway. Good job. Meet me downstairs in a few minutes. The chief needs to sign this and then I'll need you to sign it too."

CB plugged into Local Control, patted me on the back, and said, "I knew you could do it, JG," and I almost fell forward laughing. I did it!

Flight Data, Ground Control, and the SOF took turns shaking my hand and I didn't even realize when they'd come up. Evan, Kimmie, and Mandy suddenly hugged me and I felt like it was all a dream until LZ said, "They're ready for you now," and hung up the phone.

From the hall I overheard CR, "Today was all I had. She did great and she's going to be a great controller," and I smiled broader than before. My smile couldn't be sledgehammered from my face. "Sign here and here. Oh, hi JG. Come in, I'm leaving."

CR smacked my shoulder on the way out and congratulated me again which sent Satan into a greater fury as he nearly spit, "Sit down, airman," with the realization that I'd won. He hadn't been able to wash me out. He'd lost.

"The certification didn't count!" he screamed when the door slammed shut and CR was almost at his car. "And that stunt you pulled with the A-10's wasn't allowed, and then there's the runway incursion of course. I'm pulling the tapes and taking them to the Lieutenant. He'll sort this out and you'll be on the next flight out of here so you can wipe that smile off your face. You. Are. Not. Certified."

"That's funny," I replied calmly. "Because CR said I did great. And I approved the A-10's because I could. They asked me and I made it work, because that's what Air Traffic Controllers do…"

I was tempted to add, "So there," because he was not going to piss on my parade, but I was already in the best place I could be and didn't need to rub it in.

"That cert did not count!" his finger darted out accusingly, "Do I make myself clear? The Commander, the Lieutenant, everyone is going to review this! Everyone! Now get the hell out of my office!"

"Yes, sir." I jumped up, watched him squirm, and quickly glanced at the calendar to remember this day forever, the day I rose above, the day I came in for the kill and took home the carcass for dessert, the day Satan became a nobody and I became a somebody.

September 6, 2001.

What a day, I thought. A new beginning, and the best was yet to come.

THIRTY-ONE

I felt like I had it all once I was rated and yet still managed to have an unsettled feeling in my stomach when I went to bed every night. I wrestled with it for day until it hit me: I needed closure. My fight with Dad was over two years ago and no matter how hard I tried to feel the same anger, frustration, and sadness, it was no longer there, and I had to tell him, regardless of the fact that it was two in the morning east coast time.

When I heard a woman's voice ask, "Hello?" I nearly hung up, unsure if it was his new wife and unsure if I really was ready to talk to him. I didn't know what to say, and what if I said the wrong thing, or worse, he never wanted to talk to me again?

"Hi, it's Jen," my voice squeaked.

She squealed with joy, "Oh, ya fatha is not going to believe this. He's been talking about this day fo'eva." She called out, "Tony, pick up tha phone! It's ya daughta!"

Seconds later it was his voice on the other line as he sang, "Apples, peaches, pumpkin pie…" and suddenly I was five again, bouncing on his lap without a care in the world, and knew he'd forgiven me too, that we were okay from here on out, and sang back, "You were young and so was I!"

"It's you!" his voice quivered as if he was about to cry, which made me tear up too. "Oh boy, you must have been really mad at me, huh?"

"Understatement of the year," I laughed and wiped a stray tear from my face.

"I'm sorry, Apples. You know it wasn't supposed to happen like that," he said.

I replied softly, "I know," grateful for the apology I had thought would never come.

"I'm in the Air Force," I said, "And I'm an Air Traffic Controller!"

"I know, Apples," his voice lifted with happiness. "Good for you! Good for you! I'm so happy for you. Ryan's been telling me everything. I'm so happy you called me and told me. I love you, don't ever forget that."

"I won't," I said. "Never again," and I can't remember how long after that we talked or when I fell asleep.

Suddenly my alarm was going off and I leaped out of bed to throw up in the toilet, trying to remember what I'd eaten the night before. I knew I wasn't pregnant and my rating jitters were long gone and that I should probably go to the hospital. But that meant not going to work and every day I was at the tower was like a slap to Satan's face, bam! And I wasn't going to miss that for the world.

The tower was slow when I arrived, which was normal for a Tuesday. The sun crept over the horizon and flying wasn't scheduled to start for another two hours. I plugged into Ground Control and half listened as LZ briefed Sid about the runways in use and something sports related. I conducted my own checklist with the radios, pulled down the shades, and slumped into my chair, eyeing the trashcan until I hunched over it and gagged.

"JG, go to the flight Doc," Flight Data looked at me in disgust.

I groaned, "No way," and stood up to study the flight strip printer that was going berserk, printing out flight strips hours too early.

"Sid, what does "ground stop' mean?" I glanced at him, his feet on the consul and his eyes closed.

"It means no aircraft can depart," he sighed indifferently.

I protested, "But it's for airports like LAX, JFK, and BOS and I don't think there's any bad weather forecast."

This time he ignored me, but then the phone rang and he nearly fell out of his chair when he said, "What? How? Who?" and then to us screamed, "Anyone! Get the TV from downstairs. The World Trade Center's been hit."

I tried to remember which New York City building that was. Jake, Pam, Ryan and I had driven to New York City one New Year's Eve and watched the ball drop in Times Square and yet I couldn't picture the World Trade Center, least of all it getting hit. I said, "What?" as Flight Data quickly unplugged, hurried downstairs, and brought up the TV, which showed the horror footage on loop: an airplane flying directly into a building I recognized now.

"What the hell is happening?" I gripped my stomach.

Sid shook his head, "I don't know. I don't fucking know."

"There's no way that could happen, with controllers working, right?" I persisted. "I mean, it didn't just clip the building, he went right for it! What pilot would do that?"

"I'm calling the Chief." Sid picked up the phone, which sent me into a different panic, because no one called him for anything!

"Flight Data, get the evacuation kit ready to go. JG, look up the scramble procedures so we're ready to go when they call it," Sid continued after the call, and although my body was moving, my mind was frozen with the severity of it all.

Scramble procedures were something we briefly touched-up on in training, and by briefly I mean that I could recall the name and the purpose and that was about it, because it was a wartime tactic when we were in imminent danger, under attack, and needed to launch aircraft at a moment's notice.

Flight Data opened the dusty evacuation briefcase and said, "Everything's good to go," but what did he know? When the hell had we ever evacuated? On weekends when we were bored, we'd drive out to the little tower between the runways for practice, and now we were acting like it was real, like someone was going to blow this tower up and we had to launch fighters to shoot whoever was attacking us down.

I gagged into the trashcan. Sid said, "Go to the hospital, JG," without taking his eyes from the screen.

I said, "Now? When we don't know what's going on? I'm not going anywhere!"

"You'll be fine," he replied firmly. "There's nothing you can do up here. Go! That's an order."

Reluctantly, I unplugged my headset, knowing I should leave now before it got ugly in the cab, and I gripped the railing tightly as I descended one step at a time, wondering if we were going up in flames next.

I threw up next to my car, and for a moment I studied the sky. How could it be this quiet here if the world was ending on the other side of the continent?

At the hospital I counted two cars in the lot and thought nothing of it because it was only a little after six. Then I stepped inside and heard only my boots squeaking on the linoleum floor. Suddenly, I felt like the last person left on Earth, and I didn't like it.

"Hello?" I called out to no one over the counter at the Flight Surgeon's office. Usually, at least the TV is on in the corner at least a few are pilots waiting, but now there was nothing but eerie silence.

A few minutes later a startled nurse appeared and said, "Oh, hello. Have you been waiting long? The hospital is conducting evacuation procedures and I'm the only one here. Are you sick?"

I nodded, surprised that at a time like this the hospital was evacuating, and where was everyone evacuating to? Where were people supposed to go if they were sick?

"I'm throwing up, although I haven't eaten anything in a while," I said.

She spun around and said, "Follow me. It sounds like you're dehydrated."

I followed her to a back room where she hooked me up to an IV and said, "This should do it. Lie here and I'll be back in a few to check on you."

I wanted to say, "Don't leave me," but let her go and counted the ceiling tiles until I fell asleep.

When I awoke, the drip was empty. My veins felt like ice and my teeth chattered as I looked around and found a blanket I couldn't reach. I wasn't going to risk ripping out the IV for it.

"Hello?" I called out and heard nothing, and wondered if I was going to have to rip out the IV one way or another to get out of here.

"Are you feeling better?" The nurse returned breathlessly I didn't know how long after I called out.

I said, "I think so, but how would I know?"

"I think you'd better get out of here," she said. "Another plane hit! Are you able to drive home?"

"What do you mean?" I shrieked.

"I don't have time to explain. Can you get home?"

"Yes, but is it safe?"

"You don't want to be here," she said. "A hospital can be a target. Once you're home, make sure you eat bananas, toast, and rice. That will settle your stomach. Okay?"

Okay? Nothing was okay. Did she really expect me to go home and cook rice and make toast like planes weren't falling out of the sky!

From the hall I called Sid, who told me not to come back, and as I hung the phone on the cradle I thought of Ryan and how he was supposed to be back by now, and wondered if he was stuck somewhere or worse, under attack too.

Somehow I made it back to the dorm and turned on the TV. I was watching the news footage, looking for answers, when a knock at the door made me get up.

"Sid said you went home sick." Evan held up a bag of groceries for me to see and smiled sweetly, "So I called my mom and she said to make you some soup."

"For me?" I replied, feeling like the luckiest girl in the world. "Thanks! Come in!"

He kissed my cheek, walked past me, and microwaved a can of soup before he joined me on the couch, spoon fed me Chicken Noodle, and grinned. "Sid said you threw up in the tower."

"I did not!" I pushed his shoulder, which caused soup to drip onto his lap, and instead of getting angry like I thought he would, he set the bowl on the coffee table and stared at the TV.

His face went pale and I said, "Can you believe this shit? I want to hear the recordings. I want to know what those pilots are saying! Do you really think we're under attack or that the pilot just didn't know what he was doing?"

Then I thought I saw his lip quiver, which scared me too since he never cried, and I said, "We're not going to war, are we? Everything will be sorted out, right?"

He nodded, picked up the bowl, and stirred the noodles around. I said, "Hey, I'm scared too. I know this sucks, but you're scaring me! Say something!"

"She was in it."

"Who was in what?" I asked.

He clarified, "My ex was in the World Trade Center. She had just started a job there. She was in it."

"You mean to tell me the very ex-girlfriend that you never ever wanted to talk to again, even after I pressured you to look her up and you then explained to me that it wasn't necessary because you didn't love her anymore because I am the one here loving you, standing right before you, and I'm the one who will always be there for you, was in that tower?"

He nodded.

"And how in the hell, Evan, would you know that if you haven't talked to her in what, eight years?"

"Well," he shifted uneasily. "I've been talking to her for the last six months. I found her on a site."

"She is the very reason you do not cuddle with me, the reason I can't meet your friends, the reason you say you will never marry me, the reason you tell me we will not be together after the military, and the very reason you are such a complete asshole! This is complete and utter bullshit!"

"I can't deal with this right now," he pushed past me.

I said, "You? How about me?"

He slammed the door and I was left feeling indifferent about whether or not she was in that tower. Dead or alive, she'd ruined his life and was ruining mine. Then I sat down and cried, disgusted with what I'd become, how much I'd changed for him, wishing I could just pick myself up and walk away like he always did.

THIRTY-TWO

Getting on the base was hell from then on. Hours of waiting followed by twenty questions once you did finally arrive at the gate, a quick pat down then an undercarriage sweep of the car with an oversized dentist mirror, as if anyone would dare stick something to the bottom of his or her car with a giant tank pointed at him or her from the other side of the guard shack.

As if that wasn't enough, they added underground posts meant to deter rogue cars from infiltrating the shack, even though the posts were clear as day when you drove up to them. No one in his or her right mind would try it, because with the click of a button your car would be bisected and you would probably be killed.

I've been scared before, growing up in a major city and having to watch my back at night, as a kid or a woman on a subway or a bus, but never had I felt constant fear like this. There were too many unanswered questions: When was the next attack? When was America going overseas to retaliate? Were we ever going to live normally again?

Then there was Ryan, who was stuck overseas. His deployment to Italy had changed to a secret location he couldn't tell us about, except that he was fine (yeah, right), was working fourteen hour days but wasn't tired, slept in a bombed out building next to the runway in a sleeping bag, and begged us not to watch the news because they'd portrayed everything worse than what it really was. How could it be any worse?

Every time the phone rang, I thought it was Ryan, this time it was Evan, in a rare good mood.

"Oh, hi," I said.

He giggled, "I have a surprise to make you feel better."

"I doubt it," I changed the channel in search of news, but found none and started pacing.

"Oh come on," he coaxed.

I said, "I'm not in the mood for surprises, sorry."

"Well, since you're not going to guess, I'll just tell you. I'm going to see Amber tonight and she wants to meet you."

"Terrific," I snorted. "I've only been asking to see her for four months and now you want me to be ecstatic? Oh, stop the press! Let me guess, you're going to see her at the bar?"

"I know you're upset about Ryan." He liked to hit below the belt.

"You have no idea." I added and he countered, "There's nothing you can do about him being gone. He's fine and you know it. Let's go out and have a good time! I want you to meet her, okay? I've known her for fifteen years, maybe even longer."

"Who is this?" I tapped the phone against the table. "And what have you done with Evan?"

"Very funny," he laughed. "Get ready. I'm coming to get you in ten."

"Whatever," I huffed, but stared at my reflection in the mirror, wondering what I could wear to impress a Playboy bunny. Nothing, I decided. She was going to have to like me for who I was, without makeup, wearing dark jeans and a white shirt.

Evan honked the horn from the parking lot ten minutes later and when I got in the car, I asked, "Where are we going?"

He replied, "You'll see."

Then I saw it all too clearly once he passed over the strip and into the shadier part of town, and again I asked, "Where did you say she worked again?"

He put his hand on my leg as if to assure me it wasn't what I was thinking, as if he knew what I was thinking, and said, "It's close by."

"The College Clubhouse?" I asked when he parked, knowing she wasn't going to resurrect anything in this joint, especially not a Playboy career, and Evan said defensively, "It's just until she can find something else."

I replied, "Of course. I didn't mean anything by it." We got in right away without as much as a glance at our I.D.'s, adherence to dress code or payment of cover charge, a rarity in Las Vegas.

Inside it was dark, and although I'd never been to a frat party before, that was exactly what I was reminded of. The entire floor was covered in toilet paper and as I reached out my hand to keep Evan close to me, a girl nearly knocked me over on her way to the bathroom. She didn't quite make it and threw up in the trash barrel close to us. Otherwise, it looked like a typical club with a long bar counter, dance floor in the middle with flashing color lights, and an upstairs balcony area to people watch from.

I wanted to leave immediately, and as if Evan sensed my hesitation, he squeezed my hand, led me to a pub table, pulled out a stool for me, then slouched onto one across from me and lit a cigarette. When he flicked the match, I put up my hands to remind him of the toilet paper and that he could light this place on fire in a heartbeat, but he looked away as if in search for her, and I glanced at the toilet paper and wondered how many people had lost their keys in it.

"Ain't this something," he hollered over the music.

I called out, "U-huh," trying to sound upbeat, although I knew that under any other circumstance I wouldn't be caught dead here.

All of a sudden a tiny blonde in a neon pink thong bikini and knee high boots strutted past me, put one arm around Evan, and kissed his cheek tenderly, which made me straighten up, smile, and extend my hand to her once she turned around and looked me up and down. But she did not take my hand and the two of them laughed as if I'd missed the joke, and I realized she wasn't as pretty as I'd expected her to be and definitely not as tall because she was shorter than me.

Then she disappeared and Evan said, "She'll be right back. She likes you."

I put my thumbs up and said, "Great! Can we leave now?"

"Want to dance?" he caught me off guard and I said, "Yeah," thinking he really was a different person with his friends around, until he waved and said, "Go ahead," as if he'd granted me permission, and I stormed off, struggling for a reason as to why I agreed to come in the first place.

From the dance floor I pretended not to know him or look in the direction of his table until Amber swooped in. Suddenly Evan wanted me by his side and waved for me to come back, and as I kicked my way through the toilet paper I couldn't help but feel like a puppet.

"Come with me," Amber took my hand aggressively, pulling me past the dance floor as I attempted a glance towards Evan, who seemed to shrug and think nothing of it as she dragged me on stage.

A spotlight shined in my face, Amber let go of my hand and left my side, and the music went from upbeat to slow thumping guitar strings like cheesy porn music. An almost naked bodybuilder in a tiny red Speedo with a whistle around his neck appeared in front of me, threw his arms in the air as if telling me it was okay to touch him, swayed his hips, and smiled at the crowd cheering him on.

"Body shot!" the DJ screamed, and the crowd went wilder. Evan clapped mockingly, a cigarette dangling from his mouth, and Amber appeared next to him and sat in my seat.

I stepped backwards but was suddenly blindfolded and felt the naked man's hands on my shoulders as he pushed me until I was on my knees. Then he shoved a bottle of vodka in my mouth and poured it down my throat until I coughed it all up.

"Ohhhhh," the crowd screamed as if they wanted to be in my shoes, and I thought this really couldn't get any worse, until I tasted whipped cream in my mouth and seconds later, a banana.

I took a bite and chewed for a full minute until I was pulled to my feet again and the blindfold was ripped from my face.

"You weren't supposed to eat it!" Amber scowled, throwing the scarf on the ground and pulling me off the stage again like a disobedient child.

"What the hell was I supposed to do? I didn't ask for this!"

"Wasn't he cute?" she ignored me.

I said, "Evan is cuter."

That made her frown, and she said, "Aw, aren't you sweet."

"Can we go now?" I wrenched my hand from Amber's.

Evan asked, "Did you have fun?"

"A blast," I said and she walked away. "Now please, let's go. Is there crap on my face?"

"Just a little bit longer, okay?" He stuck out his bottom lip like a bratty kid and pouted, "She wants us to wait for her so we can go to another place after this and we can talk in peace."

"What is there to talk about?" I patted my sticky face and sighed, and we waited in silence, the music pounding around us, until she appeared ten minutes later in jeans and a t-shirt and her hair pulled into a ponytail like mine.

Together we walked through the bright parking lot and stopped at her Miata, where Evan said, "I hope someone walks you to your car every night," and tried to giggle.

Amber waved, threw her purse in her car and said, "Jen, don't you just love my car?" as if it was a Ferrari.

I said, "Yeah," awkwardly, unsure if I was supposed to have said something different.

"Well, I just love it. I love it so much I drove it from Maryland, right Evan?"

"Yup," he agreed, but not too convincingly. He added, "I love it too," which finally got her in the driver's seat.

She rolled down the window and waved, "See you there."

I waited for Evan to explain what had just happened, but all he said was, "Bear with me. Just a little bit longer, okay?" and kissed my cheek.

"Okay," I agreed, and observed silently as we followed her down the street and how they went down memory lane together once we sat down at the bar after Evan ordered drinks and hot wings for us.

When the wings came to the table Amber attacked them ravenously, as if she hadn't eaten in days, sneered at me when I picked up a knife and fork and performed surgery on my hot wing, and elbowed Evan. "Your girl's high maintenance, huh?"

"Uh-huh," he giggled uncomfortably, and when he didn't defend me I said, "I don't like sauce underneath my nails."

Grease dripped down her forearm as she practically flossed her teeth with the bones. I tried to ignore it and asked, "So what brought you out here again?"

She said, "I broke up with my fiancé. He wanted to settle down and get married, and have kids. I wanted a career. My brother lives here too and he convinced me to come out here."

"I didn't know you had a brother," I said, surprised we had anything in common.

"We're really close," she added, finally using a napkin. "And he supports my career. So do my parents. We're all close and that makes it easy."

"My Dad would kick my ass," I laughed, trying to picture me telling him about a career that involved me taking my clothes off, but she didn't comment.

She leaned back in her chair as if she was stuffed after two wings and said, "I'm full. I'm on the Atkins diet, have you heard of that, Jen? I already lost two pounds."

"Wow," I replied. "From where? Your earlobes?"

She chuckled, leaned sideways to pinch Evan's cheek, and said, "Where did you find this girl?" Then to me, "I've known this kid since elementary school and he still has that same silly grin. You'd love his mom, Jen, she is so sweet."

"I'm sure I'll meet her real soon, right Evan?" I raised my eyebrows playfully, thinking maybe she really was the key for me to get closer to him. "I've only seen pictures of her."

Amber punched him in the shoulder and said, "What? Evan!"

"Maybe down the road," he put his hands up to block her punches. "And maybe it's time to go and split you two up."

"We need to hang out more often. Evan's actually a nice guy when you're around," I said.

She smiled, "Sure thing," and signaled for the check, as if to make sure that I knew she was paying.

Minutes later Evan and I were back in his car, and although he turned the key, he didn't engage the clutch. He stared out the dash until her car disappeared off the lot and said, "She thinks you're nice, but she doesn't like your last name."

"She doesn't like my last name? What's not to like about Grillo? It's funny, like Brillo, or Gorilla."

"Yeah, I don't know what she meant by that, but I'm glad you came out tonight. There's a reason why I've been out with her a lot. My buddy called me after she got here and asked me to look out for her because he thinks she's doing coke."

"She's a grown woman who can make her own choices," I said, wanting to be angry because she wasn't his problem. Then I softened and said, "You're a good friend for doing that," because his caring side that emerged sometimes was what I loved about him.

"It's just 'til she gets on her feet again." He kissed my cheek as if to squander all doubt that I was first on his list and I thought, yes, this is exactly how I like him.

THIRTY-THREE

New Hampshire was the last place on Earth I wanted to be for Christmas while Evan was in Baltimore. Then again, being in my dorm room alone didn't sound so hot either.

"So tell me again why Evan didn't come with you?" Jake asked, taking Pam and me to our favorite pizza place after the flight, and starting the series of questions I knew were coming.

"Because he said his parents weren't ready to meet me yet." I unsuccessfully tried to hide behind my slice.

"After three years!" Pam nearly spit. "What are you still doing with this guy? We haven't even met him yet!"

"He'll come around," I said, sounding unsure, and Jake narrowed his eyes at me as if to say, yeah right, as if we haven't heard that one before. I said, "I know he sounds weird sometimes when I call and complain to you guys, but I know he loves me and I love him and I can't let go now that we've been together three years."

"If you say so," Jake said, and Pam switched the subject. "Ryan will be here the day after tomorrow, right?"

I said, "Yeah, he's just moving the last of his things to the new apartment."

"Four years went fast and next year you'll be done too," Pam said.

I nodded, "I can't wait. It's felt like ten," and wondered when Evan would propose, before or after I was out of the military, and where we might live together.

"And Evan will be out too?" Jake prodded, and before I could answer my phone rang, and I said cheerily, "Yes! See, there he is right now, calling me from his Mom's house! Hi Evan! I'm great," I said, sticking my tongue out at Jake and Pam as if I'd just proved them both wrong. He did love me.

Then my shoulders drooped noticeably when Evan told me he had met with his ex that night, the ex, and when I hung up Pam demanded, "What happened?" as if she'd read my mind.

I said, "Nothing. Everything's fine."

"You can't hide anything from us. Spit it out," Jake said.

I admitted, "He saw his ex. But! He said he didn't love her anymore. Now he is definitely over her."

"Isn't that exciting?" Jake said sarcastically to Pam, who seemed confused and said, "Why is he meeting with his ex?"

"I know what you're thinking, but he's great, I swear!" I said, trying to block my own doubt. "And you'll meet him one of these days and you'll love him too. I promise."

"Whatever," Pam snorted. "Since you're obviously in denial, tell me about Ryan again. Is he alright since he came back from overseas?"

Pausing for a moment because I wasn't exactly sure and didn't want to freak them out, I said, "Okay, I think. He only talked about what happened there once, on the first night when Mom and Dad flew in to see him. While we were sitting around the dinner table he suddenly talked about the body bags and all the blood and then he dug through his suitcase and found the American flag he'd bought while over there and handed the triangle to Dad, who cried like a baby, which made all of us cry too. But it's been a few weeks now and he seems better."

I didn't finish my thought, that I was afraid to ask him how he was because I didn't know what else he'd seen and didn't know what to do if he did tell me.

"Shit," Jake said with awe, and Pam nodded.

"He's better now," I reached over the table and squeezed their hands, "He got out of the military and found a job at Applebee's, just until he figures out what else he wants to do."

"Maybe he'll come back here," Pam said hopefully.

I said, "Maybe," and was distracted by my phone again. I said, "See, he loves me so much he has to call me every five minutes to remind me. Hello?"

But it wasn't Evan and I nearly dropped the phone when I heard Satan on the other end. "Airman Grillo?" I felt like I'd been punched in the gut.

"Merry Christmas," I said, hoping he'd tell me he'd misdialed and was going to hang up now, but he said nothing except, "You need to change your ticket and fly back tomorrow."

"What do you mean? I just got here," I said, wishing I hadn't picked up.

He snapped, "I don't care when you got there, you're coming right back. 9/11 retaliation efforts are in effect and you're going overseas to a classified location. Your flight leaves the day after tomorrow and you'd better get back here by morning."

"What are you talking about?" My hands shook with the realization of why he'd sent me to M-16 training in the first place. He planned my demise all along, and since he couldn't wash me out, he'd moved me to the top of the deployment list where at least ten people were ahead of me. They wanted to go overseas to re-enlist and get the sixty thousand dollar bonus tax free, which wasn't enough to keep me under Satan's regime. There wasn't enough money in the world.

"Like I said," he repeated slowly. "Change your flight, ASAP. You'll be out-processing in a day and will be gone for a year. Failure to comply will result in AWOL status. That means "Absent Without Leave," followed by a court martial. Is that clear enough? Good evening."

I dropped my phone and screamed, "He's sending me to war!"

"What do you mean?" Pam hugged me as Jake picked up my phone, but I couldn't get enough air to breathe and tell them I was going to die. I was never going to see them again! And I was never going to see Evan again either!

"I'm deploying," I sobbed. "I'm going overseas because of that asshole! I fucking hate that guy! He wants to ruin my life and won't stop 'til I'm dead!"

"It's okay," Jake and Pam tried to console me, but they had no idea what I was talking about.

"I'm his daughter's age. How could he do this to me?"

"It's going to be okay," they repeated, but I couldn't hear them.

"I have to leave right away," I said. "I have to call Ryan because I have no idea what the fuck to do."

THIRTY-FOUR

Not a minute late, I stood in front of Satan's desk the next morning wishing my face didn't resembled a red bloated balloon, which didn't matter because Satan barely even looked at me when he said, "Everything needs to be complete by 1700 hours tonight. Your flight leaves at 1900 hours and you will be on it."

He slid a piece of paper toward me that read "out-processing checklist" and had a list of places I needed to visit before I left and checked out from this base, checked out from my life. As I picked it up, I resisted the urge to ball it up and throw it in his face.

"I'll see what I can do," I said under my breath.

He suddenly roared, "You will be on that flight tonight, airman! Keep your cell phone on because I'm going to verify your progress throughout the day. Is that clear?"

The only thing clear to me was that I was supposed to be on the other side of the continent sipping Dunkin Donuts French vanilla coffee right now.

I stormed outside but was crying so hard I couldn't see my car keys or read the first item on my checklist. I calmed myself down a full minute later. Then I read "in-processing building," which was the very first building Ryan had taken me to once I'd arrived here three years ago, and I started crying all over again until I reached the parking lot.

"Where am I going?" I sniffed when I was handed a folder with a stack of copies with a scramble of letters and numbers on them. My dog tags were taped on the inside.

"It's classified," the guy behind the desk signed my checklist to confirm I'd been there, and I was reminded of Perez and his lovely details of where the dog tags were placed once our body parts were blown to bits, and Cass who'd told us in one of his speeches that ten percent of us in class would die and for us to say goodbye to each other now, which I hadn't thought was funny then. It certainly wasn't funny now, either, since I was one of the ten percent.

"I can't read this," I argued, wanting to know where my final resting place was going to be.

He said, "Follow me," as if he understood my frustration, and led me down a long hall to a room that looked like a classroom, pulled a map from the ceiling and asked, "Do you see this?"

"The map?"

"We're here," he pointed at the U.S., then slid his finger to the right. "And you're going somewhere here. That's all I know. Good luck. See you in a year."

"I was just asking a question," I said, thinking he was in cohoots with Satan.

He replied, "Sorry kid, it's just the way it goes."

It's just the way it goes for me, I wanted to say.

The chem. gear warehouse was next, and my knees were weak once I walked in and thought of the unpleasantness from basic and how I nearly died from a heatstroke.

"These are the new ones," the young blonde kid said excitedly as he signed my checklist. He was trying to cheer me up, but all I wanted to do was shove a sock in his mouth. "They're so much lighter and easier to pack than the old ones and without all the charcoal that leaks out. You'll get two suits, but only open them when you need to so they work best under an attack."

"Great," I said sarcastically, thinking at least I was done, until he said, "Oh that's the exit but you need to go to that corner, into the classroom and take the refresher chem. gear class. It's starting in a few minutes."

The dying puppy video didn't cheer me up. Neither did my failed gas mask attempts or the reminder of the godawful atropine shot.

The dentist office was next, and I stopped crying long enough to dial Ryan's number and ask him what the hell I was there for. He said, "It's easier for the military to take care of your teeth now instead of when you're 18,000 miles away."

I said, "Makes sense, okay, I'll see you soon, I've got to go," and was called into the office, trying to think of every mouth pain I could.

All it bought me was an hour and afterwards, a full minute of Satan yelling at me to get it together.

The DCU, desert camouflage uniform, was next and was the final item on the list, which almost made me throw up. Then I walked into "clothing issue" and got excited that I'd found a set of four uniforms that actually fit me, along with a pair of tan steel-toed boots, and last but not least, a Goretex coat that I saw as a badge of honor because everyone who deployed got one. They were too expensive to buy outright, were made of an all-weather material that made them look sharp. And of course, they did not have my size.

I took all of my new things next door to the seamstress and asked her for name tags. She had time to sew my name but not attach the tags, and said, "Come back tomorrow."

I replied, "I'm leaving in an hour. I don't have tomorrow," and was forced to walk away when my phone rang.

Praying it was Evan, I nearly chucked it into the garbage can in the parking lot when I heard Satan's voice requesting my progress.

"I can't get my tags sewn on," I said.

"Whatever else you need, I will send to you," Satan replied smoothly, as if this was such a sweet victory for him, and I said, "I need a Goretex coat."

"I will send it," he repeated. "More importantly, I trust you're on your way to the airport?"

"Almost." The tears welled in my eyes again.

"Call me when you get there." He hung up, and as I drove up to my dorm room, I spotted Ryan waiting for me with two large suitcases.

"One is for all of your civilian clothes," he said after I'd unlocked my door. "Believe me, when you're over there you want to be comfortable and feel normal. Change out of your DCU's whenever you can. The second suitcase is for all of your toiletries. We'll run to CVS by the airport, but we have to leave now. And you have your chem. gear bag. Just keep all your uniforms in there."

"Here are my checks, already signed. And try to sell my car while I'm gone. It's leaking oil and you know the rest." I started crying. "Damn, it's like my own damn eulogy."

"Jen, you're going to be okay," he hugged me. "Lots of people deploy all the time. Look at me! You're going to meet a lot of people and have a blast! I promise."

Then he removed one of his dog tags from his pockets, untied one of my steel toe boots, and laced the tag underneath it so that when I was wearing them all I had to do was look down and see his name.

"I'll be with you every step of the way," he said and I sniffed, unconvinced.

"Okay," I said, and watched as he zipped up the suitcases and dragged them to the car.

In less than ten minutes we were at CVS, running through the aisles and dumping everything from shampoo, soap, and tampons into baskets. Five minutes later we were in the car again, but I made him stop when I spotted Best Buy so I could buy a camera.

"You're cutting it really close," he tapped the dashboard when I got back in the car.

I showed him the box and said, "Seven hundred dollars with the warranty. It's a digital camera with three mega pixels. I had to have it. I never had my own camera and I might as well take pictures while I'm there. Wherever I'm going."

"You don't even know how to use a camera without me explaining it to you."

"I'll have plenty of time to read the manual." I unwrapped the box and shoved the charger and the camera into my backpack and before I knew it, the car was stopped and we were at the airport and I couldn't move.

"You have to get out of the car," Ryan pleaded.

I sobbed again, "I'm scared. I don't want to go. I want to run away and go AWOL!"

"No you don't," he said, and I realized that even if I did runaway, Satan was sure to find me and kill me one way or another.

"You'll be back before you know it. Right now, all you need is to get on that plane. The military owns you and there's nothing you can do about it. But when you get back-"

"If I get back."

"-you'll be out, like me, for good. I love you, and I'll see you real soon, okay Sis?"

I faked a smile, knowing I couldn't stall any longer and watched helplessly as he got back in the car and drove away.

Somehow, I managed to check my luggage and get to the gate, where I stared at my phone and wished Evan would call; his parents phone number was blocked when he'd called before and I had no way of reaching him.

Suddenly a pair of white sneakers approached me and a familiar voice said, "Hi."

I looked up and saw George, and asked, surprised, "What are you doing here, George? You weren't on the list to go either!"

"Yes, I was. On Satan's shit list." He shrugged as if it was no big deal. "And I guess that was the list he went by."

"I can't believe how calm you are," I replied. "You know we're going to be gone for a year, right? Or worse, die."

"As long as I'm away from Satan, life is good." He picked up my backpack from the floor and proceeded to get in line to board.

"But I don't want to get on," I said when I caught up to him.

He frowned, "What are you talking about?"

"I don't know," I said, realizing I better get it through my head that I was going and there was nothing I could do about it.

Then I thought maybe he was right. Maybe it didn't matter that we were going because things were going to be better without Satan and none of this was a big deal. Then I thought yeah, fucking right.

THIRTY-FIVE

George took over once we landed in Arizona, carried my backpack through the airport, got a cart and stacked our luggage, then called a cab and told the driver, "Davis Monthan Air Force Base."

He flipped through his folder in the dark, then whispered, "But after that, I'm not sure where we're going," which caused fresh tears to roll down my cheeks.

Why the hell were we in Arizona?

Once on the base, the cab driver dropped us off at the dorm. He'd done this before. We were greeted by a scrawny man with a thin mustache, dressed in BDU's even though it was past ten at night, and holding a clipboard as he greeted us. "Grillo...and...George Hanes? Here are your keys, follow me."

Inside, he pointed at an open room and said, "The laundry room is over here and the BX, pizza place, and video rental are right across the street..." but I stopped listening. I didn't want to be here and didn't care about the amenities. I wanted to go home.

I unlocked my ten-by-ten room and cringed at the sight of the depressing Government Issue desk, TV, and stand. At least I have my own bathroom and shower, I thought as George walked away and said, "See you around."

"Goodnight. Your flight leaves the day after tomorrow," Clipboard Guy said and turned to leave.

I said, "What do you mean, the day after tomorrow? I was rushed here thinking it was leaving tonight. But we're not leaving for another two whole days?"

"I don't know." He shrugged the standard military answer, and I slammed the door shut, seething at Satan, wondering why the hell he'd sent me here.

Then my phone rang and I nearly broke it in half trying to answer it once I realized it was Evan. I screamed, "Oh my God, Evan! Thank God! I've been waiting for you to call! Where have you been? You wouldn't believe where I am!"

"Yeah," he replied sleepily. "Sorry I couldn't get back to you earlier, I was busy with my parents."

"I'm in goddamn Arizona!" I interrupted. "And you haven't talked to me in two days!"

"What do you mean?" he said, and I clarified. "Satan shipped me here and I'm going overseas and I'm never going to see you again and will you please come visit me? I'll fly you out right now!"

"Wait a minute. Arizona?"

"Yes, aren't you listening? Please come and visit me."

"I don't want to fly to Arizona. I just got back from the airport. I just got back to my room. I missed my room."

"You're kidding, right? You're already back and hadn't even noticed I was gone? Did you hear what I said? I'm going to war! I might not ever see you again! What if I don't come back? I can't leave without saying goodbye to you! Please, here is my credit card number, I don't care what it costs, please come here. I'm falling apart!"

"Okay, okay" he finally agreed, and I was floored he had to think about it. If the roles were reversed he wouldn't have had to ask. "I'll look it up later."

"Stop being a selfish jerk! I'd book it for you right now but I don't have a computer. I'm begging you, please come here! I'm so damn lonely! I've missed you!"

"Alright, alright, I'm turning the computer on right now."

If I wasn't so scared for my life and didn't think I was going to die in the very near future, I would have called it quits right then and there. It had to be better to die alone than put up with his constant back and forth indecisiveness, but when I heard the sound of his fingers on the keyboard my heart leaped. He was coming to see me because he loved me, because he wanted to make me happy.

"There's a four hundred dollar ticket, but it's not until tomorrow morning. Everything else has already left and you know what, even if I do go, we'll have less than twenty four hours together. More like fourteen."

"Book it! How is this even a question?"

"Alright, calm down, I'll book it. And I know you don't want to hear this, but I'm going to hang up now because I have to smoke a cigarette and do some laundry, okay? I love you and I'll see you tomorrow."

"Aw, really?" I replied sadly, but I hung up as he wished and cried into my pillow until I found the energy to turn on the TV. I finally felt comforted once I put on ESPN.

I woke up with a headache from crying too much and was soon frantic when I realized the sun was up, fearing I'd missed Evan's flight. I jumped up and called a cab, and had enough time to shower before running outside. I was pleasantly surprised to see the cab already waiting for me.

"Please hurry to the airport as fast as you can," I pleaded to the driver and stared at the clock on the dash to calculate the minutes I had left. "My boyfriend's flight is about to land."

"Yeah," he said and floored it so that I flew into the cushy headrest.

I struggled with the seatbelt and gave up, leaning forward instead and looking through the windshield, wishing I could will the car to move even faster. I asked, "So how long before we get there?"

"Not long," he said, and once he drove off base, he weaved through the traffic as if he knew I meant business.

Studying the flat land all around us that was similar to Vegas but without the casinos, I wondered what my life would have been like if I'd been stationed here. I wouldn't have met Satan. I wouldn't be going overseas. Then again, I wouldn't have met the love of my life either.

"There it is!" I smiled when I saw the first sign for the airport, and the driver replied, "Just a few minutes, Miss," which should have calmed me down, but only sent me into a panic. What if the flight had already landed, Evan didn't have a cell phone to tell me, and what if we somehow walked past each other and then wasted precious hours looking for each other?

"Ugh," I gasped at the red light. "I need to get there now!"

And instantly, the light turned green and I relaxed, but the driver didn't move, and I said, "Hey, it's green."

"Not yet," he shook his head, and then I saw the ambulance zoom past in front of us.

But he wasn't staring at the ambulance in front of us. His eyes were focused on the rearview mirror as if he was watching something, and as I paused for a breath, I heard the screeching sound too, tires coming right at us. As I turned, it was too late. The SUV slammed into the trunk and sent me sailing into the seat in front of me, causing every vertebrae to pop.

"Miss, are you okay?" the driver asked.

I shook my head, surprised it was still attached, and said, "Yes, can we go now?"

"I have to get her information." He got out of the car. Under his breath, he said, "Stupid woman. Shit, shit, shit!" and I watched how she flailed her arms in the air, saying she was sorry, and he, without wanting to listen to her, jotted down her information.

I would have gone out there and punched her for making me later than I already was, but suddenly the ambulance pulled up next to us and a man leaped out of the back like he was Indiana Jones, opened my door, and asked, "Are you okay? Can you move? Do you need medical attention? Can you blink your eyes and look left and right?"

"I'm fine. I just need to get to the airport!" I said, which I would have said even if both of my legs were broken.

He replied, "You're in shock, and believe me, if you don't want medical attention now, tomorrow you'll feel like you did ten rounds with Mike Tyson. Promise me you'll go to the hospital if you feel bad tomorrow?"

"Sure, yes," I agreed, grateful he closed the door until I saw him step to the back of the cab and started harassing the woman and the cab driver. Couldn't he tell we were all fine?

Luckily, they told him the same and he disappeared into the ambulance and drove off, and the driver came back into the car and I said, "Please, step on it!"

"Almost there," he said, and sure enough, two minutes later, the signs appeared and we were approaching the Arrivals terminal.

"Be right back," I jumped out of the cab as soon as he stopped, knowing I should have paid him or at least promised I'd make a point to find him again, but I was in a hurry. I needed to find Evan.

And there he was, forty feet into my sprint, leaning against the building smoking a cigarette, unshowered in his usual jersey and saggy jeans and looking like a work of art.

"Oh, Evan, you came!" I hugged him and he patted my back like I was a good kid and said, "Come on, let's get out of here."

"Did you tell him about the accident?" The cab driver opened the door for me, but I shook my head.

Evan glanced at me with a raised eyebrow, but I buried my head in his chest and inhaled his smell of stale cigarettes, beer, and cologne, and thought, what if this is the last time I ever smell him?

"What happened," Evan lifted my chin, but I wiggled it free again and held him tighter in case this was the last time I ever got to hold him again.

I opened my eyes once we stopped, led Evan to the room, plopped down on the bed, and said, "Join me."

"First things first, I'm hungry. You want pizza? I saw a place when we drove in."

"No. I just want to hold you."

"You will hold me." He turned the TV to ESPN, ordered a pizza, and laid down next to me.

"Can't we put on something happy?" I asked.

"It's Seabiscuit," he said, as if that was supposed to mean something to me. "That horse is incredible."

"What's incredible is that you have tears in your eyes," I replied. "I've never seen you well up for anything and we've been through quite a lot, especially now with me leaving."

"Okay, I'll change it." He changed the station to another sports channel showing football highlights.

I squeezed him tighter and said, "Never mind. All that matters is that you're here now."

"Ugh, you're too close," he squirmed. "You know I can't cuddle. I feel like I'm being boiled alive."

"I don't ever want to leave this room." I gripped his t-shirt into my fists so that he couldn't move and asked, "What if I just went AWOL? Or what if you got me pregnant? What if you switched with George and came with me?"

"That's nonsense." He pinched my arm, hoping I'd stop smothering him.

"What is your problem?" I sat up, surprised by his insensitivity. "Why can't you share this fantasy with me for five minutes? You really can't bear the thought of getting me pregnant to save my life, or switching with George so we could be together? I wouldn't have to think twice if it was the other way around."

"Just calm down..." He pulled me close.

I said, "What do you mean calm down? What if I don't come back? I'm so goddamned terrified. Don't you know how serious this is?"

"I'll be here waiting for you," he purred. "Not here, you know, but in Vegas, ha, ha."

"It's not funny. And a year is so far away."

There was a knock at the door and Evan paid the pizza guy as I tried to remember the last time I'd eaten, not that I felt like eating now.

"You have to eat." He held a slice in front of my mouth and I said, "I don't want to. All I want is to press my body against yours."

"You can press it right after you eat." He giggled as if none of this was sinking in for him, and I took a bite then fell back onto the bed and waited until he finished his slice before he laid down again, pulled me close, and stroked my hair.

"We're perfect together," I said, not wanting to fall asleep so I could remember this moment forever.

"We are," he agreed. "Well, at least six out of seven days. It's that seventh day I don't know about."

"You mean like when you call the cops on me because I want to talk and you only want to play video games?" I snapped, recalling one of the bigger fights we had that spiraled way out of control.

He said defensively, "It's just what my dad told me to do. You know he was a cop. He was just watching out for me so I wouldn't go to jail again."

"Great advice from a guy who also told you 'the world needs gravediggers' which implied you wouldn't amount to a damn thing."

"You know how much that upsets me." He recoiled his arm from me and I said, "I'm sorry," although I didn't feel sorry at all. I was on a journey to my death and he was lecturing me.

Then he pulled me close again and said, "Don't worry. I love you. I'll be here for you, okay?"

And I nuzzled my head into his chest again and said, "Okay," because I believed him.

THIRTY-SIX

The hallway jumped to life at six a.m., and as I listened to the *hooahs* and slamming doors, I was surprised that anyone could be this excited about taking a plane today knowing we were going to whatever place it was to die.

Evan was sleeping as peacefully as though we were in a hotel room in Hawaii, and I writhed in pain as I tried to get up to take a shower because the EMT had been right. I did feel like I'd been in the rink with Mike Tyson.

"Not so fast," Evan grabbed my wrist suddenly. "I can't send you to war without having sex."

"That's the last thing on my mind," I said, trying not to cry. "This is it. This is all the time we have because you need to get to the airport and I need to get to the hospital. I can't move."

"Come on," he kissed me, and I said, "Okay," and climbed on top of him, hoping it would be over as quickly as usual, but it was a struggle. He went limp several times and I started crying, "This is the last time we're ever going to have sex again."

Finally when it was over he said, "I'm going to grab a smoke while you shower," and I cried there too wishing he had gotten me pregnant, wishing there was any way in the world I didn't have to leave today.

When he returned, he tossed my cell phone on the desk.

"Keep it with you," I said. "That way I can call you from wherever it is I'm going."

"If I wanted a cell phone I would have bought one already," he sighed.

I snapped, "You're really going to make me beg for you to take my cell phone? You're unbelievable! So when I get shot out there, wherever I'll be, and you're out drinking and smoking and laughing it up, no one will be able to reach you! I'm paying for the damned thing. You don't have to spend a dime!"

"Alright, alright I'll take it," he threw his hands up and said, "I called a cab while I was out there. It should be here any minute."

Bursting into tears, I hugged him and said, "Oh, Evan, please don't go."

"I love you. It's going to be okay." He kissed me and I got dressed.

A few minutes later, we were outside, the cab already waiting, making me wonder how time could fly so fast when you didn't want it to.

"You're going to be alright." He held me tightly, and as if we were instantly transported to the airport, the cab stopped. Evan's hand was on the door, ready to leave.

"Give me your shirt," I said, and he pulled it over his head without hesitation. I held it to my face and inhaled his smell, wondering how I'd survive without him, and watched as he pulled out a sweatshirt from his backpack and put it on.

"Bye," he said anticlimactically and closed the door.

I watched him disappear into the terminal without turning back, and I thought about running after him, running away with him and going into hiding, but I couldn't move.

"Hospital," I said, picturing Evan's life without me, smoking up his room and going out without me. It just wasn't fair. We'd come so far only to be separated like this.

Less than fifteen minutes later I was in the ER waiting room on a metal folding chair against the wall. Old people were all around me waiting as if they'd been waiting for days, and I stared at the clipboard and the paperwork I was supposed to fill out, distracted by the ticking clock above my head, reminding me that time was running out. I was going to die.

Then I noticed a phone on the wall and reached above someone's shoulder to get the receiver. I tried dialing my tower and screamed, "Mandy, it's me!" when I heard her voice, surprised the call had gone through.

"It's really you, Jen," she shrieked, and then, as if she was trying to keep it a secret, whispered, "I'm glad you're okay. Evan called about an hour ago and said you were in an accident and requested that someone else go in your place."

"He did that?" I whispered back, wishing I could propose to him at this very moment. "I'm at the hospital now wondering what they'll say because I can barely move. I'm not sure if I can go."

"Well, the Chief is flipping out and he told someone over the phone that he didn't care whether you broke your neck, that you were going because he was teaching you a lesson."

"What lesson is that?" I fell back into the chair and had the attention of everyone in the room.

"Beats me," she replied. "We've been wondering the same thing. But it sounds like you're okay and that's all that matters."

"Oh crap, they're calling me, I have to go," I said and hung up, then followed the nurse down the hall and I told her, "I'm deploying today. I mean, I don't know when or anything, but I got into a car accident yesterday and it's hard to breathe. It's hard to move."

"The doctor will see you right away." She read my pulse then flipped through my questionnaire before she disappeared.

It was another hour and a half before a doctor entered the room and said, "Stand up, airman Grillo," as if he didn't have a care in the world. Then he patted me down like he was airport security and waved at the nurse for his clipboard and said, "You're fine. I'll prescribe Motrin and some muscle relaxers, maybe some sleeping pills too. You're probably still under shock if you're feeling jittery. Just don't lift anything heavy for the next two weeks."

"I'm deploying for a year," I followed him down the hall. "My suitcases weigh a ton. Don't I need x-rays? Or maybe you want to tap my knee with a hammer?"

"Have a nice flight, airman," he chuckled.

I said, "But, Doctor…" but he turned away.

The nurse snapped her head at me and said sternly, "The pharmacy is over there and your order should be ready now," and I stopped begging. I was going and there was nothing I could do about it.

Approaching the counter, I noticed five pill bottles waiting for me, two the size of ice cream pints.

"Are these for me?" I flashed my I.D. at the technician, studied the label with my name on it, and said, "There must be some kind of mistake. This is a lifetime supply. I didn't even take anything when I broke my wrist."

She shrugged as if it wasn't her doing, and said, "I would have given you a bag, but we don't have one big enough."

"Macy's doesn't have one big enough," I said. She frowned and walked away, leaving me in this conundrum. What to do with all these pills? I'll be a junky by the end of the week.

Then I glanced at the clock. It was nearly two. I decided I'd better get back to the dorm because I didn't know what time the flight was leaving, and hurried down the hall looking for a payphone to call a cab.

"Where the hell have you been?" George ran up to me in the dorm as if he'd been waiting for me. He was dressed in his DCU's and for the first time that I'd ever seen, frantic. "Where are your keys? We have to leave now! The bus is waiting for us!"

"Now?" my voice cracked. "I'm not ready now. I got into an accident and Evan was here and I had to get meds…"

"You have to get ready." He reached into my pockets until he found my key. Then he unlocked the door and ordered, "Get your DCU's on. I'll take this suitcase already and come back for the next one and you'd better be ready. Hurry! We're the last ones."

"George!" I wanted to argue but he was already gone.

I quickly put on my DCU's and before I could button my shirt he was back, pounding on the door, "Ready?"

"No," I almost started crying, but he didn't notice. He tossed the key on my desk and reluctantly, I followed him down the hall and outside.

"Aren't you excited?" he smiled.

"Excited about what?" I asked, surprised. I wanted to hit the stop button and rewind. I wanted to go back home.

"Very funny," he said, and we boarded a bus where I didn't recognize a single face, and I sat in my own row and leaned my head against the window until I remembered my camera. I dug it out of my bag.

"Good idea," George popped his head up from the row in front of me.

I said, "Hey, give it back," as he snapped a picture of me with my eyes closed and my hand reaching up at him.

"Hey guys, smile!" he shouted at the rows behind me, and although I wasn't sure if they smiled or not, he snapped the picture.

Then the bus lurched forward and he dropped the camera into my lap. I put it back in my bag, having lost interest in taking a picture. When I glanced up, I noticed the street had turned to tarmac and on it stood a C-141, waiting for us with its cargo hatch open.

"Come on," George pulled me out of the seat. Once outside he said, "Wait here," and I stood in line waiting to get swallowed by the C-141 as George handed our luggage to the crew guys, who quickly stacked them onto wooden pallets and shrink wrapped them into place.

The line moved slowly, like how I imagined it would at the slaughterhouse, and less than a minute later we were inside the belly that resembled a warehouse, not a plane, with its exposed beams and seats along the wall, and not the middle, where there were pallets stacked high with water bottles and boxes.

George didn't seem concerned at all. He sat down and chatted up the guy next to him. The guy next to me simply nodded his head at me, starting and ending our conversation in the same second, which was fine by me.

I took off my boots because my feet always swelled on planes, and strapped myself to the jump seat and prayed my death would come fast, before I could even think about it.

"I'm Dave," one of the crew members announced through a microphone from the front of the plane, like he was a standup comedian getting ready to do a set. "Every seat in this beautiful C-141 is taken and our first stop for the night is North Carolina."

The engines roared to life and I wondered why no one else looked scared.

"As you can hear we're getting ready to go. One last thing, there might be a slight chance we divert to Canada and in that case we'll be delayed..." and I didn't hear the rest as I silently chanted, Canada, Canada, oh please let's get diverted and break down for a year in Canada. But who was I kidding. Satan had booked me a one way ticket to hell.

We lifted off and I said goodbye to Evan, my life, and my destiny, because I was no longer in control of it. It was in control of me.

THIRTY-SEVEN

It was cold and dark when we landed in North Carolina. We crossed over the tarmac, my hot breath in front of me, jet fumes and Goretex coats all around. I envied them all for being warm, for having had time to pack and say goodbye to their loved ones.

Inside the terminal, we signed a clipboard in exchange for a box lunch, a nasty Saran Wrapped sandwich, a bag of chips, and a cookie, then dispersed to different areas of the terminal, as if there was any privacy or any way to get comfortable in a place without seats.

George had found a friend and I plunked myself in front of the bathroom, wondering what Evan was doing and why there wasn't a working phone around here. Then I wondered what I was going to do for the next three hours, and rummaged through my bag for a magazine, until I rediscovered my magic pills that could make all my gloom disappear.

"What are those?" A scrawny guy stopped in front of me, stood akimbo, and studied the large bottle in my hand until I shoved it back in the bag.

"Nothing," I said as if I'd done something wrong.

"Doesn't look like nothing," he said anxiously, which made me study his pale face and dark rings under his eyes as if he hadn't slept in a month.

"You want 'em? Take them all," I handed him the bottles because I'd rather feel pain and wallow in self-pity than look anything like him.

"You mean it?" He smiled like a thief in a vault.

"Yes, but you didn't get them from me, okay?" I called after him, but he ducked in the bathroom.

Somehow, three hours passed and we boarded the C-141 for Baltimore, which might as well have been a flight to nowhere because when we landed everything was just as boring and redundant as North Carolina: dark cold tarmac, jet fumes, box lunch I still wasn't hungry for, and no damned phones.

The déjà vu returned three hours later when we boarded again, this time for Frankfurt, Germany. By the time we were airborne and I'd closed my eyes, thinking how I was sick of all this already, the chatter about the airport circulated. People said the civilian side was so close to the military side that you could practically skip a rock over to it, which meant nothing to them but everything to me.

I'd flown in and out of that airport a million times as a kid and knew the place blindfolded. I spoke the language, and without the uniform I fit right in. I could sneak over to the civilian side and no one would know I was running away from the military and the war. All I had to do was find a phone once I was across and call Mom, who'd bring me a change of clothes and take me back to Berlin and hide me there for the rest of my life, if need be. It was foolproof.

I awoke just as we touched down and for the third time in I didn't know how many hours, walked across a tarmac. It was cold and dark, as if the sun was never going to rise again, and the air was thick with the smell of bitter jet fuel that I swore I never wanted to smell again.

It started snowing, and I uncrossed my arms and watched as the snow melted in my hand as if I'd never seen a snowflake before. Then I glanced at all the warm Goretex coat wearers and felt a stabbing pain of envy in my chest until I was blinded by the lights from across the airfield. They hadn't been kidding about how close the civilian side was, I could taste the freedom like the stinging jet fuel, and my heart pounded as I fell back to the end of the line, gearing up to make a run for it.

I pictured my life in hiding for the next sixty years, either that or jail, and was brought back to reality. It was no better than the death sentence I was serving and obediently, I entered the terminal knowing that in another life, I'd have the guts to live the life of a spy.

Inside were endless rows of ugly orange bucket seats, underneath endless rows of hideous neon lights. I plopped down and stared at the Plexiglass wall across from me where behind it, soldiers like us were going where we'd just come from.

"They're going home," the guy next to me plucked a headphone bud out of his ear and said. "Before you know it, it will be us."

"When?" I gasped, excited he knew something, but the bud was back in his ear and I stood up in search of a phone and a clock that didn't seem to be moving backwards.

The only thing I stumbled upon was the guy who'd taken my pills from me two airports ago, passed out on the floor, his backpack a pillow, and drool running down his face. In the bathroom I nearly knocked into Espinoza, who stood by the door in a towel combing her wet hair, as if I'd accidently walked into her hotel room.

She was the only Hispanic girl on the flight, the other two girls were brunettes I couldn't tell apart because they'd been crying on each other's shoulders since we left.

"What?" Espinoza snapped, but I couldn't ask her why the hell she was showering and shrugged, "Nothing," and wished I'd thought to pack a towel and shampoo in my carry on.

"I don't know when we'll get to shower again," she said defensively, and I couldn't get the air out of my throat to ask what she meant by that. I almost didn't want to know.

Then I went back to the bucket seat until the announcement came over the speakers that we were ready to board. I found George at the door. He beamed, "Ready?"

"No," I followed him out.

"Lighten up," he shoved my shoulder.

"Don't want to," I strapped myself to the jump seat a minute later, untied my boots, and exhaled in preparation for the final leg of the trip.

"Jen, can you believe we're halfway around the world?" George whistled.

"I can't," I closed my eyes to tune him out and eventually he gave up and I fell asleep.

When I awoke, I wished I hadn't, because the nightmare was still reality. The plane was eerily quiet, everyone's head cocked to the side with his or her mouth agape in deep sleep, except for two guys playing with the beam of sunshine coming from a small window from the door at the front of the plane, and I thought, who knew, there was sunshine in hell?

Curiosity got the best of me. I stepped over countless sleeping legs until I was by the door where one of the guys offered, "Take a look. Isn't that gorgeous?"

"Uh-huh," I lied. There was nothing but bright clouds: no land, water, or anything that gave away where we were going.

Then my stomach dropped as we descended and Dave suddenly appeared with his microphone and woke everyone, announcing, "Good morning! Rise and shine! We're here!"

Goosebumps covered my arms as I hurried to my seat, thinking this was all going way too fast. I wasn't ready to land yet, I didn't want to be here. But the flight didn't stop for me. We landed, rolled out in a matter of seconds and stopped, and Dave hurried to the door and opened it. Sunshine flooded the cabin and I was pushed to the front, out the door and off to the side as if I was the only one blinded and paralyzed.

Through my fingers, I peeked at my new world and saw nothing but blue. Then I moved my hand and saw why. There was nothing out here but sand and sky as far as the eye could see. Sure, there was a runway, a very tiny one, and a very tiny tower with an unidentifiable flag painted on the side.

There were no clouds, birds, not even a smell, and if I was still in Vegas and drove twenty miles in any direction this was where I'd end up, this would be where the mob buried their dead, and I suddenly wished it was that easy to trick my brain into believing that. I could picture Satan on the floor of his office laughing now. It was a miracle the pilot had found this place, but that was just a fluke. No one would ever find it again.

"Come on!" George hollered, walking away as if he had somewhere to be.

I caught up, but only because I didn't want to be left alone. I searched the horizon past the few trees and buildings, but found nothing resembling civilization, and no one else seemed to care!

About a mile from the runway, we dropped our bags in the sand and everyone started talking as if this was a social function. I glanced back and noticed life on this planet. In the distance were two young kids kicking a soccer ball in the dirt, a mother looking on, and two obviously foreign soldiers in dark green BDU's smoking cigarettes. Their faces were too far away to read and I wondered, were we enemies, friends, and decided to take a picture nonchalantly until I realized I couldn't find my camera.

"My camera is gone!" I spilled the contents of my bag in the sand, but no one looked at me.

A Staff Sergeant approached me and said, "What's going on?" I read his name, "Everitt," and thought, who appointed this four striper leader of the pack?

"I left my camera on the plane," I said just as a forklift pulled up behind him and dropped a pallet.

He turned around and ordered, "Unload it guys," and everyone who'd been standing around attacked it like vultures on a carcass.

"I have to go back to the plane."

"Okay," he frowned, but my heart fluttered with the thought of getting back on the plane and accidently flying out of here, until he said, "Hey Wilson! Go with her!" and to me, "Hurry back."

I sprinted towards the airfield without looking to see if Wilson was actually behind me. I was going to search that plane high and low until I looked up and saw the C-141 over my head, airborne, and watched it until it became a tiny speck in the sky and then disappeared.

Wilson caught up to me and I said, "Just my luck."

"God wanted to teach you something," Wilson replied, and I turned away before I slapped him.

I hustled back and heard Everitt announce, "Alright boys and girls, let's build tent city!" That made everyone explode into cheer and I thought, what tents, what city? George and I are Air Traffic Controllers, why are we building tents?

Then a figure appeared in the distance, a man in BDU's like ours but with a ranger hat where the sides were pinched in, and I nearly jumped for joy that we weren't the only ones here!

Everitt intercepted him a few feet away from me and I thought I was lucky to get to eavesdrop, until I heard the Army guy mumble, "First plane here, no one else…" and wanted to die. Everitt didn't even blink and everyone else was so damned happy, as if this was a camping trip.

Then the Army Ranger tipped his head and walked back to wherever he'd come from, the forklift dropped another pallet, the last one in a row of six before it too disappeared for good, and we were left with two Port O'Potties, two pallets of luggage, one stacked with bottled water and another with those blasted MRE's I thought I'd never eat again, and two with all the tent stuff.

That was it.

THIRTY-EIGHT

Esposito stood next to her cot and combed her hair in the faint glow of the flashlight as I tried to get comfortable inside my warm sleeping bag on top of a sagging cot.

"Aren't you at all scared?" I said, trying my best to ignore Martine and Nichols, the two criers who still hadn't stopped crying, or else I'd start crying too.

"It's nothing." She shrugged as I imagined a cool Bond Girl would and cast a sideways glance when Martine and Nichols sniffled louder. "What's a year in the span of your lifetime?"

"Uh-huh." I slumped into the sleeping bag, shivering until I'd zipped it up completely, feeling like a human taco and as if Esposito and I were on two different planets.

"Goodnight," she clicked off her flashlight abruptly.

I said, "Can you turn it on again?" and dug in my suitcase until I found Evan's shirt that I could use as a pillow since I'd forgotten to pack one. "Okay, got it." I nearly choked when I smelled him. There was no way I was going to last a year out here without him.

It was still pitch black when I heard Everitt's voice. "Ladies, it's time to wake up."

His boots crunched in the dirt as he walked away and I wanted to ask him, how did he know it was time to get up? Whose schedule were we on? But Esposito questioned nothing. She got up like a well-oiled machine, clicked on her flashlight without missing a beat, stripped out of her pajamas, wiped down her entire body with a baby wipe, and stepped into a fresh set of DCU's that even had her name sewn on the pocket.

I followed her lead, minus the baby wipe, and felt better with a fresh pair of socks and underwear on. Then I cringed when I pulled my greasy hair back into a ponytail and noted that I never wanted to see my zit-loaded face again.

Martine and Nichols were still huddled in the corner, and as much as I wanted to ask how they were doing, I knew they'd drag me down with them and I'd be just as messed up as they were, so I followed Esposito outside.

There were clusters of white flashlight dots in the sand, people waiting in line by the Port O'Potties or brushing their teeth next to the water bottle pallet. I had not packed a flashlight because I didn't own one and even if I did, I wouldn't have thought to bring it. Then someone handed me his and because I didn't want to hold up the Port O' Pottie line, I felt that I couldn't argue about not wanting to go in. It beat digging a hole in the sand, but still I cursed Satan under my breath for sending me to a place that didn't even have a real bathroom.

By the time I opened the door, the sun was coming up and I saw Everitt staring out into the distance, wearing his Goretex coat and sipping from a metal cup, as if he was deep in thought and as if he'd done this before.

"Chow time!" he called out sleepily, and minutes later we walked towards the runways where off to the left stood a small white square building, our cafeteria.

I nearly ripped down the door, I was so happy we didn't have to eat MRE's and was even more excited when I saw what resembled eggs and toast, even though it was covered in curry. Four foreigners in jeans and t-shirts loaded our plates with food from behind a counter. In my case they missed the plate and plopped it onto the tray because they couldn't stop staring at my blonde hair, and I smiled curiously, were we enemies or friends?

"Come on. Scoot in between!" George waved me over to his crowded table once I'd made it into the main dining hall, but I shook my head, opted for an empty table instead, and watched the sunrise from the window.

"Hi," a bald guy with a friendly smile smacked his tray on the table. "I'm Robert. From Nebraska. Where are you from?"

"Vegas," I replied, glancing at all the empty tables around us that he could have easily chosen over mine.

"Wow, Vegas!" he marveled like a little kid, making him look even more handsome than a second ago. "That's exciting!"

"Not really, unless you're a drinker and a gambler," I shrugged, suddenly feeling the urge to do both.

"It beats Nebraska," he laughed. "Do you know what's in Nebraska?"

"No," I admitted.

"There you go."

"Well, you're certainly not in Nebraska anymore," I replied, and when he smiled I asked, "Have you been deployed before? Because I haven't."

"Don't worry," he glanced at my hand as if he wanted to touch it. "Every day, more planes will come in, more people, more supplies and equipment. Pretty soon this will be a huge tent city, with an AAFES and a gym…"

"Here? Who's going to find us out here? Doesn't that mean we'll be a bigger target?"

"Don't worry." He ate some oatmeal, which made me notice his wedding band.

"You're married?" I thought of Evan and how I ached to be with him. "Isn't it hard to be away?"

"Seven years. Four kids, three of them girls," he nodded sadly. "I've missed a few Christmases and this year it'll be birthdays. That's the hardest part. But when we get phones it'll be easier. She takes care of everything while I'm gone, she's great. You married?"

"I have a boyfriend, but it doesn't compare to what you have. What about the Army guys around here?" I changed the subject.

"I don't know," he bit into his toast indifferently.

"There are other people here besides us!" I shrieked. "It's like we've found life on mars, and you don't care?"

"No."

"Okay, what about running? Do you think we can at least get into shape while we're here?"

Evan wouldn't be able to resist me if I came back with a killer shape and much longer hair.

"I'm not sure," he said pensively, "But I'll run with you when Everitt lets us know. I need to get into shape too and I already know you won't be able to run alone here because of the Middle Eastern customs. Deal?"

"Deal," I shook his hand tightly and wondered how it could be possible for me to fight in a war but not run around in the sand by myself.

"Let's go, Jen," George walked past our table holding his tray.

"See you around, Robert," I jumped up.

Out front George stood next to a pale skinny guy with black hair parted to the side and a small purple scar on his left cheek as if he'd been stabbed with a pencil years ago.

"This is Stu," George beamed. "He does survey work, and said he needs two people to help him! We're going to follow him around today, which means we don't have to build tents."

"Hi, Stu!" I shook his hand eagerly. "I could kiss you! I hate building tents!"

"I need to get a few things from the tent," Stu said so softly that I couldn't tell if he was just really shy or hated being here as much as I did.

Fifteen minutes later I crossed off sad as he was fidgeting with one of his tools and smiled, revealing his crooked teeth. "Alright, I got it. I'll put it in the back of the truck and we'll be on our way."

"What truck?" I looked around and saw nothing. Then he nodded as if to say, of course a truck, you don't think I'm going to walk around all day, do you?

Then he disappeared for ten minutes and, no kidding, drove up with a small white pick-up truck as if he'd found a genie lamp behind the tent and wished it to be so.

"Come on already!" Stu waved at George and me as we both stood dumbfounded.

"There's even a radio?" I said as he adjusted the setting and Whitney Houston belted a tune. It was unbelievable that she was out here with us!

For no apparent reason Stu stopped the truck, hopped out, and said, "Turn up the dial and keep the doors open so we can hear the music."

From the back of the pick-up he whistled, studied his tools, and looked out into the distance as if calculating something and didn't care to share it with anyone and I thought of all the people we'd arrived with, he was by far the coolest.

"I want you here." He pointed for me to stand about twenty feet from the truck. "You'll be doing a lot of standing today. I need you as a reference point. George, you follow me and hammer the stakes into the ground behind me. We're going to plan out tent city. Bathrooms, the gym, you name it. I'm not sure of the exact number yet, but it's going to be big. Better safe than sorry."

I almost laughed because there was no way in hell anyone else was coming to this deserted place, no matter what he and Robert said, but I said nothing in case he'd forgotten that George and I were Air Traffic Controllers and had no business helping him plan a city.

"Stick out your hands." Stu pulled a big bag of sunflower seeds from his pocket and filled our palms. Then he stuffed his cheek with a handful and said, "I can't work without seeds and I don't expect you to."

Tina Turner hit some high notes behind me as I popped seeds into my mouth and watched as George and Stu walked away and hammered random stakes into the ground. I couldn't remember the last time I had sunflower seeds or that they tasted that good, and made a note to ask Evan to send me some whenever we got phones, along with a pillow.

Then my eyes fell on to the few trees and houses in the distance and I wondered about the people who lived in them and if we were ever going to see them. When I smelled cigarette smoke, I spun around thinking it was Stu, and said, "Stu, I didn't know you smoked," until I saw it wasn't him, but a foreigner wearing jeans and a plaid shirt, construction helmet and steel toed boots like mine, and most importantly, a cell phone clipped to his belt.

"Excuse me! Excuse me!" I hurried after him. "Do you speak English? Can I use your phone?"

He didn't stop or glance back so I jumped in front of him, pointed at his belt, prepared to wrestle it away from him if he kept moving, and said, "Your phone, please," as if it was going to be the last call I was ever going to make.

He looked around as if someone was watching but said nothing as he handed the phone to me. I wanted to squeeze him, but I was paralyzed. My hands shook as I dialed the area code and thanked God for having lived in Germany and therefore knowing all the right area codes to push.

"Come on Evan!" I pleaded with the dial tone, but it was my recorded voice that picked up and I almost couldn't believe he didn't answer. What if I was dying at this very moment!

I dialed his room next, but his machine picked up too and as much as I wanted to hang up, when I heard his voice I started crying. "I miss you so much Evan. You have no idea. I wish I could talk to you."

The foreign guy glanced at his boots as I hung up, so I stared down at mine and noticed Ryan's dog tag and dialed his number. Only the foreigner had had enough of me and yanked the phone from my hand and stormed off.

"Thank you!" I called after him.

"What did that guy want?" Stu startled me from behind.

I said, "I don't know. He didn't speak English," and quickly wiped my face with my sleeve.

"Huh. Well, it's time to eat," he smiled, and we followed him back to the truck and got in.

"What's going on over there?" I pointed at two large trucks in the distance dumping white rocks close to our tents.

"They're putting down limestone." Stu turned Celine Dion down and explained. "When I was deployed in Ahmahanaj," he said, "the storms hit before we could get the stone spread out and our tents and everything we had washed away in a mud river."

"Great," I said, deflated. "Not only do we have to worry about war, but natural disasters too?"

"You two should really have coats and goggles," Stu scratched his head. "You don't want to be caught in a storm without them. There's a hangar somewhere behind the revetments, where Everitt works, and that's where they keep all of the supplies. Let's head there now. George doesn't even have his own sleeping bag, he's borrowing one."

"Oh, that Satan!" I growled but George didn't say a word, not until we'd arrived at supply and Everitt shook his head remorsefully.

"Sorry, but you should have gotten them through clothing issue. I don't have the authority to order them, but once we get phones, which should be any day now, you can call your orderly room and have them send some for you."

"Don't you worry, Jen," George balled his fists, the most heated I'd ever seen him. "Once we get phones, I will call Satan every day until I get my own sleeping bag and our coats!"

"Then we'll never get them!" I laughed, but George was serious and said, "The hell we won't! He doesn't know who he's messing with."

Nodding, I let him settle with the false hope that Satan would come through for us and we got back in the truck and drove to the cafeteria, where the lunch menu was curry rice, curry green beans, and curry shrimp.

"Nasty!" George dropped his fork in disgust.

"It is not that bad," I said and Stu agreed, "Yeah," but George was on a roll.

"These shrimp haven't been deveined. There's still shit in them! We are eating shit!"

"It's really not that bad." I wished he'd calm down, because what was a little shrimp shit compared to being plucked from your life, waiting to die?

And then, as if it was divine intervention, there was the sound of an engine clear as day above us. I shrieked, "Stu! Is that a plane?"

"No, it's Superman," George snapped.

"It's absolutely amazing!" I ignored him. "A miracle of all miracles! If planes are coming in that means more will be going out, and if they're going out, I want to be on one!"

THIRTY-NINE

The crowd parted as five high-ranking officers, so high I'd only read about them in the BMTM II text book, arrived. Everitt hurried in front of them and held the tent door flap for them, then called out to all of us and the thirty new airmen trailing behind, "Everyone in the big tent for a meeting," and frowned as though he was no longer in charge.

"Don't look so serious, you guys," a Captain, the lowest ranking of the bunch, stepped forward once we were all inside and smiled. What did he know? We didn't have bathrooms, showers or telephones, and it sounded like he wanted us to enjoy it.

I wanted to hate him for being such a smartass, but he seemed genuine, and his tall lean posture strong, as if he meant business. His lips parted as he introduced himself, but I was too distracted by his Boy Scout charm and heard nothing. All I could think was, hola Capi-tahn, bienvenido to hell, and I didn't even speak Spanish.

"Be excited!" he beamed, raising his arms like a prophet. "Being here, right here on the front line, is the safest place on earth! All the weapons are here, not back home. That's why I volunteered to be here, for the mission, because we're attacking the problem head on! We're going to win this in no time!"

I wanted whatever Kool-Aid he was drinking.

"There are rules, however," he spoke sternly. "Women, you're not allowed to walk around alone or wear short sleeve shirts or pants. I know it's too cold for that now, but when it gets warmer, you'll see, but that's part of being in the Middle East. That also means no drinking alcohol, ever! And if there are any runners in the group, like myself, there's a road behind the tents that loops around, close to the taxiways. There are cars on the road, but it will be safe…"

Safe?

"…It's two point two kilometers one time around. There's also a cafeteria, there'll be three meals a day there, and there's also a school house, not sure where it is yet, but I'll keep you posted. That's where the Army is staying and they have showers we can use until our shower tents come up…"

My jaw dropped. It took a flight of ranks to tell us we had showers!

"…Everyone dismissed," the Captain finished. "Except for the Airfield Ops personnel, that's my department."

That included George and me, which meant our tent-building days were officially over, hallelujah.

George and I and three other guys I didn't recognize stayed behind and waited. I studied the Captain's crow's feet and smooth cheeks as he crossed his arms across his chest, put a knuckle to his chin, and said, "Okay. Show of hands, who is ATC? Base Ops and weather? Okay, good. Our facilities should be up and running soon. Tomorrow we have an appointment to meet the Chief Controller of the tower. The Chief is a Colonel, but that's all I know. If I find out more, I will let you know at the five o'clock meeting. We will have one every day from now on and no matter what you will not miss that meeting under any circumstances because it pertains to our mission and is the only way we can communicate right now! The meeting will be in the men's tent, which will be sorted by squadron starting today. Not to worry, it will be easy to find. You're dismissed, unless anyone wants to add anything or think they shouldn't be here."

My hand shot up and George looked away, embarrassed, and I realized too late it had been a rhetorical question, but the Captain humored me anyway and said, "What is your name, airman?" as everyone else trickled out of the tent.

"Jennifer." I patted the front of my shirt where the tags would have been and said, "JG. I didn't get a chance to have the tags sewn on because I left in a hurry."

"You didn't have time to get your name tags sewn on yet, *sir*," he corrected me. "Sir is a sign of respect and I earned that respect and you are going to give me that respect. Do you understand?"

"Yes, sirrrr," I wished I'd kept my mouth shut.

"Good," he smiled, satisfied, not having detected my sarcasm, and said, "Also, get your tags sewn on by tonight. I have a kit if you need to borrow it."

"I'll definitely need to borrow it." I stopped, then remembered, "Sirrrrr."

His smiled broadened as if he was proud of me for catching on so quickly, and for a second I wished I could be a better soldier and appease the pole up his ass, but that wasn't me. All I wanted to do was go home. Now.

"So, airman, what were you going to tell me?"

His deep chestnut brown eyes stared into mine expectantly.

I knew I didn't have a shot at convincing him, but I drew a deep breath anyway and said, "I was on vacation. And my chief controller called me and I had a day to pack and I waited in Arizona, and now I'm building tents and I don't know how because I'm an Air Traffic Controller! And he sent me to teach me a lesson and didn't care if I broke my neck after the accident and I wasn't even on the list and after all these years I was finally getting things worked out with Evan."

His hands went up to his hips and his doubtful eyes studied me as if I'd said something in Chinese. Finally he said, "I'll check it out, airman," and turned so suddenly I knew he wasn't going to check anything out, and before he disappeared through the tent flap he said, "In the meantime, you need to calm down. You've only been here two days."

"Two days!" I stepped back as if I'd been speared in the heart. "It's felt like two weeks!"

But he was gone and I hopped in the truck with George and Stu again, wondering what I could have told the Captain differently to send me home that minute. Then we drove back out into the desert and worked until the sun went down, about 4:45 and I was starving, already tasting the curry chicken and rice in my mouth for dinner.

I changed into civilian clothes and waited for a full five seconds after I called out, "George! Stu! Let's go!" and thought maybe they hadn't bothered to change out of their DCU's and had left without me.

Quickly, I hurried after a group of people with flashlights in the dark and almost felt at home once I arrived at the cafeteria. Leering eyes, curry food, and Arabic scribed cans of Coke, my new favorite thing, were there as usual, but what wasn't there was a familiar face and I somehow couldn't shake the feeling that I was forgetting something.

Then I glanced at the clock and saw it was exactly 5:00 and remembered the 5:00 meeting that under any circumstances we were not supposed to miss. I jumped up and wished I could teleport myself back to the tent. I could not believe this was happening to me on the first day of him being here, after I'd begged for him to send me home. He was going to kill me!

I ran all the way back, until my legs and lungs were on fire, and screamed, "I'm coming in!" as I burst through the tent door.

"Capi-tahn," I shrieked, but was pushed back by the herd coming out. The meeting was over and I'd missed the entire thing.

"The meeting. I'm sorry," I squeezed my way through and nearly ripped the clipboard from his hands so he'd look at me. "I'm used to eating at this time and I forgot all about it!"

"Did you just call me Capi-tahn?" he raised an eyebrow.

"Shit," escaped my lips as I tried to catch my breath. "I mean sir. I'm sorry. I didn't mean that, sir!"

"No one has ever called me that." He suddenly chuckled as if he didn't realize I'd missed the meeting, as if he didn't even know who I was. "Get with one of the guys and they'll fill you in on what you missed. If you want to go to the schoolhouse, make sure someone goes with you."

"Okay," I nodded, dumbfounded. What had happened to the pole up his ass? This guy was awesome.

Eager to shower, I couldn't wait to get back to my tent until Wright, a Tech Sergeant with five stripes on his arms, blocked my path and said, "I am not going to stand here and allow you to disrespect an officer."

"Say again?" I replied, confused. Who was this guy, besides someone who'd come off the flight today and was now trying to tower over me even though he was my height and weight but thirty years my senior, with salt and pepper hair, and squinting at me like he needed glasses?

"You are to address the Captain by his title and name, understood?"

"Sure thing," I walked around him and ducked into my tent because I had better things to do. "I'm sorry, but I need to go and shower."

Although I wasn't supposed to, I took off alone to the schoolhouse and found it immediately, with the buff and nearly bald crew cut Army guys standing outside smoking in t-shirts and towel skirts, dog tags, and flip flops.

I must have been asked ten times if I was looking for the showers, probably the new pick up line around here, and nearly took off running down the hall once I heard the sound of running water.

"Watch where you're going," an Army guy scolded me when I opened the door to the men's shower. "Females next door!"

"Got it!" I replied, embarrassed, and opened the next door where there were three girls standing in wet hair and pajamas, combing their hair and brushing their teeth.

"Hey," the tiny brunette said as I walked past. "Don't open your eyes under the water. It hasn't been treated yet."

"Thanks," I said, suddenly tired. Why couldn't anything be normal around here? Did that mean there were bugs in the water?

Then I found the four blue tiled shower stalls, moldy and with the torn shower curtains barely hanging on their hooks, but I wasn't complaining. The water was hot to the touch. I undressed, tossed my shampoo bottles into the stall and got in, and stood frozen as I let the water melt all the grease and grime from my face and the aches from my body. Never again was I going to take a shower for granted.

When I was done and couldn't wait to fall into taco cot, I dressed into pajamas and combed my hair and was about to leave when I saw that the brunette had been waiting for me.

"Oh, hey," I said, deciding to brush my teeth there instead of by the tent. I asked, "How long have you been here? I thought we were the first flight down."

"A couple of weeks," she smiled. "But we're leaving tomorrow. Remember when you landed and saw the forklifts? That's my squadron. We fly out to all the new tent city locations, get on sight and set up hangars for supplies, then move out again."

"Oh," I replied, wondering where her secret squadron slept, because their tents weren't near ours. "Sounds pretty cool," I lied. "I'm a Controller, still waiting to start."

"We work the radios too," she got excited. "We use code words for all the things that are coming in, like grapes will mean ammunition, and lettuce might mean passengers. Every day it changes though, so in case the enemy is on our freq, they have no idea what we're bringing in. I know it doesn't matter since we're leaving tomorrow, but I'm Stefanie. I hope you have a good time out here."

"Me too," I sighed. "I guess it hasn't been bad so far, except that last night I heard fireworks, and I wondered who was launching fireworks all the way out here?"

"Uhm, those weren't fireworks," she stifled a laugh. "Those were bombs. But it was in the distance and not bad at all. I've been to places where we had to duck walking out of the tents."

"Not bad at all?" I coughed. I had a bone to pick with the Captain. "Well, it was nice to meet you, I need to go."

"Bye," she said, but I was already running down the hall and outside where I slammed right Robert, who didn't seem to mind at all.

"Woah, hey," he smiled, "Good to see you too. I've got good news, we can run tomorrow. The Captain approved it. What do you say I meet you at 5:00?"

"Sure, five, sounds good, I gotta go." I hurried past him and two minutes later was in front of the Captain's tent, huffing, "Capi-tahn I'm coming in!"

"You're such a good airman, JG!" He handed me his sewing kit as if he'd been expecting me.

"Thanks, but I'd actually…" forgotten, I wanted to say, until I saw his wedding band and wondered how lucky his family must be to have someone so prepared and so caring in their lives when I had Evan who barely even knew I existed.

"Why are you still in DCU's? Isn't it past nine? Or are those your pajamas?"

"I have a meeting," he said, amused.

"You're always busy," I teased.

"What else is there to do?"

"Well, I guess I'll let you get to your meeting and I'll return this kit to you later?"

"You can put it on my bed." He brushed my arm as he walked past me, making me wonder if it had been on purpose. Then I floated back to my tent, sank into taco cot and started sewing, wishing Mom was here to do it for me.

Once I finished, it looked so awful I knew I should rip out the thick, uneven Frankenstein stitches and start again. Then I realized I didn't care if someone could tell from a mile away that I'd done them myself. Satan would kill me if he saw it, and that made me laugh out loud. And for the first time all week, I fell asleep peacefully.

FORTY

My teeth chattered in the dark cold as I waited for Robert to show. I couldn't believe I'd gotten up this early and wondered if he'd had the same notion until I saw a flashlight dot in the sand approach me.

"I thought you weren't coming," I whispered once he was closer.

"I almost fell back asleep," he admitted, coming so close he nearly touched my nose. "I thought I wasn't going to see you either."

"Let's get this over with," I sighed.

"Take it easy on me," he added, although I was the one wheezing, regretting I'd made a promise to myself to get in shape.

But after a few minutes we found our rhythm, listening to our breathing in the silence, and before I knew it, I was glad I'd forced myself to get up. Finally, something other than tents and war! Then we went our separate ways, showered, and met at the cafeteria for breakfast as if we'd been in this routine for years.

"What's with all the food?" he joked when he saw I had twice what he had. "You preparin' for some kinda fight?"

"I'm hungry," I said defensively. "And you know breakfast is the only stuff around here that isn't caked in as much curry as the rest of the day!"

"Jennifer," the Captain suddenly stopped at our table as if he'd noticed Robert and I were having too much fun. "Meet me by the tents in fifteen minutes. We have official business today!"

"Ay, ay Capi-tahn," I replied.

The Captain walked away and Robert kicked me under the table as though he couldn't believe how casually I'd spoken with an officer.

"Ouch? What? He's so gung-ho in the morning and he never even sleeps. I guess I'll see you tomorrow, same time?"

"See you," he shrugged, and I left my tray and walked back to the tents and found a white van parked outside, with the Captain in the driver's seat waving me to come on already.

"This is ours?" I climbed into the front passenger seat and said, "Hi guys!" to George, Wright, and Simon, a shy guy who'd been on Wright's flight, sitting in the back.

"Yes," the Captain shifted into gear and stepped on the gas. "It's for the controllers and we'll get another one for Base Ops soon. The tower is exactly three point four miles from tent city and we'll be using the vehicles for shift change, once we figure out a schedule."

"It's nice," I replied, wanting to turn on the radio but restraining myself. Amazing how we could get trucks and vans at the drop of a dime, but no phones.

We traveled on a narrow crumbling street with few buildings and trees along the way. The gas station was the only thing I recognized, and as we zoomed past I wondered if the foreigner nationals, I just called them foreigners, who were getting gas even knew that Americans were on the base.

When we turned into the tower driveway the road turned to gravel, and we parked next to an old tan Mercedes under an overhang that looked like it would fall if I sneezed.

"Base Ops is next door, but we don't have the keys for the office yet." The Captain pointed left before he effortlessly opened the door to the base of the tower, which didn't have a single lock or code like I was used to.

The hallway was white marble and the solid double doors the Captain tried to open were a beautiful dark wood.

"It's locked. Let's try upstairs," he said, and we took the white marble staircase upstairs into a tower cab decked out with a large red Persian rug, a futon-style sofa with a wood frame, two chairs, pictures of Middle Eastern officials and a clock on the wall, and nothing on the consul but a wind dial and a fax machine.

The fifteen or so fat foreigners with dark skin and black mustaches snapped to attention and waited to shake the hands of the Captain and the guys in front of me, until it was my turn and I was treated as though I had leprosy.

"JG," the Captain coughed when he saw my bewildered expression. "Sit with me."

I sat and said nothing. Most of the foreigners cleared out, leaving three controllers and an old guy who I assumed was the Colonel from all the ribbons on his chest, and up the stairs came a man with a tray who wore a long white t-shirt like a dress and seemed almost too afraid to look at any of us.

The Colonel barely opened his mouth when the tray was placed on the table, but the servant jumped anyway as he quickly arranged shot glasses on all corners of the table, filled them with boiling hot tea the color of honey, bowed, and disappeared downstairs again.

"I am Colonel Salem," the old man said in surprisingly good English, reminding me of the Middle Eastern version of the Godfather. "Salem, because my name too hard to say. Chai?" he asked, but no one said a word.

"Don't be shy, drink chai," he chuckled, and we all laughed as if it was just what we needed to break the ice.

"What is your name?" he looked at me.

"Jennifer," I replied.

He smiled, "Genie? Your name we have in Arabic too, it mean ghost."

I nodded, hesitant to tell him that I knew all about Aladdin and Genie, because I still didn't know how much conversation we were allowed to be having. No one else said anything besides their names either and then Colonel Salem whispered something in Arabic, which made the three Amigos turn around and stare at the floor as if they were being disciplined.

"Bilal his name." Salem pointed at the guy in the middle who was the darkest and shortest from the bunch with a very black narrow mustache. "We say, Bolbol. It mean bird. Because he our little bird." All of them chuckled like school children then stopped abruptly when the Colonel said, "Moses," and the eldest stepped forward. His head was the size of a watermelon and his voice boomed, "Hello."

He made a point to nod at everyone but me, but no one seemed to notice.

"And that one Sami," the Colonel said, and the last one stepped forward. "That's his short name. If you look at his name written on his shirt, it's long. That his grandfather name, father name, and his name too, but we just say Sami."

Sami smiled at everyone, including me, which nearly made me fall out of my chair. Suddenly, I was fascinated and wanted to know everything about him, if he had a wife and kids, where they shopped, what they did on the weekend, what kind of car they drove, and what they liked to eat.

"All controllers are officers," Colonel Salem explained. "They do not live here. They fly here every week and only stay a few days. All controllers speak English because we send them to America and England to study, but speak English to them so they can practice."

The controllers turned around as if there were planes in the sky or even on the taxiways and the Colonel drew a breath as if he was about to start a lecture, until the Captain interrupted him.

"Colonel Salem. We are here to conduct exercises, training missions for the next few weeks." I nearly spit my tea across the table, "What is usual in situations like these is that we work together. When our planes come in, we talk. Your planes, your controllers talk. Two controllers for you and two for us until they get comfortable, then we'll just need one each."

Colonel Salem shook the Captain's hand and then both stood up as if they had something better to do although I wondered if the Colonel knew that the Captain had been lying. It wasn't that we were conducting exercises, we were moving in and building a city that was quite visible from the tower!

"Thank you for your time Colonel," the Captain nodded. "I have another meeting as well."

Once we were situated in the van again and on the way back, I couldn't keep my mouth shut any longer and asked, "What was that back there? How come I couldn't shake their hands and why are we lying to them if we're on their base?"

"First of all you're not allowed to work there," the Captain replied calmly, although my jaw dropped in protest. "Let me finish. And if you do work there you're not allowed to use the bathroom. I'm working on it. You can't take it personally, it's their custom."

"If that's their custom, then why am I here?"

"Remember, JG, we're at war," he ignored my comment. "My instructions are to be politically correct. I can't mouth off our business to the foreigners, especially when I'm still waiting on the mission."

"We don't have a mission yet?" I replied, dumbfounded. All this rush to get here for nothing, and what if our mission turned out to be killing everyone we just met?

"It will all come together," the Captain explained without explaining anything at all. "I'll see all of you at five."

Everyone dispersed into different directions. I opted for my tent and got the surprise of my life when I saw Esposito, Martine, and Nichols had moved out and six new girls had moved in.

"Hi?" I said like a question rather than a salutation.

"Hi, I'm Melanie," the first girl on the left said, rearranging her clothes in her suitcase and smiling as though she's waited her entire life to come here.

"Sweep the tent every time you come in!" the fat girl snapped.

I glanced behind me to make sure she really had been talking to me, and sized them up as Ying Yang twins. Both wore glasses and had pale skin, except that one was tall and skinny and the other short, fat, and snotty.

"I've been deployed before and that's how you keep the dirt out," she continued. I bit my tongue so as not to say, "Leave, that's how we kept the dirt out before you got here," and took a step forward, when I was confronted by an overweight black girl who looked me up and down as if she wanted to know what business I was there to conduct.

"You look just like Queen Latifah," I smiled. "You know, the rapper?"

"Well you look like a dumb cheerleader," she snarled. "Who the hell made you the welcoming committee?"

"Well, I did, since I was on the first plane here, but I guess you can figure out everything for yourself." I stalked away to my corner of the tent, wondering what kind of misfits had landed here, until I met the tall blonde who smiled sweetly and said, "I'm Joanne. I hope you don't mind, but the tent was a little smelly so I sprayed your perfume around."

"I guess not," I said in awe as to why she couldn't have used her own perfume, and moved on to the last two who, were in a shouting match about the temperature inside the tent.

"Lena," the skinny Hispanic girl shouted as if I wasn't there. "It's too hot in here! The thermostat isn't yours because your cot happens to be next to it!"

"No way Rosie, it's cold in here," the short chunky Hispanic girl replied with the most soft-spoken voice I'd ever heard. She combed her hair, unfazed by Rosie clucking like a chicken, and I was frozen for a moment, not only by her smooth skin and big black eyes, but at the diversity of the group.

How the hell were we going to fight a war like this?

FORTY-ONE

It was George and I who were assigned to work the first tower shift. At almost 5:50 a.m. the Captain handed George the keys through the front window of the van as we got in and smiled encouragingly. "If you need anything, I'll be at Base Ops. If I leave for a meeting I'll let you know. There's a box of MRE's in the trunk, if you can bring them upstairs. For just in case you can't leave the tower for lunch."

"Do you mean just in case the base gets blown up and we can't make it to the cafeteria?" I replied seriously, scanning the backseat. "How about some M-16's? I had to retrain to use them and I don't see any."

"Very funny, JG." The Captain tapped the side of the van as if he'd heard enough, and said, "And you shouldn't have any more bathroom issues. They've been resolved. Enjoy your day, airmen."

I made a thumbs-up and smiled as George gently accelerated, but meant it sarcastically because the bathroom was the least of my worries if I was still a leper to them.

When we arrived the two youngest soldiers were there, Sami and Bolbol and they seemed less excited about seeing us than we were about seeing them. They snickered as we sat down on the futon behind them and together we sat in silence, them with their eyes out the window and us studying the walls as the rising sun illuminated everything orange and yellow. Under any other circumstance I would've been in awe at how big the sun was on the horizon, but it reminded me of home, driving to the tower in the mornings, and made me feel invincible, which I clearly was not. I never wanted to see another sunrise as long as I lived.

Suddenly Colonel Salem crept upstairs, smiled, and asked, "Chai?"

We nodded, then he whispered something in Arabic, which made Bolbol and Sami jump up and join us immediately. A minute later a servant soldier came up with a tray, tea, and shot glasses. He left the tray on the table, bowed slightly, and left.

Salem reached for a glass and we followed suit. Then I caught a whiff of Bolbol and recoiled from his body odor. It was as though he hadn't showered in eight weeks or ever, but no one else noticed and I lifted my glass to toast and held my breath as I sipped the tea.

As if George's glass had given him courage, he said, "Are those your radios over there?"

"Yes, come!" Bolbol jumped up and waved him over excitedly.

Sami and I looked at each other indifferently. I didn't want anything to do with him and his archaic equipment, and he didn't want anything to do with me.

"Check this out, Jen," George cooed.

"Maybe later," I smiled at Salem, who stood up to leave.

He winked as though his mission was complete, he'd started us talking and now had to go, and then all hell broke loose.

The phone rang and Bolbol jumped up and down, laughing, "Look, look!"

Sami and I jumped up, and although Sami started laughing too, George and I couldn't see what was so funny about an old green pick-up truck doing circles in the middle of the air field with a rifle sticking out of the window.

Suddenly a shot fired and George and I ducked.

"Dog," Sami tapped my shoulder so that I'd look up.

"They're shooting a dog?" I peeked over the consul and saw a dog running for dear life, the truck after it as if it posed some kind of threat.

"Who cares about the dog?" George screamed. "They're pointing that rifle all over the damn place and waving it back and forth, pointing at tent city and the tower. They're going to kill someone!"

"No, no," Bolbol shook his head as if we'd misunderstood. "He try to scare dog, not kill."

"Oh boy," I sighed. What a bunch of knuckleheads we were sent to work with. These guys didn't care if they shot their own planes down!

Finally the truck sped off and a flight of two foreign F-4's taxied to the runway. From the speaker I heard the pilot request in Arabic what I assumed was takeoff, but as soon as Bolbol put the microphone to speak, Sami pulled it away from him and they took turns play-slapping each other until Sami got the upper hand, put Bolbol in a headlock, won the right to speak, and cleared the aircraft for departure.

The rinky dink fighters took off, thick dark smoke lingering way past after they disappeared, and I stood silently wondering what this circus was all about. How could we declare war on a country so primitive?

Then the radio sprang to life again, this time with an American pilot. "Tower this is Reach41, twenty miles out," and I wanted to jump up and down.

Bolbol handed the mic to George, who said, "Reach41, tower, wind calm, report five mile final," and I held my breath in anticipation, watching as the C-17 appeared in the sky and landed then rolled out on the runway, the Captain's truck hot on its trail so he could get their download information.

The Captain hopped up the short flight of stairs, where I pictured him negotiating my departure: yes I was ready to go, no, I didn't need my luggage. But minutes later skipped back to his truck and our radios didn't crackle. I was not going home.

The new troops made the walk to tent city and the C-17 closed its door and made the turn to take off.

"I'm going to the bathroom." I was ready to cry and hoped I could hold out until I got downstairs and could sob as loudly as I wanted to.

When I descended the marble staircase the C-17 engines rumbled past the tower, and for a second I thought about running outside and alongside it until it stopped, opened its doors, and took me with them. Then the sound was gone and I was downstairs, smack in the middle of a long narrow hall that reeked of old vinegar and cheese.

From all the windows along the ceiling it was brighter than I'd expected. I turned left, determined to open every door if I had to to find what I was looking for, and realized too late that all the doors were open and that I was in the servants quarters. I made eye contact with one of the servant soldiers boiling water in the kitchen. No wonder they didn't want me there- I wouldn't want some stranger in my living quarters either!

I hurried down the hall, but it was too late. Heads popped out from every door as if a silent alarm had sounded to witness the blonde soldier running down the hall.

The first door I tried was just a white tiled room with a hole in the middle of the floor and a vase standing next to it. My hand went to my mouth, I pinched my nose and tried not to throw up, and then let my hand fall again when I turned and saw the crowd and noted that their curiosity about me had doubled.

I opened the second door and ducked inside even though it resembled a concrete dungeon. There was a toilet- at least something that was once white and porcelain, perhaps a donation from Alcatraz, and I knew I shouldn't complain about something the Captain had fought so hard for, but why was it too much to ask to get a normal toilet around here?

When I dropped the toilet paper and flushed it swirled in circles, and I realized too late that's what the little trashcan on the right was for. Then I washed my hands from the trickling faucet, broke the gray sliver of soap into three pieces, and accidently pulled the frail nail from the wall that had been holding the rag I dried my hands with, making me feel like a bull in a china shop.

I took a deep breath before I opened the door and pushed my way through the crowd, then hiked up the stairs two at a time and found George and Bolbol still by the window and Sami with his feet on the consul, reading an Arabic newspaper. I peeked over his shoulder to get a better view of a picture of a woman and asked, "Who is that? She's beautiful. Doesn't she have to wear a scarf?"

I moved my hand in a circle around my face in case he didn't know the word for scarf. He nodded and said, "Varry be-you-tiful." His face turned serious and he said, "No scarrrf. Woman we-ar scarrrf only if she want to we-ar scarrrf. Many woman no we-ar scarrrf in the city."

He rolled his r's as if he was pronouncing them for the first time, and stifling a smile, I replied, "Oh," because I'd pictured it all very differently.

"What about him?" I pointed at a guy in jeans and a t-shirt in a movie ad, and he shrugged as if to ask, what else would he be wearing?

"George, are you hearing any of this? Women don't wear scarves and the guys wear jeans. I guess he'll tell me they go to college too."

George turned away as if to say "whatever, Jen" and Sami nodded, "Yes, school, of cour-rse!"

"What? That's not how we see it on TV."

"Okay," Sami stood up as if he was about to get serious and said, "TV, 90210. Everrryone be-you-tiful. Everrryone in Amerrrica be-you-tiful."

"You mean the show 90210 on TV?" I was surprised he'd seen it. "And you're asking if everyone in America looks like that? No, no, no, that is not America!" I laughed. "You think everyone eats hamburgers too?"

"Yes, hamburgers," Sami smiled as if I'd reassured him he was an expert on the U.S. I put my hand on my stomach and shook my head, "No, no, no!"

"Yes!" Sami insisted, and I said nothing because all I could think about was how lucky we were to work here. No one else from tent city got to work with the foreigners. No one else was having this much fun.

"How about you go to lunch first?" George said. "I don't feel like leaving. I'm not hungry but might have an MRE later."

"Suit yourself." I took the keys, excited to take the van and blast the radio on my own, but lost my thunder once I got to the cafeteria.

Al-Jazeera, the Arabic news channel, was silently broadcasting images of the country we were in and I was reminded how far away from home we were and that no matter how much we laughed together and shared stories, the soldiers in the tower and the civilians serving food in the cafeteria were not our friends.

When I returned to the tower Bolbol and Sami were gone. Moses and a tall officer named Omar were there, sitting at the table eating pita bread and hummus and listening to music that sounded like a whining bumblebee in my ear.

I sat down opposite George in one of the chairs but said nothing when they didn't look up in my direction. Even George was trying to look busy by looking out the window until a servant brought tea.

Moses said, "Here, chai," slid our glasses across the table, and added, "Try," and lifted the breadbasket in our direction.

It was the softest, fluffiest pita that I had ever tasted, and the hummus, loaded with garlic and spices I'd never tasted before and knew I'd never be able to emulate even if I did recognize them in the grocery store, ignited my senses. It was simply amazing.

Then Moses offered me an orange, but I shook my head apologetically and said, "I don't like the juice under my nails," and he retracted the offer. Effortlessly, he peeled the orange as if to show me there was nothing to it and handed it to me.

"Thank you." I took the orange, more confused than ever. A controller in the states might have peeled it for me, but one of them?

A few hours later the shift was over. George left a few minutes before 6:00 and drove to the city. He dropped the key off at the men's tent, where Queen Latifah and Simon retrieved it and drove back to relieve me.

I couldn't wait to fall into taco cot and sleep, dream that I was anywhere but here, but Rosie and Lena were chatting loudly. Rosie stood behind Lena, who sat Indian style on her cot, and combed her hair.

"Yeah," Rosie shrieked halfway through her story. "I thought I was checking in to a hotel until we stopped in front of the tent. I mean, what the hell! My boss said I was going to a paradise in the Middle East!"

I smiled, knowing that feeling well.

"I didn't know what to expect either," Lena sighed. "But I guess it's okay now. All I need is my soap to be happy. I feel so dirty here."

"Can you believe this shit? I was expecting a hotel!?" Rosie laughed louder, but my smile faded.

We were going to be stuck here forever, in this damned tent, in this damned country for absolutely no good reason whatsoever. I had a life back home, a boyfriend, friends, and now, nothing.

FORTY-TWO

A well-over middle aged man with a white Santa Claus beard, sunglasses, flip flops, and a Hawaiian shirt came up the tower stairs like he owned the place. I was on my own now, working with Omar, abiding by our unspoken agreement: if a foreigner came up, he dealt with him, an American, however, was all mine.

"Hi," I said enthusiastically, curious as to why he was dressed for the beach.

"Hey," he smiled back. He removed his sunglasses, revealing a deep tan line, and asked, "Is this where I file my flight plan?"

"You're a pilot?" I took his flight plan and stuck it in the fax machine, the only reliable equipment in the tower.

"I've been in the business for a while," he chuckled. "I fly the old Russian helicopters around here."

"Huh," I replied, because I hadn't noticed any helicopters and if I had, wouldn't have known the difference between a Russian or an American one. I said, "It'll be a minute. The machine is a little slow." I avoided his gaze and hoped he wasn't thinking what I was thinking: how the hell do we control traffic with all this old stuff that looks like it had been salvaged from an old World War II bunker?

Our radios were the size of a suitcase atop the consul and our computer, although newer, was just a souvenir from my former life because, just like the phone sitting next to it, it didn't work.

"Here you go." I handed Beach Santa his confirmation.

"Are you okay?" he surprised me by asking, because usually-astute Omar hadn't noticed a thing.

"I'm fine, really."

I hoped he'd leave, but he persisted. "You're not fooling anyone, you can tell me."

"It's my birthday tomorrow," I confided. Omar, absorbed in his bumble-bee chant music, didn't hear a thing.

"Well, in that case, Happy Birthday!" he sang.

"It's not happy at all," I snapped. "I've been here four weeks. I've missed my brother's and my dad's birthdays and who knows what else. Have you seen tent city? It's huge and getting bigger! We're never going home!"

"I'll bring you something tomorrow, okay? You'll be here, right?"

"I'll be here, but please don't bring anything. I didn't mean to vent like that."

"Nonsense," he waved. "It's your birthday. I have to bring you something."

"Where do you plan on going?"

"Leave it to me." He winked as if there was a secret mall in the distance I couldn't see.

Then he disappeared, and by the time I was on my way home and saw the new candy cane striped guard gate pole, a jovial pole that wouldn't deter a child, much less a terrorist who wanted to storm the city, I'd forgotten all about him.

"Are you open yet?" I stuck my head into the large post office tent a few hundred yards from the gate. Conveniently, it was located next to the gym and AAFES, which weren't open yet either, and although I figured they weren't open yet because the Captain would have told me if they were, it didn't hurt to check on their progress.

"Not yet, but…"

"Any day now?" I finished the woman's sentence, which made her laugh and made me want to cry. "Thanks anyway."

I drove past the new chow tents that were dark and depressing compared to the cafeteria but had to be built to accommodate all the new soldiers coming in. Next door was the new laundry tent; the old was forced to shut down as soon as the washers were turned on and the sand instantly clogged the pipes and permanently stained our clothes yellow. Now our laundry was picked up from one central tent and driven five hours to the nearest city, where they came back neatly shrink wrapped, covered in white powder as if we had fleas, and, as if something was in the water that just couldn't be avoided, yellow.

After I parked the van on the side of the tent, dropped the key in the men's tent and was ready to enter mine, I heard Rosie scream, "Wait, don't come in here!"

"Is everything alright?" I froze. "What's going on? Do you need help?"

"Just hang on!" She whimpered as if she'd broken her leg, then said, "Okay, now you can come in," as if it was nothing.

"What happened?" I glanced at her in her pajamas, holding her usual cut-off water bottle that she kept juice in. "You scared the crap out of me."

"Nothing." She stormed off, which wasn't hard to do since half of our tent had moved out- or rather, moved on.

Fatso was caught having sex with a guy in his tent, which was hard for me to believe because her attitude and body were so unappealing.

"It's true. I sent her away," the Captain had confirmed when I asked him about it.

"Why her and not me?" I'd argued. "You know I want to go home!"

"I didn't send her home, JG. I sent her to a more desolate place than here because she's married and fraternization is a direct violation of the United States Code of Military Justice. I don't tolerate that."

That kept me quiet until I walked into the tent and discovered Melanie packing her bags.

"I'm pregnant!" she'd beamed. "All this time we were trying and I didn't think to check before I left, and if they didn't waste three STD checks on me here, I would have found out sooner."

"Congratulations," I'd said, and although I could tell she wanted a hug, I'd been deep in a trance, reminded of how Evan and I had had the chance to get pregnant and didn't.

"You too?" I'd asked Joanne, who had nearly finished arranging her suitcase but unlike Melanie, who'd started humming, looked close to tears.

"Test results," she'd said, barely audible. "The Captain told me I had to leave and take care of it now, and all I want to do is stay and serve my country…"

But I'd walked away before I could hear the rest, wishing I had some bad test results that could have gotten me sent home too.

With that in mind, I was still in disbelief about Rosie and the kind of people I'd been put in a tent with and said, "That wasn't nothing," and followed her all the way back to her cot.

She stomped like a little kid in a temper tantrum. "You screamed at me not to come in here!"

"I couldn't make it to the Port O'Pottie, okay?" She spun around and thrust her hand in my face.

"No, not okay!" I smacked her hand away. "You're thirty years old and you can't make it to the bathroom, so you decide to pee and dump it right outside the tent that we sleep in? Are you out of your mind?"

"It's not a big deal," she turned away. "I took a nap and I couldn't make it, that's all."

"I don't know what to say to you right now." I wanted to storm off, but couldn't think of a place to storm off to. Then I stopped dead in my tracks when I saw Queen Latifah lying sideways on her cot like Cleopatra, reading a magazine and sucking her thumb.

"Are you sucking your thumb?" I was fired up.

"Yeah," she shrugged. "It relaxes me."

"You are what, twenty nine, thirty, and outrank me, but that, that, relaxes you?"

I left, ducked into the chow tent where I was pleasantly surprised to the see the Captain sitting by himself for a change.

"Capi-tahn!" I sat down across from him.

"JG, not now." He looked up from pushing curry peas around the plate and said, "I'm expecting some high-ranking officers here for a meeting."

"Figures." I folded my hands on the table, wondering what it would be like to sit across from him at dinner every night. "You know you should take care of yourself and not focus on the mission so much."

"I do. I run in the morning," he looked annoyed, which made me want to test his patience.

"Too bad, I haven't seen you, but moving on, it's my birthday tomorrow, can you send me home?"

"Oh, yeah, sorry I forgot, happy birthday and very funny, but no." He handed me a cookie from his tray and repeated, "Have a nice birthday, but you need to go."

"There was some old dude in the tower today," I bit into the stale cookie. "In shorts and flip flops and he had a white beard. Do you know who he is?"

"Probably CIA," he shrugged as if he didn't care. "They're all over the place."

"They're all over the place?" I sat down again. "The CIA. Is here? This guy was old, though!"

"JG, beat it!" The Captain glanced around and shooed me as two frowning men approached the table.

"Ay, Ay Capi-tahn!" I jumped up, suddenly excited about Beach Santa.

The phrase, "be careful what you wish for," didn't occur to me until later, when he indeed came back up to the tower the next day, handed me a paper bag, and said, "Told you I'd come back. Happy Birthday, enjoy!"

"Wait! Thanks," I called after him, but he was already gone. I nearly fainted when I opened the bag and saw the six-pack of Heineken.

"Genie, you okay?" Omar asked as I tightened the bag and unsuccessfully tried to stuff it under my shirt.

"Yes, fine, fine, fine!" I scrambled. The Captain was going to kill me for this! He wouldn't bother sending me to another base; he'd have a special kind of punishment lined up for me. He expected higher of me and therefore would be even more disappointed if he found out I had alcohol in a country where one drop got you the death sentence.

I could see the headlines: "International scandal caused by airman who wanted to have a Happy Birthday!"

He'd sent me straight to Leavenworth. And where was I going to hide six-pack in a city of a thousand alcohol deprived soldiers? They'd sniff it out in a second. Oh God, why did I have to be so sour? What had I gotten myself into now?

FORTY-THREE

"Lena, my underwear is missing!" I shrieked, standing in front of my cot and comparing my pile of yellow, powdered clothes to my receipt. "I mean really, all twelve, every single pair except the one I have on, are gone."

"They've got to be there," Lena chuckled as she stuffed her pile of clothes into her suitcase. Then she plunked herself on my cot, took the receipt from me as I rummaged through the pile again, and said, "That's the funniest thing I've ever heard. Are you sure you're not imagining things?"

"Who the hell would want used underwear? What kind of operation are they running here? I can't wash my clothes in the sink like you do. I don't have the patience anymore."

"Hey, my clothes are clean," she said defensively. "I let them soak all day and night, then scrub them until my hands prune."

"Because you're OCD," I replied. "It's not normal to get a box the size of a TV filled with Tide and body wash. You know that, right?"

"I'm not OCD." She glanced at the big box of soap her Dad had sent her. Recently divorced, she said he had to work two jobs. I couldn't imagine what the shipping cost had been, but it didn't bother her in the least because she couldn't live without it.

"It's not a bad thing," I said. "It's just surprising, that's all. Don't your clothes turn to rags from all the bleach and vinegar?"

"How'd you know?" She was stunned.

"Just a guess.. I hope Evan got my letter and sends the pillow I wanted. I can't believe it's taken almost six weeks to get the post office running, and the phones still aren't done!"

"Yeah, I'm going to have to send my Dad another request list too." Lena glanced at her package again. "That might last me two weeks."

"You're kidding, right?"

"I wish," she shrugged, and I wondered if I was as crazy as everyone else who was deployed here.

I asked, "Want to come with me to the laundry tent?" and knew she would because there wasn't much else to do to kill time. Even I had to lay off from the reading because I was starting to narrate everything in my head as if my life was a book.

"I'm sorry," the laundry girl said indifferently after I asked her what might have happened to it.

"What do you mean, 'sorry'?" I eyed her name tag to file a complaint until I realized it would probably be thrown into the trash. "All I want to know is how this could happen and how I'm going to get them back!"

"Here's a voucher that you can cash in when you get home." She tore a note from a receipt booklet as if this happened all the time and there was nothing else anyone could do about it.

"Oh, please," I slid it back towards her. "We both know we're never going home."

"That's nice." She marked the note and slid it back. It said, "value at eight dollars" and I almost jumped the counter and strangled her.

"What am I going to do with eight dollars on a receipt? I need underwear now!"

"AAFES will be open soon," she smirked.

"I'll take it for her." Lena stepped in front of me when my cheeks flushed, took the receipt, pushed me towards the door, and said, "We'll figure something out." Once we got outside and I screamed, "What a dumbass. Seriously, what the hell am I going to do with this? I need a damned phone." I kicked the dirt.

"I know," she replied, walking in the direction of our tents. "But there's nothing you can do now. Are you coming or what?"

"I need to cool off." I shoved my hands in my jeans pockets. "I'll see you in a while."

But a while turned into much longer when I discovered a long line outside the comm. Tent, right next to the bathroom and shower tents. Those had been a giant letdown, just like the chow and laundry tents if you asked me, because you still couldn't open your mouth and eyes in the water, which really made me want to do it. Scalding hot was the only temperature, and it was always dark because people felt the need to steal light bulbs.

"What's going on here?" I went to the back of the line as if I owned the place and yet somehow hadn't gotten the memo.

"Didn't you hear?" Two guys glanced at me, annoyed I'd interrupted their conversation, then turned back as if that had answered my question.

"No, what?" I stood on my tiptoes and saw nothing.

"Phones are working."

"Are you sure? Because I hadn't heard, the Captain didn't even mention they were close to being up. I mean, really sure? Because I don't think I could handle it if you weren't sure."

"Yeah." The guy on the left pointed at an easel by the door and read out loud, "One call per person, fifteen minutes only."

"Oh, my God, it's a miracle!" I wanted to do cartwheels. I wanted to run and scream and tell everyone, especially Lena, but then I got scared that if I left, I'd jinx it and the lines would go down. I couldn't risk leaving. It was selfish, but I couldn't help it.

One by one I watched as people came out smiling like they'd seen Jesus, and I couldn't wait to look like that. I'd tell Evan how much I loved him, Ryan, Pam and Jake how much I missed them, and Mom and Dad not to worry, that I was okay, although I sure as hell wasn't.

Then a man started yelling in the tent, "Who is he? How could you do this to me?" and my jaw dropped as he stormed out of the tent and sent my mind reeling. What if Evan had moved on and didn't love me anymore?

"Next," the technician called out, and I walked in a lot slower than I'd imagined, picked up the receiver on the desk, and dialed while holding my breath.

Every wall had a piece of paper taped to it that read, "15 minute calls only," and I closed my eyes, trying to picture what Evan was up to and how he was going to break up with me.

"Evan!" I couldn't help but scream when I heard his voice. "You answered!"

"Jen! Jen! It's you!" He screamed back so happily that I knew if those were the last words I ever heard I would die happy.

"Hang on, I'm at the bar and it's loud," he killed my smile. Just once, couldn't he be sitting in his room missing me, awaiting my call and/or arrival?

"I miss you so much, you have no idea!" I clutched the receiver with two hands as if that would make the distance between us seem a lot less.

"Hang on, hang on," he repeated, then I heard a door slam, silence, and his drunken giggle. "I love you, you know that? I love you and I miss you!"

I had to fly halfway around the world for him to tell me that. "I know, I know," I wanted to smile and couldn't.

"Mandy is getting a package together for you."

"Thank God for Mandy," I replied sarcastically, since I'd sent the letter to him.

"If there's anything you need, let me know."

"Well, now that you mention it, all of my underwear was stolen."

"Your underwear?" he repeated.

"Yeah, it's a little primitive here. I guess someone didn't have her own. Can you get me some?"

"Sure, what kind you want? Let me get a pen. What color, what size?"

"Whatever is on sale and how come you don't know my size?"

"I'm sorry." He paused not because he didn't know my size after three years, but because he couldn't stop giggling. "It's just so damned funny."

"Do you want to move in together when I get back?"

"Together?" he blurted out.

I couldn't believe I'd said it out loud either and stumbled to defend it. "Because, you know, we're losing a year of being together. I just thought you might want to."

It was so quiet I thought he'd hung up, lit an entire pack of cigarettes, and started pacing the sidewalk in front of the bar. Then he exhaled and I realized how much I missed him, wanted to hold him and smell him.

"Okay," he sighed. "But I'll need your checks. To cover rent. I'll get them from Ryan, okay?"

"You mean it?" I was too surprised to question why he couldn't afford rent on his own for the next year. He loved me. We were moving in together!

"Uh-huh," he purred, and then the line went dead.

My fifteen minutes were up and I couldn't have been happier because we were going to live happily ever after. All I had to do was get home!

FORTY-FOUR

"JG." Lena ran into the tent breathless as if she'd run all the way from the airfield and not the van right outside the tent to come get me. "The Captain says you need to take your shot records and go to the hospital tent as soon as you can."

"Now? For what?" I was almost afraid to ask, but knew it probably had something to do with the Anthrax and Small Pox vaccines everyone had been talking about. No one wanted to take them because they were so painful. Even the news reported a story of a group of marines who'd refused them and ended up in in Leavenworth for insubordination, which didn't instill a sense of confidence that they were safe to get.

"He said you're the last one out of all of us, so please go. I'll see you later," she huffed and disappeared, and I searched for my empty shot records, wishing I had a way to get out of getting them.

I devised a plan to sign in and leave, but when I arrived the tent was empty except for two male nurses sitting at a table and laughing.

Hoping they didn't know why I was there, I said nothing and turned to leave but male nurse A said, "Shot record," and I handed it to him as his smile turned into a frown.

"Why haven't you received the first anthrax shot yet?"

"Anthrax?" I feigned surprise. "Oh, I, uh, already got that before we left. It's because I was in a car accident. They didn't have time to write it in there."

"You'll just have to get it again then." He slapped my shot record on the table impatiently, which caused male nurse B to cop an even bigger attitude.

"Roll up your sleeve," male nurse B said, getting a sterile syringe from a cabinet.

"Now?" I cringed as he tore the plastic.

"Right now, airman," male nurse A chimed.

"But-" I hesitated, but male nurse B didn't. He plunged the needle into my arm and I howled, "That hurts!"

"Yeah, it does that." He tossed the syringe into a biohazard box and said, "If it swells up, come back immediately. It means you're allergic and..."

"And I'll be sterile?" I wondered if the rumors were true, but neither replied. "You mean swells up more than this?" I showed them the big red lump that had formed.

"Hmm," male nurse B studied my arm pensively.

Male nurse A joined him and said, "Yeah, more than that. And make sure you come back in a month to get the second shot."

"There's more?" I whined.

"Six to be exact."

"Six?"

"It's time for the video," male nurse A interjected. "In the back room, we're about to play a video about Small Pox. You'll get that shot after, but it will be in the other arm, don't worry."

"Great." I shoved my record into my pocket, walked to the back room where at least forty of fifty other people sat on the floor in front of a microwave cart with a TV on top, and made my way to the back. I didn't recognize anyone. New people were coming in and no one was leaving. It felt like this was going to be our home forever.

This time a female nurse walked in, pushed "play" on the VCR, and said lackadaisically, "This should only take twenty minutes," before walking away to wherever she came from.

The screen went black before a black and white documentary started, starring a 1961 man in a lab coat and thick black glasses. He smiled as though he knew more than he was going to let on, crossed his arms, and leaned on his desk as he waited for his footage to cover the screen: puppies and kittens that'd been exposed to small pox and slowly died in the corner of a room. How many animal shelters had the military raided in the sixties for all these re-enactments?

The nurse returned and said, "There's a small chance, about two percent of you, of having a negative reaction to the vaccine. Just wanted to let you know that. So roll up your sleeve and form a line."

I scanned the room and calculated my chances of dying at .04 to .08%, or 100% with my luck, and couldn't get myself to roll up my sleeve with the throbbing in the other arm still fresh.

"Roll up your sleeve, airman," male nurse A prompted impatiently a few minutes later.

"I can't," I replied without a plan.

"Do you have acne?" he asked.

"Yes!" I pushed at random spots on my face. "Right here and here, see?"

"No, I mean on your back?"

"Yes," I nodded a little too enthusiastically.

"You have large open sores on your back caused from acne?" he replied skeptically.

I stuttered, "Uh, yes," feeling queasy, but unbuttoning my shirt to show him.

"Big red infested blistering welts that ooze puss?" he asked again, and I nodded, which made him wave me away and me dash to the exit before he changed his mind about checking my back.

I ducked into the mail tent just to get out of plain sight and to my surprise, there were a few packages waiting for our squadron.

"They were delayed a few weeks because of a heavy snow storm in Delaware that made the warehouse collapse. Biggest snow storm in their state's history, supposedly!" The woman behind the counter said.

"Of course," I shook my head knowingly. "Because those packages were for us. I always get lucky like that."

"There are four," she chuckled. "But one is very heavy. Do you need help?"

"Pile it on," I encouraged her, and noticed that all the boxes had water damage. It was a miracle they'd made it all the way over here. I said, "Getting mail here is better than ten Christmases combined. I don't like making two trips."

I almost regretted having said those words as I wobbled back to the tent, and was excited for the guys, who had two packages, as well as Lena and I who had the other two.

"Finally!" Lena smiled when I gave her her package and plunked my box onto taco cot.

"I know what you mean!" I opened my box, ripped the bag of Lay's Potato Chips open, and said, "Lena, potato chips!"

I pulled out a jar of Ranch Dip that I'd dubbed "crack in a jar" because it was so addictive and slowly unpacked the rest: four bags of sunflower seeds, gum, a bright beaded handmade necklace, a pillow, and another small box that said, "To Jen, my love, from Evan" that made me fight back tears.

"Come sit with me, Lena," I said as she held up a few new bottles of soap.

"Oooh." She marveled through my box and pulled out a gossip magazine with someone on the cover I didn't recognize. It was like I was in prison and had been cut off from the real world. Never again would I take another gossip magazine about pop culture for granted!

I placed the beaded necklace around my neck and read the Hallmark card signed by everyone in the tower except Satan. The necklace was from Mandy and I couldn't help but laugh when I thought about Satan seeing me like this, plastic beads around my neck and no dog tags. Then I fluffed my new pillow. Never again was I going to take a little thing like that for granted either, and puffed out my chest at my little kingdom. All this stuff, even though it couldn't have cost more than ten dollars, made me feel like I had it all, like I was queen of the desert!

Last but not least was Evan's box from Victoria's Secret. I held it in my hands for a few minutes and visualized how he'd bought them, packed them and sent them, to me. They'd once been in his hands and were now in mine. If only he could send himself, I thought, a little disappointed he hadn't added anything more personal, but this was what I'd asked for and couldn't complain.

"Oh no!" I gasped when I pulled back the tissue paper.

"Those are so beautiful!" Lena plunged her hands into the box and pulled out a pile of neon, leopard and feather thongs.

"What the hell am I going to do with thong underwear in the desert! My ass is going to chaff in our DCU's. They're like sandpaper!"

"Come on, these are gorgeous." Lena inspected all the details, making me question what had happened when he walked into the store. He'd meant well, but had probably forgotten the note he'd written.

"Maybe you're right," I said. "I should see the bright side of this. Do you still have your disposable camera? I'll buy you another one as soon as AAFES opens up."

"Sure," she stood up, found it in her suitcase easily, handed it to me, and asked, "What's up?"

"What do you think about taking pictures of me wearing these so that I can send it to Evan? I know it's a lot to ask, but maybe that's why he bought them."

"I don't mind at all," she surprised me, and I quickly undressed, modeled the underwear with nothing else on, and hoped Evan would like it.

"Thanks." I got dressed again, took the camera, and walked to the post office to send it off. Then I walked to the phone tent to surprise Evan and tell him there was a special package on the way for him.

"Hey, honey," he slurred as usual.

"Hi." I wondered when the day would come when he wouldn't be lit all the time.

"I'm out partying with my Dad," he said as if that justified why he was drunk. Then, as if he knew it would keep me from pouting, said, "He flew into town to see how I was doing and he wants to say hi to you, hang on."

"Wait! I've never met him! I won't know what to say!"

"Listen, Jen is it?" his father's voice boomed drunkenly in my ear. "You watch out over there, you hear?"

"Yes, sir." I tried to ease up on the man who'd encouraged his son to call the cops on me when we got into an argument instead of trying to settle it.

"I'm proud of you kid, so is my wife. We're proud of you for defending this country. You're brave, you know that, right?"

"Thank you," I whispered, and before I knew it, Evan was back giggling, "My dad says you sound cute."

"Does that mean I'm going to meet him?"

"Of course, baby," he cooed.

"I got the underwear," I sniffled. "And I sent you something too."

"Oh, yeah, the underwear." He sounded angry suddenly. "Just don't come home pregnant, okay?"

"What?" I nearly fell from the chair and he repeated it again, "Just don't come home pregnant," and I wished I could reach through the receiver and strangle him.

"How fucking dare you!" I screamed, hung up, and stormed out of the tent, wishing there was a punching bag around.

My eyes fell on the rec. tent I'd never stepped foot in. What better time to take a look than now?

I walked in and saw pool and ping pong tables and a small semi-circle of people half asleep around the TV. It reminded me of an elderly home, people biding their time to die. It was way too depressing to stay, and I turned to leave until I spotted Robert sitting by himself reading.

"Haven't seen you in ages," I said, sitting down across from him. "How's the gym treating you?"

"I miss having a buddy." He smiled, closed his book, and asked, "Are you busy? Do you want to play chess?"

"Sure," I lied. I was tired of games, but he hurried and got a board and quickly set it up.

"You're not even trying," he said after he beat me in five moves.

"I am," I protested. "I'm just not very good, okay?"

"You're a controller, aren't you supposed to be good at this?"

"I've heard the analogy before, but all I do is work planes. I can't predict what you're going to do, sorry."

"Don't waste my time," Robert snapped.

I snapped back, "Hey, I'm sorry, but I just got off the phone with my boyfriend and he said something unpleasant."

"What did he say?" He tilted his head and smiled as if he was excited.

'Don't come home pregnant.'

"Ouch." he set up the board again and grinned. "What if me and you?"

"What if you and me what?" I glanced at his wedding band.

"You know..." His eyebrows danced. "You go down on me and I'll return the favor. It's not cheating, you know."

"See you later." I stood up but he caught my arm and said, "Calm down. Everyone out here is doing it. You see those two over there? They're married and having sex with several people. And those two? Same thing."

"Whatever," I said, but suddenly saw what he was talking about, people sitting closely together and laughing. "That's nice, but I have to go," I wrestled my arm free.

"Capi-tahn!" I thanked my lucky stars when I saw him marching in a hurry in the opposite direction, "Wait up! Where are you going?"

"There just aren't enough hours in the day to go to all the meetings I have, JG."

"Enough hours?" I glanced around incredulously. "There are way too many!"

"Make it quick, JG."

"Uhm, okay, you remember that bald guy I used to run with?"

"Robert?"

"Yeah, him. Wow, I'm surprised you remembered."

"Well?"

"Yeah, uhm, did you think we were an item? Because he seemed to think so."

I thought the Captain would berate me for wasting his time, but started laughing so hard he bent forwards and nearly dropped all of his papers.

"I didn't need you to make a scene Capi-tahn," I tugged at his arm to get him to stand upright again. "This isn't funny! Please, I need to know. Why would he think I'm interested in him?"

"Oh, JG." He mockingly wiped a tear from his eye. "It's funny because you treat everyone here like they're your brother and guys can't handle that. Guys are guys. You say hi to them, they think you want to sleep with them."

"You're kidding, right?"

"You're in the middle of the desert with a thousand guys! And you're one of fifty girls. Of course that's it. You want me to say something to him?"

"No, thanks," I smiled at the thought. "I'll just avoid him."

Then a guy walked past us, nearly tripped when he stared at me, and the Captain said, "See?"

"I thought it was all because I have bad skin," I replied.

"I'm off," the Captain waved.

As I watched him leave, I knew that if he'd proposed what Robert had, I wouldn't have hesitated. Then I kicked myself for thinking about a married man with kids, who also happened to be my boss, and much worse, an officer, in that way.

I wished he'd send me home, I was obviously losing my mind. Get me out of here before I can't take it any longer.

FORTY-FIVE

Of all the ways I'd woken up in the desert, the tent wall smacking me in the head was definitely a new one. I licked my dry lips and tasted sand. I rubbed my eyes and realized I had an entire layer on my face. The last time a storm had passed through like this I was at the tower with Moses with less than a mile visibility, as if someone had hung a tan-colored curtain in front of the window.

Moses went off on a tangent about how sandstorms were bad in the city because a fine layer of dust settled in the fridge even if you didn't open the door. I bit my tongue so as not to mention that he had a wall, and of all luxuries a fridge, and I had sand lodged in my ears so far down Q-tips would never reach to get it out.

It was late morning- I could tell by the way the sun indirectly flooded the tent and because everyone was at work. I forced myself out of the cot even though I could have slept all day, but it was already March and getting hotter by the minute, and if I wanted to enjoy one of my last running days before I was forced into the gym like a treadmill lab rat, I had to get up.

No one except me was outside, not even on Runner's Road, and as I turned the corner I found out why when a gust of wind almost knocked me down. Loose strands from my ponytail smacked my face telling me to turn around, but I was up now! I wasn't going back!

Then I thought the winds would subside, that it had only been a strong gust holding me back, but the winds just kept coming. Tears involuntarily leaked from my eyes and my face stung, and as I turned my head to evaluate how far I'd already run and still couldn't force my way back, my ears hurt from all the pressure and I temporarily turned deaf. The only way to run through this was one step at a time, and by running, I meant kicking my knees up, putting my head down, and pushing my way through.

By the time I glanced up again there was a beat-up white pick-up truck half a mile up the road that I was sure wasn't there before. I was also sure it wasn't one of ours because all of our trucks looked brand new. The foreigners' were old and dented, but there was no reason for it to be out here. This road was the back of the flight line, as well as the border between our city and theirs, and there most certainly wouldn't be any flying today.

As I squinted I counted five distinct silhouettes crammed inside, all staring in my direction. Forcing myself to glance back, I realized I'd gone too far, that I couldn't just turn around and go back even though the wind was behind me. They could sneak up on me easily and my cries for help would die in the wind. My only option was forward and toward whatever they had planned for me. I'd go down fighting.

My big idea was to cross the road, which seemed to work. I was on my side and they stayed on theirs and I wanted to kick myself for being so paranoid because obviously they did have official business and I happened to be on the road at the same time as they. But then the headlights turned on and I watched in awe as they crept across the road, turned off the lights and shut off the car as if they really were waiting for me.

I crossed again and felt pretty clever until they did the same. I was out of ideas, I had nothing except regret I hadn't gone to the gym like Robert did and that I was going to get raped, kidnapped, or killed all because I'd made a promise to get into shape for Evan.

When I crossed a third time, the truck was less than a quarter mile away. It too crossed again as if to tell me they meant business. I calculated my odds if they all attacked me at once; I could break a couple nuts with a kick or two, maybe a nose, but five guys were just too many and I was just too exhausted from fighting the wind. In minutes I'd be dragged into the trunk and would disappear forever and there was nothing I could do about it.

By the time I was parallel to the hood of the truck I was ready to fight, and I threw my hands up to show them I was a force to be reckoned with.

But nothing happened. No one jumped out of the car, not even the lights turned on, and so I lowered my arms just as the front driver's side window lowered too.

"Hi," the foreigner, a guy I'd recognized from the chow hall, waved.

"Hi?" I replied, staring back at the guys staring back at me, trying to climb onto the driver to get a better view.

The driver stuck out his hand and said, "Fo' you," and I nearly lost my balance when I saw four Arabic candy bars in his hand.

"For me?" I graciously bowed for my fans and took the candy bars. "Thank you, I love chocolate!"

"Yes," the driver nodded, and for a minute we stood there staring at each other, me not knowing what else to say that they'd understand and them probably feeling the same.

"Okay, thank you, but I really have to go."

"Okay, okay," the driver rolled up the window again, but didn't start the car until I turned around and jogged away, wondering who would believe me if I told them this.

By the time I made it to the tower I was on such a sugar high that I barely noticed Simon's sad face, how he was slouched in the chair, and that he hadn't moved after I'd handed him the keys to the van.

"What's up?" I ran over to Bolbol and Sami, my two favorite guys to work with because they brought me newspapers and seeds from the market, and knew that it was going to be a fun night.

"Waz up?" Sami echoed back and handed me a bag of seeds I didn't hesitate to open and stuff my cheeks with.

Bolbol turned his head in disgust because he thought that I ate seeds unladylike, with a cup in my hand for me to spit the shells into, but how else was I supposed to eat them?

"What is that?" I pointed over Sami's shoulder at a picture of a dome with a point on top that was clearly the top of a mosque, but also very clearly built to resemble a woman's breast, which seemed comical in a no-nonsense country.

Sami read my mind and laughed so hard he couldn't hold onto the newspaper. Then Bolbol stood up to see what was so funny and became so enraged he couldn't look at me.

"That is religious mosque," Bolbol pointed his finger at the sky. "Allah does not think it's funny!"

Sami, however, thought it was funny and laughed harder, which made me laugh too, although I tried to calm Bilal down. "Bolbol, I'm sorry. I didn't mean it."

"Tsk," Sami frowned as if to say, "he's uptight, forget him," then nodded towards the couch where Simon was still sitting, staring out into nothing.

I thought I knew the look of despair until I saw him.

"Oh my God, Simon, are you okay?" I knelt on the floor, picked up the keys, and shook his arm.

He had tears in his eyes and now that I was up close I could tell he'd probably been crying for quite some time.

"I'm sorry," he sighed as if he were tired, but not from lack of sleep, more like lack of desire to breathe.

"Simon, talk to me." I squeezed his clammy hand, thinking I should run and get the Captain, but I couldn't get myself to leave his side.

"Every time the anniversary date comes around," Simon whispered cryptically. "The pain is as deep as if it happened yesterday."

"What anniversary? What do you mean?"

"JG!" The Captain's voice suddenly boomed up the stairs and was followed by his quick energetic steps.

"Yes, sir!" I let go of Simon's hand, shot up to greet the Captain and stepped in the line of sight so the Captain couldn't see Simon and ask questions.

"I have a mission for you, listen very carefully." He handed me a picture with a cell phone on it and some kind of toy lying next to it.

"Is that a cell phone?" I turned the page over as if there were more pictures.

"JG, shush for a minute, I need you to listen!" He ripped the page from my hands. "It's for size comparison! This is very important!"

"Ay, ay, Capi-tahn, I'm listening!" I smiled, thinking he was cute when he was serious.

"This is a picture of a bomb..." He handed me the picture again.

"A bomb?" I screamed, staring at the picture and trying to make sense of which was which. "Where?"

"JG!"

"I'm sorry, I'm listening. Go on."

"This is a picture of an undetonated bomb. It's in the range. Nothing can fly to the range until we get it, copy?"

"Copy, sir."

"I'm downstairs by Base Ops with the Colonel and a bomb expert. We're waiting on the foreign bomb expert, okay? Hand him this picture and tell him to meet us downstairs, northwest side, okay?"

"Yes, sir," I folded the picture a few times and shoved it in my pocket, unsure what side he meant exactly. I also wanted to ask him how he thought he was going to find a little bomb in that huge range, but he turned and left before I could open my mouth again and my eyes fell on Simon, who looked like he needed to be carried out.

"Simon, what happened?" I sat down next to him.

"I live in Florida now..." he sighed. "But before the accident, we were in Washington."

I didn't like where this was going and was glad that at least Sami and Bolbol weren't paying attention.

"Eight years ago, I had a beautiful baby girl..."

Now I really didn't like where this was going.

"And I was late for work that morning. You know how it is, getting two kids ready." He smiled apologetically, as though I understood, but I didn't. "And I had just started at the tower and couldn't keep being late all the time, and I kept telling her to hurry up! because I still had to bring them to the hospital for their doctor's appointment."

Simon paused to breathe and swallowed his tears, and I wondered how many times he'd told his story and if maybe the Captain knew about it.

"I dropped them off and as soon as I got to work my supervisor pulled me aside. Not because I was late but because the hospital had called for me and requested I get back there immediately. I asked my Sup what was going on but he said he didn't know. And when I got to the hospital I saw that the very same spot where I had dropped them off was blocked off with yellow caution tape, and I asked the cop what had happened but all he said was, 'Stay calm.' How could I stay calm when I didn't know what was going on? No one in the crowd could tell me either and we stood there waiting, wondering why we'd all been called in the first place."

Suddenly, the downstairs door opened again, followed by running footsteps. This time, it was a foreign man in a suit dabbing at his sweaty forehead with a cloth napkin as he tried to catch his breath.

"I, I, I...where am I supposed to go? I'm here. For the bomb."

"Yes," I interrupted him, wanting to throw him out so I could hear the rest of the story. "Don't worry, you're not late. They're waiting for you downstairs, on the side of the tower."

"Thank you," he said, turning to go back from where he came from. "Thank you!"

"Okay, keep going." I sat down again.

"Then I was screaming at the cop, 'Why did I have to leave work if you're not going to tell me what's going on?' but all he said to me was 'Sorry, there's nothing I could do,' and he walked away. Can you believe that?"

I shook my head in disbelief. Tears flowed down his face, but he didn't seem to notice.

"Well, they pieced it together. A twenty year old airman wanted to re-enlist but the psychologist told him he was unstable. So what did he do? He took an M-16 to the hospital and killed the psychologist and attempted to kill everyone in sight, including my wife, my son, and my baby."

"Oh my God," I said, unable to say anything else. I'd never met anyone who should have had his own 20/20 special.

"She was shot from behind, through the chest, holding our baby girl. Our baby died first, then my wife's lung collapsed, but by some miracle, they brought her back to life. An older woman laid down on my son and took five bullets in the leg. Her leg was amputated but she lived."

Then he stood up, picked the keys off the floor, and walked downstairs as if he hadn't just shaken me to my core, and I called after him, "Where are you going? What happened to the guy? How is your wife? How old is your son now? Is he okay?"

"That son of a bitch was shot in the head by a cop who made it to the scene later. He saw the piece of shit reload and so he shot him in the head from across the parking lot."

"Wow." I pictured the scene in my head.

"My son is fourteen and still in therapy," he added. Without a doubt, I thought.

"I'm sorry, the phone's ringing," I said, and he disappeared through the door.

"Hi Capi-tahn," I cleared my throat. "Sure, I'll bring you an MRE. Any kind? You got it."

Minutes later, I stood in front of the Captain's desk and placed the MRE on his desk.

"Thanks," he stopped typing. "I'm swamped and can't get away."

"Oh, before I forget." I reached into my pocket, pulled out the bomb picture and placed it on his desk.

"JG," he roared, and I stumbled back, realizing my mistake. "I hope that isn't what I think it is."

"It's not!" I coughed, backing up. I'd never seen him that angry and didn't want to see what he was capable of either.

"All you had to do was one fucking thing! You told me you understood, what the hell happened?"

"I'm sorry, Capi-tahn," I shivered.

"Get the fuck out of my sight, JG, because I don't know what the fuck I'm going to do!"

FORTY-SIX

Three high ranking colonels trailed behind Queen Latifah when she came up to the tower for shift change.

"Have you seen the Captain?" she snapped.

"Maybe he's in his office," I replied indifferently. I hadn't seen him for weeks following the bomb picture incident and I didn't intend to. "Maybe a meeting?"

"He has a meeting with us," the first Colonel replied sharply, and I bit my tongue not to question him. How was it my fault he was MIA and spreading himself too thin?

"I'm sorry, sir, then I'm not sure where he is." I took the van keys, ready to head out for the night, until I thought about how this might be my redemption. If I found the Captain and brought him to this very important meeting, he might send me home. I offered, "I'm heading to tent city now. I'm sure he's there if he's not in his office. I can drive you there."

"We'll wait here," the second Colonel replied softly, as if he'd taken a group vote and thought that the Captain would walk up any minute. But I knew better. The Captain might stretch himself thin but he never missed a meeting. Something was wrong.

"Here," the third Colonel scribbled a note and handed it to me. "Everything he needs to know is on that note. We will wait for him here, please see to it that he gets it."

"Yes, sir!" I folded the paper in half so that he knew he could trust me not to read it and then hurried downstairs.

A gust of wind startled me, tore the door open, knocked me into the dirt, and sent the note sailing. For a second I stared at the note in disbelief before it disappeared in the night sky. When I stood up I didn't know what to do. Although I should have gone upstairs to get another note, they'd think I was an idiot- who'd believe that a gust of wind ripped a note from my hand? I jumped in the van and decided that what I lacked in information I'd make up in speed, and was grateful no one else was on the road but me.

"Slow it down!" the gate guard called after me, but all I saw was sand in the rear view mirror and called out, "Sorry," although I wasn't. This was important! My going home depended on finding the Captain! My life depended on it.

"Capi-tahn!" I hopped out of the van in front of the tent and ran in, not caring who was in there.

Inside it was dark, except for a faint light in the back corner coming from the Captain's desk. I realized then that his cot was exactly across from mine in the neighboring tent and smiled, then held my breath when the overwhelming smell of dirty socks started to choke me. How did the guys sleep in here?

Although no one seemed to be home I thought I'd find a clue, a calendar, something on his desk that would help me find him. Instead I found the Captain passed out on his cot, sleeping with his hands across his chest as if he was in a coffin. He was fully dressed in DCU's and more handsome in the faint light than I'd remembered.

I was the only one in the entire city who knew where he was and I wanted to keep him all to myself. I couldn't take my eyes off him: his smooth skin, his perfect hair, and his lips that seemed to beckon me to kiss him.

"Capi-tahn," I tried to snap myself out of the fantasy. He was my boss, I couldn't think of him that way, but he didn't stir, which only intensified my desire for him.

Leaning in, I thought this might be my only chance to kiss him. Then he opened his eyes as if I'd shaken him awake and he stared at me, sniffing the air and wrinkling his nose as if I had something to do with the stench.

"There, uhm, are some guys waiting for you at the tower," I finally said.

"Jen?" he asked as though it was common for someone to be staring at him in his sleep.

"Yes."

"Jen?" he sat up, confused, so I repeated, "Some guys came to the tower to see you, sir."

"Who came to see me?" He patted his head as though he couldn't believe his hat wasn't on it.

"I don't know." My cheeks flushed and I looked away, grateful that it was dark and he couldn't tell.

"Well, what did they want?" He stood up, caught his balance, and patted the side of his pocket as if looking for something.

"I don't know, but please don't kill me."

I handed him the keys to the van and he said, "Thanks, I was looking for those. Well, what did they say?"

"I'm not sure."

"You're not sure what?"

"I'm not sure what they said because I had a note but it blew away and so I came to get you."

"They gave you a note and you lost it?" He scratched his head.

"Yes," I whispered.

"I dozed off," he yawned, not hearing me. "But only for a few minutes," and he suddenly spun and took off through the dark tent.

I struggled to keep up and said, "You're not going to kill me, are you?"

He stopped so suddenly that I bumped into him, and although I gasped, "I'm sorry, Capi-tahn," he said nothing as his hot breath gently stroked my forehead and his chest touched mine every time he inhaled, so rapidly I couldn't tell if he was angry or turned on like I was.

"Now, I remember the meeting with the Colonels!" he blurted out. "JG, that message was terrible!"

"What?" I said, realizing he'd left the tent. "Hey!" I called after him, but he was already in the van and drove off.

I fell into my cot, exhausted and in a daze, and thought I was dreaming when, hours later, Lena was in my ear. "Jen, get up, we have to go!"

"No, Lena," I groaned.

The air raid alarm was going off in the distance, but I didn't care. Ever since the first time I heard the practice siren and thought I was going to die from bombs falling from the sky and nothing happened, I lost interest. Now, I didn't care whether I died by bomb or not. Death was the only way I was getting out of this place and if that was the way it had to be then that was the way it had to be.

"We have to go!" She pulled my leg so that half of me slid from the cot.

"Lena, let me die," I pushed her arm away. "I don't care anymore. I'll roll under the cot and lay close to the sandbags!"

"You are coming with me whether you like it or not," Lena pulled on the other leg until I barked, "Alright, alright. I'm up!"

"We're the last ones out!" She shined a flashlight in my face as if that was going to make me move any faster. "It's three a.m. and you know how much I love my sleep, but we have to go!"

"I didn't think the bunkers were done yet," I said because I knew they weren't, and even if they were, you could hardly call an abandoned train cart that was open on either end and only slightly buried in the sand a bunker. "So where are we going? If a bomb drops we're dead no matter what."

"This isn't a laughing matter." She pulled my arm forcefully. When the bunkers came into view she let go of my arm because it was completely crowded and obvious we wouldn't fit.

"Lena, next time let me die!" I walked away.

"Jen, where are you going?" Lena hissed.

I said, "Anywhere but here."

The siren sounded again, the raid was over, and the crowd dispersed around me as everyone hurried back to his or her tent. But I knew I wouldn't be able to sleep yet and took the long way back, only to find the Captain, or someone who liked like him in the moonlight, sitting on the sandbag wall in front of the tent.

"Do you have a minute to talk?" He looked up at me sadly.

I couldn't tell if he'd been waiting for me or just any familiar face, but I was glad to join him and said, "Minute? I have all night."

His lips curled into a delicious half smile, but his eyes stared out into nothing as he inhaled deeply through his nose and said, "I called home today. I talked to my parents and they said one of my oldest friends, someone I've known since high school, is dying of cancer."

"I'm sorry, Capi-tahn." I was tempted to put my hand on his until I thought of Wright and what he might say if he saw us.

"She was the prettiest girl in school." He drifted into a memory and I was right along there with him, trying to picture him younger, even more handsome if that was possible, and how he probably had every pretty girl from three surrounding counties hanging off his arm.

"She was a cheerleader and I dated her for a while. Even our parents thought we were going to get married. And now this? Cancer? They say she's not going to last through the night. They're giving her hours to live. Hours! She was so young."

"I'm sorry, Capi-tahn," I put my hand on his forearm and didn't give a damn who saw it. The man worked over two hundred hours a week and deserved a little comfort now that his best friend was dying.

Then I caught a whiff of his aftershave and let go of his arm before I nuzzled his neck. I suggested, "Why don't you try to call her family and tell them how you feel about her?"

"No." He looked away as though he was embarrassed to cry, and I remembered how he hardly ever called home because he knew his wife could handle things without him, which was why he couldn't understand why I felt the need to call home every five minutes or felt that my life was slipping away from me more each minute.

"Listen, you deserve to call," I said. "You can't beat yourself up. You have to say goodbye. If you don't, you'll never forgive yourself."

"It's too late anyway." He drifted off again, which made me stare at him again in the faint moonlight and fantasize about kissing him, wishing he'd take me in his arms and pull me close until he said, "I always have been attracted to brunettes."

"Huh?" I replied, surprised the conversation had turned to this.

"Brunettes," he repeated, which made me want to both slap him and disappear into my tent. Didn't he realize I was throwing myself at him?

"I remember being deployed in," he said, naming a country I didn't recognize, "And in the elevator was the most beautiful woman I'd ever seen. Tall, long dark hair, brown eyes, exotic looking, you know what I mean?"

"Uh-huh," I held my hand to my aching chest and wished he'd stop torturing me.

"We made eye contact and she just smiled and I just smiled and we just knew, and then she gave me her room key, can you believe it?"

"No," I pictured the scene and wished I was not only a brunette, but that brunette.

"But I couldn't do it. I got to my room, laid on my bed thinking of what she must be thinking, and thought it would be too weird if I went. I can't explain it and yet I think about her a lot."

"Obviously," I replied and stood up so that he couldn't give me another brunette fantasy. When he said nothing I added, "I'm sorry for your loss, Capi-tahn. I hope you know you can talk to me anytime."

"Aren't you off tomorrow?" He stood up quickly as if he wasn't ready for me to leave yet.

Staring at him, I didn't know what I was working. All I wanted to do was run my fingers through his messy hair, unbutton his shirt, and press his body against mine. Then I shook my head and wondered if maybe Bilal had had a point when he said that I was turning into a man. Of course he'd meant it in the physical sense that my legs were getting too muscular, and he felt that a woman wasn't supposed to have muscle, she was supposed to be soft, but now I took it differently because all I ever thought about when I looked at the Captain was sex.

"I think you are," the Captain answered his own question and moved in so close I thought he was going to kiss me.

"You make the schedule, Capi-tahn," I croaked, my throat dry. "You know I'm off tomorrow."

"Very funny, JG." He smiled as if he was toying with me, and I reminded myself that was all he wanted to do because he liked brunettes, not blondes!

"How about you join me for one of my meetings in the officer's tent?" he swayed closer.

"Me?" I moved backwards before I lost my self-control. "Isn't that where you plan missions and highly confidential top secret things? What am I going to do there? Serve coffee?"

"Yeah." He stepped even closer so that my cheeks flushed and said, "Actually, every Sunday night we play Risk."

"Risk?" I stepped back again. "As in the board game? You play board games? Not plan out how we're going to defeat Saddam? That's what you do every week? No thank you. I only played it once, ten years ago. You don't want me there."

"I'll teach you," he smiled seductively, or my mind was playing tricks on me.

"Do I have a choice?"

He stared at me.

"Do I have a choice, *sir*?" I repeated.

"No, you don't," he grinned.

"Okay then, I'll see you there at six, bye." I ducked into my tent, relieved to be away from him.

Even though Evan thought of me as a cheater I wasn't, and I only hoped that the game of Risk brought me one step closer to home, because if it didn't, I was going to go nuts.

FORTY-SEVEN

A gust of wind blew my hair into disarray as I waited in front of the top secret tent.

"Hello?" I called out, and was checking to see if my clothes were too wrinkled when the Captain unzipped the tent flap as if he'd been standing there waiting for me.

"Come in, come in," he said giddily, looking handsome in a simple navy polo and jeans and making me feel underdressed in a t-shirt and shorts.

Trying to brush past him as though he didn't make me nervous by standing so close, I was pulled back by the faint smell of his aftershave and followed him to the card table in the middle of the tent where a group of middle aged guys in polos, some in glasses and some bald, were seated setting up the game.

"Hi," I waved as the Captain pulled out a chair for me. I nearly missed it and said, "I'm Jen."

"They know who you are," the Captain snapped.

No one said a thing, someone coughed, and I glanced around the room at the folded metal chairs and piles of rolled up maps on the floor, wondering what went on in here after hours. The guys themselves looked harmless, not the big powerful men they were rumored to be. I couldn't even place them outside of here. Why was everyone so afraid of bigwigs?

"That's Mayler, he goes by LT," the Captain sighed as if it was a chore to introduce them to me. "General Nelson, just call him Nelson. Captain

Romero, call him Romero, and Major Finsberg goes by Fin…and don't forget, always address them as sir!"

"Yes, sir," I replied seriously.

"Gosh, JG, you're so uptight," the Captain giggled, but no one else thought he was joking either and I wondered why he'd invited me here if he was going to be so snooty.

"Pick a color," the Captain barked as if to prove he was in charge of me.

"Red." I reached for a box filled with red toy soldiers, but he plucked the box from me mid-air and said, "Sorry, that's mine. Pick anything but red."

"It's one game, Capi-tahn."

"He's always red," Romero sighed as if he too was sick of his crap and I thought good, because I needed allies if I wanted to teach the Captain a lesson.

"I guess I'll take green then." I put my hands on the table to tell him I meant I wasn't backing down. My mission was to beat him, wipe that smug smile off his face, and remind him he should have sent me home when he had the chance.

By the way Nelson pursed his lips I could tell it was his color but he said nothing, handed me the box like a gentleman, and shuffled another deck. Then Romero picked up the die and rolled them across the board, explaining, "This is how you fight an opponent, with the die. The goal is to take over all the other countries. There are cards too, some with missions and some that get you additional soldiers. And that's the gist of it. It's easier if we play and explain as we go along."

"Roll the dice to see who goes first," LT handed me the die and I rolled against the Captain.

"Oh!" The Captain screamed, offended when my five beat his two. "Beginners luck."

"Geez, I'm sorry," I replied sarcastically.

"You should be," he smirked. "Nobody beats me. I win every week."

Everyone confirmed this with a slight nod.

"Then I take it back. I'm not sorry," I snapped, which made everyone gasp. "It's on Capi-tahn. You asked for it and you're going down!"

"Whatever," he shrugged casually.

"What I meant to say was," I cleared my throat for emphasis. "I'm sorry guys, because I didn't come here with the intention to win tonight or to strategize. I only came here to kick the Captain's ass!"

Now the shuffling, rolling, and setup stopped. I had gone too far, put my foot in my mouth, and there was no taking it back. I stared at the Captain, who stared at me, and I knew he was going to punish me by making me low crawl the flight line for two weeks for disrespecting an officer in front of officers.

"Whatever, Jen, I'm unstoppable!" the Captain suddenly snapped. I could have sworn a collective sigh went around the table and everyone glanced at each other as if they sided with the Captain and were thinking, "How do you deal with her?"

"I don't care who's with me." I felt emboldened and put my fist on the table. "But I'm taking him down if it's the last thing I do!"

"You think they're going to listen to you?" The Captain snorted, rolled again and said, "Take that!" as he knocked one of my soldiers to the ground.

"We've only just begun, Capi-tahn. You can surrender now or make it a slow and painful death. It's up to you."

"Keep dreaming, honey." He stuck his tongue out at me which made LT, Nelson, Romero, and Fin laugh as though it was the ice breaker we needed. This was the game I'd come to play!

It only took a few minutes for the die to make it all the way around the board and every player to lose just one toy soldier, as if they were testing each other's weaknesses. It was obvious I was the weakest, which didn't bother me. I just needed a way for them to band with me because I couldn't annihilate the Captain alone.

"Red," I said nonchalantly.

The Captain glared at me as though he couldn't believe what I was saying but said nothing.

"I was serious, Capi-tahn. No mercy. No prisoners. You're going down."

"Alright then." He rubbed his hands together as if he needed to change his game plan, but it didn't work.

"Ha!" I rolled the higher number. "See, it's meant to be!"

"This isn't fair!" he stammered. "Attack someone else."

"I'll let you recover. For now," I passed the die to LT because I didn't want to push my luck, and besides, watching the Captain lose his cool was kind of fun.

"Thanks," LT smiled as though he was happy for me.

"Attack red please," I batted my eyelashes playfully.

"He's not like that," the Captain crossed his arms. "He's not going to listen to you! No one's going to listen to you. I win. Every. Time!"

LT scanned the board and weighed his options as if deep in thought, and I said, "Here's your chance LT," pointed at the Captain as if to make it clear who the enemy was, and added, "This is your time to shine! This is your time to conquer! He's mean to everyone I work with," I laughed. "He deserves it."

"Red," LT hesitated, as if he regretted his decision, and I clapped excitedly.

"What?" the Captain's jaw dropped. "You're going to listen to her? Come on!"

LT grinned, convinced he'd made the right decision, but he didn't win against the Captain. Then he passed the die to the Colonel next to him and the Captain said, "I told you not to mess with me."

"Red." the Colonel winked at me.

"Listen, you guys, this is not fair!" the Captain whined.

"It's just a game," the Colonel laughed. He rolled but also lost, and then he passed the die to Romero. "Everyone is tired of you winning every single week."

"Green, green, green," the Captain chanted, but Romero didn't even blink as his eyes locked onto mine and sparkled in the dim light as if to reassure me, yeah, we've got his ass in the bag, sweetheart. "Red," he said coolly.

"Yes!" I threw my hands in the air.

"No!" the Captain screamed and pursed his lips as he realized everyone had banded together. "This is so unfair! Unfair!"

"Aw, Capi-tahn," I mocked him, and I would have felt sorry for him if it wasn't so funny to see him lose his self-control so quickly and over a game!

All of it lasted about an hour and a half. All the red pieces had been cleared from the board and the Captain sat with his arms crossed, fuming. When I lost a few minutes after the Captain had, I stood up and said, "It's been fun, gentlemen. Thank you for having me."

"The pleasure was ours," the Colonel stood up and squeezed my hand in both of his.

"Oh, please," the Captain huffed as everyone else stood up and shook my hand as well. "Let's go, JG."

Then he took hold of my arm and pinched it as he led me to the door. I almost thought he was going to kiss my cheek when he leaned in so close, but he hissed in my ear instead, "This was the last time you're invited, you know that, right?"

"It's been great!" I hollered across the tent to piss him off even more. "Thanks again for having me!"

"The only reason I asked you to come here," his lips grazed the side of my ear, "was because they wanted a closer look at you. They thought you were cute."

"Send me home Capi-tahn," I snarled back, but he let go of me, unzipped the tent, pushed me out, and said, "Get the hell out!"

"It was a pleasure watching you get your ass kicked!" I screamed, but the tent zipped shut again and I was dumbfounded by the size of his ego.

Deciding it was a good time to talk to Evan again, I marched to the comm. tent and was surprised he answered.

"I'm so glad you called."

He sounded desperate, but I was in no mood for manipulation and said, "How about an apology, Evan?"

"What do you mean?"

"I mean, the last comment you made to me was out of line. About you not wanting me to come home pregnant?"

He paused a long time before he admitted, "I must have been very drunk. I'm sorry if I said anything like that. I didn't mean it. I love you. I miss you so much it hurts."

"You need to stop drinking so damn much. You have no idea what I'm going through. It's hell here, I am literally in hell, and it's hell without you. Never mind the distance between us, I could die any fucking minute and we're constantly fighting!"

"I know," he whispered. "I love you and I don't want to lose you."

"I love you too," I softened. "How have you been holding up without me?"

"I've been okay." His voice was raspy, like when he spoke on the radio, which I loved, and it made my chest ache with longing until he added, "Hanging out with Amber a lot."

"That wasn't exactly what I wanted to hear."

"She took me to a Playboy party. And I got to hang out in the dressing room with her and all these girls kept coming up to me asking me if they looked fat…"

"Evan, do you really think they need your opinion and more importantly, that I want to hear this? Are you really that naïve or are you willing to do anything to see a piece of ass?"

"Hey," he said confidently. "When Amber said one of the girls wanted to sleep with me and handed me her number I said no."

"That's just so fucking fantastic, Evan."

"Well, she said not to do it."

"Uh-huh, tell her I said thanks."

"The girl had chlamydia or something."

"I'm glad you didn't sleep with her only because she had chlamydia! As if I don't have enough shit to worry about here! Be with her if you want to, just let me know."

"No. I love you Jen, you know that, right?"

"I don't know," I snickered. "I don't know if we should break up or stay together, and I should hang up for now. Goodnight, Evan."

"Wait!" he screamed. "You're the one, you know that right?"

"What?"

"You are, Jen. You're the one! I want to be with you forever and I can't wait for you to get back."

"Really?" I nearly dropped the receiver. No one had ever called me their "one" before. "What happened to never getting married?" I asked.

'Shalalalala la means I love you,' he sang quietly, then sniffled as if he was crying and didn't want me to hear it, "Do you remember when we heard that song when I picked you up in the morning? After our first date?"

"Of course I do," I replied. "But I don't know if I'll ever see you again. Your t-shirt doesn't smell anymore and I can't remember what you smell like. Do you know what that's like?"

"You'll be home soon, baby," he cooed. "I love you."

FORTY-EIGHT

Waving a flyer over the Captain's desk, I expected him to pause his maniacal typing and look at me.

"Capi-tahn," I said when he didn't. "Can I switch my shift tomorrow and take the day off so that I can run the 5K race tomorrow? I would have asked you sooner but I haven't seen you in ages."

"You want to run a race?" He suddenly eyed me.

"I admit I'm not very competitive, unless I'm playing Risk, of course."

"Very funny, JG."

"I've been running a lot and although I'd never race under any other circumstance, I think I might have a shot at winning."

"Sure. Then I'll have Simon cover your shift, and sign me up too. I'll run it with you."

"You'd cancel a hundred meetings just for me?" I was suddenly flattered.

"Why not?" He smiled as though he wanted me to believe that was true.

"Maybe because you're always busy? Or do you feel guilty for not sending me home?"

"You belong here," he said. "I've been falling behind on my running, and you know I always make time for you."

"Oh, I know you do," I said, expecting to run the race alone tomorrow. "Just make sure you're there tomorrow and not stuck in a meeting, alright?"

He nodded as though he was listening, but resumed his typing as if the conversation had never taken place, and the following morning I stood at the finish line and watched as random people strolled in behind me, everyone about to race, except for him.

"Why are you wearing those sweat pants?" he asked suddenly coming up from behind me.

"They're from George." I tugged at the strings to make them tighter. "The laundry service isn't exactly reliable around here. They've stolen almost every type of clothing from me, even my underwear. And I can't get the strings tight enough so now I have to hold them while I run."

"Let me see." He took the strings from me as though it was second nature for him to be tugging at my pants.

"There, better?" he pulled them so tight they dug into my flesh.

"Yeah," I winced, and he said, "You're so funny, JG."

"I am?"

"Oh, the stories you'll tell when you get home."

"Are you sending me home?"

"No," he laughed, as though I'd asked a ridiculous question. "But when you do get home, the laundry story will be funny."

"I doubt it."

"Glad you all could make it to the 5K," a rec. guy said, blowing a whistle then sauntering off to the side so he could see all the participants. He held up his clipboard and said, "The race is simple. Around the cones, loop the track twice. Any questions?"

The Captain, with his hands on his hips, winked at me and whispered, "You got this."

"Let's do it," I smiled, grateful he was by my side.

Then, without warning, or because I had been staring at the Captain and had temporarily forgotten about the race, the whistle blew and the Captain was off without me.

Leaping forward, I realized instantly that there was no way in hell I could keep up with his gazelle like stride. My running style was completely opposite of his; start out slow, and maybe if I found some fuel in the reserve tank, finish strong.

"Wait up!" I gasped, but he couldn't hear me. I'd started out wrong, too fast, and my lungs couldn't keep up. They burned and my legs, not used to sprinting, felt tired.

"Come on!" The Captain glanced back and I wished he'd run ahead without me so I could fall back into the dirt and just lie there.

"I can't!" I wasted my last breath and he finally slowed down, as if he remembered that he was my support system and not the other way around.

"I thought you've been running?" he asked, and I wanted to kick myself for thinking I was someone I was not. I had asthma. I wasn't competitive for a reason: it could kill me.

I glanced around me. Only a snake or scorpion bite could get me out of this nobly, but there was nothing.

"Go, Jen!" One of the people standing on the side suddenly called my name, but I didn't know who, and didn't recognize anyone, but suddenly I felt like I'd been given a push.

"Wait up, Capi-tahn. You're so fast!"

"I haven't even broken a sweat," he said defensively.

"You're like eight feet tall. Look at those legs."

"Nonsense," he said. "Look, we're almost done with the first lap and we're in the lead."

He was right. I quickly turned my head and saw that we had at least half a lap in between us and everyone else, which surprised me since everyone who was running were people I saw running outside frequently.

"My legs are numb. I can't go on."

"Don't give up now."

"Uh-huh," I grunted. I'd never run this fast in my life.

"Keep it up! You're almost done!"

It was hard to believe, but when I looked up, the rec. guy whistled, the Captain who'd been in the lead the whole time stepped back as if he had a pebble in his shoe, and I finished first.

"You're first!" the rec. guy cheered.

"Oh my God!" I coughed, putting my hands on my hips and wondering if my lungs would ever recover.

"See, you did it," the Captain slapped my back. "Wasn't that easy?"

"You let me win, but I did it!" I wheezed.

"Of course you did." He raised his arms as if he wanted to hug me but then lowered them again. "I knew you could do it. That was nothing."

"Maybe nothing for you because you're some kind of cheetah giraffe mix," my lungs wheezed. "Tell me, who were those guys on the side of the road? I swear they were cheering for me and I've never seen them before in my life."

"JG, of course they know your name. You're still in the desert surrounded by horny guys!"

"That can't be your answer to everything."

"I've got a meeting to go to," he glanced at his watch, annoyed. "I'll see you tonight at the five o'clock meeting."

"See you," I replied, and he disappeared and I was left to revel in the satisfaction that I had won a race, and even though I didn't have a trophy or a t-shirt to prove it, I didn't care.

"Airman Grillo!" Wright called from behind me as I was about to duck into my tent a few minutes later.

"You scared me! Sir." I faced him, saw his angry glare, and almost asked, "What did I do now?"

"I've been meaning to talk to you about the Captain. You know, calling him by his incorrect title, still, and talking to him once in a while on your off time, and now racing together."

"What are you talking about?"

"Tell me, what's going on with you two?" He put his hands on his hips as if to tell me he meant business, but I knew for a fact the Captain didn't like me in that way and asked, "Going on?"

"Do you know the consequences of fraternization?"

"I barely even know the guy!"

"Oh, I beg to differ."

"I really don't know what you're talking about. What did I do?"

"I can write you up with an Article 15, and get you kicked out of the military."

"I don't know what you're talking about, but go right ahead. I'm ready to get out of this place anyway."

"Excuse me?"

"You heard me," I snapped back. "Now if you'll excuse me, I need to shower."

"I'll be watching you!"

"Good!"

I showered but could not seem to find the happy place I'd been in that morning. I called home, thinking it would make things better, but it didn't. Ryan sold my car months ago and hadn't collected the money yet, but he assured me he would. Mom lackadaisically explained her new silk curtains to me in great detail while Jake and Pam couldn't figure out where to party that night. Evan didn't answer, and I, with nowhere to go, listened to all of my old messages and cried at the sound of familiar voices, until I heard Amber's.

"Evan, how dare you ditch me every time we go out? You never answer your phone..."

I skipped forward to the next message.

"Evan, I've called you ten times already. Where are you?"

Then I hung up before I could hear the rest, because I'd heard enough and knew all I needed to know. If I didn't get back home now I was going to lose my life, my friends, and my boyfriend forever. I already knew the Captain wasn't going to send me home, not ever, not until the mission was done, the war was won, and certainly not because I wanted my cutesy life back.

I needed something drastic, something more serious than the fraternization I wasn't interested in anyway. I needed an international scandal and I had the six-pack of Heineken hiding under my cot, just right for the occasion.

Running back to my tent, I dug the beer out from between my suitcases, stood outside of the Captain's tent, and raised it in the air like a hunter's trophy.

"Capi-tahn! Capi-tahn!"

He appeared a second later, and to my surprise, looked hurt.

"JG! What are you doing with that? Where did you get that from? You know that's illegal here!"

"Please, Capi-tahn. Please send me home. I can't take it anymore. Please, I have to go."

"Do you know the penalty for having this?" He yanked the pack from my hands. "I could send you home for this right now!"

"That's the idea." I pawed after him but his reaction time was better, and when he turned I fell forward into the sand.

"Trust me, JG, that is not the way you want to leave here! Now tell me, where did you get this from?"

"Send me home," I glanced up.

George and Simon had joined the party, and if they'd been curious before, they were sympathetic now, shaking their heads apologetically like they knew we were stuck here forever and that I should just give up, and I looked away, wishing the bombs would drop and just kill me already.

"I'm not messing around, JG, this is serious. Where. Did. You. Get. This?"

"Why can't you send me home? I'm going crazy! I'm losing my mind more and more every day. Why do you like to see me tortured like this? Haven't three months been long enough? I wasn't supposed to be here longer than a day."

"Where?" he demanded.

"It was a gift."

"A gift from whom?"

"Some guy."

"I'm not in the mood for games, JG."

"Neither am I. Haven't I been here long enough?"

"JG!"

"Please send me home. I have nothing left. My car is gone and my boyfriend might be too. I can't lose him, Capi-tahn. He's all I have."

"I've heard enough about Evan these past few months. Evan is ridiculous and you know it. I'm not sending you home in the middle of a deployment. It will end your career. And we're in stop loss now anyway. I was going to tell you at the meeting tonight. You're not going anywhere. Even if I did send you home, you are stuck in the military until the President lifts it."

"What? But my contract is up in August. I'm supposed to be out of the military in August!"

"Not anymore. It could take years before it's lifted, and by that time everyone will get out who was supposed to, but since you're low-ranking my guess is you will be one of the last."

"How long will I be stuck here, Capi-tahn?"

"Tell me who gave you the beer!"

"A pilot, but I don't know his name," I said, ashamed.

"It doesn't matter." The Captain marched up to his truck, opened the door, and said, "They're all going to get it!"

"You okay?" George and Simon helped me up and I sighed, "Well, I guess that completely backfired."

The five o'clock meeting started as scheduled, although I couldn't look the Captain in the eye, even when he said, "The war is scheduled for next Wednesday. We'll have MRE's in the tower and I'll let you know what the flying schedule is going to be like."

My eyes fell on Lena, who looked more afraid than I did, and visions of the tower, the entire city on fire, flashed before me.

"You'll have to carry your chem. gear with you at all times," the Captain rambled on casually, as if he was reading from a TV Guide. What the hell was wrong with him?

"That's all for now. Dismissed."

I hurried over to Lena, put my arm around her so I couldn't see her quivering lip and start crying too, and took her next door to our tent and said, "Don't be afraid."

"Are you nuts," she sobbed. "We're going to die!"

"We're going to be alright. We're here where all the action is, we have all the weapons in the world. We're safer than anyone back home." I unsuccessfully tried to recite the Captain's speech, but Lena wasn't buying.

"Sounds like bullshit to me."

"Maybe. But there's nothing we can do about it."

"We're going to die and I don't even know how to use this stupid mask!" Lena held up her chem. gear mask.

"If that's your only worry, that's nothing. I can help you with that, but please stop crying or I'll start crying." I took the mangled mask from her and laughed, "No wonder you're scared to die. Did you tie this thing in knots?"

"I don't know," she said sheepishly.

"Do you have a stopwatch?"

"Yeah," she showed me her wrist.

I said, "Take it off. I'll time you. See, doesn't this look a little better?"

"I don't know." She shrugged, wiped the tears from her face, and exhaled as if she felt better already, which made me feel kind of better, but only because I wasn't thinking about the death sentence next Wednesday.

"Gas, gas, gas," I hit the stopwatch, but she dropped her mask on the ground.

"Lena, we're going to be okay." I hugged her and thought, how in the hell could the military send all of us kids here to die? "Take a deep breath and we'll try again. Ready?"

"Yes."

"Good."

At least one of us had been fooled.

FORTY-NINE

Lena and I sat huddled on her cot in the dark and trembled. I waited for the bombs to drop, any minute now, for the tents to burn down, and prepared myself for a vision of bloody bodies everywhere, and couldn't decide if the Captain had left us here for our safety or our demise.

Lena sniffled next to me, but I had no more tears left after today. I'd walked around the deserted base wondering what I should do with my last day on Earth and came up with nothing. This was my fate. This was how my life was going to end. And there was nothing I could do about it.

Then I'd called Evan to say goodbye again but couldn't do more than sob uncontrollably, which prompted him to tell me everything I wanted to hear: "It's going to be okay baby. I can't wait for you to get back and see our cozy little apartment. Just stay strong." meaning "Just stay alive."

Suddenly someone stuck a flashlight in our tent and whispered, "It's been called off, the war's been postponed," and was gone.

"Lena, did you hear that?" I whispered. She whimpered back and I said, "Stay here," and went after whoever was outside.

"Hey, what do you mean 'postponed'?" I found him next door, sticking his head into the men's tent I knew for certain was empty, along with our entire block. "We've been sitting here for hours and now you're telling me it was for nothing and that this is going to happen all over again?"

"I don't know." He moved onto the next tent as if he wanted go get rid of me so that he could carry on with his very important job. "Something about the full moon."

"Doesn't that sound absurd to you?" I wanted to punch the Captain for doing this to us. "With all of our technology, we had to stop because of the moon? I'm not saying I want World War III or anything, but come on."

"It's too bright for our fighters." He delivered the message to another empty tent, "The enemy can see our fighters in the sky. It's on again in two weeks."

"Thanks." I finally let him off the hook, because I would only get the real answer from the man who'd caused all this.

I found the Captain the next day, marching around the base with energetic determination. I wanted to think he was running away from me because he was about to get it, but I was out of breath by the time I caught up to him.

"Capi-tahn!" He finally stopped. "What happened yesterday?"

"JG, I'm busy."

"I know, I know, but is it true it's going to happen all over again in two weeks?"

"Get to the point."

"Is it true about the moon?"

"Another time. Not now. Is that all?"

"Since I know you won't send me home, for the next time, I thought I didn't want to be in the tower but now I think I do. I don't want to sit around waiting to die."

"For Chrissakes, JG, you're not going to die."

"Can you schedule me to work next time though? I want to see the action and if we get blown up, it'll be quick."

"Sheesh, I'll see what I can do." He stormed off as if he wasn't going to see about it at all, but two weeks later the war was rescheduled, and I knew I'd put my foot in my mouth for good this time.

The tower was pitch black when I walked upstairs. So was the entire airfield. I'd heard glow sticks were strewn all along the runway so pilots could use their night vision goggles, but still it seemed way too dark for anything to happen out there. Then my eyes adjusted and I spotted what Sami had been looking at, a C-130 with soldiers loading jeeps and supplies like a busy ant colony.

It made me forget about bombs, destruction, and bloody bodies as I watched their shapes move swiftly in the night. We had the best damned Air

Force in the world. No wonder the Captain wanted to be here. Who was going to mess with us?

Then I glanced at Sami as he handed me the binoculars. He smiled, like he too thought this was cool, and I felt a stab in my chest because he had no idea what the hell was going on. For the last three and a half months I worked beside him and gained his trust and now he was going to help me bomb the hell out of his own country because he thought this was a routine exercise, when in fact this was a planned war and we unfortunately were stuck in the middle.

Hours went by, aircraft took off and came in, but not a single firework ignited. I laid in taco cot that night wondering if the war had been postponed again, and the next morning I took off with the same determination as before to find the Captain.

"Where do we stand now, Capi-tahn?" I found him in the chow tent eating breakfast, very relaxed, I noted.

"We won," he shrugged.

"But nothing happened, how did we win? Our bunkers still aren't even done and I know half of the equipment we wanted still hasn't arrived. Just like that, we won?"

"Isn't it amazing? Even when we don't have everything we need, we're still far superior in firepower than anyone," he winked. "We're at the safest place on Earth."

"Does that mean we dropped bombs and we just didn't hear it?"

He nodded as though it was obvious, and my stomach turned to mush as I pictured all the destruction and lives lost- women, children, soldiers- and whoever was left alive was left without a home. "So what am I supposed to do now, Capi-tahn? I have to work tonight. What do I say to Omar, or Sami and Bolbol? How do I act?"

"Nothing. Act normal. That's the mission from now on."

"But we're going home soon, right? We came here to win and we won. When are we going home?"

"Oh, JG," he giggled like I was a naïve little school girl. "Now that we won, you'll see the morale go down. We have nothing to work towards except keeping the peace, and we might have to do that for years."

I left without another word, made it to the tower a few hours later, and realized for the first time since we'd been here Moses, Omar, and Bilal spoke Arabic to each other intentionally to exclude me.

I wasn't in the mood to talk either, I decided, until Moses jumped on the table, waved the newspaper in my face, and said, "Genie, look."

On the front page was a picture of an American soldier bound and tied to the bumper of a car, being dragged on a dirt road, I gasped, "Moses. It's not my fault! I'm sorry. It wasn't supposed to happen like this."

He stared at me as if he thought this was exactly how it was meant to happen, then raised his hands in the air, and clapped and whistled and danced on the table so hard I thought it was going to shatter.

"Dead American," he sang while I pleaded, "Moses, really, I'm sorry," and for a second I hated the Captain for telling us this wasn't going to be a big deal.

"Dead American!" He bent over and laughed in my face. "You kill our families and now Americans dead!"

When he jumped from the table, I jumped out of my seat and ran downstairs to Base Ops and told the Captain, "Don't send me back up there. They are dancing on the table and laughing at us."

"I already told you, JG," he tried to explain calmly as if that was going to calm me down. "Stay professional at all times. Be the better person." then he looked away as though the notes he was typing were more important.

I snapped, "Capi-tahn, you don't understand!"

"No, you don't understand," he stood up angrily. "We're under contract to work with them for the next however many years. They don't have a choice and neither do you. I know it's hard, but do your best."

"I can't do this for however many years!"

"You have to. I'll let you go back to the city for today, but from now on, it's just how it has to be. You have to do your best."

But back in the city I saw what the Captain had meant by the morale and the mission changing. Hardly anyone was dressed in DCU's; those had been replaced by Hawaiian shirts and flip flops. Someone was smoking a cigar, two other guys sat in front of their tents sucking on a hookah and I couldn't believe it when I saw a group of girls dressed in short shorts and tank tops, bikini strings hanging out at the back of their necks as they sauntered past the guys with the hookah, who called after them, "Going tanning?"

They played shy and giggled, then one guy smacked the other in the shoulder and said, "Come on," and I knew immediately the girls were going to the fenced off area to tan, I'd heard of it but had no idea where it was, and the guys were going after them to leer.

I decided I'd make my own tanning area behind my tent and changed into my bathing suit, laid down a towel in the small alley created by the generators and the back of other tents, and marveled at how peaceful it was to soak up some rays and forget about the rest of the world.

"What do you think you're doing?" Wright towered over me as I was about to fall asleep.

"What does it look like?"

"Grillo, you can't." He almost sounded sorry.

"Read?" I lifted my book and hoped he'd leave me alone.

"I don't care what the other women do around here, but as long as you're under my command you're going to respect the rules of this land. You will not suntan, period. If you don't get dressed this instant, I'm writing you up."

"No one can see me. It's not fair."

"I know." He extended his hand to help me up. "And I'm sorry, but the rules are the rules."

Reluctantly, I let him pull me up, took my towel and book, and wondered why all the assholes, the sticklers for the rules, were always in charge of me. Then I went to the post office where I found a huge package addressed to George and me, and although I hadn't thought about it at first, after seeing his reaction when I brought it back and placed it on the cot I said, "It couldn't be, could it?"

"It sure could." He frowned as he tore at the box and pulled out two Goretex coats, goggles, and scarves.

"It's ninety degrees outside now! Just in time!" I laughed.

"I'm going to call the Chief and thank him for the rush delivery," George scoffed.

I put my coat on and walked up and down the aisle and said, "I'm never taking it off. I don't care how hot it gets."

Then George put on his goggles and scarf, walked behind me, and said, "I'm never taking these off either! They're my favorite."

"I guess better late than never." I took the coat off when a bead of sweat rolled down my temple.

"I'm going to cuss him out." George balled his fists, making me realize Satan had beaten us both.

Then I slipped out of the tent with nowhere to go and nothing to do and with the stone cold reality sinking deeper. I was never, ever, ever going back home.

FIFTY

Someone had sandwiched a cot between mine and Josie's and although I wanted to blame the girl sitting on top of it typing on three different laptops, she looked completely out of place with her long, smooth brown hair and pale skin, so much so I could tell she wasn't military.

"Hi?" I stepped over her large suitcase in the aisle and asked, "Are you Air Force?" Even if she'd said yes, I wouldn't have believed her. She glanced at me, surprised, and shook her head. "Civilian?"

"Yes," she said shyly, but also as if she was amused.

I said, "Out here? So, may I ask what someone like you is doing here?"

She shrugged.

"Where are you from?"

She stared at me as though she wanted to answer and couldn't because the tent might be bugged.

"What are you doing here? How old are you? What's your name and what are you doing with three laptops and enough luggage to live out here for three years?"

"Megan, twenty two, and I can't tell you anything else."

"I hope you don't think I'm nosy, but I am. Nothing new ever happens around here."

"It's okay. You're fun," she replied, turning her attention back to the laptops.

"I'm guessing you can't tell me exactly why you're here, but can I ask you yes or no questions?"

She nodded.

"FBI?"

"No," she replied, which led me to believe she was CIA, just like the pilots. What a badass. She was the female version of Jason Bourne, only much skinnier. If I was a guy I'd have a crush on her.

"CIA?"

Her eyes grew wide. Bingo.

"Is your mission top secret?"

She ducked so that her face was hidden behind one of her screens, as if that was going to make me lose interest, but I waited. Finally, she said, "You can sit," and lifted one of her laptops.

Sitting down, I covered my face with one hand and said, "I don't want to get you into trouble."

"Trust me, you won't understand what you're looking at," she giggled.

I stared at the graphs on the screen and said, "You're right. Looks like hieroglyphics. So how long are you staying for?"

"I don't know. I'm here with six guys, but they're in another tent with all the equipment. We travel all over the place and how long we stay just depends upon how quickly we can get the data we need."

"More equipment? You must have needed an entire plane to get all this here! You've got to be the coolest person I've ever met."

"Thanks," she smiled, turned off all her laptops, and said, "I'm done for the day if you want to show me around."

"Well, around isn't much, but I do have keys to the van if you want a tour of the city and the tower?"

"Sure, I've never seen a tower."

"Then you've come to the right place."

At the tower, Simon was kind enough to explain all the sand dunes and F-4 fighter aircraft on the ground to Megan. As soon as Moses could, he pulled me aside and said, "Genie, I'm sorry."

Still a bit shaken by his actions, I didn't accept his hand right away, looked at him skeptically, and asked, "What made you change your mind?"

"My people stealing from museums. They don't deserve this country."

I nodded as though I understood what it must be like to have your hometown blown up and everything in it ransacked, then shook his hand and said,

"I'm sorry too," and guessed that was what the Captain meant when he said to stay professional. But professional didn't always cut it when you sat in a tiny room with someone all day, learned about their families and their religions, and ate their food and drank their tea.

Then, as if not to make a scene, he nodded for me to go and turned around as if nothing happened, and I rejoined Megan and said, "If you've seen enough, let me show you Base Ops."

The office was deserted when we got down there. All the computers were off and the only source of light came flooding in through the blinds, casting strange shadows on the walls, which was how I discovered the Captain face down on his desk.

"He works a lot," I whispered when we approached him.

I was unable to take my eyes off him even though a puddle of drool had collected on the table, and I was reminded of when I had him all to myself the night I lost the note. I suddenly wished Megan wasn't with me.

"I guess I should wake him up in case he has a meeting." I pinched his arm.

He awoke with a jolt, looked at Megan, but said, "Jen?"

"Yes, Capi-tahn," I waved my hand to get his attention. "This is Megan. I'm showing her around the base. I know you're busy so we'll leave you alone."

"Oh, hi!" He stood up, flattened his uniform shirt with a little too much enthusiasm, and said, "I'm not busy at all. I can show you around the airfield."

"No, it's okay, really, we were just leaving," I interjected, but he said, "Follow me," and Megan didn't waste any time getting right behind him.

The Captain opened the passenger truck door for her as if they were on a date and she smiled as if she wanted it to be so. Like a child, I slid into the back seat and crossed my arms, upset she got the front seat next to the Captain and I didn't.

"These are the runways, taxiways over there, the lighting system, and let's drive over to the revetment area," the Captain said.

"You never gave me a tour of the revetments," I said, fascinated by the large concrete domes used to house broken aircraft. The concrete shielded from engine run blasts or bombs in case one didn't drop during flight and then accidently went off. "They are really cool looking up close, like something out of a sci-fi movie."

"You never asked." The Captain winked in the rear view mirror as if he could tell I was upset, and I looked away, embarrassed, bit my lip, and blushed. "And here's where I catch people having sex all the time." He elbowed Megan to get her to smile, but she didn't think it was funny, which made me want to kick her out of the truck.

"Aren't they embarrassed?" I leaned forward, trying to picture two naked bodies behind a concrete road block uncomfortably attempting to have sex. "What do they say to you? What do you say to them?"

"I hope you're using a condom," he replied matter-of-factly.

"You're so funny." I leaned forward and pushed his shoulder until I became distracted by three camels behind the fence along the runway and screamed, "Look, camels!"

"They're here all the time," the Captain replied. "Those are Bedouin behind the camels. They herd them."

"Can we go outside the base and get a closer look? I was six the last time I saw a camel. In Tunisia."

What I wouldn't give to be a kid again.

"It's not safe, JG," he crushed my dreams as he parked the truck at Base Ops, right where we started. "And I have to get back to work. Do you need a ride back to tent city?"

"I have the van," I showed him my keys but he couldn't take his eyes off Megan. He took her hand in his as if he were about to kiss it, and purred, "Come back anytime."

"Goodbye Capi-tahn." I tugged at Megan's sleeve so her eyes would unlock from the Captain's, but they didn't until we turned the corner.

"The Captain was really nice," she said dreamily when we climbed into the van. "I like him."

"He's the best," I agreed, not mad anymore. It wasn't her fault he was awesome and that I would give anything to have him look at me like that. And she was the best thing that had happened to me here, the first person my age who wasn't weird and I felt I could really talk to. I wanted her to stay forever. "What do you want to do next?"

"How about I show you my tent?" she sat up confidently.

"I didn't even know you had one." I drove through the gate, parked the van and dropped the keys, and followed Megan's lead to a camouflaged tent I couldn't remember if I'd ever seen before or not.

"How long has this been here? Look at all these containers out here. I can't even begin to imagine what you're doing here."

But instead of answering, she said, "Come on," ducked in the tent, and shouted, "Ready or not, we're coming in."

Inside it was cold, much colder than in any of our tents, and as dark as a cave. Computer screens were scattered across three different tables along with a flat screen TV, the largest I'd ever seen, DVD players, video games, and so many crisscrossed cables on the floor I thought I'd fall if I didn't lift my knees high.

Simultaneously, six chairs swiveled in our direction and I saw six geeky smiles.

"Everyone, this is Jen," Megan said flatly. And as if she'd trained them to do so, they sang in unison, "Hi Jen!"

Megan pointed left to right and acted as if it was a chore to introduce us. She said, "Tim, Dave, Lou, Andy, Rick, and Dave number two, who we call Meatloaf so it doesn't get confusing."

"Are you working now?" I squinted at no one in particular. Most of them were in flannel shirts or jogging pants and undershirts with holes, as though they were about to sleep. Some had scraggly beards as if they hadn't been able to shave in this wilderness, and all had thick black framed glasses on and stared at me expectantly. "I hope we're not interrupting."

"Has Megan told you anything?" Tim smiled.

"No, she scared me half to death earlier with all her laptops. I don't want to know anything."

"Suit yourself," Lou sighed, making me feel like I'd missed out on some top secret stuff.

"Put on a movie and stop talking so much, Lou," Megan ordered, no longer the meek and shy person she was around me or the Captain.

"I got them right here," Rick shuffled through a pile of DVD's. "How about Daredevil, is that alright with you, Jen?"

"Sure," I replied. "Anything will be great, believe me."

"Good choice." Rick loaded the DVD player, unplugged a computer screen, and connected the player to the TV. "It's not even out of the movie theaters yet," he giggled.

Meanwhile, the other guys moved all the chairs into a semi-circle and Megan asked me what I wanted to snack on. "Cashews, Doritos, sunflower seeds, Pepsi?"

"Pepsi?" I asked, surprised. "I never liked it before, but all we have out here is Arabic Coke. I'll take it."

Seconds later the commercials jumped to life, so loudly I wondered what people must be thinking as they passed the tent. I took a sip from the can, thinking this was the best soda I've ever drank in my entire life, and suddenly I was homesick, or whatever you called it when you want to live a normal life again. When the movie started and Ben Affleck and Jennifer Garner lit up the screen, I couldn't remember the last time I'd been to the movies or the last movie Evan and I had seen. My former life was slipping away more and more each second.

As soon as the movie ended and the credits rolled, Megan jumped up and said, "Ok guys, that's it, we'll see you later," as if she was in some kind of hurry to get back to our boring tent.

"You don't want to play cards?" Dave tried to get us to stay.

I nodded, "Yeah, cards would be awesome," because the last thing I wanted to do was leave. It was like being in an oasis, around civilians who didn't have anything to do with the war, and for the last two hours I'd completely forgotten where I was.

"No, we gotta go. Right, Jen?" Megan insisted and I agreed, waved, and followed her outside.

"I'm sorry if you wanted to stay longer," she said once we were away from her tent. "But I've been around those guys every day for the past six months and I can't handle being around them for any large amount of time."

"I know what you mean," I replied, because if the choice was hanging out with her or anyone else here, I'd choose her every time. "I hope you never have to leave," I added, but she said nothing, as if she didn't hear me or didn't want to answer, and I let it go, thinking it might be better not to know.

FIFTY-ONE

"Where is she?" The Captain glanced past me, looking for Megan because we'd been inseparable for an entire week before she disappeared into thin air and had me thinking I'd made her up.

"I'm fine, thanks Capi-tahn," I let my tray smack the table. "You've never asked to see where I was!"

"Very funny, JG, but I always know where you are. Now seriously, she's never far from your side, where is she?"

"I don't know, gone." I stirred the curry rice on my plate.

"There's just something about brunettes," he said, as if that was what I wanted to hear. "I think I had a dream about her the other night. I couldn't stop thinking about her. She really was different from anyone here, don't you agree, JG?"

"Yes."

"So, where did you say she went?"

"She has a boyfriend," I snapped.

"Well, I don't like her like that. I'm just saying she was interesting. Really, where is she?"

"Lay off, she's gone, okay?"

"As in, left?"

"How's your game of Risk going?"

"Very funny," he narrowed his eyes. "I have to go, but if you're working tonight or tomorrow, can you get some toner from Base Ops for the tower fax machine? I keep forgetting to bring it up."

"Sure thing, Capi-tahn," I waved, happy that he was leaving for once. "I'm going there right now."

But the Captain had obviously forgotten to tell Neill and Ed that I was coming, because as soon as I opened the door to the office they stared at me from behind their desks with wide eyes as if I'd interrupted something very important.

"I'm just here for some toner." I glanced at Ed cautiously, but couldn't tell why he looked like a deer in head lights.

He was a fat kid from Ohio with beady eyes and glasses and I hardly ever saw him because he insisted on working graveyard shifts only. He hated the sun and loved scrambled eggs and therefore could only eat one meal a day, breakfast, at the chow hall so that his day solely consisted of sleep, work, and eating.

Neill was the exact opposite of Ed. Tall, lean with reddish blonde hair he combed to the side, and male model-like cheekbones. If he didn't act so shy about everything he'd be drop dead handsome, but he rarely spoke, nothing more than hello, and usually averted his eyes so that I still didn't know the color.

"What's going on? Am I interrupting something? Didn't the Captain mention that I was coming? He said the tower needed toner. Is that alright with you two? You're looking awfully weird."

"Yeah, sure fine, why wouldn't it be?" Ed said.

"Yeah, why wouldn't it be?" Neill added.

"You guys are being very strange."

"We are?" Ed looked at Neill. "No we're not."

"Yeah, I mean no, we're not," Neill repeated.

"Seriously guys, what's up? It smells in here."

"No it doesn't," Ed shook his head.

"No way, what are you talking about?" Neill chided.

"You got your toner right? Have a good night, Jen," Ed smiled.

"No really, it smells in here, like food or something, but not food from the chow tent. This is different."

Suddenly I was Pepe Le Pew, the cartoon skunk who floated in the air when he smelled something delicious, and I ended up in front of Ed's desk. He was holding on to his desk drawer so tightly I saw white knuckles.

"You can tell me, what's the big deal?" I stepped closer.

"There's nothing to see." He attempted to shove me to the side, but as soon as he lifted his hand I pulled the drawer open and saw a personal sized Pizza Hut box, an empty McDonald's French fry container, and a crumpled Burger King burger wrapper like a cherry on top.

"What the hell?" I gasped. "Is this the Twilight Zone? How did you get this, where did it come from, do you have more? I would kill for a burger, please, tell me!"

They stared at each other and telepathically came up with an agreement not to say a word.

"I don't know you guys very well and you don't owe me a damn thing, but someone better start talking! I've been stuck in this hellhole eating shit food while all the while you guys are eating like kings? No wonder you're not losing weight!"

They averted their heads, as if that was going to make my pleas any softer or my arm-waving any less intense.

"Come on, guys! Just tell me where you got it from. I have to know. I just want one measly little burger, something, anything!"

"Italy," Neill sighed.

"Neill!" Ed hissed.

"Oh, come on," Neill shook his head. "Who is she gonna tell?"

"Yeah, I won't tell anyone! Promise!"

"When the C-17's fly in at night they come from Italy and we ask them to bring us stuff," Ed confessed.

"That is absolutely brilliant," I muttered in a daze as I pictured the operation. "I hope you guys are thanking the pilots. A lot!"

"We do," Ed nodded. "But you wouldn't want it anyway. By the time it gets here, it's cold, stale, and gross."

"The hell I don't!" My mouth was already foaming at the thought of a thick, greasy, gooey burger. "If it's good enough for you, it's good enough for me. Please, I'll do anything. Just a bite next time they bring some in. Pretty please. I'm ready to rip my hair out, I want it so badly!"

"No," Ed replied firmly, but Neill stared him down as if to say, "Come on, all she wants is a bite." He finally agreed, "Alright, alright, we'll see what we can do. Now get out."

By the time I made it back upstairs, the phone was ringing and on the line was Ed, who told me his radios had just gone out but that he was expecting a cargo aircraft.

"He's twenty minutes out, and I was talking to him when the radio died. When he comes up your freq. I need you to ask him if he has anything to download. It's Cargo 189 and we have nothing for him to upload, you need to tell him that and then call me back so I know. Got it?"

"Got it," I jotted the info on a notepad and read it back to him.

Like clockwork, Cargo 189 called me a few minutes later. "Tower this is Cargo 189, ten miles out."

It took me a second to reply because the pilot's thick, scratchy Southern drawl made him sound just like Bill Clinton, and I wondered if anyone had ever told him that.

"Cargo 189, Tower, report three mile final." I laughed as I pictured Bill Clinton flying the plane. It was obvious I was laughing at his voice, but I couldn't keep a straight face. "Say download."

"No apples, no oranges, no grapes," he replied annoyed, and for a second I was stumped until I remembered the little brunette from the schoolhouse showers who'd told me about the radio codes that changed daily.

"Say upload," Bill Clinton prompted me, but I didn't know the codes and didn't have time to call Ed. Trying to be creative, I said, "No goat, no sheep, no camels," but since he was probably already annoyed at me for laughing he didn't respond for a long time, and I was grateful he couldn't see my cheeks flush with embarrassment.

I called Ed back with the info, cleared the C-17 to land and was surprised when the Captain came running up the stairs a few minutes later.

"JG!" He took a second to catch his breath and smiled as if he was really excited about something. "Funny thing with that C-17 pilot," he said. "He asked about the female in the Tower and said you were a piece of work. I agreed, but wondered how he would know that?"

"I have absolutely no idea, Capi-tahn."

"Huh, well, have a good night," he said, leaving.

I almost thought he'd come back five minutes later when someone opened the door and screamed, "Yoohoo!"

Ed slowly walked up, held a wrinkled brown Burger King bag in the air, and said, "You want it?"

"For me? Are you sure?"

He tossed it at me like a basketball and said, "Take it before I change my mind."

"What do I owe you? I don't have a million dollars, but that's how much this means to me."

"Like I told you before, it's cold, and don't tell anyone! Oh, and here's a Pepsi," he pulled an American Pepsi can from his cargo pocket, making me feel like I'd hit the jackpot.

"Ed, I can't thank you enough. I don't know what to say!"

"Nah, we've got plenty, don't worry about it," he waved as he descended the stairs.

"I love you," I called after him, but the door already slammed shut.

Gently, I set the bag on the table, popped the Pepsi can open, and took a swig without swallowing right away. Every taste bud was in overdrive and I wanted to hold on to that sugary taste as long as possible.

"For you?" Omar wrinkled his nose. "Burger? Burger King? Yech."

"Yes, Omar, isn't it beautiful?" I turned the dilapidated burger by the wrapper so he could see it from all sides.

"No," he turned away as though he couldn't believe I was about to eat it.

"I agree, it's not much to look at." I studied the deflated bun, lumpy ketchup, mayo, and cheese mess. "But it smells fantastic, doesn't it?"

Trying to waft the scent to my nose, the burger was so cold it smelled like chemicals with a hint of ketchup instead of food, but my senses were already heightened and I was ready to taste it. I picked up the Whopper with two hands, stuffed it into my mouth as far as it would go, and took a bite.

"Genie, no!" Omar said disgusted, but it was too late, I'd taken a bite, made it through the stale bun, wilted lettuce, warm mayonnaise and ketchup, hard cheese, and spongy beef, and had left this Earth.

"Oh yes!" I mumbled and took another bite even though I hadn't finished chewing yet.

Omar turned his face away as if it was too much for him to witness me lose my self-control over a burger, but I didn't care. I'd been sent here to die and was granted a dying wish, a burger, a piece of home. Who gave a shit whether I ate it with manners or not?

"It's just a burger," Omar wrinkled his nose.

"Oh no it's not! It's a Whopper!"

"Wha-ppar?"

"Yes, best burger ever." I picked hardened cheese from my teeth with my tongue.

Then I glanced at the clock. My two minutes of absolute happiness were over. My stomach gurgled in protest because even back home I didn't eat fast food. Here, it was all I could think about.

Omar stared at me and I at him, and we thought the same thing. I was mad. I'd lost my sanity for good and there was no turning back.

FIFTY-TWO

The Army moving in from one day to the next felt like a rat infestation.

"Why are they here Capi-tahn?" I caught up with him in the chow tent. "They're disgusting! The women spit in the shower, not like they have toothpaste in their mouths, like they're truck drivers with hair balls stuck deep down in them, and they don't conserve water! They do chest bumps and push-ups in front of the chow tent with the guys, and what is with the reflective gear group fitness? Are they trying to get killed and make it easy for snipers to find them?"

"They're only here for a month, JG," the Captain said, amused. "It's for our protection, a new Air Force policy. The Army goes where we go."

"Where was our protection when we first got here? And their tents are huge, like hangars! It's just a matter of time before we get blown up because of them. They're just so, so different from us. Can't you send them away sooner?"

"No, JG. They'll be moving on soon enough, going to the front lines."

"I don't necessarily want them to go there," I replied sadly. "How about you send me home? You're sending everybody else- at least, sending them away when they land."

"No," he said sternly. "And that's different. The more people I send away, the less people need to leave home."

Why couldn't I have been one of those lucky people? I'd be sitting at home right now, none the wiser.

"One of their officers propositioned me to sleep in his tent with him. Is that their policy too?"

"That's their policy." He glanced away as if he wanted to say something different but changed his mind. "I guess, save money and house them all in one big tent. They don't believe in fraternization."

I wished he didn't either. "So, when's it going to be our turn?"

"Bye, JG," he shooed me away, and I suddenly felt old, like four months had taken forty years to pass, and watching this entire squadron come and go was going to make me feel worse.

I went to the gym to clear my mind, but couldn't shake the feeling that I was a hamster in a cage never able to escape no matter how fast I ran. The TV's in my face only made it worse, blasting all the bad news from around the world as if that was going to give me any hope of ever leaving.

But suddenly the scene changed to a young, blonde hotshot reporter on the outskirts of our tent city and I almost fell off the treadmill. It was unmistakable, our little tower, the fence, and the rows of tents, and she was broadcasting it to the world as if we didn't already have a target on our back!

I would have walked outside and hopped the fence to punch her myself, until the screen changed to "This just in," and I became transfixed by dark and grainy night vision goggle footage of an American girl being rescued from a hospital.

Her name was Jessica Lynch, and I repeated her name over and over again so I'd never forget it, so I'd be able to find out what really happened to her beyond the cockamimi story on the subtitles. I didn't doubt for a second she was ambushed and everyone was killed. What I did doubt was that she was going to be fine, that she didn't remember a thing behind that wave and brave smile.

All I kept thinking about was that I could have been her, any American girl who wanted to go to college right after high school could have been her, and this was the thanks she got after she sacrificed her life: dead friends and a fucked-up life because of poor and faulty leadership.

I wanted to leave this place so badly I could taste it. And it didn't help when a week later Saddam Hussein was captured and the Captain laughed at me and said, "We definitely can't go home now. You know better than that."

"But we succeeded," my voice cracked unwillingly over the clacking of his keyboard. "This doesn't make sense anymore."

"Actually, JG," the Captain paused as if to emphasize there was not a snowball's chance in hell that we were leaving. "More tent cities are being built in the theater because there will be more uprisings."

"Is this ever going to end?"

"It's already over. We're here for peace."

"We're in the middle of nowhere. They don't need peace here! The days are all running together, Capi-than. I'm finding it hard to remember things."

"That's good." He'd lost interest and started typing again.

I put my hands on his desk in protest and said, "Why are you trying to push me over the edge? There is only so much I can take, and I couldn't take it three months ago!"

"Lighten up, JG. If you haven't noticed already, tent city is coming down. Any day now we'll be back at the cafeteria. The post office, gym, and AAFES are coming down tomorrow, and didn't you notice the trailers? We're moving in there."

"Those are for us? They look like trailers in a trailer park. Why?"

"They're to protect against sandstorms."

"They're ugly and a few months too late, don't you think?"

"Trailers are a good sign."

"If it's a sign that we're going home, then it's a good sign."

"It means we're here to stay," he cut me off. "The next step, maybe in a year, they will build barracks and then we'll be able to rotate out, knowing that everything is secure."

"Next year?" I pictured construction crews plowing over the desert then thought of Evan, who was sitting alone in our apartment waiting for me. "What if Evan won't wait a year?"

"JG, go!" he snapped, and I left his office in a daze, not paying attention while driving on the road until I saw the gate guard chasing after the van with his gun raised.

"Airman! Stop the van!"

"I'm an American!" I put my hands in the air. "What's going on?"

"Well, America," the cop gasped when he caught up to me. "Your sticker expired. Who are you and what squadron are you with?"

"What sticker?" I replied, and he tapped the windshield with the tip of his gun. I shouted, "You were going to kill me over a sticker?"

"It's not just a sticker. It needs to be renewed."

"I don't know anything about a sticker! Call the Captain, he'll explain everything!"

"I don't have a phone. Park the van over there." He pointed with his gun and I thought I'd take matters into my own hands. What kind of guard shack doesn't have a phone?

I parked the van and was headed towards the comm. tent until the gate guard raised his gun again and said, "Get on the ground, airman, or I will shoot you!"

"I'm going to call the Captain!" I said, panicked.

"I told you to park it over there and not move!"

"I'm on your side! Do you see my uniform? I am an American, why are you trying to kill me over a sticker?"

"Get in the van, airman!" he screamed, putting a walkie-talkie to his mouth and calling for backup as I crawled back to the van.

Within seconds, as if this was the most exciting thing that had happened in weeks, four mock cop cars with flashing lights skidded to a halt in the dirt. Eight cops got out and pow-wowed for a second, until the eldest one with salt and pepper hair decided to brave it to my van.

"Why are you being uncooperative, airman? State your name."

"My name is Grillo," I sighed.

"Face forward!"

"I was just coming back from the tower and I'm hungry and tired and I wasn't thinking about any sticker."

"Stop being argumentative."

"I'm answering your questions."

"I don't like your tone!"

"Call the Captain. He'll explain everything."

"What Captain?"

"I don't know *what* Captain. *The* Captain!"

He studied me for another second before he stormed off, and I watched as all of them became engrossed in a deep discussion and wondered what the hell they could be talking about until the Captain's truck appeared. My hero had come to save me!

With his hands on his hips he listened to them for a minute, which I was sure was protocol, before he ripped them a new one. Finally, he came over to the van and I opened the door to hug him and said, "Oh, Capi-tahn, I'm so glad to see you!"

He pressed the door shut and hissed, "What the hell are you doing?"

"Me? What did they tell you, Capi-tahn, because it's a misunderstanding! They tried to kill me!"

"JG, quiet," he barked. "Don't you know better than to argue with these guys? Do you have any idea how much trouble you're in?"

"What?"

"I'm writing you up, just as soon as I can calm down and calm those other guys down too."

"Traitor!"

"JG, go to your tent, now!"

"Go ahead and write me up!" I got out of the van and slammed the door and screamed loud enough for all of them to hear. "I don't care anymore! You can go to hell and while you're at it, send me home and end my career because I just don't give a damn!"

But he didn't send me home. He sent Lena and Josie instead and gave me the day off so I could watch them pack. They were mostly packed anyway, and therefore cracked jokes about who they'd see first and what they'd eat and where they'd go once they got home.

My mind drifted as I pictured Evan picking me up from the airport, sweeping me off my feet and kissing me until we got to the car where he'd have sex with me right then and there because he'd missed me so much...

"Stay in touch, okay?" Josie and Lena hugged me as though they'd already forgotten about me, and I envied them for the fact they would no longer eat curry food and have to take scalding hot showers in the dark or brush their teeth with a bottle of water that had been fermenting in the sun for weeks on a pallet. No longer would they have sand in their ears, yellowed laundry, stolen laundry, or nights so lonely you thought you were the only living creature on earth. And best of all, no more asshole Captain.

"Yeah, I'll stay in touch." My eyes fell on my cot, my grave, and I swallowed my tears, wanting nothing more than to choke Satan out for sending me, and the Captain for keeping me hostage here.

FIFTY-THREE

"The Captain wants to see you, ASAP!" Queen Latifah ran up the tower stairs, hours before my shift was up.

"Do you know what it's about?" I replied, afraid to leave since I'd managed to dig myself in the hole deeper since the gate guard incident when last week I left the Captain stranded at the tower.

He'd told me he'd be right down and I waited in the van for an hour and left when I assumed he'd forgotten about me. Then he'd caught up with me at the cafeteria and was so pissed he couldn't unclench his jaw to speak.

"No," she said, looking annoyed to be there.

I said, "I guess it had to catch up with me sometime."

At Base Ops, the Captain was on the phone. I sat in the metal folding chair in front of the Captain's desk and attempted to peer over his keyboard to read the papers in front of him, but couldn't tell if it was a Letter of Reprimand or an Article 15 that would end my career, like I'd dared him to give me. Then I glanced at Neill and Ed, who seemed to be amused, and I wondered how badly the Captain was going to kick my ass.

When the Captain finally hung up he stared at me until I said, "Well? What did I do now?"

"Stop loss has been lifted," he shrugged.

"What does that mean, Capi-tahn. You know I don't understand all that military lingo."

"It means you can go home. Unless you don't want to."

"Do I want to go home?" I leaped out of the chair. "Me? Yes, yes, yes, Capi-tahn, when, yes, thank you, yes, when?"

He pried my hands from his shirt and said, "Calm down. It was just a question."

"Capi-tahn, you can't do that to me!" I grabbed his shirt again. "How can you mess with me like that? I'm going to cry! Are you serious? What is it really? Please tell me, am I going home?"

"I'm not messing with you," he grinned. "There's a C-5 coming in tomorrow and they have two seats open. I want to send you and Ed, but I called Dover Air Base and they seem to be full. No rooms available because of NASCAR weekend. The next flight will be here in two weeks. That's when George and I are scheduled to leave."

"What? I don't want to stay another two weeks longer than I have to. I'll never get out of here. No, please, send me now, I have to leave, I want to go, my bags are packed, I'm ready. Damn NASCAR! I don't need billeting, I'll sleep on the floor, I'll walk home, just please, don't reconsider."

"JG, you are way too excited," he suddenly frowned. "Get out of my office. I'll take care of everything, just please, go!"

"You mean it, though? You won't change your mind?"

"Git!"

"Ay, ay!" I saluted him, but if Ed and Neill weren't there, I would have kissed him. I was going home. Home, home, home!

I went to my tent and went through my suitcase even though I knew everything was packed. Then I thought about all the things that could go wrong, like they had when Ryan had tried to get back, and I sat on my cot in that horrible tin can trailer and tried not to cry because it would just be my luck that a storm would come or the plane would break or Evan wouldn't remember what I looked like and we'd pass each other in the airport like strangers.

I woke up with a jolt, remembered what day it was, and quickly showered and attempted to drag my suitcases out of the trailer.

"Hey, JG." The Captain got out of his truck as if he'd been waiting for me and said, "I can drive you," then put my luggage in the back.

For a second he looked as though he was going to miss me, and I realized I was going to miss him too and that I was no longer mad at him for keeping me here. His hands were on the steering wheel so tight I almost regretted not staying the extra two weeks with him and George, and felt maybe that I was abandoning not only them, but the foreigners too, since I hadn't had the chance to say goodbye to any of them. I cared about what they thought of me, but not enough to stay. It was time to go and see what was left of my life.

"Hey, Ed, hop in," the Captain rolled down his window when he saw Ed dragging his suitcase on the side of the road as if he was more eager than I to leave.

Ed tossed his own luggage in the back and sat in the back seat. I was about to ask him how he'd dragged his fat suitcase so far until the Captain turned off the truck and the parked C-5 stared me right in the face.

"See ya." Ed hopped out as if the backseat was on fire, handed his luggage to the crew guy, and disappeared up the ladder.

The last time I'd seen a C-5 was when Ryan dragged me to an airshow I couldn't have cared less about. He'd made me go up the cargo hatch to see how big it was, because it wasn't nicknamed "the Galaxy" for nothing. That thing could carry tanks, busses, and helicopters. Now it was going to carry me.

"Thanks for sending me home, Capi-tahn." I said, ready for the beginning of the end.

"There were two seats available and I figured I'd at least give you the option."

"Bye." I put my hand on the door, but he held onto my arm and said, "Wait, before you leave, I can tell you, I think you're beautiful."

"What?" I pushed his hand away in disgust. "You're about five months too late! Didn't you know I liked you?"

"You were working for me. I couldn't tell you that."

"Is that why you kept me here?" He didn't answer, but his smile told me everything and I repeated, "I lost six months of my life because you thought I was beautiful? Thanks."

"Wait," he pleaded when I opened the door.

"The engines are on and I'm not missing this flight because of you."

"You were right about your Chief, Satan, as you call him. The day you told me you weren't supposed to be sent here, I talked to George and he confirmed everything you said."

"He did?" I whispered, surprised that George defended me and even more surprised the Captain could stab me in the back more ways than one. "And still you kept me here?"

"I called Satan and gave him regular updates on you and you know what, he's not half bad. I think you might have been exaggerating a little."

"You called the Devil himself and told him about me? How could you do this to me? I trusted you!"

"I told him what a wonderful asset you are that you are, a dedicated and hard-working airman, and he said nothing but great things about you too. I like the guy. I'm still not sure why you call him Satan."

"That's how he is Capi-tahn, a liar, a manipulator, he's the Devil! I call him that for a reason. Believe me, you have no idea who you're dealing with."

"Don't you think you're being a little extreme?"

If his plan had been to befuddle me to keep me there longer, it wasn't going to work.

"Goodbye." I slammed the door shut and didn't look back.

The engine was loud, and I stood stunned for a moment as the crew guy who'd helped Ed with his luggage approached and helped me with mine. The sun caressed my face and then a slight breeze seemed to push me forward, as if beckoning me to get to the ladder already.

I hurried to the ladder, climbed as though my life depended on it, and looked down even though they always say "don't look down." I nearly slipped, not because of a fear of heights but from the element of surprise at seeing the empty cargo area where there was nothing besides our luggage and a wooden crate. Then I thought, what do I care? I'm going home!

"Hey," I smiled at Ed, comfortably seated in a cushy pale blue airline seat. "Now this is a way to fly!"

Ed didn't look up from his magazine. I sat down unfazed and untied my boots and smiled when another crew guy arrived.

"Hi!" he said over the roar of the engines, handed Ed and I earplugs, and said, "Put them in your ears because the entire flight will be loud."

Satisfied we'd jammed the foam pieces in our ears correctly, he left and I sank back in my seat, ready to witness every minute of my journey home and still not believing it wasn't all just a dream.

FIFTY-FOUR

Ed's gaze was on the clouds when I awoke. I knew right away where I was, out of hell and homebound, and realized I'd never even asked where we were going.

"Ed?" I waved my hand in front of his face. "Where are we?"

He shrugged as if he didn't know or care and pointed at the seat next to me that was piled high with chips, candy, and soda to get me off his back. Without hesitation I tore into the Oreos and Doritos and felt like a pig until I saw four empty bags next to Ed.

I stood up and stretched, found the bathroom right around the corner and marveled at its size, easily ten times bigger than that of a usual airplane bathroom. I could dance the tango in here. I could live in here if I had to. Then I studied myself in the fake mirror, which was of a far superior quality than what I had been used to these last six months, and couldn't believe how well-rested I looked. I wondered if Evan would think the same when he saw me.

Not wanting to think about that yet, I opened the door and nearly knocked one of the crew guys over.

"Were you in the bathroom without your boots?" His lip curled in disgust when he looked down at my feet.

"Yeah," I shrugged.

He covered his mouth and laughed, "This plane does evasive maneuvers! The insides of that toilet have been all over that floor countless times! You're gross!"

"How was I supposed to know?" I asked defensively, but he hurried away as if he couldn't wait to tell everyone else what he'd just seen, and I thought, go ahead. What was a little toilet water on my socks when I was going home?

"Did he tell you where we're going?" I hollered at Ed as I felt the butterflies in my stomach.

"Nah," he replied, and I waited patiently because I couldn't see anything other than the wing from the window.

When we finally landed, we taxied for what felt like an hour and I said, "This has got to be the biggest airport in the world. It never takes this long to get to the terminal."

Ed finally muttered, "We're in Spain. Some naval base, can't remember what the Captain said."

I'd been to Spain many times as a kid but I was always by the ocean, and judging by the way the last six months had gone, I didn't expect to see any beach or water when we got out.

"Come on," the crew guy beckoned us to follow him.

He descended the ladder first, then Ed and then me. I froze when my eyes fell on the wasted empty cargo space and still couldn't move once I smelled clean air and the scent of freshly cut grass, my favorite smell in the world.

"Take your bags. It's going to be three hours for the maintenance check, maybe longer before we fly again," the crew guy said once my boots hit the tarmac, but I wasn't listening.

As soon I turned around and saw the field of sunflowers as far as the eye could see I was stunned. I thought I'd died and gone to heaven. Nothing could have prepared me for such beauty, the bright and vivid colors, and the peace I felt at that very moment, as though the last six months of hell had been worth it to see this.

Van Gogh's ghost suddenly whispered in my ear, "See why I paint these?" and I said, "Yes!" and wished I could run across the tarmac and touch every blade of grass and every petal, lie in the dirt and gaze up at the sky with the flowers all around me to soak it all in.

"Hey, Jen, hellooo, are you there? Jen! The car is waiting!" Ed put two fingers in his mouth and whistled.

Coming back from my trance, I stumbled backwards and said, "Do you see that? Isn't this the most beautiful thing you've ever seen?"

"It's lovely."

"I could kill whoever stole my camera," I climbed into the van, but no one knew what to say about that. "Why are we so far from the terminal? Is that normal?" I asked after a few minutes, and Ed burst into a fit of laughter.

"Duh, we're transporting nukes. Why do you think there were only two seats? In case we blew up!"

Every crew member glanced at me expressionless and didn't bother to answer as I recalled all the bomb procedures I'd learned in training. Now it all made sense: the long flight to avoid populated areas and the long taxi to a remote part of the airport.

"The Captain didn't tell you?" Ed laughed harder.

"Does it matter?"

"No, but it sure is funny. You should see your face right now."

"You've got three hours," one of the crew guys opened the van door for us. "It's not a huge terminal but the burgers in the cafeteria are the best and if you don't know what else to get, you should at least get a bottle of wine. It's real Spanish wine. Everyone buys at least one."

I followed Ed into the terminal until I spotted a row of phones and said, "Don't wait up," but just like all the terminals from the past none of them worked, and I reminded myself that it wasn't time to call home yet and let everyone know I was coming because the minute I did, something would go wrong and I'd never make it back.

When I caught up to Ed he was already in the 1960's retro cafeteria. Even the fat guy behind the register looked like he was an original and was extremely put off that we were in there and wanted to order.

"I guess I'll have the burger and fries," I said. "And one of those," I pointed at the wine bottle on the counter. I pictured Evan and I toasting together in our new apartment and wished I could buy a case.

"Here you go," the fat guy slid the tray towards me.

I took the tray and started eating at an orange and brown trimmed table. When Ed joined me he took one bite, let the burger fall onto his plate, and said, "Too greasy."

"I guess we're not used to this food anymore," I said, not wanting to waste the burger no matter how much it hurt my stomach.

Ed pulled a magazine from his bag and didn't reply so I was stuck with my own thoughts about Evan and what I'd say to him when I saw him. I thought back to the night before we left tent city when the Captain had sent us to an out-processing briefing.

It was supposed to prepare us for our departure, but only annoyed me when I was handed a stack of papers and forced to watch a cheesy video about couples arguing over what chores to do when they got back. That was not Evan and me, no matter what the psychologist with the flaming red hair and thick black glasses said. She didn't know us, didn't know everything we'd been through and that we were stronger than ever. We had our own apartment now, something I never thought we'd have, and our entire future ahead of us. This was only the beginning of better things to come.

But then why was I so worried?

FIFTY-FIVE

It was three a.m. when we landed in Dover, Delaware. I knocked Ed out of the way when the C-5 door opened and inhaled the air, the smell of freedom. I would have known we were home even if I was blindfolded, which I practically was since the only light posts were in the distance illuminating grassy fields that separated us from the dark terminal.

"Head that way," the crew guy pointed, and we were off, dragging our luggage through the mud until we stumbled into a curb.

"Wait here," Ed said, leaving me at the edge of the parking lot as he tried to enter through the automatic door. "It's closed," he came back a second later. "I'll try to find a phone and call a cab."

I sat down at the edge of the parking lot, stared up at the mosquitos dancing in the light, and thought about how lucky I was to be alive.

"Be here in a minute," Ed sat down and lit a cigarette.

Then it started to rain lightly, our foreheads and shoulders instantly covered in droplets, but neither of us moved. I couldn't remember the last time I'd seen rain or the last time I'd smelled the beautiful aroma when concrete was cooled by rain.

Sometime after that a minivan pulled in and a soccer mom hopped out and said, "Taxi?"

"That's us," Ed said and helped her load our luggage into the trunk.

"Strange taxi," I said when she got back in the van.

She said, "It's my car. I just work nights to make extra money."

"Is there a Dunkin' Donuts around here?"

"Not sure," she replied. "Never heard of it."

"It's alright," I sank back and studied the white picket fenced houses that we passed, wondering which one Evan and I would live in if we lived around here.

"How about that Circle K?" Ed asked, and Soccer Mom suddenly veered off the road and into the lot.

"I'm buying everything," Ed smiled, and we raced down each aisle until our arms could no longer hold all the candy bars and chip bags.

"I need a coffee." I tried my best to make it like Dunkins would, but it didn't taste the same and I forced myself to drink it anyway because I didn't have the heart to throw it away.

Ed was on his third candy bar by the time we got back to the van, but fell asleep almost as soon as his head leaned against the glass. I kept my eyes on the pretty houses and didn't realize until it was too late that Soccer Mom had been trying to talk to me.

We pulled into the Philadelphia airport around 6:45 and with the sun coming up, but I'd seen enough sunrises not to pay attention. All I cared about was the airport and getting the hell out of here.

"Good luck. See you." Ed caught me off guard when he hugged me quickly, then dragged his suitcase on wheels through the automatic door.

"He already paid," Soccer Mom said, waved, and drove off.

I stared at the terminal doors, alone for the first time in six months, and bravely went inside to find my American Airlines flight that left at nine.

"Thank you, soldier," a little boy suddenly hugged my leg.

I bit my lip not to cry when I saw his big blue eyes. When I looked up to thank his parents, he started running back to them and I searched for a bathroom to change out of my DCU's so I wouldn't be sobbing all day.

By the time I made it to my gate, I still had two hours left to kill. I left my bags in search of a magazine from the bookstore, but didn't recognize anyone on the covers. Then I sat down again, the payphone staring me right in the face, and the first people I thought about calling were Sami and Bilal to tell them goodbye, and George and the Captain to tell them sorry for leaving without them, although I wasn't. I was terrified to dial Evan. What if he didn't answer, what if he couldn't pick me up, what if he didn't want to?

I nearly laughed out loud when I picked up the receiver and heard a dial tone. Never again would I take a phone for granted. I mustered up the courage to call him.

"You're coming home baby?'" he said sleepily. "You're almost here? Of course I'll pick you up," he finished my sentences as I sniffled. "I'll call Ryan right away. I love you. I'll see you soon, okay?"

"Okay." I hung up and let my nerves settle as the terminal filled up with people drinking coffee and reading their newspapers.

I envied them for their normal lives and felt sorry for myself because I'd never have that. I was twenty two going on ninety, was used up and empty. Esposito had said "what was six months compared to a lifetime," but it was more like a lifetime had gone by and I knew nothing. If given the chance to run across that tarmac in Frankfurt Germany again, I would rather have run than to come back and feel this out of place.

My hands fidgeted with my pants the entire flight as I waited for an announcement that said we'd be diverted to somewhere and would be stranded for three hours for a maintenance check.

But the speaker remained silent, and once we landed and taxied to the gate my heart started pounding like when I'd run the race with the Captain and thought I was going to die. I had to see Evan. I had to get off this plane.

I unfastened my seatbelt even though the sign was still illuminated and made my way up to the front of the aisle, ignoring the dirty glares and the elbows as soon as the light went off. No one was going to get in my way.

Then the door opened and I was off, down the jet bridge, through the terminal, on the tram trying not to break through a window to get there faster, and once it finally stopped, through baggage claim to find the man I loved more than life itself, the man I was going to marry, the man who'd waited for me all this time. But he was nowhere.

Tears flowed down my face as I realized he wasn't there, or if he was, didn't recognize me. Like a lightning flash I saw him a second later, leaning against the wall with a backwards baseball cap and jersey and a crooked half-smile.

He opened his arms wide and I bolted towards him, burying my head in his chest and cried as if I'd never cried before. I inhaled all of him: the stale cigarette smoke, faded cologne, and beer and thought, oh yes, I am definitely home.

"Oh my God, Evan," I couldn't stop the tears. "Oh my God, I never thought I'd see you again."

"Good to see you too, baby," he shook my shoulders as if he was making a joke, but I couldn't laugh. All I could do was cry.

"It's alright baby, you're safe, you're home, everything's okay." He took my face in his hands. "I can't wait to show you our beautiful apartment, okay?"

"I thought I was dead."

"But you're here," he sounded confused. He tried to pull his hand away, but I wouldn't let him. I was never going to let him go again. "You have to let go of my hand, just for a second. I think I see your bags on the carousel."

"I can't. I can't lose you again."

"I'm not leaving you, I promise." He pulled at my hand, but he would have had to saw it off. "I'm only going a few feet."

"Hold my sleeve so I can get your bags," he said as though I was a child, and once he'd stacked them up he said, "Okay, now take my hand. The car isn't far away, okay?"

But I quickly realized nothing was okay. Everything was too loud, the crowd too close and too smelly.

"Get me out of here," I screamed, but outside it was worse as I nearly choked from the secondhand smoke and the oppressive Las Vegas summer heat.

"Get in," Evan unlocked the door and tossed the suitcases in the trunk. I would have walked right past it if he hadn't reminded me it was his. Then he blasted the radio and lowered the windows because he thought it saved gas when he didn't run the air-conditioner.

"Please Evan, I know this sounds weird, but I can't handle the noise right now and it's like a thousand degrees. Can you put on the A/C?"

"It's just the radio," he said, perplexed. "It's Nickelback, our boys, remember we love them?"

"Please," I said, and he sighed, turned the radio off, lit a cigarette, and puffed a few times before he tossed it out the window and turned on the air.

Billboards and streets I recognized but couldn't name flew past me. When he pulled into our apartment complex I knew where we were and yet didn't.

"Ready?" He parked the car, led me up the stairs, and opened the door. "Here's the living room, tada."

Tada, nothing, the place was empty except for his frumpy futon, and I thought we'd been robbed until he took my hand and said giddily, "Come in, come in."

In the bedroom was nothing more than his king sized mattress, not even sheets, just his tiny twin-sized comforter and two bare pillows. The trashcan next to the bed, however, was stuffed to the brim with tissues that told me instantly that his porn collection was alive and well, although he'd promised to throw it away. In the spare bedroom was nothing more than a cheap particle board desk and a computer. The fridge was bare except for beer and ketchup. And that concluded the tour.

"It's small, but it's ours," he nudged me, but it was hard to look at him.

"There's nothing here, Evan. What happened to all the money you were getting from my checks? Where is the furniture? You don't even have groceries."

"Oh, you know, I thought you'd take care of all that." He opened the patio door nervously, showed me the lawn chair on top of the fake grass rug next to the overflowing ashtray, lit a cigarette, and said, "This was where I sat and talked to you at night."

"Well, I'm feeling a little overwhelmed right now," I admitted. I'd pictured it all a little differently: bigger, cozier, sexier. Why wasn't he whisking me off my feet and carrying me to the bedroom? He could barely stand to send me off without having sex, now he didn't seem to want to touch me.

"I still need to get my car," I said when I was sure we weren't going to have sex. "Ryan sold it and never collected the money. Can't remember if I told you that or not, but I know I still have the spare and I'm getting it back. I'll show that punk."

"Let's just settle in for a bit." He stubbed the cigarette out so that ten butts fell onto the fake grass. Then he put his arms around my waist and said, "Things are going to be different now with us. I'm going to cut down on my drinking and like I promised, I'm getting rid of my porn too."

"You want to do it now?" I glanced at the bare bed.

"Maybe not right now," he kissed my cheek. "But definitely tonight, okay?"

"Okay, tonight," I agreed, knowing it wasn't going to happen.

I rested my head on his chest, surprised he didn't mention how good I looked and then again not surprised at all. What had the psychologist said? "Reintegration takes time. Work your way into your loved ones' schedules slowly.'

"I'm going to shower," I let go of him. "I can't wait to open my eyes under the shower and stand under lukewarm water!"

"Huh?" he looked at me quizzically.

I said, "Never mind, I'll explain later," knowing I wouldn't be able to.

How could I ever explain to him what I'd been through and what it felt like? I could barely explain it myself. From one day to the next I was ripped from my life while he carried on as if nothing happened. Now it was six months later, after what had felt like twenty years in a time capsule, and I was back. Just like that.

I didn't even know where to begin on how to reintegrate.

FIFTY-SIX

I gazed at Evan all night, unable to sleep. Had he awoken and caught me staring at him I would have said it was the jetlag, or that I was too excited to sleep, but in reality, I didn't want this to be a dream. What if I fell asleep and woke up back in the tent?

At six a.m. Evan's alarm sounded like a siren. I leaned over him to turn it off and he smiled at me and stretched.

"You set it by accident," I kissed him.

"No I didn't." He yawned, but I could tell it was fake and he was about to tell me something I didn't want to hear. "I'm golfing with the guys today. Thought I told you."

"Maybe you did, but come on, I've been gone forever. Can't you cancel?"

"We've had it planned for a week."

"But I just got back." Tears stung my eyes as the words "slow reintegration" flashed before me. "I haven't seen you in a very long time. Please."

"It's just a few hours."

"Your few hours could turn into all day when you drink beer." My stomach felt queasy.

"I gotta go." He stood up, picked the clothes he wore yesterday off the floor, and went into the kitchen to grab a beer. "I'll see you when I get back, baby. We'll do something fun."

"Evan, please," I begged, but the door slammed shut and the ground beneath me seemed to move.

I fell to the floor on all fours for balance, then crawled to the window just in time to see him peel out of the lot. Although I knew something was wrong when I started sobbing uncontrollably, I didn't know what. There was no reason for me to feel this afraid, especially after I'd survived six months of war, and yet I couldn't stop shaking, couldn't stand up, and couldn't shake the feeling that I was never going to see him again. What if he got into a car accident? He barely even said goodbye!

Then I opened the door, about to run down the street after him and stop him, but every building looked the same and I feared I'd get lost, and what would I do then? He didn't have a cell phone and wasn't coming back for hours! How could he do this to me?

My eyes fell on the open phone book where he'd put a star next to the golf course he was going to. He must have told me when he made the tee time reservation, but I simply couldn't remember. Had I known, I would have asked him not to.

I calmed my breathing long enough to dial the golf course number. Then I realized I was pacing, I never paced, and found it hard to breathe although I wasn't having an asthma attack. What the hell was going on with me? Okay, he went golfing and I didn't like it, but I was feeling as strung out as if I'd just witnessed a car accident, blood pumping through my veins and praying to God no one got hurt. Why the hell was I so scared and why the hell did I think he was about to get killed when he'd been drinking and driving since I met him and had never gotten into an accident before?

"Hi, I'm looking for Evan," I started crying again. "I'm sorry, but it's an emergency. Have you seen a tall guy, backwards baseball hat, and football jersey? If you could, can you have him call home please? He doesn't have a phone and I need to talk to him."

The receptionist sounded sympathetic, like she wanted to come over and help me with whatever it was I was going through, which only made me feel worse. What was I going through? What was happening to me?

I hung up, patted my legs, my stomach, my face. It was me, but I didn't feel like me. I glanced in the mirror. It was me, but it wasn't me. Why did I feel so different? How was it possible to understand that I was afraid but not know what I was afraid of?

"Baby, what's wrong?" Evan called twenty minutes later and I started sobbing harder than before because I couldn't put my fear into words and if I could, he'd think I was crazy.

"I'm sorry, I really am. I'm so embarrassed, I don't know what's going on with me, but please, can you come back. I'm afraid. How could you leave me like that? What if I never saw you again?"

"I shouldn't have left," he muttered regretfully. "Sorry guys, but I gotta go," he said to his friends. Then to me, "I'm sorry, I'll be right back, okay?"

I somehow said, "Okay," but didn't want him to hang up.

"I have to or I can't come home. Don't worry, I'll be right there."

I should have called Ryan, or anybody really, but all I could do was grip the phone in my hands and sob. Whatever this was, this ridiculous fear, this unknown panic, I could handle it. I could handle anything. At least, that's what I kept telling myself every time I was alone and my body convulsed with heart attack symptoms. And at least no one was around to witness it and run the other way.

On day fifteen of my arrival it was time to go back to the tower as if I'd never left. I put on my green BDU's and pretended I hadn't died and been reborn a freak, and wished I could erase the last six months as though they didn't really happen.

"Airman Grillo, have a seat." Satan's familiar voice lured me into his black hole as soon as I walked into the foyer at the base of the tower.

He studied me with a bemused smile, like he was the scientist and I his rat, and I thought of all the times I'd wanted to strangle him, jump over his desk and choke that smile off his face while I was gone. Now that I'd made it back I could actually do it, although I'd end up in jail with my life worse than ever, and with the same end result: him winning.

"So how do you feel, airman?"

I felt like punching his face regardless of the consequences. I felt like I was dead although there was blood pumping through my veins. I felt like I didn't recognize my life although nothing had changed except my address. And I felt like I couldn't say a word, couldn't even move a muscle in my face that would give it away and give him the satisfaction.

"I mean it, I want to know," he repeated, and for the first time I saw something other than mockery in his eyes. He truly was curious about what

I'd been through because that chickenshit had never been deployed and didn't know what it was like to be so close to death and survive.

"Fine," I managed.

"The Captain spoke to me on several occasions."

Hearing it from him almost stung me as much as when I'd heard it from the Captain, but I wasn't about to break now.

"I know he spoke to you," I took the upper hand. "What's your point?" He shifted uncomfortably and seemed to be searching for the right words to put me in my place, but said nothing. "I know everything. I know you wanted to teach me a lesson and I know you wanted me dead."

"He told me what a great asset you were," he interjected. "That's why I sent you. I had nothing but faith in you."

"I. Bet."

"Well, aren't you glad I gave you the best training possible?"

"That's funny, because I got rated all by myself and I sure don't remember you teaching me anything about being deployed."

"Can you tell me anything?"

I can tell you Evan touches me less than before, but for some strange reason wants to cuddle just as I finally fall asleep, although that makes me feel claustrophobic now. I can only sleep after I've tossed and turned for hours and only once I've surrendered onto my back as if I'm lying on taco cot, and once I do fall asleep, I have nightmares about being back there.

I can tell you that I hate leaving the house and when I do, I get lost, even if it's right around the corner, and get anxiety from hearing noises that I'd forgotten existed, like something as simple as a cash register or screaming child.

I can tell you that I know I cheated death and really, the entire war altogether, and can't even say that I was deployed because I never even saw a gun or pulled out the chem. gear, and still I can't shake the fear and I can't talk to anyone about it because I don't even know what it is I'm feeling besides trapped in my own mind.

And I can tell you that I'm scared as hell you'll send me back, because I know you can and even if you don't, even if I make it through my last four weeks in the Air Force, I can still get called back because in the tiny fine print of the United States Air Force contract it reads that the Air Force still owns me for four more years and can call me back at will.

"There's nothing to say," I shrugged.

"Nothing?"

"Good day, Chief," I stood up and excused myself. "I need to get upstairs and get my ratings back."

"I sent the coat as soon as I could," he called after me, but my finger was on the elevator button and my teeth clamped down on my tongue before I could say "Fucking asshole motherfucker, fuck you!"

If only everything in life was as easy as going back upstairs and getting my ratings back, I thought, coming home to an empty apartment that afternoon. I curled up in a ball on the couch and wondered if Evan was gambling or drinking or both, and didn't realize I'd fallen asleep until the phone rang.

"Hello?" I didn't bother to look at a clock until Evan said, "Jen, it's me," as if he was about to cry.

He never called when he was out and he certainly almost never cried.

"Evan? Are you crying?"

"Please, you have to help me," his voice slurred. "I hit a car. I'm at a gas station and coming home. My car is fucked up. Meet me downstairs with a screwdriver. I don't know what to do!"

"Please don't tell me you killed someone," I said. "Did you kill someone? Evan, you have to tell me!" I got off the couch and turned on lights.

"Just help me."

"Did you hurt someone?"

"I don't know, damn it Jen, please, not now! You have to help me!"

"Did you call the cops?"

"No."

"Evan, you have to call them now!"

"Okay," he said, although I knew he wouldn't. "I love you Jen and I'm sorry I've been such a dick. You're always there for me and I don't know why I take advantage, but I love you, okay?"

"Okay," I said. "I love you too." I hung up and dialed 9-1-1. It was the only way he was ever going to learn. It was a miracle this phone call hadn't come sooner. Someday he'd thank me.

Then I hung up before the operator answered, put on pajama pants, and dug through the kitchen drawer in search of a screwdriver. If Evan went to jail there was no hope of us ever having a future together, and if we didn't have a future together I'd have to move out and couldn't start school like I wanted to, and wouldn't be able to start my new life with Evan in three months when he got out of the military, and together moved to New Hampshire or Maryland and lived there happily ever after. Wasn't sticking together what relationships were all about?

Downstairs I waited in the dark parking lot for what seemed like hours until I saw his car roll in without headlights. I still didn't believe it was him behind the wheel of that crushed thing until the door opened and he stumbled out and I could smell the alcohol wafting towards me.

"Evan, how did you drive this thing home?"

He was so drunk he couldn't hear me. He dragged his feet to the back of the car and started prying the license plate off, and pulled so hard he lost his grip and fell backwards and started cursing.

"Evan! Talk to me!" I shook his shoulders once he gripped the plate again. "What are you doing?"

"Oh God, please help me, Jen. I know someone saw me. They're going to call someone. I'm in deep shit!"

"Tell me what happened." I pretended to feel sorry for him but I was really sorry for me. I should have left him years ago. I deserved better than him and now it was too late to walk away because I loved him and wanted him to get better.

"They won't find me if they don't have a plate."

"Your car is totaled!"

"Don't remind me."

Without warning, he let go of the plate and hobbled upstairs as if his insides were killing him.

"Did you kill anyone?" I said with my eyes on the cordless phone. It wasn't too late to call the cops.

"No."

"You're sure?"

"I was on the strip and I remember being stopped at a light and then I looked up and it was green and then *boom*, I think I fell asleep for a second, and the next thing I know my front end is in the back of a red pickup! I know people saw me. My life is over!"

"It's not over," I said unconvincingly. There were a million people on the strip in the summer. Lots of people saw him.

"Pray with me." He sat up again, took my hands in his, and closed his eyes. "I swear to you right now, I will never, ever drink again. I swear it!"

I awoke when I heard the front door slam shut and someone quickly walking through the living room with grocery bags.

"You went shopping?" I said, walking into the kitchen and deciding not to mention the obvious, that he'd taken my keys. "I actually can't remember the last time you went grocery shopping, if ever."

"Yeah." He faked a smile and with jittery hands emptied the bags that weren't filled with food, but with glass candles with Jesus and the Virgin Mary painted all over them. "I took your car."

"Do you think you maybe shouldn't be driving?"

"Help me light these." He handed me a candle and a lighter. "I'm fine. And don't worry, I'm looking at a used car today."

"You don't have any money."

"Stop questioning me! I need you to pray with me."

Evan set up candles around the room as if every piece of furniture would now serve as a shrine. Then he took my hands in his, bowed his head, and closed his eyes.

"Evan you're shaking."

"It's nothing. Withdrawals," he replied, and I thought of Nicolas Cage in the movie *Leaving Las Vegas*, where he tried to quit drinking towards the end of the movie but couldn't stop shaking. I didn't know it actually happened like that for real. I didn't know Evan drank that much or that he had that much of a problem until now.

"Pray with me that no one saw the accident. Pray that no one will call here looking for me. Pray that the military doesn't find out. Pray that I don't lose my license and go to jail. Promise you'll never tell anyone and don't answer the phone unless the answering machine goes off first."

"This is getting a little crazy." I let go of his hands, found the phone, and handed it to him. "Make the call, face your guilt. Call the police. You're not going to go to jail."

He whipped the phone into the couch, wrapped his arms around me tightly, and closed his eyes as if he was reliving a slow dance from his prom.

"You have to call the police," I wedged myself free. "Take responsibility and this will all go away."

"I can't," he whispered. "I'm scared."

"I'm scared too Evan, but you could have killed someone!"

"Stop saying that!" he said, picking up the phone and putting it back on the charger. That's when he saw a red flashing light that told him there was a message waiting. And that's when he exploded, "Why didn't you tell me anyone called?"

"I didn't know, I swear. I didn't hear anything."

"I can't listen to it." He bit his knuckle and pushed play anyway.

When he heard the stern voice of a female car insurance adjuster, he said, "Bitch." To me he said, "You knew!" and gripped his greasy hair.

"I didn't! But here's your chance to make it right. It's a good sign! Call her back!"

"Fuck her." He deleted the message.

"What are you doing?"

"I don't ever want to talk about this again!" He took my keys from the counter, punched a hole in the wall by the front door, and slammed the door shut when he left.

"Don't do this, Evan," I called after him, but he flicked me off, got in my car, and sped out of the lot, to the nearest bar, I was sure.

I wanted to leave, wanted to pack my suitcase and have Ryan pick me up and bring me to the house he was renting with Winston and Joe. They'd gotten out of the military months ago and were leading regular lives and working regular jobs, which was exactly what I needed.

If only I could've gotten that first shirt off the hanger and into the suitcase, then maybe it would have been easier. I just couldn't get over the fact that if I left, I'd be giving up on him and on us, especially after he stood by me while I was gone for six months. I couldn't just up and leave now, I had to stay. I owed him that much. That was what strong relationships were all about. That was how they stood the test of time.

FIFTY-SEVEN

I woke up with the sun shining so brightly in my eyes I thought I was back in the desert until I saw Evan sleeping peacefully next to me. Trying to do the same, I closed my eyes but couldn't get past my pounding heart, and gave, up wondering when I'd feel back to normal again. When would I feel like I'd been home for months and not since yesterday?

"I'll be right back." I gently climbed over Evan, my intention, to watch TV like I always did, until I caught sight of my running shoes in the closet and thought, if it helped me there, why wouldn't it help me here too?

The fantasy blew up in my face, however, as soon as I stepped outside. My body protested every step as if my limbs and organs knew what my brain was thinking: I had enough new things going on right now and sure as hell didn't need this too.

But I didn't want to turn back. The sun on my face felt comforting and if Evan was up, I wouldn't know what to say to him because it seemed like we were drifting farther apart every day, especially now that it was crunch time. He was getting out of the military next week and not once had he brought up when we were moving or where.

I had also started school again and didn't realize until halfway through the semester that I'd bitten off more than I could chew. In my defense, it was only so I could get my degree done this year, which had given Evan the idea that he should slip out of the house every minute he could, gambling and drinking the night away, so he wouldn't "interfere" with my homework.

To my surprise, everything suddenly made sense. I found a groove, found serenity, and for the first time in a long time felt in control as I inhaled, listened to my shoes on the pavement, left right, left right, and exhaled steadily.

I closed my eyes and saw "runner's road" right in front of me, felt the wind and the sand on my face, and then saw the white beat-up car that had waited for me, with the guys cramped in there to give me candy bars, and I had to stop running and started laughing so hard I held onto my stomach.

Oh the stories I'd tell, the Captain had said, and it was only a year out of my life, Esposito had said, and now I realized they were both right. I was home, I was alive, I had stories to tell and the rest of my life to live and I'd been too scared to live it. And it wasn't too late to start now.

I ran back, opened the door, and shouted excitedly, "Evan," kicked off my shoes and hurried into the bedroom to discuss our future.

But he was obviously not ready to discuss our future as he quickly turned off the TV, turned to the side, and pulled the covers up to his shoulders as if he was sleeping.

"Hey," I snapped, my good mood gone. "I saw you. I'm not stupid, you know. I thought you said you threw all your porn away. Don't you think I want some once in a while? You haven't touched me since I've been back!"

"Oh, hey." He faked a yawn as if still trying to pull off the charade, which infuriated me more.

"What is your problem? I'm in the best shape of my life and all you can think about is jerking off!"

"Jen." He took hold of my hand to pull me onto the bed, but I was tired of his lies, so I undressed and turned on the shower instead.

"I'm sorry, Jen," he said from the other side of the shower curtain.

"No you're not." I stifled my tears because tears had a way of drawing out Evan's complete indifference that he then used against me to make me think that this was all my fault. "It's the same old shit with you."

"You know I'm used to being alone."

"You're not alone," I ripped the curtain open. "I'm right here. I've been back for almost three months and we've been dating almost four years. When were you ever alone?"

"I don't know Jen, but I told you from the beginning we're never getting married."

"What is that supposed to mean?" I toweled off and put on a pair of shorts and a t-shirt which made him leave the bathroom, go in the kitchen, and get a beer from the fridge. "You also said we're never living together and guess what, we're living together!"

"Only because you forced me into it."

"What are you saying?"

"If you really want to know, I was thinking of moving back with my parents."

"As in next week and without me?" He nodded. I wanted to wring his neck. "When were you going to tell me? When I was driving you to the airport?"

"I never said we were going to get married," he repeated defensively, and I nearly fell to the floor to beg him to stay.

"But we've been through everything together. You're the only one I want to be with!" my voice softened.

"I don't know how to say this, but you nag too much," he shrugged.

"You mean to say I nag too much about drinking?" I was angry again. I could not believe what I was hearing. "Since you almost died and nearly killed someone?"

"It's your voice. Like nails on a chalkboard. I can't take it anymore."

"You can't take it anymore? I stuck with you through everything and now you're throwing me out like the garbage and walking away. You're killing me, you know that? Literally killing me."

"Forget it," he turned to leave.

"Fuck you! You'd better talk to me! You can't just leave from one day to the next!"

"All I'm saying is," he ran his fingers through his greasy hair and took a swig of beer. "I'm going back to my parents, start over and maybe get an FAA job, who knows?"

"Who knows? I've been trying to get you to apply to the FAA with me for the last two months and you kept saying you have to think about it and now you're saying you're doing it, but without me, like we haven't shared the last four fucking years together?"

"I never asked you to." He sighed as if he felt deflated, but it was me who was deflated.

"How could I have gone so wrong? I mean, everything I've done in the past four years was wrong or for nothing. I joined to make a better life for myself and ended up with you and Satan. You said I was "the one" Evan, what the hell did that mean to you?"

"I thought you were going to cheat on me."

"So you lied to me?"

"I do love you, Jen." He pursed his lips together so that more lies wouldn't fall out, then said, "I just think we need time apart."

"Time apart?" I gasped. "Could you say anything more hurtful to me? What have I done to you to make you hate me this much?"

"I don't hate you, Jen."

"No, you do. No one would do this to another human being. You don't even know I exist. You can't even tell how stressed out I've been. I haven't slept, I haven't eaten."

"I was gonna say, your legs were looking a little thinner."

"You son of a bitch!" I screamed, and as if suddenly possessed, walked into the kitchen, grabbed a knife, held it to my wrist, and said, "Well, let me make this easy for you!"

"Jen, stop! What are you doing?"

"You never loved me. I did everything for you and it was all for nothing!"

"Jen, stop!"

"Fuck you." I tossed the knife because it would indeed be too bloody, sprinted into the bathroom, and found his sleeping pills in the medicine cabinet.

"There's just no more fucking point." I swallowed the last of his pills and smiled, until I glanced up from the sink and saw his slack-jawed reflection in the mirror and instantly regretted what I'd done.

He wasn't worth the dirt under my shoe and yet I was going to give up my life for him?

"You crazy bitch!" He fumbled for the phone and I stuck my finger in my mouth and tried to throw up the pills. "I'm calling the cops."

I couldn't hear him as I gagged over the toilet, but nothing came out. My stomach was a steel trap. I could eat a huge meal and go on a rollercoaster with not so much as a hiccup.

"The cops will be here any minute. Yeah, you think you're so smart, think you'll swallow pills and just throw them up? It doesn't work that way!"

I hurried out of the bathroom, swiped my keys from the table, and made it out the door before he called after me, "If you go, I'll tell the cops your license plate and you'll get a DUI."

"Fuck you," I ran down the stairs two at a time, but it was too late. The first cop car pulled up as soon as I unlocked the driver's side door, and Evan pointed, "That's her officer."

"Everything's fine." I put my hands up, but the cop wasn't buying it and said, "Hand me the keys, ma'am, and come with me."

Suddenly I felt the pills working, felt whoozy and struggled to stand.

"Is this her?" the EMT opened the door to the ambulance. "Are you okay?"

"Officer, I'm fine, really, please let me go."

"Tell me what's going on," the cop said as the EMT took my pulse and nodded that I indeed was going to be fine.

"It was an argument," I replied. "He likes to overreact, that's all."

"They're going to take you to a hospital and check you out. Standard suicide call response," the cop said as he backed up and the EMT strapped me to the gurney.

"But I wasn't-" the door slammed shut and I watched through the little window as the cop went upstairs to join Evan.

"So how many did you say you took again? How long ago?" the EMT asked.

"Two," I said to shut him up. "Where are you taking me? What about my stuff? I don't have keys or anything!"

"You'll be fine. Just enjoy the ride. You'll be out of here in no time."

For a second I thought about bursting through the door, running back home to fight for my man, my life, but what was the point of fighting for something that didn't love you back? He was probably cracking another beer open this very second and joking with the cop.

"Your pulse is slowing," the EMT frowned. "Don't worry, we're almost there."

When the doors swung open, he unbuckled the seatbelt and helped me up, walked me through the emergency room and through a thick door that said "Psych Eval," which made me think I was in an Edgar Allan Poe novel because this was my worst nightmare: being locked up and no one knowing where the hell I was.

"They'll take good care of you," the EMT said. Then he signed some papers and left.

"Please wait in the room," a nurse said as I stared down at her phone. I needed to call Evan to get me the hell out of here. "Over there," she repeated sternly, and I wished I could rewind the last hour of my life, the last four years, all of it.

"I'm sorry to make you wait so long," a man in a white coat finally strolled in, sat down, and flipped through my paperwork.

"How long have I been here?" I looked at him from the hospital bed and he said, "A little over three hours," and I couldn't help but cry again because my cell phone was at home and I probably never was going to see it again either.

He handed me a tissue but my face was so raw I could only dab at my skin, which only made me cry harder.

"Jennifer, is it?"

I nodded.

"You're having problems with a significant other? Can you tell me more about it?"

"There's nothing to tell. I love him and he doesn't love me. I didn't just fail at this relationship, I messed it up from the beginning, trying to make something from nothing and had completely wasted my time."

"Do you want to die?"

I almost said, "Yes, what is the point of living if the person you love doesn't love you back?" but I said, "No." When that didn't seem to satisfy him I added, "It was drastic, I know. I'm a fool. I knew better but I'd convinced myself it would end up differently and it didn't, okay?"

"You look like a smart young lady," he said as he scribbled something on his clipboard.

I laughed, "Am I missing something? No smart person would have done what I've done or wasted all those years on a loser."

"That's not for me to decide," he said. "But I am going to release you." He stood up.

"You are?" I sat up too.

"Yes, but you have to take care of yourself. Forget about this guy and you'll be fine."

"Just like that? Are you kidding?"

"No. Walk away from him. Is there anyone you can live with?" He handed me a pen and then showed me where to sign.

"Yes," I lied and calculated how many pillows and blankets I'd need to make the backseat of my car comfortable. I was not telling Ryan about this no matter what.

"Good. Then this is the last I'll see of you. Take care."

"Yeah." I followed him out, hurried past the nurse's desk and outside before he changed his mind.

When I realized I didn't have money for a payphone, I went back inside and had the ER nurse call me a cab. It arrived thirty minutes later and I got in although I had no idea how I was going to pay him.

"Do you know that guy?" the driver asked when he pulled into my apartment building. I saw Ryan, looking worried as he stood up from the curb as if he'd been sitting there for quite some time.

"You okay, sis?" he asked as soon as I opened the door. I was embarrassed.

"I don't have any money," I muttered. "My wallet's upstairs and I don't even know if I can get it."

"I got it." He paid the driver then hugged me as if he wasn't ever going to see me again.

"You're cutting off my air," I gasped.

He squeezed harder and said, "Evan told me what happened."

"Oh," I replied, and wished I could slip through his arms and lie in a puddle on the ground for the rest of my life. "It was a misunderstanding."

Finally, he let me go, looked into my eyes until I turned away, and said, "You're coming with me. What do you say to that? We have plenty of room. You don't have to be alone. Evan said he'd be gone for a few hours so you can get your things. Whatta ya say?"

"He said that? What an asshole! I can't move out, not now!"

"He said the cops told him that you guys had to split up, for a while anyhow, so come on."

"What?"

"Yeah," he followed me upstairs.

"Asshole!" I repeated, opened the door and wished I could stay angry, but I couldn't.

This was Evan's and my home. We were supposed to be together forever.

Then I packed my bag and wiped the tears from my face because tomorrow was a new day, and in a few days Evan would call me and ask me to come back and everything would be back to normal. We'd pack our bags together and move to the East Coast like we'd planned and then get married.

All I had to do was make it through the next three days.

FIFTY-EIGHT

All I could think about was Evan as I followed Ryan's car through the small gated community, how I should be with him at this very moment and how we could easily have lived in one of these houses and started our own family. Then Ryan opened the garage door and reality set in. I was in a fraternity house.

"Come on, Jen." Ryan waved me out of the car, but I didn't know where he wanted me to come over to since the entire garage was a makeshift bar complete with stools, dart board, ping pong table, bikini posters and empty kegs along the wall.

"Hey, Jen." Winston and Joe appeared at the door and didn't let on they knew about Evan, although I knew they did.

"Thanks for letting me stay," I said, painfully reminded of Pam's basement. Somehow, I had pictured this all differently.

"Nonsense," Winston said.

"Yeah, whatever," Joe shrugged.

"Help me with her mattress!" Ryan said, and they ran past me as if that was the most exciting thing they'd heard all day, untied it from Ryan's roof, and carried it inside.

"Your room is next to mine," Ryan said after they dropped the mattress in the downstairs living room, now the only piece of furniture in it. "Here's the bathroom and outside is the patio and small backyard. That tree and grass is pretty much it."

"It's nice," I replied, wondering what Evan would think. "What happened here?" I said when I noticed a crack in the stair tiles.

"We've been meaning to fix that," Winston explained. "When we moved in we were trying to move the couch and slid it on the banister, then it took off on its own and fell."

I already missed my quiet apartment with Evan and wondered who he was with and what he was doing.

"I'm afraid to ask, but that's a pretty big hole in the wall." I remembered the hole Evan punched into our wall, which was tiny compared to this.

"Joe dared Winston that he couldn't smash his head through it."

"And he did it?"

"Yeah," Ryan replied as if he couldn't believe I'd even asked the question.

"But it's huge! I could fit in there!"

"He got a little carried away."

"Can we have a couple of rules now that I'm here?"

"Boo!"

"No!"

"All I'm saying is, you guys might do well with a little order, that's all."

"Who invited her here, again?" Winston joked, and they shrugged at each other like a "Three Stooges" skit.

"The living room is upstairs," Ryan opened his arms like a magician and kept walking towards the kitchen.

It was hard for me to move. I was stunned into silence by the silent porn on the oversized TV, the mismatched furniture, and the entire wall covered in neon bar lights that emitted so much heat I thought I was getting tanned where I stood.

"Uhm." I pointed at the TV, but no one glanced at me so I said, "You sure do have a lot of lights in here. How's the power bill?"

"We don't even need regular lights," Winston said. "Or heat."

"Oh," I replied, but only because I was so startled by the messy kitchen. It was if they hadn't done dishes since they moved in six months ago.

"So who's the Iron Chef around here?"

"Me," Joe shrugged. "I was gonna clean it."

"Last week," Winston joked.

"They don't complain when they eat," Joe added.

"He sure does get creative," Ryan admitted.

No one was bothered by the smell of rotten food.

"So who does the shopping?" I held my breath.

Joe and Ryan shrugged, then Winston said, "I don't know, we kind of all do, like what, every few months or so?"

"Sounds right," Ryan said. "When we get a chance."

"So who feeds the lizard?" I glanced into the glass terrarium.

"We take turns," Ryan said, but I could tell none of them remembered when they'd last fed him and that it was a miracle he was still alive.

"Let's go downtown and celebrate Jen moving in," Ryan smiled.

"I'm not really in the mood to go out," I said. What if Evan called? I needed to be close so I could leave at a moment's notice.

"Yeah, I thought we were staying in?" Joe rummaged through the pantry and said, "Maybe not." He held up a bag of Oreo cookies, "This is it."

"I'm really not hungry," I said even though I couldn't remember the last time I'd eaten. Sulking on my bed sounded like a better idea.

"No, no," Ryan ignored me. "Let's go downtown."

"We can stay local," Winston winked as if he was working a plan.

"The usual?" Joe asked in on it, whatever it was.

"Yup, let's do it," Ryan and Winston agreed.

I said, "Really guys, I don't feel like it," as they pushed me out the door and into the car.

"Why are you taking a raincoat, Joe? It's like a hundred degrees out!" I said when he got in the backseat with me. All of them laughed, as if I'd told a joke, but I didn't get it.

"I feel cold," he finally said, which had everyone cackling again.

I wanted to ask them what they were up to, but then Winston parked the car, opened the door for me and said, "After you," like a perfect gentleman and I forgot all about their inside jokes and thought I had them pegged all wrong. Sure, they were messy, disorganized and had jokes I didn't understand, but they had manners, they were all like brothers, what did I have to worry about?

For about an hour I sat and watched them play darts and drink beer. I nibbled on a slice of pizza, glanced at the drunk couples in the bar, and wished Evan and I were one of them until Winston suddenly said, "Alright, it's time to go," as if we were in some kind of hurry.

I wanted to make sure the guys left a big enough tip, but Winston insisted, "Jen, now," took me by the arm, and gently walked me to the door and held it open for me. But once outside he took off, as did Ryan, as if they were racing each other and for some strange reason wanted me to join in.

"Let's go, Jen!" Ryan opened his car door after Winston opened his and I said, "I'm here, what's going on? Where's Joe?"

But no one answered me. I barely had my leg in the door when Winston slammed into reverse and I fell forward. He rolled down the window and screamed at Joe, who was running through the lot with his raincoat belt flapping on the sides, "The trunk is popped!"

"What the hell, guys? Ryan, you're a server and you guys left without paying the bill?"

The trunk of the car suddenly slammed shut, Joe got in breathlessly, and Ryan screamed, "Go, go, go!"

"Yeah, man, yeah!" Joe turned his body and stared out the back window. "Coast is clear."

"Is someone gonna tell me what the hell happened?" I looked around anxiously, but Ryan, Winston, and Joe were laughing so hard they couldn't answer.

"Ryan, you work at Applebee's and you complain about people not paying all the time! Joe, I could have sworn you left money!"

"Joe took a sign," Ryan finally caught his breath enough to speak.

"What do you mean, a sign? What sign?"

"I didn't take it," Joe argued. "I simply carried it out."

"Whatever, it was Winston's idea."

"Hey!" I interrupted, "Come on, tell me!"

"Haven't you ever wondered why we have so many neon signs?" Winston laughed. "We collect them. From this place."

"You mean you steal them?"

"Yeah," Winston nodded.

I asked, "You don't have enough? I feel like I got sunburned just sitting in the kitchen for ten minutes," but this only made them laugh out loud again.

"Never enough!" Ryan joked. "Winston, you still up for going downtown?"

"Yeah."

"Let's do it," Joe agreed and I threw my hands in the air, thinking of Evan, who called the three of them "Goonies" for a reason and that if this was just the beginning of the night, I didn't want to see the end.

I said, "Wait, guys, guys, please. I love that you are taking good care of me, but I have to get home and do homework. Please, just drop me off."

"Aw, Jen," Ryan said.

"Party pooper," Joe said.

"Wuss," Winston added, and I prayed, please, Evan come back to me and get me back to our normal life and out of this constant frat party. Please!

FIFTY-NINE

For the life of me I couldn't figure out why the media said the FAA was hiring, were in dire need of new controllers because the baby boomers were getting out, but didn't call me even though I'd submitted seven different applications.

My savings had dwindled substantially and I was desperate when I scoured the newspaper and called the first thing that popped out at me, Personal Assistant, excited that it might be for someone famous and I'd be able to pay my bills on time again.

"Hello?" some guy with a thick New York accent answered as if I was bothering him.

"I'm calling about the job posting in the paper," I replied, ready to hang up.

"Oh, yeah, the job postin'," he said. "Yeah, can you interview tomorrow about seven in da mornin'? Unless that's a little early for you, most people I know are still partyin' at seven, ha, ha."

"Seven is great," I tried to place his voice. Did I know it from a movie, a TV show? Who was he that he knew people who partied until seven a.m?

"Okay, let's, uh, say we meet smack in the middle of the strip, at the Excalibur Hotel. It's my favorite."

No one over the age of ten would call the Excalibur Hotel their favorite, but I didn't want to judge if he was going to pay my bills, and said, "Okay," hoping he paid well so I could move out of the frat house sooner rather than later and into my own place.

"I'm Neil." He smacked his lips together loudly as if he was chewing gum and I said, "I'm Jen," with the realization that I didn't know any famous Neils.

The following morning I arrived a few minutes early, got out of my car and walked through the hotel, unsure of who I was looking for. As I heard another phone ring, I saw him: a short fat man with a black mullet, sporting a neon pink track suit.

"Who is dis," he answered and I paused, turned to leave to get out of there, because unless he was Danny Devito's twin brother, he wasn't famous, and by the sloppy way he dressed, probably didn't pay well, which wouldn't help my situation.

"Uh, It's me, Jen, remember we were going to meet at seven today?" I felt bad for wanting to ditch him and turned back.

"Oh, hey," he hung his phone up when he saw me and extended his greasy hand. I bit the inside of my cheek and shook it, couldn't take my eyes off the scary purple scar on the side of his cheek that looked like he'd lost a bar or prison fight and had me reeling for an excuse to get out of here. "What are you doing awake so early? Most people aren't up this early!"

"I thought we had an appointment," I replied, perplexed.

"Oh, yeah," he ignored me. "Change of plans. Let's go to the Excalibur café. It's my favorite."

"Yo honey," he called to the hostess as he pushed his way past an elderly couple a few minutes later.

He was not the kind of man I wanted to be seen with and I made eyes at the hostess to tell her I was sorry, but she didn't care and seated us anyway.

"I already know what I want!" he said, quickly glancing at the menu.

The hostess replied flatly, "Maria will be right with you."

"Broads," he shrugged at me. "You know what you want?"

"I'm not hungry." I slid the menu back at him.

He said, "Get something.' Most important meal of the day, you know."

"Uhm, yeah, but I already ate," I replied.

The waitress appeared and he said, "Pancakes, sausage, toast, and two eggs over easy," as if he hadn't eaten in three days.

"Just toast," I said when he glanced at me.

The waitress left. He took a toothpick from the dispenser in the middle of the table, caught me staring at his scar again, and said, "You wanna know about it?"

"No, that's ok."

"Do you know who I am? You recognize me, don't you?"

"Uhm. Yes?" I lied.

"Sure you do," he raised his eyebrows playfully. "I'm Neil Gregorio, the boxing champ."

"Yes, of course," I said unconvincingly and started fidgeting with my hands.

Fuck Evan for not taking me with him and putting me in a stupid situation like this. What the hell did I think I was going to do for a has-been boxer?

"I know I look a little different now." He was pleased with my answer. "I don't hit the gym like I used to and I gained a few pounds," he smiled and put a hand on his gut.

"You look great." I studied all the different jelly varieties on the table.

He raised his fists to his face and jabbed the air, "Oh, I was great. I was great!"

"I believe it," I replied, wondering when the bullshit session would be over so I could leave and go on a real job search.

"You know what? I forgot my resume in the car. Let me go get it." I stood up, proud of myself for coming up with a pleasant exit strategy.

"It's fine, it's fine." He waved me back down, just as food came and said, "I need someone to help me organize my business and help me with some personal things. I'm impressed you're up this early."

"Most people are up this early if they have a job," I replied, annoyed.

"Most people your age have been up all night doing drugs or something, but you look like a good kid."

"Thanks?"

"I need help moving today," he continued. "Things from my apartment and to my new office. I pay ten an hour and I can take the tax out if you like, or you can do that at the end of the year."

He shoveled pancake into his mouth but only half made it. Some stuck to his face. The other fell to the table.

"I prefer you take it out." I buttered a slice of toast and glanced the other way, wondering if anyone thought we looked weird sitting together.

"Or maybe you can," he spit pancake across the table. "Just deduct the standard Nevada tax. Moving on, I have a lot of sports memorabilia from fighters like Mohammad Ali and Tyson and plan to have them signed by them when they came to Vegas. Ali will be here next week and Tyson the following week."

"How do you know?" I considered who he might know, but judging by his appearance came up with nothing.

"I just know." He tapped his temple as if he had telepathy and asked, "Do you have a car?"

"Yes," I replied and regretted my answer when he said, "Good," and stuffed his mouth with toast dipped in egg. "Because I walked here this morning and I got stuff to move."

"Oh," I replied, instead of "how." This was not the sort of town you easily could walk anywhere to.

"Can you take me to Wells Fargo?" He flagged down the waitress. "I'm getting some money wired to me."

"Am I on the clock?" I asked skeptically, and he said, "Of course," which I supposed was our agreement that I was hired.

"Nice ride," he whistled after I unlocked the car door.

"It's a Hyundai," I replied, surprised that a famous boxer was impressed by that.

"That way," he pointed out the window and buckled his seatbelt. "Just a few blocks east."

"East?" I pulled out of the lot. I didn't want to be caught dead east of the strip with all the run-down motels.

"Yeah," he replied, then said, "That's the Wells Fargo."

I parked the car and said, "I'll wait in the car."

"You're my employee and I'm telling you to come in!" he replied angrily.

"Okay, I'm coming." I got out of the car and followed him in, wondering where the temper had come from.

Inside were an elderly couple and a young woman in line and the teller was in the process of opening her window.

"It's about time you opened up!" Neil elbowed me as if he was being funny.

"Neil!" I hissed, embarrassed.

"I'm trying to motivate her!" he ignored me. "Come on, we don't have all day, missy!"

The elderly woman stepped aside so that Neil could be next and I pulled his arm as he moved forward and said, "Please, Neil. It's going to take less than a minute. You can't go around yelling at people. We're not in a stadium."

"I want my fucking money!" he screamed.

"I'm out of here." I let go of his arm and turned to leave, but he pulled me back hard and said, "The hell you are. I need money and you're waiting with me!"

"Alright, just calm down." I glanced at my car in the lot and calculated how fast I could outrun him and get the hell out of here.

"How can I help you, sir?" The teller waved him over, but he seemed to have forgotten all about his money and asked sweetly, "What are you doing tonight, honey?"

She took his account slip and smiled as if she heard those words all day long which encouraged him. He leaned over the counter, oblivious that he looked and smelled like he'd slept in a dumpster the night before and cooed, "Do you know how sexy you are?"

"He's my boss," I replied when she glanced at me curiously. "He's got a lot of energy."

Silently, she opened her drawer and counted out the money that had Neil drooling. I took another glance to see how many hundred dollar bills were on the counter and nearly fell backwards when I saw a grand total of twenty two dollars.

"Thanks, sweetheart." He stuffed the money into his back pocket and headed for the door.

"We came here for twenty dollars? You made a scene in there for twenty dollars?"

"Twenty-two," he corrected me. "There's more where that came from."

"I'm not sure if this is going to work out." I purposely didn't unlock the car door.

"It's right up the street." He stuck out his bottom lip as if he was about to cry. "My place is right around here."

"What do you mean here? You're staying at Motel 6?"

"I'm in between apartments," he shrugged. "I don't have a lot of stuff either. It'll be quick. Please don't go."

"There'd better not be." I unlocked the car door, my patience wearing thin.

Less than a mile down the road, I turned into Motel 6, got out, and waited as he unlocked the door to his room.

"Pardon the mess," he chuckled, but there was nothing to chuckle about.

The mattress was off the bed, the sheets in a pile on the floor. One of the table lamps was knocked over, the other had a shirt on it as if he'd gotten kinky the night before, which I did not, under any circumstance, want to think about. Random cardboard boxes were scattered all around the room and on the bathroom sink I could see a toothbrush, deodorant, and a cheap bottle of cologne.

"Here." He handed me a laundry basket, picked some clothes off the floor and threw them in the basket, handed me some quarters from his nightstand, and said, "I have enough quarters for the first load."

"Isn't this a little too personal?" I replied when I glanced down and saw his stretched out underwear only inches from my face.

"Not at all. This is what I hired you for. This is what Personal Assistants do," he said, and I bit the inside of my cheek instead of telling him he needed a mother, not an assistant.

I walked through the parking lot and dumped his clothes into the top loading machine, grateful I didn't have to touch any of them, put in the quarters, and cranked the dial even though I didn't have soap. When I got back to the room, Neil was splashing water on his face. I picked up one of the chairs that had been tossed over, sat down, and said, "Hey, maybe later we'll have time to get you a haircut and some new clothes, if you need help with that too?"

"What?" He suddenly stood up, came over to me, put his dripping wet face close to mine and said, "Who the hell do you think you are? Don't you know who I am? This is my signature haircut!"

Feeling trapped in the chair, I leaned back and said, "I'm sorry, I just thought, never mind. You look great. That's your signature haircut, okay!"

He backed away, ran his fat fingers through his thick greasy hair, and started pacing in front of me.

"You're stressing me out! I've been up all night! I haven't slept! And now you, you, with your smartass mouth!"

"I'll just wait outside." I stood up but that only set him off more, and I thought that for a short fat man he sure moved quickly. He slammed the door shut, locked it with the chain, and said, "Oh no you don't! Sit down!"

My hands gripped the armrests of the chair as I realized my phone was in my car and that this lunatic could do whatever the hell he wanted to me and no one would ever know what happened to me if I ended up missing.

"I need to figure this out!" He paced nervously, sweat dripping from his brow.

"There's nothing to figure out. I'm not a problem. I can help you." I wanted to distract him, but he wasn't having it.

"Shut up!" he screamed. "Sit down!"

"I'll sit! Okay," I put my hands up and eyed the door, knowing that if I didn't get out really soon things might get really ugly really fast.

Then he reached under the bed so quickly I thought he was reaching for a gun, until the paper plate came into view with a pile of white powder on top.

"No! Please, please, please let me go!" I screamed. "I can't handle the sight of drugs!"

"I just need one hit," he pleaded.

"Don't!" I leaped up as he put his nose to the plate, unlocked the chain, and tore the door open.

Neil followed me out and for a second we stared at each other as if we were about to duel until he realized his plate of powder might fly away and stepped back inside. I opened my car door and left it open as I started the car with the intent to back the hell out and never look back.

"I can't let you leave," he whimpered, torn between taking a hit and following me. "Not with my things in the car. I just need one hit to feel better."

"I can't do this." I put my hand on the clutch.

"I know your plate number. I'll call the cops and say you stole my stuff!"

Before I could answer, a big black Expedition with limo tinted windows rolled up next to me and had me so enthralled I couldn't move. As if I was in the middle of a low budget movie, a big, bald, muscled guy in a black suit and sunglasses got out of the car and approached Neil, who was visibly shaking. Then a scrawny, clean-shaven, skinny guy in jeans hopped out of the car, lowered his sunglasses at me, and said, "Oh, hello Miss," as if he was a country music star, and walked past me as if he had bigger fish to fry.

The bodyguard said nothing, only stood in front of Neil to intimidate him, which worked because Neil cowered and said, "Oh, her, she's my new assistant."

"A new one, huh?" the country star replied as Neil and the bald guy exchanged envelopes, like a corny drug deal, making me wonder what kind of ad I answered. What drug dealer or druggie needed a personal assistant?

"Enjoy your day, little lady." The country star nodded again, climbed into the back of the car.

The bodyguard followed suit, they backed out of the lot as quickly as they'd appeared, and I hit the roof.

"Neil, what the fuck kind of an operation are you running here? What are you getting me involved in? I need to go. Whatever it is you still need from in there, get it now because I have to get the fuck out of here!"

"Keep it down." He glanced around to see if someone was watching us.

I screamed, "Stop being ridiculous. No one is here except you and me!"

"You get the laundry and I'll load the last of the boxes," Neil said, excited, as if the drugs had kicked in. "My new place isn't far..."

"Hurry up!" I screamed through the lot as I headed through the laundry room. "I am not getting arrested for you!"

His laundry was soaking wet, but I tossed everything into the basket anyway. When I got back to the car, I threw it into my trunk and Neill looked at me with puppy dog eyes and said, "Thank you for sticking with me. You're a cool girl."

"Listen," I backed out of the lot, my knuckles turning white on the steering wheel. "You have no idea what kind of pressure I'm under and I certainly don't need this shit on top of it!"

"I'm sorry," he whispered, but I said, "Shut up," which made him snap to attention. "Do you know what it's like to live with three guys while trying to go to school? Huh, do you? Well, it was supposed to be a few days and I'm going on six months now and do you know what I get when I open the door at night? Parties, orgies, you name it. It's non-fucking-stop. The cops come, tow trucks come, and some nights I sleep in my car, but do you think they care? No. The other day I woke up and tried to microwave some oatmeal, and you know what, Neil?"

"No," he shook his head, ready to cry.

"I'll tell you what. The microwave, the blender, the toaster, practically every kitchen appliance was outside when I glanced down through the open window. That's because they bought a trampoline, a big one like in the movie "Big," and that's what they told me. The movie was on, it looked like fun, and they went out and bought one. Now it's become the new hangout, the nap place, and where our appliances go to die because when Ryan gets drunk he thinks he wants to see appliances leap out of the second story window and bounce back in, and of course he misses."

I paused, thinking, why was it so hard to just have a normal life?

"Where to now, Neil?" I snapped.

He pointed left and I turned.

"You know what my brother's one night stand did last week?" I couldn't stop. "She used all my make-up, perfume, and my toothbrush. You know how I knew, besides the fact that I heard her rummage through my things at eight a.m. when I knew Ryan had already gone to work? He told me afterwards that he'd given her permission to use my stuff, but why she used my toothbrush and not his is beyond me. I put everything in a Ziploc bag and drove to Applebee's to give it to him to give to her because I wasn't touching it ever again!"

"Right," he whispered.

My hand slapped the radio dial but Nickelback was on, which reminded me of Evan, so I smacked the dial to turn it off again and said, "My asshole ex-boyfriend left me, can you believe it? And I let him go and the sad thing is I keep thinking he'll come back to me, any day now, he's going to make the call and realize what he's left behind because I was the better person. He asked me to show up at the apartment and help the movers, and instead of lighting his things in a bonfire and celebrating, I did it. But guess what? He's not back!"

"It's right there," he said.

My tires screeched through the lot and I huffed, "Another shithole? How can you take me to another dump? What is wrong with you?"

"I wanted to stay at a nicer place," he shrugged, and when I looked at him to see if he was serious about this being a nicer place, it dawned on me how lucky I was still to have the rest of my life ahead of me. Neill had completely blown his. He knew and now I knew and I was complaining about useless Evan.

"Will you come in with me?" his voice squeaked.

I said, "Sure," and turned off the car.

"I want to show you everything and explain the business to you." He smiled excitedly and I remembered the horrible partnership we were in: me, his assistant who hadn't found an exit strategy as he wasted my day, and he, my boss who didn't have any money.

"Can't wait," I tried to sound upbeat.

But then at the front desk he signed the paperwork and lifted the keys to his new motel room and smiled, "Got it. Penthouse," which made me feel even sorrier for him.

Neil is quite the optimist I thought when we each took a box and walked upstairs to room 205, unlocked the paint-chipped door, and he waved his hand like a magician and said, "See."

"See what?" I glanced around at the ordinary motel room impatiently.

Neil dropped the key on the side table, crouched next to the wall and said, "See this crack on the wall right here, it's unacceptable, this is what I need you for."

"What are you talking about?" I crouched next to him and after a second, did see a tiny crack that must have been magnified with the drugs he was on.

I waited for the punch line. Finally he said, "I need my office to look impressive, professional. I have a business to run. I can't have customers coming in and out of this filth."

"What business are you trying to run out of this motel?"

"I'm glad you asked." He lifted one of the box flaps and gently pulled out a magazine with Mohamad Ali on the cover and not the gold and diamond encrusted watches and sports rings I'd been expecting.

"You can get those anywhere, 7-Eleven, gas stations, any corner," I replied, stunned. "How long did it take you to collect all these? Is that what you're going to sell?"

"I told you," he shook his head patiently as if I just couldn't see his vision. "I know when Ali and Tyson are coming here and where they're staying. I'm going to get them to sign all these. Do you know how much they're worth?"

"No," I shook my head and slowly backed up to the door because it was time to call it a day.

Then his eyes grew wide when he realized I was about to take off, and then I did.

"I knew you wouldn't stay!" He shook his fist in the air as I glanced back at him from the end of the hall.

By the time I made it to my car and knew that his fat ass hadn't followed me, I was so furious I started crying. And I couldn't even blame ignorant Neil. This was Evan's fault for leaving me so damned vulnerable and desperate to make ends meet that I had now sacrificed my safety.

I tossed the laundry basket and the rest of the boxes into the lot and sped away, realizing I might never get out of the frat house. And that caused a whole new wave of tears because I couldn't understand that why, if I was working so hard to get myself out of a rut that I was really only treading water and getting nowhere.

SIXTY

It took almost a month for a car dealership to call me back and hire me as a receptionist. My trainer was a woman with a bright orange afro and bright green eye shadow who didn't want to train me at all.

"You'll see," Maggie fished for her red lipstick in the drawer. "As soon as you get the hang of working here, they'll fire me, just to save money, and before you know it, they'll do the same to you."

"I'm sure that's not true," I said, surprised. "I really need this job."

"Oh, it is, honey. No, no, you're doing that wrong, these copies are stapled together and this one is for the customer." She helped fix my paperwork and nodded when it was correct and I could file it.

The paperwork was the easy part. It was the people, not just Maggie, who were hard to get used to. Customers were happy until you handed them the repair bill, and car salesman coming in and out of the office to check their internal mailboxes were either snippy because of a deal gone sour or too chatty for me to get any work done. The supervisor, however, scheduled me around my classes and I was allowed to do homework when it was slow, which was worth its weight in gold since I couldn't get a moment's peace at the frat house.

"Oh, it is! Mark my words," Maggie muttered to herself, making me wish they'd fire her already and shut her up.

"You're doing fine," Debbie, the other receptionist, smiled encouragingly. Her desk faced mine so that each of us worked a separate window, and if it hadn't been for her kindness, I would have left a long time ago. Debbie was older than I, had two kids, and was divorced and was always keeping an eye out for someone to date.

"'Fine,' nothing," Maggie added. "You'll be gone too, missy," and Debbie shook her head at me as if Maggie was full of it.

That semi-training and banter went on until the dealership closed at ten. By the time I got home that night, all the guys were out and had left me a kitchen so stacked with dirty dishes, I had nowhere to sit. Finally, after an hour the dishwasher was going, the kitchen table was clear, and I had enough room to spread out my text books and study. Then Joe and his girlfriend Candy came home.

"Hey," I said as they drunkenly walked up the stairs.

Neither of them answered, which didn't surprise me. Candy was a drunken stripper with neon white and rainbow hair, tattoos and piercings that had you wondering which trailer park she stripped at. Joe was her love-sick puppy and followed her around wherever she went. They giggled and fell onto the couch. Joe first, so that all I could see were his feet and his elbows poking out on the side as Candy sat on top of him.

Then he took the remote and blasted the TV so that I looked up and said, "Hey! I'm trying to study here."

"Oh, hey Jen." Joe peered out from behind Candy, but I could tell he was half asleep and high on something. "Sorry, didn't see you there."

He turned it down, but not quite enough. I let it go until I was forced to walk over to them and study the scene up close; both of them were passed out and drooling on themselves. Candy was asleep in mid motion of zipping up her hooded sweatshirt, making me think she'd died in her sleep.

"Hello?" I waved my hand in front of their dead faces and felt sorry for all the money they'd spent on getting high, but this was not the place for them to crash.

"Joe, are you okay?" I tugged at his arm, feeling nauseous. He had his whole life ahead of him and all he wanted to do was please Candy. And I knew about self-destructing your life for someone else all too well.

"Joe," I shook him urgently.

"What's going on?" he awoke. "Oh, yeah, hey Jen."

"You have to go," I pointed at Candy. "The party is over. No drugs in this house. I'm not going to jail for you guys."

"Who the fuck is she?" Candy suddenly woke and nearly spit on my face.

Once she realized I wanted her out, she stood up and attempted to clock me in the face but missed. Joe stood up too and pulled her back.

"All I'm saying is you guys can come back when you're sober. You're freaking me out."

"Fuck you, bitch!" she lunged again and Joe, suddenly coherent, pulled her down the flight of stairs and to the front door by her waist.

"I'm really sorry, Joe," I said.

He glanced at me sadly, as if he knew this wasn't how it was supposed to be but couldn't help it, then slammed the door shut. I didn't know what I thought about it until Ryan called me on the phone and screamed, "How can you kick him out? He's one of us!"

"Just hang on," I said, and glanced at my phone when I heard another call. "Winston's calling me too."

"Jen, how can you kick him out?" Winston said heatedly. "How are we supposed to pay the bills?"

"They're on drugs. I almost thought they were dead. You know the rules," I sighed. "Everyone knows the rules."

"You're lucky I have a friend. He's always wanted to move here."

"I hope he doesn't eat as much as you. All my free time is wasted on trips to the grocery store!"

"His name is Jason," he ignored me. "I'll call him right now. You'd better cross your fingers."

I did, because the last thing I wanted was a house in even more chaos and uproar and the guys mad at me. But I didn't have to worry. Jason arrived a week later with two suitcases, one filled with white sneakers and the other with plaid shorts and crisp polos as if he was a golfer, or so I was told by Ryan. When I actually met Jason he was being ushered out the door.

"Hi," I said, stunned by his surfer body appearance: tall, tanned, built, blond hair, and a perfect smile.

"We're going downtown," Winston replied for him.

"You know, show him around," Ryan said.

"Oh, I know," I waved. My first two weeks of their showing me around was still very clear in my mind and I hadn't been to the strip since.

A few weeks later, I finally saw him up close and nearly fainted. Thinking I was alone, I went upstairs for breakfast and was surprised to see Jason sitting at the kitchen table in his boxers eating a bowl of cereal. I backed down the stairs immediately. I did not want him to see me in skimpy shorts and a t-shirt, unshowered, and my hair a mess.

"Oh, hey Jen," he said cheerily.

"I'll be right back," I waved. "I need to shower."

"Oh, stop it," he flashed a perfect smile. "I haven't showered either. We're roomies, it doesn't matter."

It matters to me if you look like that, I thought, but walked into the kitchen anyway.

"I've never seen anyone up before ten around here, even when they have to go to work."

"We were out late, I don't know why I couldn't sleep." He stared at my short shorts, making me feel self-conscious.

"I take that back." I opened a cupboard in search of a cereal bowl until I became distracted by the beautiful shape of his back and the two dimples smiling at me right above his waistline. Evan's body did not look like that. "They used to get up early and start drinking from the keg fridge, but they haven't filled that thing in a while and now that you're here, they've been going out. What happened to all the bowls?" I opened the dishwasher and saw that it too was empty.

"I did the dishes." He suddenly stood up and came right to me, gently pressing his body into mine, but stepped back when he realized he'd come too close and stuttered, "I wasn't sure where they go so I put them here."

"That's okay." I inhaled the smell of his coconut tanning lotion and wished he hadn't stepped back. I couldn't remember the last time I'd been that close to a man. Evan hardly ever touched me, and when he did his body felt like a cold board.

I set the bowl on the table and forgot all about eating cereal as I stared into Jason's crystal blue eyes.

"So how do you like Vegas so far?" I almost smacked my forehead, wishing I had something better to say.

"What's not to love? Sunny every day. I've been working on my tan, see?" He flexed his bicep so that I could see the difference between his dark bicep and white tricep and I nearly lost my jaw.

"Looks good," I pursed my lips together. "I'm surprised that trampoline isn't broken yet. You wouldn't believe how many appliances we lost because of that thing. At first Ryan would jump from the window, I don't know how he didn't kill himself, and when that didn't do, he emptied the kitchen."

"Oh, Ryan." He shook his head and smiled as if remembering something, but didn't elaborate.

"What are you going to do about a job?"

"Not sure," he shrugged. "I might go to school, might work at Home Depot with Winston. Haven't decided yet and my parents will send me money until I figure it out."

"Nice parents." I envied him.

Who wouldn't love it here if he didn't have to worry about bills or where he was going to end up in life?

"Thanks for getting groceries," he said.

"No problem," I smiled. "Although they don't last long when Winston comes home for lunch. He'll take a loaf of bread, a pound of turkey, and a pound of cheese, and eat it until it's gone and then tell me he needs calories for the gym."

"That's Winston." He agreed. Then he asked, "How's your job at the car dealership? Did I get that right?"

"Yeah. It's not bad. I just hope I'm not there for the next ten years."

"Boyfriend?"

"Actually, no," I said, trying to remember the last time I'd mentioned Evan without tears streaming down my face. "We broke up. I'll never date again."

"My girlfriend and I broke up before I came here."

"I'm sorry," I said, although I wasn't. He was gorgeous.

"Don't be. It wasn't going to last much longer anyway."

If he wasn't so damned polite, I would have put him into the same category as Evan. It wasn't fair that guys were over girls like it was nothing.

"Yo, Jen? Did I say something wrong?" Jason touched my arm.

"No, not at all." I reached for the box of Cheerios on the table and wished I could erase Evan from my mind permanently.

"I finished that one." Jason smiled sheepishly, closed the lid, and set the box at the end of the table.

I said, "It's fine," and stood to get another one.

"No, let me," Jason stood up too, and together we reached for the same box of cereal, his body against mine, my heart about to explode out of my chest.

"Sorry," he said when I turned around and glanced up at him with wide eyes.

"It's not that," I replied, but his lips were already on mine and as I tasted sweet milk in his mouth and felt my knees get weak, the cereal box fell from my hand and spilled all over the floor.

"Listen, I can't do this. I'm just not ready," I said, thinking how good it felt but how I wasn't ready for another heartbreak.

"I'm sorry, I didn't..."

"No, the kiss was great. It's just that I can't do the relationship thing, the jealousy, you know?"

He smiled and kissed me again and said, "Whatever you want is fine with me."

I pushed him back and said, "No one can know. I mean it. I don't want it to be weird around here, especially with my brother."

"I promise," he whispered in my ear and licked my ear lobe. "I'm game for whatever you want."

SIXTY-ONE

No one ever rang the doorbell because everyone knew the door was always open, and I thought I'd have to shoo away a salesperson when I opened the door annoyed.

"Apples, peaches, pumpkin pie!" my Dad sang, stretching out his arms and hugging me, and as he made the dance around me, invited himself in.

"Is that your U-Haul?" I asked, looking into the cul-de-sac, confused. I couldn't remember the last time we talked, but it didn't involve him driving cross country with all of his things.

"Are you surprised to see me, Apples?"

"Well, yeah," He squeezed the air out of me again before I could close the door.

"How long did it take you to get here?"

"I don't know, a week? Nice place you guys got here. Looks big."

"Thanks, but how come you didn't call? Is your divorce final yet?"

"Ah, never mind that." He waved off the divorce talk then pointed at the cracked tile and asked, "What happened there?" I answered the standard couch-on-the-railing reply and explained the hole in the wall that still hadn't been fixed before he could ask about that.

"I thought I'd surprise you guys. Oh, I've missed you! We haven't spent any time together in years. Holy moly, that's a big TV! And those speakers, I'm sure you can hear them from space!"

"Look, Dad, I'm about to leave." I hoped he wouldn't get too comfortable, but he sat on the couch, tested its buoyancy, and asked, "Do you mind if I sleep on your couch? You know until I find a place of my own. You think the guys will mind?"

"Uh, well, we're four people in a three bedroom house," I said as if that should have explained it all: No.

"I'll just take the couch, no one will notice."

"But you can't smoke. No smoking in the house." I followed him into the kitchen.

"It'll take me a while to regrow anyhow."

"No smoking at all," I said sternly, but he grinned at me as if to say "whatever," and said, "Okay, Apples. It's okay, you look like you're in a hurry. Go to work, I'll see you later."

"Okay, love you." I hugged him, hurried downstairs, and didn't bother to check my ringing phone to see who was calling because I expected it to be Ryan.

"Hey, Jen," Evan said coolly. I checked the caller I.D. which said "blocked," and was about to hang up when he said, "You there?"

"What do you want?" I snapped. "You only call when you need something and now you're blocking the calls so I answer."

"Just calling to say hi, can't I call and see how you're doing?" he replied, offended.

"If you cared how I was doing you wouldn't have left!" I replied and I bit the inside of my cheek before I admitted how much I missed him and how I still wanted him back.

"Oh, that," he giggled. "You know I love you. I just had to get away and figure some things out."

"Good for you. I gotta go."

"Wait. I'm coming to Vegas next week. Can you pick me up from the airport? I want to see you. You know, I think we have some unfinished business."

"As in what?" My heart suddenly raced. All this time I'd been waiting for him to come back and get me and now he was coming back to get me. I'd go with him, of course I would. Jason had been fun, but he wasn't Evan. No one would ever be Evan.

Back in Two Weeks

"Can you pick me up from the airport?" he repeated.

"I'll think about it." My head was spinning.

"Okay, I get it. Payback. Because it wasn't enough when you had all the movers pack all dirty dishes. Can you imagine how badly it stunk when I opened them?"

"That was the idea," I smiled. "It was the least I could do."

"I'll call you with my flight information next week, the day before I get there."

"I won't answer."

"Okay," he laughed, which made me laugh and almost break down and tell him that there was no sunshine in my life even if there weren't any clouds in the sky. All I ever wanted was him.

Then he hung up and I was tortured for a week as I waited for his flight to arrive.

I'd tried to be late and ended up in the parking lot right on time. As soon as I opened the car door, he was there with a cigarette in his hand, backwards hat and football jersey, as if no time had gone by, except that his face looked gaunt and pale, as if he'd aged ten years without me.

"You look good," he hugged me.

"Oh, you too," I lied, and coughed when I smelled his faded cologne, beer, sweat, and cigarettes, reminding me of a homeless guy.

"Oh, sorry." He flicked his cigarette away and grinned apologetically, as if that was going to make me forgive him for the year of hell he'd put me through.

"How about the Bellagio for dinner?" he looked at me.

"The Bellagio?" I replied stunned.

"Yeah, you remember, the one from Ocean's Eleven, the one you always wanted to try."

"Oh, I remember!" I replied, sarcastically. "I asked you to take me there a million times and you said, "someday," which I learned meant "never," and if this is our someday, I hope that carry-on bag of yours is filled with money because I sure can't afford it."

"Tonight," he whispered. "Say yes."

"Okay, but what time? I need to change, obviously."

"Seven. I already made reservations."

"What happened to you in Maryland, you've never been this organized? The only planning you ever did for me was when you took me to meet Amber. What's this all about, Evan?"

But I already knew the answer: he'd come back to marry me and I was going to say yes because, despite his smell and ratty appearance, this was what I'd dreamed about this last year. He was all I ever wanted.

"I take that as a 'yes.'" He kissed my cheek as I stopped in front of his hotel. "See you in a few hours."

"See you," I said, unsure if I was ready to change my entire life in just a few hours and fly back with him in a day or two.

Dad said, "You know you don't have to go," when I got home and changed, and I knew he was right, I didn't, but I did, because I had to see how this was all going to end.

Then I pictured myself on Oprah, sitting in the leather chair next to hers while she said, "Girl, you need to forget about that silly boy, hm, hm," while Dad, Ryan, Jake, and Pam smacked their foreheads in the audience and screamed "boo" at me as I tried to defend Evan with the usual, "But I love him!"

Evan seemed nervous when I pulled into the valet hours later, and I watched him puff his cigarette as he paced back and forth in a nice suit. When he finally saw me, he jammed the cigarette into the ashtray, flattened his suit coat, and hustled over to the car as if we were late.

"You look great." He kissed me and my heart fluttered as if the last year had never happened, he never left and broke my heart, and I was still crazy about him.

"You too," I said breathlessly.

"All I did was iron this old thing." He smiled, took my hand in his, and said, "Let's go to dinner, shall we?"

In less than ten minutes we were parked at the Bellagio, walking hand in hand, my head nuzzled on his bicep as if we'd rediscovered love again. His old confident stride was back and I was putty in his hands and couldn't wait for him to whisk me away.

"Right this way, sir," the host winked at Evan, as if he was in on the surprise.

I nearly kicked myself for wasting all those tears and sleepless nights, wondering what I could have done differently and when and if he was ever coming back, when he'd planned to come back for me all along.

Evan let me follow the host first. My black heels quickly sank into the plush carpet and my mouth hung agape as I tried to take in all the beautiful oil paintings, lit up on every wall as if we were in a small museum. The tables were intimately spaced, everyone seemed lost in their own world as the Bellagio fountains danced in the background through the windows and I couldn't wait to be one of them. This was exactly where I wanted to be.

Then I bumped into a table in the middle of the restaurant and stood for a moment face-to-face with twenty huge glass vases filled with big vibrant sunflowers, and I was instantly transported back to Spain. I smelled the fresh cut grass and wet soil, and felt the breeze on my face and remembered how precious this one life we have to live is, and how I'd wasted it being miserable.

"Over here, miss," the host pulled out a chair for me. "Complements from the chef," he said, and a large plate with a tiny cracker was put in front of Evan and me.

"How are you supposed to eat this?" Evan frowned.

"It's just a cracker." I stabbed it with my fork, popped it into my mouth, and said, "See?"

"Well, I might as well tell you why we're here." He put the fork down, agitated. "I'm here because I'm filing bankruptcy."

"Huh?" My throat went dry because I'd obviously been played as the fool again. "You mean you're trying to clear up your debt, for the future?"

"All my gambling debt caught up to me and I owe more than a hundred grand. They wanted me to fly here and explain some things." He smiled as if it was funny that I'd misread his signals.

"Who wanted you to explain what things?" My fingers dug into my thighs.

"The IRS."

"So what was our unfinished business?" I asked hopefully, but he crushed the last bit of hope I had when he said, "Well, this restaurant," and opened his arms as if he'd given me the world. I smiled, thinking if this wasn't so damned sad, I'd be laughing my ass off.

"So who's paying for dinner if you're broke as a joke? Because it sure as hell isn't going to be me."

"It's the last thing that's going on the card," he said proudly.

"Is there some jewelry that's going on there with it?"

I stared at him and he put the card away as if I was going to take it from him and said, "Don't push it." He leaned across the table, reached for my hand, and said, "Are you okay? I mean really, you know, since I left, have you been okay?"

"Of course, I've been great!" I pulled my hand away, trying not to cry. What wasn't great about living in a frat house, working at a job that didn't have a long-term gain, or getting a degree in psychology I couldn't use?

"You know what," I shook my head. "No, I'm not great. I'm not good at this charade like you are. I haven't been fine at all. It's been so hard without you. Every day is torture. I've missed you so much, you have no idea."

"I missed you, too." He took my hand again and squeezed it as if he was sorry for all the hurt he'd caused, but then he opened his mouth and pushed the dagger deeper and said, "You know we're not good for each other. You know how much I hated how much I affected you."

"Why wouldn't I be affected by you? I thought I was going to marry you!"

He sat up straight and looked at me as if he wanted to say something but changed his mind.

"Evan," I closed my eyes and regretted telling him how I felt. "Honestly, I'm fine. I'm almost done with school, I have a job, and I'm waiting for the FAA to hire me."

"That's another thing I wanted to talk to you about," he shifted uneasily. "The FAA picked me up in New Hampshire."

My fork fell from my hand and crashed against the plate before it fell to the floor. I picked it up so I could ram it into his throat but a waiter took it from my hand and placed a new one next to me.

"What do you mean by New Hampshire, Evan?" I hissed. "As in my home state, as in the place you told me you were never going to go and it was one of the reasons we broke up, because you couldn't see yourself living there and were never, ever, ever going to live there because you wanted to live in Maryland and nowhere else. Do you mean that New Hampshire?"

"Yeah," he chuckled nervously. "Isn't that funny."

"You have some nerve," I crossed my arms. "I'll tell you what's funny: your card getting declined and me leaving you here. I think I've heard enough. I'm ready to go."

But as I stood up the food arrived, and I sat down wishing I hadn't come here with a guy who couldn't appreciate any of it. His card, for whatever reason, did not decline, and I drove him back to the hotel where we sat in the valet driveway for at least ten minutes before he said, "Want to come up?"

If he hadn't looked so sad, I would have said no. Instead I said, "Only for a few minutes," and pulled away from the valet and into the parking garage.

Upstairs he immediately kicked off his shoes, hung up his suit because he'd put all that effort into ironing it, turned on ESPN like old times, and got under the sheets wearing only his boxers. He patted the side of his bed and asked, "Do you want to do anything?"

"No," I said sadly, because I knew that all the love I felt for him was gone for good and that he'd succeeded in turning me into stone like he was. I was probably never capable of loving anyone again. "I came up to thank you for dinner."

"No problem," he fake yawned. "I owed you."

"You owed me a lot more." I opened the door and stared at him. I couldn't even remember his birthday, only that he was a Scorpio, and knew that we didn't belong together and that no matter what happened, I was doing the right thing.

"I wish you all the best," I said. And I did.

I wished that he found all the loved and happiness he could find in this world because it would be a miracle for him to find someone who loved him as much as I had. And I closed the door and decided I was going to be single forever. And that was totally fine with me.

SIXTY-TWO

Nine months to the day I was hired at the car dealership I was fired, just like Maggie had said I'd be.

"We're downsizing," they'd said after I was called into the office to sign the pink slip.

Then I ran out the door and cried in my car until I could finally see and was able to drive to the nearest 7-Eleven to get a newspaper. That's when I saw the ad: "Canvassing, no experience necessary, $10 tax free," and thanked God it was right down the street.

As I walked into the packed conference room I stood off to the side with the rest of the overflow people, and soon realized I was overdressed and that canvassing had nothing to do with art and canvas and had to do with politics.

"Here's how it works," a skinny bearded man with glasses, cargo shorts, and flip flops said in front of the packed room. He looked like Shaggy from Scooby-Doo and it was hard not to laugh. "You're going door-to-door to drum up political business. Get people to vote! Get people involved in the community!"

Although I knew nothing about politics, I knew that he was motivated and that it was tax free and that I needed the money.

"Team leaders like myself will drop a group of you in a neighborhood to scope out potential voters. Knock on doors, ask about their concerns in the community, and bring questions back to us. We will provide you with sunscreen, bottles of water, and palm pilots to keep tallies and addresses for yard signs. Anna," he pointed at the girl next to me who'd obviously done this before, "and the next six, come with me." That included me, and together we followed Shaggy to his silver blue van.

"Hi, I'm Brian and I love Ozzie Osbourne." A guy with blonde hair and freckles, looking like an overgrown Boy Scout, sat down next to me.

"Me too," I said hoping he wouldn't quiz me on a song.

"Anna, do we have everything?" Shaggy got in the driver's seat and looked at her in the rearview mirror as she got comfortable on the other side of Brian.

"We're cool," she bobbed her head like she was half asleep.

"Hi Anna. I'm Brian. I like Ozzy Osbourne."

"Everyone, that's Dan, Mitch, and Garcia," Shaggy pointed over our heads as three guys got into the back. It was obvious I was the only new one on the crew, but no one said a thing. "Brian, Jen, and Anna in the front. Everyone have cell phones?"

"Right on," Anna bobbed. The rest of us nodded.

"Alright, then we're off."

Brian whispered in my ear as I buckled my seatbelt, "Dan lives in a motel. He doesn't have a cell phone."

I turned away, not wanting to look at him because I didn't care, but happened to catch a glimpse of his bloodshot eyes and felt trapped when they locked on to mine.

"Hi," I said, but Dan didn't answer, and I noticed Mitch, the handsome bodybuilder next to him, who didn't have the time of day for me.

Garcia on the end, however, said, "What's up," but I could tell he was ex-military with his crew cut hair and perfect smile and thought that although he was cute, he was not the guy for me.

"I love Ozzie Osbourne!" Brian beamed at me again, and Dave turned up the radio, presumably to appease him. I said, "That's Nickelback," and pushed all thoughts of Evan away.

"I just love Ozzie Osbourne." Brian swayed his body side-to-side and I thought I wasn't going to last another hour, and definitely not an entire day, with him, and that I should have searched a little further through the classifieds.

About twenty minutes later Shaggy parked the van in a neighborhood I'd never seen before. If I'd decided to walk away I couldn't, and I decided that even if I did make it until the end of the day that I wasn't coming back.

"Okay, we're here." Shaggy folded a large road map in half, drew on it in blue pen, and said, "Everyone sync your palm pilots, take some sunscreen and water, and Jen, tag along with Brian, since everyone else in the van has been doing this for a couple of weeks already, just until you get the hang of it." Then he glanced at his watch as if we were about to tandem dive out of the van and said, "See you guys around, let's say, noon for lunch."

"Watch me first," Brian beamed when the van pulled away.

The others dispersed and I followed Brian and watched as he chose his first house and knocked on the door. To my surprise, an elderly woman opened the door and Brian smiled even bigger and said, "Hi, I'm Brian and we are in the neighborhood to find out-" and then *boom*, the door was shut.

"Not interested," he shrugged as if it was no big deal. "We'll try the next one."

It was almost the same reaction from an elderly man, but this time, Brian saved it with, "Just a few minutes of your time, sir, to get your opinion because we want to be involved in your community," and the man lit up like we had made his day. Whadda ya know, I thought. All that junk about Ozzie Osbourne, but he was a natural at this.

"And you'd like the yard sign? We can get that for you right away. Another crew delivers them, is this weekend good for you?"

Brian typed some kind of Morse code into his palm pilot while I glanced at the yard I wouldn't be caught dead having a yard sign in. Politics was personal, why did you have to advertise?

"How about you try the next house?" Brian said encouragingly.

"I'm not ready," I replied, but he knocked on the door and waved his hand as if to say ladies first, and when the door opened, I said, "I'm Jen," and the door smacked shut.

"You just have to keep trying," Brian smiled.

I didn't have the heart to tell him I wanted a real job, not to be walking around in the Vegas summer heat sweating like an animal. Then I worried, what if I'd made a mistake by leaving the Air Force? But then I thought of Satan and deploying and almost pushed Brian out of the way. I said, "I think I can do this on my own now," as I knocked on the door and reminded myself, this is only temporary, something to pay the bills.

Hours later Shaggy met us at the rendezvous point, collected all of our palm pilots, and skimmed through the information to monitor our progress.

"How'd you do?" Shaggy asked without looking up from the palm pilots in his hand.

"Fine, I think," I replied thirstily. "But my forehead and nose are burnt. All this sweating wore off my sunscreen."

"Right?" Anna bobbed her head as if she was part of the conversation which annoyed the crap out of me.

"Your next task is to collect signatures for a petition," Shaggy said once we'd eaten lunch.

He parked the van in front of a Walmart parking lot, on another side of town I'd never been to, and handed us clipboards weighed down with petition signature booklets. "If the cops come, find another location and call me and I'll pick you up from there."

"What do you mean, cops? I don't want to go to jail." I stayed put as everyone else got out.

"You're not going to jail," Shaggy laughed. "But big companies usually don't like us loitering so they call the cops and then we move."

"That's not very convincing."

"It'll have to be. I'll see you later."

We stood a few feet apart but didn't speak to one another. It was hot and bright. I used my hand as a visor and was hoping to God no one recognized me, when someone said, "Grillo, is that you?"

"Oh, yeah, hi." I shook his hand and remembered the guy from the Air Force dorms, but couldn't remember his name.

"Tyler," he offered.

"Jen." I stared at his flannel shirt, the same one he wore in the Air Force off duty. "You don't have to call me Grillo anymore. And this is just a part time gig, if you're wondering. I'm kind of in between jobs."

"It's cool, Gillo. I'll sign your petition, but only if you'll go out with me Friday night."

"This Friday?" I couldn't believe he was asking me out.

"I don't see why not." He ripped a corner from the petition booklet I handed him, wrote down his number, and said, "Call me. We'll go out around seven, okay?"

"Okay," I stared after him. He was cute, in a farm boy sort of way, with dark hair and freckles and a better body than I'd remembered.

Friday night around seven, I drove to his house and parked the car.

"Do you like country music?" He asked when he met me in the driveway.

"No" was at the tip of my tongue until he smiled sweetly, opened the passenger door of his pick-up truck, and said, "There's a great country bar, we'll do some line dancing. They have bull riding and cheap beers on tap and good wings."

"Great," I replied sarcastically, but his engine was so loud when he turned the key he didn't hear it.

"They sure like to keep the music loud," I said once we arrived. We stood waiting for the hostess, who appeared seconds later in a cowboy hat, daisy dukes, black boots, and a black leather vest without a bra underneath.

"What are you having, Grillo?" He eyed the waitress behind the bar and when he couldn't hear my order, took the liberty of ordering a drink and a shot for me.

"Jen," I screamed over the music and he nodded as though he understood, although I could tell he didn't.

The drinks arrived a second later and he lifted his glass as if we were toasting to something so I lifted mine and together we downed the shot and chased it with a beer, which made me cough.

"Did you hear that announcement?" He pulled me from the chair and took me across the crowded bar to another waitress holding a clipboard.

"I can't hear anything," I said, feeling tipsy already. I read her lips when she said, "Sorry, the list is full."

"What list for what?" I screamed, and Tyler's shoulders slumped as if his whole night had been ruined and said, "Mud wrestling."

"For me? Oh no, I can't do that." I backed away, all the way back to the bar stool where he appeared a few seconds later pouting as if I'd kicked his dog.

"Maybe next time, okay?" I patted his hand because there wasn't going to be a next time.

But then the waitress with the clipboard pushed her way between us and said, "There's another spot open, someone just dropped out."

"That's okay," I shook my head.

"She'll do it." Tyler signed my name to the list.

"I'm not sure if I'm ready right now." I felt queasy. I didn't know a thing about mud wrestling.

"Come on, Grillo, why are you being like this?"

"Like what?"

"Never mind, I thought you were cool."

"Alright," I said, wishing I didn't have to impress him to get him to like me.

The waitress smiled, "Right this way," and I followed her through the bar and down a long hall where a Samoan bouncer stood with his arms crossed, guarding a beat up door.

"Good luck," he said as he opened the door.

I croaked, "Thanks," when I glimpsed inside and saw an old, saggy, dimly lit hotel room that had been preserved from the 1970's.

"I think I'm in the wrong place," I said to no one in particular.

Five very short and very skinny girls dressed in bikinis fixed each other's make-up and hair.

"Oh, girl," the oldest and skinniest, with protruding cheek bones, long brown hair, and big boobs approached me. "You can borra one o' my 'kinis. There's a bathroom right ova there."

"I can't fit into that." I lifted it up so that she could see what I was seeing, but someone else said, "You don't have a choice. We're going on soon," and I was pushed towards the bathroom.

"It's not working. I can't come out," I stared at my reflection in the mirror, ready to cry.

Under no circumstances was I fat, but in this stretched out ensemble I had a muffin top and my nipples were barely covered.

"We gotta go!" one of them shouted, and opened the door so quickly it hit me in the shoulder.

"Are you sure I look okay?"

"Showtime." The bouncer opened the door and everyone glanced at me, seemingly happy not to be me, and walked out.

At the edge of the hall I peered out into the crowd that couldn't see us. Tyler was nowhere and although I couldn't see the wrestling arena, there was a part in the crowd where I assumed it would be, and a man in a light suit and cowboy hat with a microphone.

"Cowboys and gals," the host said when a spotlight lit him up.

I glanced down at my trembling body, flabby compared to the others, and watched as a bead of sweat rolled from my armpit down my side and wished I'd drank a hell of a lot more than I had.

"Come on down, girrrrrrls!" the host said, and two girls in front of me stepped forward, waited for the spotlight to guide them to their places, and waved as the crowd went wild.

"Please welcome Loola and Lani!" The host paused for applause. "Quick rules of the match: no standing up, no dirty fighting, no biting, no clawing, no pulling hair, just pin 'em, got it? Any last words, Loola?"

Loola waved, flicked her hair back, and purred something sexy but inaudible. Lani did the same, and more sweat started rolling from my pits as I wondered why the hell I'd agreed to this if Tyler wasn't even here, and if it would be weird if I called a cab and the driver picked me up looking like this.

Then the spotlight blinded me and the host said, "That was a fast round, let's hope this girl can make it last!" and although I was sure I was supposed to move, I couldn't get myself to make the first step.

"Go!" Someone pushed me from behind and I stumbled forward without a wave and almost didn't see Lani on her side of the arena, on all fours and growling at me like a rabid dog, her hair, skin, and bikini slicked in brown shiny water.

"Yourrrr name little gal," the host asked, and I screamed, "Jen!"

"Alright Janet, arrrrre you rrready?"

One more time I glanced out into the audience, because it didn't matter whether I was ready or not. Lani wanted to destroy me and the guy who'd put me in this predicament had vanished.

Then Lani dove headfirst into the center of the arena.

"Ahh," I screamed when I dove forward.

A million goose bumps appeared on my skin. I expected mud to be thick and warm but this was oily and freezing cold.

Lani wrapped her arms around my waist and pushed and pulled me towards her.

"What are you doing?" I gasped when she pulled my hair, but all she did was grunt.

Then she sat on top of me like I was her horse and waved an imaginary lasso in the air until the crowd howled for more.

"Please," I gasped when she put me in a headlock, and I let her pin me, hoping this was the end of it.

"Therrrrrre's one!" the host announced.

Lani sneered at me as if she'd only had a taste of me and wanted more. Again I searched for Tyler, wondering why the hell I'd let him convince me to do this, until the host said, "Round two!" and I was forced to dive in again.

Like a canine statue, I sat on all fours and let Lani twist herself all over me. When she pulled my hair again I screamed, "Hey!" to get the host to tell her to stop, but he was busy swinging his microphone by the cord, trying to impress a woman who was actually watching this.

That's when I saw Tyler chatting with the rink girl, a tall brunette in a bikini holding the number two trying to be coy with him. If she looked anything like me I might have thought I was his type, but it was obvious, I'd been played and was old news.

Somehow our eyes met, just as Lani pinned me again, and as the host screamed, "There's two!" I got onto all fours and sloshed through the slime to my corner just as Tyler crouched down to me and said, "You're doing great!"

"I am?" I asked. "I didn't know they had number girls here like a real wrestling match."

"Word of advice, Grillo," he spoke into my ear. "You need to do something sexy like spank her or something."

"Spank her?" Mud flew from my lips and he rushed back to the rink girl before he could elaborate.

"Round three!" the host said, and my heart pounded with anger as I saw Tyler hand his phone number to the girl like he'd done to me.

"It's on, bitch." I dove for Lani's shoulders and spun her around.

"Oof," I knocked the wind out of her and tried to pin her, but my hands slid right off her shoulders.

"I was just kidding before." Her eyes bulged as if she was suddenly afraid of me.

Then Tyler, back at my side, whistled and clapped loudly and said, "Go, Grillo!" which made me lose my grip for good.

Lani grabbed my waist again and this time, I reached my hand around Lani and started spanking her ass.

Tyler and the crowd went nuts, which infuriated Lani so that she maneuvered herself behind me pulled me up by my hair until she could reach her forearm around my neck. I glanced up and saw the movie like screen on the wall, recognized my muddy body, and to my horror, my left breast that had slipped out of my borrowed bikini.

I let my body fall forward so that she could pin me for the last time and was relieved when the host screamed, "That's three! Let's hear it for Lani again." I wanted to fix my bikini top and get the hell out of there.

Feeling like the discarded girl I'd turned out to be, I sprinted past Tyler and his new girl and into the hall, where I decided I was never, ever going to date again for as long as I lived!

"Hey, Janet, they just loved you! Did you hear that applause? I think you should consider coming back." Loola toweled her hair dry in the dingy hotel changing room.

"I just want to get out of here if you don't mind," I said, taking a fresh towel for the shower.

"You never know if you don't try." She shook her head as if disappointed I wasn't jumping up and down at her review. "If you leave, you could be wasting your talent."

"Oh, Loola," I sighed. "You have absolutely no idea."

SIXTY-THREE

Like every Friday evening, I stood in the office and signed for my awesome four hundred dollar tax-free check, then searched for Shaggy to tell him that I wasn't coming back. I couldn't argue with the money, but even though I was walking around neighborhoods all day and getting people motivated to vote, it wasn't motivating my life in any kind of direction. I needed a real job.

I lost my nerve again when Anna pulled him aside first, and I decided that first thing Monday morning, I'd tell him, and went out the door.

"Hey Jen, wait up," Mitch called after me.

"What's up, did I forget something?" I glanced past him, surprised he knew my name.

"Uh, what do you say I take you out tonight?" He stared at his feet nervously.

"Oh, thanks, but no, I can't."

"You have other plans?"

"No, it's not like that. I just don't date anymore."

"Well, it doesn't have to be a date only because it's a Friday night," he stuttered. "I wanted to take you to the Italian place right across the street. You've got to be hungry."

"I am," I agreed, considering his offer only because I didn't want to go home quite yet. God only knew what kind of party was in the making. "But this is not a date, okay?"

"Okay." He smiled confidently then took my hand in his and walked with me across the street, where he opened the door for me and asked the hostess to seat us.

"I had you pegged differently." I scanned the menu although I already knew what I wanted. Spaghetti with meat sauce was my thing.

"Like what?" his eyes wouldn't rest on a single page, making me nervous. Something wasn't right with his eyes.

"I don't know, a bodybuilder guy?"

"I'm a school teacher. A sub, actually, and I should be getting my own classroom soon. I just do this for extra money on the side in the summer."

"Exciting." I tried to sound enthusiastic as he stared past me and into a mirror behind me and flexed his pecs and biceps subtly.

"I can't imagine teaching kids in Vegas." I glanced around the empty restaurant. "Aren't they rowdy? Isn't the dropout rate really high?"

"Yes, but hopefully I can change that, be a good influence, you know?"

"That's really cool."

"The kids aren't so bad." He pushed his fork and knife around the table. "I love to teach. I do this job in the summer for extra cash, but I miss those kids when I'm not around them, the way I captivate their attention, motivate them, and teach them things, everything from the lesson plan to staying away from drugs."

"Hm," I studied his shaking hands for a moment as he stopped pushing his utensils.

"I did have a drug problem, but I've been clean for six months now," he whispered.

"Oh," I replied. When he turned his head away, embarrassed, I thought he might really want to talk about it and asked, "What drugs did you use?"

"Meth," he pursed his lips together. "I loved Meth. Have you ever done meth?"

"No, I haven't done any drugs," I replied, already having lost interest in having a conversation with a drug addict about his self-inflicted problems.

"Well, meth is awesome! Meth makes you feel like Superman, like you can do anything and you are on top of the world. But then you can't sleep and at night, when everyone else is asleep, you feel lonely because everyone is sleeping and then three days later once it wears off, you crash. And you can't move. You can't do anything but sleep for three days. And I got caught up in the nasty cycle even though I told myself every weekend it was time to quit. It was just too easy to get."

"But you're okay now?" I asked, but he didn't answer. His eyes bounced back and forth from the table to the glass to the silverware. "I'm really not into drugs, or secrets."

"I didn't mean to," he said, surprised.

"I'm sorry, I didn't mean it like that. It's really none of my business."

Thankfully, the waitress came and took our order. I took huge gulps of water and hoped it would wash down my intruding questions. I tried to lighten the mood and said, "Let's talk about the weather, or do you watch CSI or something. I mean, I don't, but maybe you want to talk about that?"

"I don't get to watch much TV. I'll have it on when I'm grading papers but I don't pay much attention."

My guess was he couldn't keep his eyes steady enough to watch, even if he wanted to, and I said, "Me neither," but only because the guys hogged the TV with their "programs."

"Do you have a boyfriend?"

"No," I shook my head. "Vegas is a special place for guys; they're never honest, and let's just say the last few dates had turned disastrous."

"Well, then I do need to be honest with you." Mitch paused.

"I don't know why I keep saying this stuff," I said quickly. "You don't have to tell me anything."

"I do," he said. "I've never said this to anyone, you're the first, but there's nothing wrong with taking responsibility and acting mature, right?"

"I guess so."

"I have chlamydia."

I bit the inside of my cheek, nearly through it. The first cute guy to ask me out and he had a sexually transmitted disease. My dating life was one big prank.

"That must have taken a lot of courage to tell me," I finally said. "I've never met anyone who had chlamydia. I'm okay with it."

"Seriously, you don't mind?" His shoulders came up as if a weight had been lifted.

"Of course not," I said, because I'd already decided I wasn't ever going on another date again and because I was quitting Monday and would never see him again. "How did you get it? Are you in pain? Is it painful?"

"No, nothing like that," he laughed, as if it was something to joke about. "I'm on meds, it's curable. You can look it up on the internet if you want."

"Sure."

"I remember when I got it too. It was on one of my binge weekends, up all night, wanting to have sex with everyone and everything."

"I really don't need to hear this."

"No, it's fine," he said losing all shyness. "This girl called me and told me she had it and that I should get tested, which I did, and it turned out I had it too and I had to take responsibility and call everyone I remembered sleeping with."

"Good on you." I made a thumbs up, grateful the food had arrived.

"I knew you'd understand." He bit into his pizza as I motioned at the waitress for the check and twirled spaghetti onto my fork.

"You want to leave?" he asked hurt.

"It's just that I have homework and I need to study. You can understand that, right?"

"I guess so. When do you want to go out again?"

"I don't know, but I really appreciate dinner." I patted his hand, trying to figure out when I could tell Shaggy that I wasn't coming back.

"Let me walk you to your car at least," he said twenty minutes later, and reluctantly, I agreed.

Outside it was already dark, but not dark enough to avoid Garcia and Anna, who caught sight of Mitch opening my car door and giggled as they walked past.

"I gotta go," I said, embarrassed, closing my car door and backing out of the spot even though Mitch screamed, "Wait!"

But I was sick and tired of waiting. I deserved more and I deserved better.

Caught at a red light as soon as I got out of the lot, I shook my head because I couldn't even get my great escape right. Once I started moving again, I realized I wasn't too far away from my former car dealership and definitely was not ready to go home yet.

I parked the car and hurried through the deserted showroom, where I saw a few straggling salesmen who waved and I could tell wanted to know where I'd been, but I avoided them, ducked into the back office, and said, "Hey Debbie!" I made her jump as she sat silently flipping through a magazine.

"Oh my God, where have you been?" Debbie leaped out of her chair. "Come over here! I can't believe you just disappeared! Are you at another dealership?"

"No." I suddenly wished I hadn't come here and opened this can of worms. "I'm in between jobs right now."

"No one could figure out if you went to another dealership or what, and speaking of what you've been up to, I want you to meet someone. One of the salesmen's sons, he's so cute…Let me page him."

Before she could put her mouth to the receiver, I snatched it from her and placed it back on the cradle.

"Please, no. It's been a long day and I don't want anyone to see me looking like this, and I've sworn off dating."

"Oh, stop," she flicked her hand at me. "You're young and pretty, look at you, I'm an old bag, but you, you need to get out and enjoy life a little."

"I think I need a break from enjoying life."

"Come on." She looked at me dubiously.

"Next time. I promise. And you're not an old bag. Why don't you go for him, whoever he is?"

"He's for you," she winked, picking up the phone. And before I could stop her, she paged him.

I put my head on the desk and sighed while she stood up and glanced through the glass window to see if she could spot him.

"Remember Bob?" she giggled. "When he surprised you behind the photocopier and started sucking on your earlobe?"

"Gross! How could I forget? Just thinking about it makes my skin crawl. Did he retire yet?"

"Almost, but not yet. It was so funny!"

"Ha, ha, it's so funny I want to throw up just thinking about it. So whose son are we talking about anyway? I don't know anyone around here who had kids as old as I."

"I don't know," Debbie said as if it wasn't important. "One of the Middle Eastern guys."

"Well, I kind of need to know." I silently ran through the list of the guys I'd hung out with at some point and said, "You know I partied with all of them. It wouldn't be right."

When she didn't reply I said, "The Morrocan guy?" and pictured the offspring of the tall bald guy with glasses who always sprinted through the dealership as though he was an Olympic runner.

"Not him." She shook her head and resumed looking through the glass. "I know he was here."

"The Egyptian?" I thought of the short, fat, curly-haired guy who had a gambling problem and sold cars like they were bottles of water on a hot day when he needed money.

"Not the Caveman," I said, thinking of the quiet Lebanese guy who'd been in the States twenty years and still had a rough accent as if he'd stepped off the plane yesterday.

"Oh yeah, maybe him," she shrugged.

"I didn't know he was married." I thought back to the night we went out on a date that wasn't really a date in my eyes because we didn't have one thing in common and nothing to talk about and sat there stirring ice cubes around in our glasses. "I didn't even know he had a son. I can't date his son!"

"Nothing happened, right?" She folded her arms expectantly. "Going out for a drink doesn't count. Hell we all do it here."

"I swear I'll come back another time." I stood up and hugged her.

"I'm not sure if he went home yet but I could swear I saw him a few minutes ago," she tried again.

"Bye," I smiled and left, and sat in my car for a minute and thought about how great my bed sounded right now, how I could curl up in a ball and cry myself to sleep. What sounded even better was if I could rewind the last four years of my life and have a do-over. I had gotten nowhere and had nowhere to go except to the frat house after a hot and sweaty day around the town.

I backed the car out of the spot and wiped the tears from my face, feeling sorry for myself. Someday it had to get better. It just all had to make sense. Then I glanced up and caught a glimpse of my greasy face in the mirror and saw the wrinkles around my eyes that Evan had single-handedly given me and hadn't been worth a single tear.

Suddenly I was hot, even with the air conditioner on, and despite the fact it was still a hundred degrees out, I inhaled the air. I adjusted the mirror and thought that crying in a parking lot on a Friday night wasn't going to get me anywhere. Tomorrow was another day and that's all I could focus on right now. My future was out there, somewhere.

And then the craziest thing happened. I turned the corner and caught a glimpse of a tall figure at the top of the stairs, at the main entrance to the dealership, and for whatever reason felt compelled to slam on the brakes and stare at him as he slowly descended the stairs towards me as if he too was wondering who the hell I was.

My hands gripped the wheel as he moved closer, as if I expected the car to flip over somehow, and still, no matter how I tried, I couldn't get a good look at him with the parking lot light directly shining in my face. I knew I should have left- what did I care about a figure walking down the stairs- but I couldn't. I had to see who it was because I sensed I already knew. The Caveman's son. The guy I was supposed to meet.

When I was able to release my wheel, I shielded my eyes from the light and saw that he was only a few feet from my door, and I suddenly felt a cold rush of air around me and felt paralyzed, as if a cosmic force had taken control over me. I could not move. I could not breathe, and when I saw his big beautiful brown eyes staring down at me and a smile so warm it could melt the polar caps, I knew I'd died and gone to heaven.

"Hi," I croaked.

"Hi." He made the earth move.

"I wasn't talking to you," I fired back, and wished I could kick myself. "Hi, Ivan," I waved at the old Russian salesman who'd been standing on the side smoking a cigarette and watching, us amused.

"Don't look at me." The Russian flicked his cigarette and walked away, and again I was locked in a force field.

The smell of lemons and soap wafted towards me, making me want to push the door open and pull him close to me and never let him go. Then I remembered how greasy and tired I looked from being in the sun all day, and my foot floored the gas pedal and I sped out of the lot, onto the road in the opposite direction I needed to go, until I pulled a U-turn and got on the highway and felt that I was far away and safe enough to breathe.

The Caveman's son had made me feel more alive in the last few minutes than I had in my entire life, and I knew it sounded crazy, but I felt it in my bones that he was the man I was going to marry. And I, in my usual panic and haste, had run away.

SIXTY-FOUR

The only thing I could do to get the Caveman's son was to go to the car dealership Monday morning and beg the manager for a job. At seven a.m. it was too early for customers to come walking through the door, but the manager would definitely be there.

"J.D.," I leaned over the counter in the middle of the showroom floor breathlessly. "Hire me. I want to sell cars."

J.D. was an extremely handsome older Italian man with black hair, tanned skin, and green eyes, and had been in the car business for twenty something years and had sold cars on his looks alone. He saluted me, like he always did when he saw me, and I said, "J.D. I'm not an officer and even if I was, you don't salute indoors," but he wouldn't put his hand down until I saluted him back.

"You know my Dad was a B-52 pilot," he sighed.

"Yes, I know, but that doesn't mean you have to go saluting everyone who served in the military."

"Yes, it does."

"So, can you hire me or what?"

"You're an Air Traffic Controller," he shrugged. "Why do you want to sell cars?"

"Can you even hire me back even though I was fired from the office?"

"The office is separate. And you know I can do whatever I want. Why do you want this job?"

"I don't know. I just do. I need it because the FAA isn't hiring. Good enough reason?"

"Suit yourself," he shrugged again, "Get an application from Debbie and go get drug tested, the address is on the application, then I'll call you in three days when I get the results."

"Three days!"

I'd barely slept all weekend, and for the first time it wasn't because of my crazy roommates and their parties. I couldn't wait three days to see the Caveman's son again. I couldn't wait three more minutes!

"Want the job or not?" J.D. asked, and I hurried to get the application, which had Debbie squealing with excitement.

I didn't get excited until I was about to leave and saw the Caveman himself sipping coffee at his desk and reading a newspaper.

"Mo," I sat down across from him eagerly. "Hi."

He didn't respond, didn't even give me a glance when he turned the page. I remembered him as being a man of few words, but come on! This was a life and death situation!

"Uhm, I met your son the other day." I stopped talking because it sounded crazy. Then I thought, screw it, remembered how alive I felt at the sight of him and said, "I met your son and he's beautiful. He's the most beautiful man I have ever seen. Is he here today?"

"Oh, hello." He took a sip from his coffee and went back to reading his paper. I nearly slid across the desk to get his attention.

"Please Mo," I begged. "I have to see him again or my heart is going to stop. Please!"

A smile appeared on his lips as if he was having too much fun with this and he said, "Oh."

"I know it sounds crazy," I stood up when he still hadn't flinched. "I don't know what's gotten into me. Have a good day."

"He saw you too," the Caveman suddenly said, and my voice echoed through the showroom, "What? Is that what he said? Tell me!"

"Nutting," he shrugged, but I was hooked.

"What do you mean, 'nothing.' Spit it out!"

"He say he see you and I say you worked here while ago."

"Thank you, thank you, thank you." I clapped my hands together and spun in a circle. "When is he working again?"

"Later, now scuse me. Go," he said, already having lost interest in my silliness, but I didn't care. I was on cloud nine.

From there I left and did the urinalysis, which was stricter than any Air Force pee test I ever had to take because it included cutting my hair, and for the next few days I could barely focus on school or even eat, and by Thursday evening when I heard from J.D. that I could come in Friday morning, I nearly fainted.

Friday morning I stood on the porch at 6:50 a.m. with wet hair, wearing a button down shirt and dress pants, and stared down at my shoes to verify for the millionth time that I looked presentable.

All the other salesmen who were already there, were huddled to the side, eating donuts from the service department and sipping coffee with their eyes still half shut, but the Caveman's son was nowhere to be seen.

Suddenly I realized my mistake. I was gullible Alice from Alice in Wonderland, always chasing after something only to realize I'd been chasing the wrong thing. Instead of a rabbit, however, it was always the wrong guy who, no matter what, I was going to do anything for so he'd like me. I was an Air Traffic Controller, soon to be have a psychology degree, and now I was out selling cars to meet a guy because I thought he'd made the Earth stop moving under my feet.

I turned to leave, to tell J.D. he was right and that this wasn't for me, until I heard, "Hey," behind me and knew it was him before I completed the turn and dropped my purse.

The Caveman's son went down on one knee immediately and scooped up my notepad, pen, and Chapstick. I should have helped him, but just like the last time when I was near him I couldn't move or breathe, and I was forced to stare at his perfectly gelled hair and then his smile as he looked up and handed everything back to me.

I forgot my name, what the hell I was doing there, and whether or not I was supposed to be nervous or excited, because I was both. This was how the universe had written it and I just had to go with it. He smiled, his eyes sparkled, and his body emanated such heat that I had to fight the urge to pull him close and inhale his smell of fresh lemons and soap.

"I didn't mean to scare you. I'm Sal," he said.

"Sale?" I joked, but my heart skipped a beat as if Cupid had shot me through it. I knew his name!

"S-A-L, Sal," he laughed, and I laughed too.

"Sal, of course, Sal, got it. I'll never forget it, now. I'm, uh, Jen."

I nearly fell over when he said, "I know."

Then we stared at each other in silence for a moment as if neither us could believe we'd finally met each other, and he said, "First day?"

"Yes, and I don't know what I'm doing. I don't how to sell a car." I hoped he'd never leave my side ever, even if it meant we had to stay on this front porch all night and sleep standing up.

"It's simple." He leaned against the railing, pointed at the street and cars speeding by, and said, "When a car comes in, you say the color of the car and that means it's yours, that's called an 'up.' Then you walk the customers around the lot, have them drive the car, and bring them inside. Once they're inside, J.D. or my Dad will take care of them. You'll do fine. The new people always do well."

His name suddenly came over the speaker and he said, "I have to go."

I looked at him as if to say "please don't" and asked, "What if I can't find a car?"

He laughed and said, "Are you saying you want my number?" and pulled a notepad from his pocket, wrote down his number with a smiley face next to it, handed it to me, and said, "All you had to do was ask, but I don't mind."

"You like that?" I blushed, but it was too late to feel embarrassed. I wanted him and I wasn't going to back down.

I didn't bump into him again until noon, after I sold my first car and was stuck making photocopies and he surprised me from behind and said, "What do you say we go out for dinner tonight and celebrate your first sale?"

Dinner? I wanted to elope.

"Okay, meet me at my car when we're done around five or six?"

"Sounds like a plan," he winked, but our plan didn't pan out at all when we got in the car and sat there for thirty minutes trying to decide where we wanted to go.

"You pick," I insisted, but he was too damned agreeable. He shrugged, "I don't care. I'll agree to anything as long as that will get you to stop messing with the radio."

"Oh," I sat up straight and realized how nervous I'd been.

"I'm just kidding," he smiled. "Are you always this uptight?"

"Yes, I am. Here's your chance to get out of this and never look back."

"Not a chance." He squeezed my hand and I finally started the car and headed towards the strip, hoping to find a restaurant that would make this night memorable.

"How about sushi?" I suggested and pulled into the restaurant parking lot.

"How about yuck."

"It's not that bad," I parked the car and opened the door hoping he'd follow.

"I've never had it and I don't want it."

"Well, that's perfect then," I said. "What better way to start something different than now?"

"Okay, whatever you want," he got out. "Where are you from, by the way?"

"New Hampshire."

"I've never met anyone from New Hampshire before," he said as we were seated.

"I get that a lot. You?"

"Michigan."

"You're the first person I've ever met from Michigan," I said, and we laughed so hard I'd almost forgotten what my life was like before I met him.

"My mom, brother, and sister are still there, but my Dad is here, as you know."

"Speaking of that," I sat up right again. "There's something I need to tell you. I went out on a date with your dad, not really a date, but he tried to kiss me, and I swear I didn't know he was married or had kids. He never mentioned you before."

"He told me," he glanced away. "But his version was a little different. That you didn't stop calling him."

"It's not how it happened, I swear!"

"Sit down, don't go. I know how he is. I'm not mad at you."

"I've never met anyone like you," I sat down again. "You're a nice guy. There's got to be something wrong with you. Tell me now, what is it? STD? Criminal record? Girlfriend?"

"Actually, I'm married," he said.

I replied, "Figures," and wished the Earth would swallow me whole.

"I'm just kidding," he squeezed my hand. "We have to work on you being so uptight."

"Not funny!" I snapped. "I know you can't imagine the dating scene around here, but Vegas is a dating nightmare and I don't want to date. I'm looking for a husband."

"Well, I'm looking for a wife."

"Oh, really?" I crossed my arms. "You trust me enough to marry me?"

He shrugged as if he hadn't given it much thought at all until now, but was going to play my silly game anyway.

"Would you let me shave your face?" I challenged him.

"You got a razor on you? Try me." He crossed his arms mockingly.

"What if I cut your jugular?" That's what Evan feared when I'd asked to shave his face.

"You'll drive me to a hospital."

"How about a haircut? Would you let me cut your hair even though I don't know how to cut? It's just something I've always wanted to do."

"Why not?"

"Why not?" I repeated. "Who are you? No one would let me do that. I begged my ex to let me for years and he never gave in."

"I would," he shrugged. "It's just hair, but do you mind if we don't talk about your ex, because I have one too and I'm trying hard to forget her."

"Old habit," I replied sheepishly.

He showed me his phone and said, "This is how I deal with her," and scrolled down the menu until a phone number with the words "don't answer" appeared.

"That's so clever. Why hadn't I thought of that?"

Because Sal was perfect that's why.

"I think they're kicking us out," he said when the waitress brought us the bill. "It's almost two a.m. I'll pay, you get the car."

By the time I pulled the car out to the restaurant entrance, Sal was walking out. He got in the car and tossed two fortune cookies in the cup holder and said, "For later."

"Do you know how to drive a stick, by the way?"

"I don't." He admitted.

I said, "So that's what's wrong with you. Wanna learn?"

"Now? People are going to think we're nuts if they see us!"

"I guess we're nuts then," I opened the car door so that we could switch places, and to my surprise, he did exactly as I instructed and made it out of first gear so smoothly that I asked, "Are you sure you haven't driven before, because you're driving like a pro?"

"No, I promise," he maneuvered the clutch and stalled.

"You did that on purpose!"

"No I didn't. You're just a good teacher." He wiggled the clutch. "I don't even own a car, I drive my Dad's."

"What do you mean, your Dad's? You don't have your own car?"

"I crashed my car in Michigan, got caught in a bad rain storm and flipped it on the highway. I'm under twenty five and the insurance is too high for me to get my own here so I'm going to wait a few years."

"How old are you?" I studied his face.

"Nineteen, why?"

"Nineteen? How is that possible? You're, like, a six-foot-something giant!"

"Six-foot-six."

"Six-foot-nothing. Get out so I can drive you back to the dealership."

"What is the matter?"

"I'm twenty five, that's the matter, and this isn't going to work out. I'm, I'm too old, too damaged. I know you don't understand, but this was a bad idea. I can't afford to date right now. It would literally kill me."

"I know that look," he said. "My ex did a number on me too. That was one of the reasons why I moved here."

"See, now I'm crying," I said. "And I don't want to cry, but I can't help it. I'm messed up, and when I saw you I thought I was ready to move on, but just the thought of everything I went through is too much. I've had the best time tonight, but I can't do this to you. I'm sorry. We can stay friends but nothing more."

"My ex was crazy too." He got out of the car as soon as we pulled into the empty dealership lot.

Without saying a word, I watched him leave and wished he hadn't. Then, as I always did when I didn't have a clue, I turned to fate. I opened a fortune cookie.

"Look no farther, happiness is right beside you," I read out loud, smirked, tossed it on the floor, and read the next one.

"Look no farther, happiness is right beside you," I read it aloud again, and although I thought that they'd misprinted an entire batch, I saw that one was written in red and the other in black in another font and with different lucky numbers.

Oh my God, what the hell had I done?

SIXTY-FIVE

At nine in the morning my phone rang and nearly blasted me out of bed.

"It's me, Sal," he said before I could say hello. "I had to talk to you. I couldn't sleep."

"Me neither." I frowned, knowing I was being selfish for talking to him. My stomach cramped up just thinking about his smile and how I had to let him go.

"I couldn't stop thinking about you. What do you say we go to the movies or something?"

"I thought I told you yesterday that this wasn't going to work and that I just wanted to be friends?"

"All I'm asking you is if you want to go to the movies."

"We really shouldn't."

"Come on, matinees start in another hour or so. I know you want to."

"Listen, I can't."

"I understand," he sighed. "If you're not ready then you're not ready."

"Thanks for understanding," I said, knowing the heartbreak would be easier now than down the road. "I'll see you at work." I hung up, feeling like all the walls were about to cave in on me. Evan had been out of the picture for a year and still I felt pinned under his thumb.

Then my phone rang again and when Sal said, "Hi," again I said, "I thought I said, 'see you at work,' as in, I'll see you in a few days?"

"You did," he chuckled. "But I want to go to the movies with you right now. I'm outside. We can drive around for a while, what do you say?"

"You're here?" I hurried to the door, peeked out the side window, and saw him in his car in the driveway wearing a backwards baseball cap looking like one of those sexy jocks from high school: guys who never glanced in my direction, guys who were always out of my league.

"Come on, let's go."

"Do you need an answer right now?"

"You have two minutes. Starting now. No, now."

Butterflies swarmed in my stomach as I pictured myself on top of a cliff like the Grand Canyon and looking down at him waving at me to jump because he wanted to catch me. He was absolutely nuts. I. Could. Not. Jump.

"Jen, are you still there?"

"Yes."

"Yes, you're still there or yes, you're coming out?"

"My hair is a mess."

"I doubt that. Your hair is perfect."

"You say all the right things, I give you that, and I appreciate all this, but I can't. I'm sorry. Goodbye."

I hung up, feeling like I'd made the biggest mistake of my life. He deserved better, but then again so did I, and how long was I going to live with the fear of living? I had to jump or I was going to die old and alone.

I put on my shoes and opened the door and made it to the car just as he leaned over to open the door for me from the inside. The sight of him smiling up at me made me realize I didn't want to spend another day without him.

"Glad you could make it." He put the car in reverse.

Reaching for the oh-shit bar, I suddenly realized I had overstated my readiness to jump. I hadn't been ready at all and needed to climb right back up that cliff, go back inside, and think about this a while longer.

"You okay?" Sal stopped the car and reached for my hand.

"Can you open a window? I'm not feeling too good."

"I picked out a good movie, I promise!" He laughed and I let go of the oh-shit bar, let go of the branch on the side of the cliff and let myself fall into his arms, because for the first time in four years, I knew I was going to be okay.

EPILOGUE

Sal and I married in 2004, eight months after we met. We redid the ceremony one year later. Jake, Pam, Lena and Mandy were all a part of the wedding party. Joe, Jason, and Winston attended. I saw Amber while I was dress shopping, she was buying her wedding dress too and I almost didn't recognize her. Las Vegas did not resurrect her career or do her any favors.

I still work at an airport in Las Vegas with Satan who is no longer my boss. He is pleasant to work with and has sincerely apologized to me for the events that took place in this book.

I'm in touch with some of the foreign controllers and hope to go back and visit someday. I still talk to George, once in a great while, and the Captain, who still thinks I'm funny.

Evan and I spoke years ago, he has also gotten married and asked to come visit me and my husband, and sent a request to be my Facebook friend.

I declined.

www.ingramcontent.com/pod-product-compliance
Lightning Source LLC
Chambersburg PA
CBHW071223290426
44108CB00013B/1278